Timothy Taylor

slay the
Spanish!

weapons against the Ruy Lopez

EVERYMAN CHESS

Gloucester Publishers plc www.everymanchess.com

First published in 2011 by Gloucester Publishers plc (formerly Everyman Publishers plc), Northburgh House, 10 Northburgh Street, London EC1V 0AT

British Library Cataloguing-in-Publication Data
A catalogue record for this book is available from the British Library.

ISBN: 978 1 85744 637 1

Distributed in North America by The Globe Pequot Press, P.O Box 480, 246 Goose Lane, Guilford, CT 06437-0480.

All other sales enquiries should be directed to Everyman Chess, Northburgh House, 10 Northburgh Street, London EC1V 0AT
tel: 020 7253 7887 fax: 020 7490 3708
email: info@everymanchess.com; website: www.everymanchess.com

Everyman is the registered trade mark of Random House Inc. and is used in this work under licence from Random House Inc.

To my beautiful wife Liz

Everyman Chess Series
Chief advisor: Byron Jacobs
Commissioning editor: John Emms
Assistant editor: Richard Palliser

Typeset and edited by First Rank Publishing, Brighton.
Cover design by Horatio Monteverde.
Printed and bound in the US by Versa Press.

Contents

Bibliography and Acknowledgment

Books

Opening for White according to Anand, Vol. 2, Alexander Khalifman (Chess Stars 2003)

My Best Games of Chess, Vols. 1 & 2, Alexander Alekhine (G.Bell and Sons 1969)

New York 1924, Alexander Alekhine (Dover 1961)

My 60 Memorable Games, Bobby Fischer (Simon and Schuster 1969)

The Games of Robert J. Fischer, Wade and O'Connell (Batsford 1972)

Grandmaster of Chess, Paul Keres (Arco 1972)

Easy Guide to the Ruy Lopez, John Emms (Everyman 1999)

Nottingham 1936, Alexander Alekhine (Dover 1962)

Chess from Morphy to Botvinnik, Imre König (Dover 1977)

World Championship Interzonals, Wade, Blackstock and Kotov (Batsford 1974)

My Best Games of Chess, Vassily Smyslov (Dover 1972)

Counter Gambits, Tim Harding (British Chess Magazine 1974)

The Life and Games of Mikhail Tal, Mikhail Tal (Everyman 2003)

Practical Chess Endings, Paul Keres (Doubleday 1974)

Spanisch bis Französisch, Paul Keres (Sportverlag Berlin 1969)

Play the Ruy Lopez, Andrew Greet (Everyman 2007)

The Siesta Variation, D.N.L. Levy (The Chess Player 1971)

Computer Programs and Databases

ChessBase.com; Fritz 11
MegaBase 2010 with updates through 2011
MegaCorr4 (Chess Mail)
Correspondence Database 2010 (ChessBase)

Acknowledgment

Very special thanks to Grandmaster Michael Han.

Introduction

The Spanish Inquisition lasted from 1478 to 1834, but chessplayers have yet to escape the Spanish Torture! First studied by the priest (later bishop) Ruy Lopez de Segura, 1 e4 e5 2 ♘f3 ♘c6 3 ♗b5 (the Ruy Lopez or Spanish Opening) has tormented Black players for five hundred years, and there's no end in sight. According to Chessgames.com Opening Explorer, the Ruy is more than three times more popular than the Italian Game (3 ♗c4) and about five times more popular than the King's Gambit.

Bottom line, if as Black you wish to defend classically and meet 1 e4 with e5 and 2 ♘f3 with ♘c6—you will face the Ruy Lopez.

And you will face it again and again. I always try to play any opening that I write about, but sometimes it's not so simple. As I noted in my book, *The Budapest Gambit*, in the seven months of preparing the manuscript I was unable to get a single Budapest Gambit, even though the opening started on move two! Obviously it was easier to get the subject of my next, *Alekhine Alert*, with the "get it in one" 1...♘f6, but the Ruy Lopez is so popular among White play-

ers that it was just as easy to get as an Alekhine, even though the opening starts on the third move, not the first.

I advocate the Modern Steinitz against the Ruy, and this is the subject of this book: the basic tabiya occurs after the moves **1 e4 e5 2 ♘f3 ♘c6 3 ♗b5 a6 4 ♗a4 d6**.

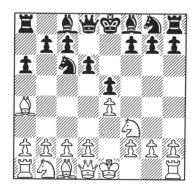

White's only way of avoiding the Modern Steinitz (once he's started with the Ruy) is the Exchange Variation, where White plays 4 ♗xc6 instead of 4 ♗a4. In order to give Black players a full repertoire I've covered the Exchange in Chapters Ten and Eleven.

One advantage of the Modern Steinitz is that it is learnable, even if you are starting from scratch—but just try a repertoire based on the Marshall Gambit! I like this sound sharp gambit, and I used to have great success with it—but since "my" opening only *started* after the moves 1 e4 e5 2 ♘f3 ♘c6 3 ♗b5 a6 4 ♗a4 ♘f6 5 0-0 ♗e7 6 ♖e1 b5 7 ♗b3 0-0 8 c3 and now 8...d5—move eight!—in practice, after a few gambit successes as Black, I never got the Marshall again—just a huge assortment of Anti-Marshalls. I faced extraordinarily boring lines like the DERLD (delayed exchange Ruy Lopez deferred) where, on the sixth move, White avoids Marshall for the sleepyland line 6 ♗xc6 dxc6 7 d3 (see *True Combat Chess* for a miracle win from a dead-drawn position resulting from this opening).

You get the Modern Steinitz in four, with only one deviation, the Exchange Variation that goes with the territory—instead of a laundry list of deviations right up to move eight (need I mention later Anti-Marshalls like 8 h3 and 8 a4).

With the Modern Steinitz one gets a sound opening where, in most lines, you get *your position* and Black can play for a win. I can't say it's a walk-over for Black—but you *will* get rich play with excellent chances to equalize and more importantly, be able to counter-attack!

Before we begin the book proper with my traditional World Champions retrospective, it's worth going through the basic variations that will be covered, chapter by chapter. One thing that surprised me as I studied was the

great variety of play under the MS umbrella: there are two positively savage gambits, the Siesta and the Yandemirov, where Black sacrifices a pawn or a piece, respectively, for purely speculative reasons—and there are two rock solid positional lines. Yet even the positional lines sometimes feature wild attacks—unlike almost all other variations of the Ruy, in the Modern Steinitz Black frequently castles queenside; see, for example, Games 4, 23, 28 and 36. Besides all this, there are short forced draws and long endgame grinds. There are even two completely different ways of meeting the Exchange Variation! In short, there's something for everyone. Here's a preview of the lines that I will cover:

1. World Champions

Every World Champion (with the sole exception of Kramnik) has either played the MS or played against it. Capablanca and Alekhine were great advocates of the defence, but the ultimate MS star of world-class players was someone who never received the title of World Champion, Mr. Forever Second, Paul Keres. According to the *MegaBase*, Keres played 59 games with the MS, using it throughout his career against foes such as Tal, Spassky, Euwe, Geller, Bronstein, etc. He won 27 games, drew 28, and lost only 4, for an astonishing winning percentage—against top level competition—of nearly 70% *with Black!*

With that kind of record, I've made Keres an honorary World Champion and hero of the entire book. The first chapter, as well as all the others (except for Chapters Six and Eleven, which feature lines he never played) will start with a Keres game—there is no better way to understand the Modern Steinitz than to study his games.

Going back to the first chapter, we'll see the great predecessors win one by one with the Modern Steinitz (Steinitz himself, Lasker, Capablanca, Alekhine, Euwe, etc) until finally, in the modern age, we find a certain Fischer who never played the MS with Black—but discovered its strength when he lost to it as White! Even Kasparov, who was never seen on the black side of the MS, had to concede a short draw in a World Championship match when Short uncorked the MS! By the time we get to Anand, all the variations covered in the book will be seen.

2. Solid Line 1: The Knight Defence

The great divide in the MS is between the solid lines, where Black defends e5 against an early assault, and the gambits, where Black is willing to pour oil on any central flames and fight fiercely in the chaotic blaze that ensues. Needless to say, the latter is not to everyone's taste, so I begin with the solid knight defence of the centre: an ideal example is the sequence 5 0-0 ♗d7 6 c3 ♘ge7 7 d4 ♘g6 from Oim-Keres (Game 21).

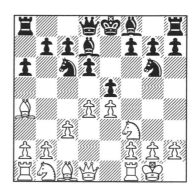

3. Solid Line 2: The Bishop Defence

Here Black defends e5 with the fianchettoed bishop, much like a King's Indian Defence: Black's basic set-up is seen after the moves 5 0-0 ♗d7 6 d4 ♘f6 7 c3 g6 8 ♖e1 b5 9 ♗c2 ♗g7 as in Parma-Keres (Game 25).

4. The Siesta

This fierce gambit occurs after 5 c3 f5!?—Black eschews solidity and opts for an unclear pawn sacrifice in one of the critical lines, which continues 6 exf5 ♗xf5 7 d4 e4 8 ♘g5 d5 9 f3 e3; see the rest of this wild encounter in Euwe-Keres (Game 34).

5. The Yandemirov Gambit

Why sac a pawn when you can sac a piece? The Russian GM Valeri Yandemirov is the primary advocate of just this kind of madness. He reasons that if White tells you where his king lives (answers the MS move 4...d6 with 5 0-0) then you might as well attack him immediately and ferociously. A typical line is 5 0-0 ♗g4 6 h3 h5 7 d4 b5 8 ♗b3

♘xd4 (Black sacrifices a piece on move 8!) 9 hxg4 ♘xb3 10 axb3 hxg4 11 ♘g5 ♕d7 and Black has compensation for the bishop with the open h-file and trapped white knight on g5; see Aseev-Yandemirov (Game 50).

6. Delayed Exchange Variation

White can enter a version of the Exchange Variation a tempo down by waiting for Black's 4...d6 and then taking on c6. This kind of tempo-loss variation is only good for White if the Black player is not prepared—but Keres, for example, brushed this line off with ridiculous ease: he scored seven wins for Black and only five draws, with no losses! My analysis also shows that Black has nothing to fear; e.g. 5 ♗xc6+ bxc6 6 d4 exd4 7 ♕xd4 c5 8 ♕d3 ♘e7 9 ♘c3 ♖b8 10 b3 ♘g6 11 0-0 ♗e7 12 ♘d5 ♗f6 and Black had equalized in Mecking-Keres (Game 53).

7. Duras Variation

This is an attempt by White to force the position into a Maróczy Bind structure, but the Ruy and the Bind are two different animals that don't get along well. 5 c4 (the Duras move) is met easily by Reshevsky's 5...♗g4, targeting the hole at d4, and Black has no problems; see Keres-Reshevsky (Game 60).

8. White Plays an Early d2-d4

Here White tries to take over the centre without preparation by c2-c3—he simply shoves his d-pawn forward on move five or six. The first variation has long been refuted as a winning attempt, and is nowadays only played to draw. Playing d2-d4 on move 6 is a little better and usually transposes back to Chapter Three, although independent lines are possible, if not dangerous: 5 0-0 ♗d7 6 d4 ♘f6 7 dxe5 ♘xe5 8 ♗xd7+ ♘fxd7 9 ♘c3 ♗e7 shows easy equalization for Black in Hermlin-Keres (Game 72).

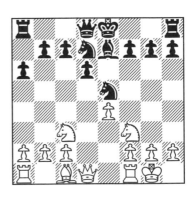

9. Four Fishes

It's possible—even probable—that you will meet players who do not want to get an advantage with White—they want only to play defensively and hope to draw. With this "goal" in mind, one is likely to run into any of the following four fishes on move five: 5 ♘c3, 5 d3, 5 h3 or 5 ♕e2. All of these defend against non-existent attacks, and all give up the advantage of the first move—but when you're playing to draw anyway, what does that matter? A typical example is 5 h3 (if Bobby Fischer saw such a move, he'd be rolling over in his grave, and not just from DNA testing!) 5...♘f6 6 0-0 b5 7 ♗b3 ♘a5 and Black was already at least equal in Paljusaj-Nei (Game 76).

10. Ruy Exchange:
Main Line with 4...dxc6

The Exchange Variation is White's only way to both play the Ruy Lopez and avoid the Modern Steinitz. White gives up the two bishops but damages Black's pawn structure; generally speaking White hopes to win the ending, while keeping the draw in hand. Keres always took back with the d-pawn (the popular way) and nowadays Magnus Carlsen does so as well—but both these great players draw almost all their games in this variation. A typical position is reached after 4 ♗xc6 dxc6 5 ♘c3 f6 6 d4 exd4 7 ♘xd4 c5 8 ♘de2 ♕xd1+ 9 ♘xd1 and White is minutely better in a drawish position; see Khachiyan-Taylor (Game 80).

11. Ruy Exchange:
Larsen's Variation, 4...bxc6

One of the great discoveries I made while working on this book is that the recapture with the d-pawn (away from the centre, which lames Black's queenside pawns into the ending) is *not* obligatory, and in fact the natural recapture towards the centre is quite playable! Yes, Black reaches Chapter Six a tempo down, but it's hard to see what White does with this tempo—while Black's winning chances are much higher than in the dull fashionable lines with 4...dxc6. World Champions like Lasker and Alekhine used to play 4...bxc6, then it was forgotten; then revived by Larsen—then forgotten again, and even vilified: Krzysztof Panczyk and Jacek Ilczuk in their recent book *Ruy Lopez Exchange* call taking towards the centre "unjustified" and add, "This variation is played only once in a blue moon, and it doesn't have much value. White has a few strong continuations that cause serious problems for Black."

But I disagree with these modern commentators, or rather I agree with the great Alekhine, who called this variation "eminently practicable". Having played the boring 4...dxc6, I can't wait to surprise my next exchanging foe. I imagine him chopping my knight, looking for the quiet game; he feels he has at least a draw is in his pocket—and then I go all Larsen on him with 4...bxc6!.

A pretty example is 5 d4 exd4 6 ♘xd4 c5 7 ♘f3 ♗b7 8 ♘c3 ♘e7 9 0-0 h6 10 ♖e1 ♘g6 11 ♗e3 ♗e7 and Black has completed her development Chapter Two style, with no endgame problems to look forward to: this is Herrero Crespo-Monllor Garcia (Game 83).

Not every potential Modern Steinitz player will like every line in the book, but as you see, you don't have to: the opening is so rich that you can build a repertoire to suit your taste.

And one final note before we go to the World Champions' games—how did I do with the Modern Steinitz myself? There are two answers to this: in preceding years I used to play the MS from time to time, without benefit of any study, and my results were up and down as one might expect, hovering around 50%. Then I began to actually study the variation in preparation for this book, and aimed for the MS every time I had Black. I quickly discovered that few White opponents were prepared for this line (they were all booked to the gills against 4...♘f6 of course). Meanwhile, I was getting the advantage straight off; I was often better before move ten.

And the box score? Of my seven "post-study" games with the Modern Steinitz, *I won all seven with Black.*

Chapter One
World Champions

As mentioned already, every official world champion except Kramnik has played on one side or the other of the Modern Steinitz—but before we follow these great players, let's start this chapter with our hero, honorary champion and Modern Steinitz mentor, the great Paul Keres.

1 e4 e5 2 ♘f3 ♘c6 3 ♗b5 a6 4 ♗a4 d6

The two *almost* World Champions have reached the basic tabiya of the Modern Steinitz.

5 c3 ♗d7

5...f5 is the Siesta Gambit: see Chapter Four.

6 d4 ♘ge7

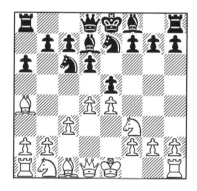

One of Black's two solid lines: this system will be fully covered in Chapter Two, where I point out that this move order is actually slightly inaccurate. The ...♘ge7-g6 manoeuvre played here works much better when White has committed to kingside castling with 5 0-0 (see Games 19-20 for the explanation).

I prefer 6...♘f6 here, followed soon by ...g7-g6, which will be covered in Chapter Three.

7 ♗b3

Threatening 8 ♘g5; but the positional 7 ♗e3 is probably best, which guarantees a slight edge for White (see Game 20).

7...h6

Necessary, as 7...♘g6? 8 ♘g5 wins material.

8 ♘bd2

White can also attack in gambit style with 8 ♘h4 (see Game 19).

8...♘g6 9 ♘c4 ♗e7 10 ♘e3

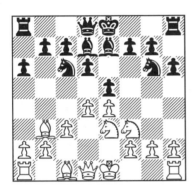

10...0-0

Later Keres played the improvement 10...♗g5! and won quickly: 11 0-0 (or 11 ♘xg5 hxg5 when one sees the key idea: Black takes advantage of his delayed castling to activate the rook on the now open h-file) 11...♗xe3 12 ♗xe3 ♕f6 13 ♕d2 ♘a5 14 ♗d5 c6 15 ♗b3 ♗g4 16 ♘e1 0-0 17 f4 ♘xb3 18 axb3 exf4 19 ♗xf4 ♕e7! (in the next phase of the game Keres exploits not only the loose centre pawn, but also the doubled pawn on b3—then finishes with a classic back rank attack!) 20 ♘d3 ♕xe4 21 ♗xd6 ♖fe8 22 ♗g3 ♕d5 23 ♘f4

♘xf4 24 ♕xf4 ♖e4 25 ♕d6 ♕xb3 26 ♖f2 ♖ae8 27 h3 ♖e1+ 28 ♖xe1 ♖xe1+ 29 ♔h2 ♕d1 30 ♗f4 ♗e6 31 ♖f3 ♖h1+ 32 ♔g3 ♕e1+ 0-1 W.Unzicker-P.Keres, Hamburg (7th matchgame) 1956.

I will thoroughly cover the key ...♗g5 idea—which is even stronger if White has castled early—in Chapter Two.

11 0-0 ♖e8

Not long before this game, Keres had played 11...♗f6 12 ♘d5 when he felt that he had "scarcely anything better than to surrender the centre" with 12...exd4, when White had a small advantage in space after 13 ♘xd4 in M.Euwe-P.Keres, World Championship, The Hague/Moscow 1948. Nonetheless, the text "improvement" also fails to equalize and 10...♗g5 must still be preferred.

12 ♖e1

Keres remarks that 12 ♗c2 was superior, leaving the rook on f1 to support a later f2-f4.

12...♗f8 13 ♗c2 ♘h4

An important resource in this variation: Black exchanges the active white knight and gains kingside room for his pieces. See Game 24 for another example of this motif.

14 ♘xh4 ♕xh4 15 ♘d5

Keres feared 15 g3 ♕d8 (not 15...♕h3 16 ♗d3 and Black's queen is in danger) 16 f4—and with good reason: White is better after 16...exf4 (or 16...exd4 17 cxd4 ♘b4 18 ♗b1 c5 19 d5 and Black's knight is in danger on the queenside, while White owns the centre and kingside) 17 gxf4 ♗e7 18 ♖e2 and White's central pawns and half-open g-file give him excellent attacking chances.

15...♖ac8 16 ♖f1?!

This loss of a tempo allows Black to equalize, and soon play for a win.

16...♘e7

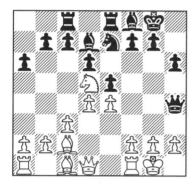

Black is fine, as Keres ejects White's best piece.

17 ♘e3 ♘g6 18 g3

18 ♘d5 ♘e7 with a draw is not inspiring, but probably best: now Keres takes over the advantage as White's attack comes too slowly.

18...♕h3

The other defect of 16 ♖f1 is that it robs the bishop of that square—so Keres can keep his queen, safely, near White's king.

19 f4 exf4 20 gxf4 f5

Not a bad move, but not the best either: the thematic 20...♘h4! is on yet again! After 21 ♖f2 c5 White's shaky position is pressured from the centre and queenside, while the threats of

mate and ...♘f3+ tie down his rook. Black is better; in fact White must watch out that he doesn't lose almost immediately; e.g. 22 dxc5 (or 22 d5 f5! and Black smashes the white centre) 22...d5! 23 ♕xd5 ♗xc5 24 ♕d3 ♗b5 25 c4 ♗xc4! and wins.

This variation shows the strength of the MS as a counter-attacking system: even after some opening inaccuracies Black's position was rich in resources; and when White was inaccurate in turn, Black could have taken the advantage almost immediately.

21 ♖f3 ♕h5 22 exf5 ♘h4 23 ♖f1 ♕xd1 24 ♖xd1

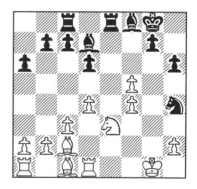

24...c5

As Keres pointed out, 24...c6! is correct (to block any check from b3) and Black has a good game: 25 ♗d2 ♗e7 (with the idea of ...♖f8 and taking the pawn on f5) 26 ♖f1 d5 27 ♖ae1 ♗d6 28 ♖f2 ♖f8 and Black recovers his pawn with a slight edge due to White's broken kingside. Note that 25 ♔f2 ♗e7 26 ♗b3+ (as in the game) doesn't work here. Black counters with 26...d5 27 c4

②xf5! 28 cxd5 cxd5 29 &xd5+ &f8 when he has splendid activity and a lead in development, while White suffers from weak pawns. The position must be assessed in Black's favour despite the pawn minus; e.g. 30 &xb7? &h4+ 31 &f3 &xc1! and Black wins.

25 &f2 &e7 26 &b3+ &h8

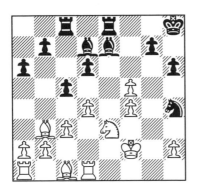

27 &e6!

After Keres missed two chances (20...②h4 and 24...c6), it's Bronstein's turn and he now transforms his weak doubleton into a mighty passed pawn.

27...&xe6 28 fxe6 cxd4 29 cxd4?

White wants to play d4-d5 and win with his protected passed pawn—but he won't get that chance. Instead, 29 &xd4! targeting d6 gives White a big advantage. Keres gives 29...d5 (29...&d8 30 &e4 is considered to be winning by both Keres and *Fritz*) 30 &xd5 &c6 31 f5 g6 with some counterplay as Black's only chance, but White can squelch this with the exact 32 &d7! gxf5 33 ②d5 &xe6 34 ②xe7 (not 34 ②c7? &c5+ 35 &g3 &g8+ 36 &xh4 &e4+ 37 &h5 &f2 38 &d4 &xd4 and it's Black who wins)

34...&8xe7 35 &xe7 &xe7 36 &xh6 and Black has no compensation for the pawn.

29...d5!!

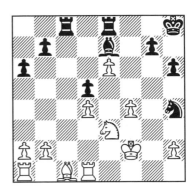

Necessary, to prevent d4-d5, but very strong as well: Black vacates d6 for the bishop, while the c-file is an avenue of attack.

30 ②xd5

Bronstein could draw with 30 f5 ②xf5 31 ②xf5 &f8 32 &g3 &xf5 33 &f4 &c6 34 &e1 &f6 35 &ac1 &fxe6 36 &xc6 &xe1 37 &c8+ &h7 38 &e5, but he is material up and playing for a win...

30...&d6

...which is good news for Keres, who now has excellent compensation.

31 &d2?!

White should probably run for equality with 31 &g3 g5 32 &g4 &xe6 33 fxg5 &e4+ 34 &h5 ②f3 35 ②f6 &h4+ 36 &g6 &xh2 37 &d3 ②xg5 and White holds the draw.

31...&xe6 32 &ac1 &f8 33 &e1 &g6 34 &g1 &f5 35 &xg6 ②xg6 36 ②c3

Even now 36 ②e3 &xf4+ 37 &e2 &xd4 38 ②f5 &e4+ 39 &f3 &e6 40

♘xd6 ♖xd6, as given by Keres, should be enough to draw after 41 ♖c8+ ♔h7 42 ♗c3.

36...♘xf4 37 ♔e3 ♘g2+ 38 ♔d3 ♗xh2 39 d5 ♖f3+?

Time pressure. After the correct 39...♔g8, rushing towards the passed d-pawn, Black would be clearly better.

40 ♔e4 ♖f2 41 ♖d1

Thanks to the tempo gain at the time control, now it's White who has compensation for a pawn!

41...♔g8 42 ♘a4 ♘h4 43 ♗e3 ♖g2 44 ♘c5 ♖xb2 45 ♖d2! ♖b4+ 46 ♖d4 ♖b6 47 ♘e6 ♗d6 48 ♗f4

I am well aware of the strength of a passed centre pawn in rook + knight endings—see my win over GM Vasquez in my *Bird's Opening* book. Bronstein has energetically used his chances—but the critical moment is coming soon...

48...♘g6 49 ♗xd6 ♖xd6

...and he makes a fatal error.

50 ♔f5?

If White attacks with rook and knight (but not his king!) he should draw: 50 ♖c4! ♖d7 51 ♘c5 ♖e7+ 52 ♔d4 ♖e2 (or 52...♘h4 53 d6 ♘f3+ 54 ♔d3 ♘e5+ 55 ♔d4 ♘c6+ 56 ♔c3 ♖f7 57 d7 and the passed pawn gives White compensation) 53 ♘xb7 ♘e7 54 d6 ♘f5+ 55 ♔d3 ♘xd6 56 ♘xd6 ♖xa2 57 ♘f5 and I think the rook and knight can hold against the rook and three pawns.

50...♔f7 51 ♘c5 ♖f6+

Black drives the white king back with gain of time.

52 ♔e4 b6 53 ♘xa6

53 d6? loses to 53...bxc5 54 d7 ♖f4+ 55 ♔e3 ♖xd4.

53...♔e7 54 ♘c7 ♘f8 55 ♘b5 g5 56 d6+ ♔d7 57 ♔e3 ♘e6 58 ♖b4 ♘g7 59 ♘d4 ♖xd6 60 ♖a4 ♔e7 61 ♖a6

Against 61 ♖a7+ Keres had prepared the following pretty win: 61...♔f6 62 ♖xg7 ♖xd4!.

61...♔f6 62 a4 ♘f5+ 63 ♘xf5 ♔xf5 0-1

After 64 a5 ♖e6+ 65 ♔f3 bxa5 66 ♖xa5+ ♖e5 Black consolidates and wins easily with the two extra pawns.

Now it's time for the official World Championship games, in order of the title-holders, with the aforementioned exceptions of Vladimir Kramnik. To illustrate all the variations in the book, some champions are featured in more than one game.

Game 2
D.Baird-W.Steinitz
New York 1894

1 e4 e5 2 ♘f3 ♘c6 3 ♗b5 a6

The first official World Champion is the namesake of the entire opening. Steinitz's original system, still called the Steinitz Defence today, was 3...d6. However, White can force Black to "give up the centre", that is, exchange his strong point pawn at e5 for the white pawn on d4. This is hardly the end of the world, but usually White gets some space advantage and Black is often left struggling to draw: one pure Steinitz Defence, Game 68, can be found in this book, in which the above points will be elucidated.

The improved Steinitz—the Steinitz Defence Deferred, or as I'm calling it, the Modern Steinitz—was a discovery of the champion's later years, when he found that the insertion of ...a7-a6 enabled Black in most lines to "hold the centre"—that is, maintain a black pawn at e5. However, from my 21st century vantage point, I must interject that modern chess has no room for dogma—so on occasion Black does well to take on d4 anyway (but with the useful tempo ...a7-a6 included); for a good example of such unprejudiced thinking see Game 71.

4 ♗a4 d6 5 d4

The best answer to this, 5...b5, can be found in Game 13 in this chapter, and will be fully analysed in Chapter Eight.

5...♗d7 6 0-0

As Black did not go into "move order punishment" mode, White has been allowed to transpose to a main line.

6...♘ge7 7 ♗g5

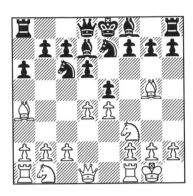

7 c3 is correct, with a normal Chapter Two position—whereas now White must beware the Noah's Ark trap, which is very common in the MS.

7...h6 8 ♗e3 b5 9 ♗b3 exd4 10 ♗f4

Now we see why White needed to be able to take back with the c-pawn! After 10 ♘xd4? ♘xd4 11 ♕xd4 c5 12 ♕xd6 c4 Noah's Ark wraps up White's Lopez bishop with a win for Black.

10...g5 11 ♗g3 ♗g7

"A pawn is worth some trouble!" Steinitz said.

**12 ♗d5 0-0 13 c3 ♘xd5 14 exd5 dxc3!
15 ♘xc3**

Not 15 dxc6? cxb2 and wins.

15...♘e7

Black has consolidated his extra pawn and soon acquires more material.

16 ♘d4? b4 17 ♘ce2 ♘xd5

Black has two extra pawns and *no* trouble!

18 ♕b3 ♘b6 19 ♕c2 f5 20 f4 c5 21 ♕b3+ ♔h8 22 ♘f3 ♗a4 23 ♕d3 ♗b5 24 ♕c2 g4 25 ♘h4 ♕f6 26 ♖ad1 ♘c4 27

♗f2 ♖ae8 28 ♖fe1 ♘e3 29 ♗xe3 ♖xe3
30 g3 ♖fe8 31 ♖d2 ♖3e4 32 ♔f2 c4 33
♕d1 c3

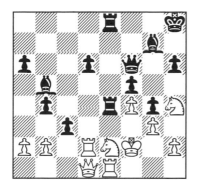

34 bxc3 bxc3 35 ♖xd6 ♖xe2+ 36 ♖xe2
♖xe2+ 37 ♔g1 c2 38 ♕xe2 c1♕+

Two queens reduce trouble to a
minimum.

39 ♕d1 ♕d4+! 40 ♖xd4 ♗xd4+ 41 ♔g2
♗c6+ 42 ♔f1 ♕xd1 mate

A drastic win that clearly shows the
difference between the Steinitz and the
Modern Steinitz. The latter, with ...a7-
a6 inserted and a thematic ...b7-b5 expansion in the works, means Black can
push back the Ruy bishop with ...b7-b5,
...c7-c5-c4, and clearly demonstrates
that an unsupported d2-d4 by White is
not to be feared.

Game 3
F.J.Lee-Em.Lasker
London 1899

---

1 e4 e5 2 ♘f3 ♘c6 3 ♗b5 a6 4 ♗a4 ♘f6
5 d3

Unimpressive, but often played.

5...d6

Of course 4...d6 5 d3 ♘f6 reaches
the identical position via the MS order—this is a common transposition.
See Chapter Nine for more examples of
this kind of quiet play for White.

6 c3 b5 7 ♗c2 g6

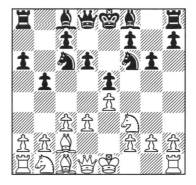

At this point it's worth considering
the modern game V.Anand-
S.Mamedyarov, Wijk aan Zee 2008,
which started like this: 4...d6 5 c3 g6 6
d4 ♗d7 7 0-0 ♗g7 8 ♖e1 b5—note that
the great Lasker played the exact same
pawn structure as Mamedyarov, only
109 years earlier!

8 a4 ♗b7

The double fianchetto has a very
modern appearance. Also good is another plan, seen in a more recent GM
game: 8...b4 9 a5 ♗g7 10 ♗a4 ♗d7 11
♗xc6 ♗xc6 12 cxb4 ♖b8 (Black has very
good compensation with the two bishops and attack against White's split
pawns) 13 ♗d2 0-0 14 ♕c2 ♗a8 15 0-0
d5 16 ♖e1 ♖e8 17 ♘a3 ♗f8 18 ♖ac1
♗d6 19 ♗c3 ♖e7 20 d4 dxe4 21 dxe5
exf3 22 exd6 cxd6 23 ♖xe7 ♕xe7 24

♘c4 ♘d5 25 ♕d2 ♕e4 26 ♘e3 ♘f4 27
♕xd6 ♖c8 28 ♖d1 and now in M.Go-
dena-Ch.Gabriel, Swiss Team Championship 2003, Black played 28...♖xc3
and won with a little help from his opponent—but 28...♘e2+! 29 ♔f1 fxg2!
would have won quickly and cleanly.

9 ♘bd2 ♗g7 10 ♘f1 d5

Already Lasker is better.

**11 ♕e2 0-0 12 ♘g3 ♕d6 13 0-0 ♖fe8 14
h3 ♘a5 15 ♗d2 c5 16 ♖fd1 ♕c7 17 ♕e1**

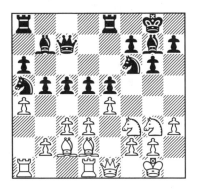

17 ♖a2, preparing to double on the
a-file, at least has a positive function—
better some plan than none! White's
retrograde move is equivalent to sit-
ting and waiting for the axe to fall.

**17...c4! 18 d4 ♘xe4 19 ♘xe4 dxe4 20
♘xe5 ♗xe5 21 dxe5 ♕xe5**

A pawn down against Lasker...

**22 ♗e3 ♘c6 23 b3 ♘a5 24 b4 ♘c6 25
♖d7 ♖e7 26 ♖dd1 ♖d8 27 ♖xd8+ ♘xd8
28 axb5 axb5 29 ♕d2 ♘e6 30 h4 ♗c6
31 ♖a6 ♖d7 32 ♕e1 ♗b7 33 ♖a5 f5 34
g3 f4!**

...means no hope! Now Black breaks
through and finishes with a few powerful blows.

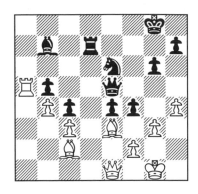

**35 gxf4 ♘xf4 36 ♗d4 ♕f5 37 ♕e3
♖xd4! 38 cxd4 ♕g4+ 39 ♔f1 ♕g2+ 40
♔e1 ♕g1+ 41 ♔d2 c3+ 42 ♕xc3 ♕xf2+
43 ♔d1 e3 44 ♗b3+ ♔g7 45 d5+ ♔h6
46 ♕e1 ♗c8! 0-1**

After 47 ♕xf2 exf2 Black queens.

5 d3 didn't make much of an im-
pression, but we will see it again!

Game 4
R.Réti-J.R.Capablanca
Berlin 1928

1 e4 e5 2 ♘f3 ♘c6 3 ♗b5 a6

Some sources give a different opening move order: 3...d6 4 c3 (of course 4
d4 is correct and compels Black to stay
in the old Steinitz) 4...a6 5 ♗a4 f5, and
also a different course at the end, with
White playing on for a few more
moves. I have followed the usually very
accurate *Chess from Morphy to Botvinnik* with the Modern Steinitz move order and the more plausible resignation
on move 18—why drag it out against
Capa?

4 ♗a4 d6

According to the *MegaBase*, Capablanca played the MS twenty times in tournament play, and won a little over 50%—that is, 11 wins and 9 draws! No losses of course, but Capa hardly lost at all, with any opening. Besides Réti, he also defeated strong players of the time like G.A.Thomas and Tarrasch.

5 c3 f5!

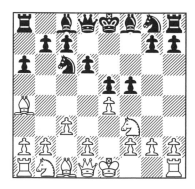

I like the story that the great Cuban champion was having a siesta one day, when he suddenly dreamed up this variation! While this does explain how the Siesta got its name, like a lot of great stories it overlooks one bothersome historical fact: the Siesta had actually been played before, and against Capablanca himself! Yes, Marshall played it in their match (see below) and got a quick advantage with Black, though Capa made a draw with his great defensive skill. So it should be another Marshall Gambit—but it seems Marshall only got his name stuck to a gambit when he lost!

In any case, after this original "Mar-

shall Gambit" no strong player took it up—until Capablanca himself took a second look, liked the other side, and reintroduced the opening with great success at Budapest in 1928.

Perhaps Capa's "Siesta dream" had him playing the black pieces!

6 d4

Against Marshall, Capa played 6 exf5 which is still considered best, though he quickly went astray in the unfamiliar position: 6...♗xf5 7 d4 e4 8 ♕e2 (8 ♘g5 is correct and critical; see full analysis in Chapter Four) 8...♗e7 9 ♘fd2 ♘f6 10 h3 d5 11 ♘f1 b5 12 ♗c2 ♘a5?! (the opening has gone wrong for White, and now the simple 12...0-0 is clearly better for Black, who has f-file play and the better centre—but after this unnecessary knight manoeuvre Capablanca conjures up queenside counterplay and makes his draw) 13 ♘e3 ♗g6 14 ♘d2 0-0 15 b4 ♘c4 16 ♘dxc4 dxc4 17 a4 ♘d5 18 ♘xd5 ♕xd5 19 axb5 e3 20 0-0 ♖xf2 21 ♖xf2 exf2+ 22 ♕xf2 ♖f8 23 ♕e2 ♗xc2 24 ♕xc2 axb5 25 ♗e3 ♗d6 26 ♗f2 ♕g5 27 ♕e4 h6 28 ♖e1 ♖xf2 29 ♔xf2 ♗g3+ 30 ♔g1 ♗xe1 31 ♕xe1 ½-½ J.R.Capablanca-F.Marshall, New York (14th match-game) 1909.

6...fxc4 7 ♘g5

The sacrifice 7 ♘xe5 is good for a draw at best (see Game 42).

7...exd4 8 ♘xe4 ♘f6

Also good is 8...♗f5 (see Game 43).

9 ♗g5 ♗e7 10 ♕xd4

10 ♗xf6 is the only move, but Black

is still better: 10...♗xf6 11 ♕h5+ g6 12
♕d5 ♗d7 13 0-0 ♕e7 14 ♘xf6+ ♕xf6
15 ♖e1+ ♘e7 16 ♖e6 0-0-0 (16...♗xa4!
is even stronger) 17 ♗xd7+ ♖xd7 18
♕xb7+ ♔xb7 19 ♖xf6 ♘d5 20 ♖e6 and
now, instead of 20...dxc3 which led to a
draw in V.Andreev-V.Yandemirov,
Ekaterinburg 1997, Black had 20...d3!
with a very dangerous passed pawn.
10...b5

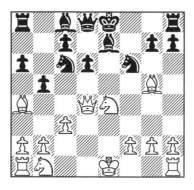

This key MS move shakes off the pin
and gives Black the attack—and on the
next move we will see...
11 ♘xf6+ gxf6

...that the white queen and both
white bishops are hanging! Naturally
there is no way out for White. It's
rather nice to see a decisive advantage
for Black—in a Ruy Lopez!—after just
eleven moves.
12 ♕d5 bxa4 13 ♗h6

Or 13 ♕xc6+ ♗d7 14 ♕f3 fxg5 15
♕h5+ ♔f8 16 ♕h6+ ♔g8 and White
runs out of checks.
13...♕d7

Capa must be cheating, every move
is *Fritz*'s number one pick!

14 0-0

White can also lose with 14 ♗g7
♕e6+ 15 ♕xe6 ♗xe6 16 ♗xh8 ♔f7 as
Black gets two pieces for the rook; and
14 ♕h5+ ♔d8 15 ♗g7 ♖g8 16 ♕xh7
♕e6+ 17 ♔f1 ♕f7 is even worse!
14...♗b7 15 ♗g7 0-0-0

Unlike almost all other Ruy lines, in
the MS Black can often castle queenside and play for an attack on White's
king—something I like very much!
16 ♗xh8 ♘e5!!

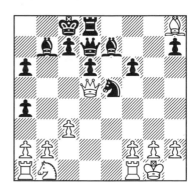

Capa doesn't need White's divagat-
ing bishop.
17 ♕d1

Another demonstration of the attacking power of Black's position is
seen after 17 ♕a5 ♖g8 18 f3 ♕f5 19
♔h1 (no better is 19 ♘d2 which loses
the queen to 19...♘xf3+ 20 ♘xf3 ♕xa5)
19...♕g5 20 g3 ♘xf3 21 ♕xg5 ♘xg5+
22 ♔g1 ♘h3 with a pretty mate.
17...♗f3! 18 gxf3

If 18 ♕c2 ♕g4 forces mate.
18...♕h3 0-1

White has no defence to ...♘xf3+ or
...♖g8+.

The Siesta is a terrifying gambit unless White is very well prepared!

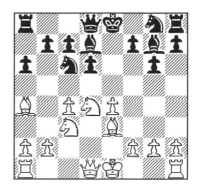

1 e4 e5 2 ♘f3 ♘c6 3 ♗b5 a6 4 ♗a4 d6 5 c4

This is the Duras Variation, where White tries to set up a Maróczy Bind—but it's no longer any kind of danger to the Modern Steinitz. I think Keres liked to play this rare line so he wasn't "playing against himself" with the main moves 5 c3 or 5 0-0.

However, Capablanca shows here that Black can equalize rather easily with a kingside fianchetto; then in Chapter Seven, Reshevsky and Yandemirov show how Black can play for a win with the even stronger 5...♗g4, which has essentially put the Duras Variation out of business.

5...♗d7

For 5...♗g4 see Games 60-62; for the rather doubtful 5...f5 (the Siesta doesn't work well here, as we will see) go to Game 63.

6 ♘c3 g6 7 d4 exd4 8 ♘xd4 ♗g7 9 ♗e3

There are two reasons why this Maróczy Bind position is much easier for Black than the usual "dreaded bind" positions: First, the white king's bishop is misplaced (normally in the Maróczy it's on e2) and it's due to be exchanged for the d7-bishop, easing Black's cramp.

Secondly, Black can develop with ...♘e7, so in the long run (as we see in the game) ...f7-f5, breaking the bind, can't be prevented. That said, the Maróczy Bind is a very solid system, even in a non-aggressive form like this, so Keres never has to worry about Black taking over the advantage, and can exert some light pressure until Capa fully equalizes, when a draw must ensue in view of reduced material.

9...♘ge7 10 0-0 0-0 11 h3 ♘xd4 12 ♗xd7 ♘e2+!

Capa cleverly disorganizes his opponent's pieces: if White takes with the queen, Black will threaten pawn structure demolition with ...♗xc3, while ♗e3-d4 is prevented. In the game, of course, the white knight is misplaced and must soon move again.

13 ♘xe2 ♕xd7 14 ♗d4 ♗xd4 15 ♕xd4

After 15 ♘xd4 Black equalizes easily; e.g. 15...♘c6 16 ♖e1 ♖ae8 17 ♕d3 f5 18 exf5 ♘xd4 19 ♕xd4 ♕xf5 and a draw could already be agreed.

15...♘c6 16 ♕d5 ♖ae8 17 ♘c3 ♕e6 18 ♖ad1 f5

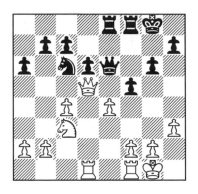

The key break: Black is fully equal.

19 exf5 ♖xf5 20 ♖de1 ♖xd5 21 ♖xe6 ♖e5!

White was hoping for 21...♖xe6?? 22 cxd5 winning a piece.

22 ♖xe8+ ♖xe8 23 ♖d1

If 23 ♘d5, Black takes over the seventh and the advantage with 23...♖e2.

23...♔f7 24 ♔f1 ♘e5 25 b3 ♘d7 26 ♘d5 c6 27 ♘f4 ♖e4 28 g3 ♔e7 29 ♘e2 ♘c5 30 f3 ♖e3 31 ♔f2 ♖d3 32 ♖xd3 ♘xd3+ 33 ♔e3 ♘b4 ½-½

As one sees, Black had no difficulties in this variation, provided he played within the position. So far so good, but why stop with equality? I think 5 c4 is really anti-positional in combination with the Lopez Bishop—so Black should play not just to equalize, but to win: see more in Chapter Seven.

Game 6
F.Yates-A.Alekhine
New York 1924

---

1 e4 e5 2 ♘f3 ♘c6 3 ♗b5 a6 4 ♗a4 d6 5

0-0 g6

Already inaccurate, but the game was played in the early days of the variation. My research indicates that if Black wants to fianchetto his king's bishop, he should play a move order like this: ...♗d7/...♘f6/...g7-g6. I'll go into all the details in Chapter Three. Note as well that the coming development of the black knight to e7 also seems inaccurate, for as Alekhine himself pointed out, White could have gained some advantage by exploiting the pin that Yates achieves on said knight.

6 c3

Allowing the move order error to go unpunished! Since this game, White has made a huge score with 6 d4!.

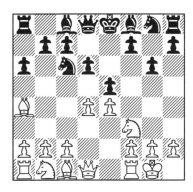

Now Black has to deal with the threats of d4-d5 and d4xe5. Black can try:

a) 6...♗g7 7 dxe5 (7 d5 b5 8 dxc6 bxa4 9 c4 also looks good for White) 7...b5 (or 7...dxe5 8 ♕xd8+ ♔xd8 9 ♘c3 and White is clearly better in the queenless middlegame) 8 ♗g5 ♕d7 9

♗b3 dxe5 and now, instead of the overly fancy 10 ♕d5 of I.Zubairov-P.Bacherikov, Russian Junior Championship 2001, White had the simple 10 ♕e2 with a big plus, as one sees a rook coming to d1 soon.

b) 6...exd4 7 ♕xd4 f6 8 ♕d3 ♗d7 9 ♘c3 ♘e5 10 ♘xe5 dxe5 (or 10...fxe5 11 ♗b3 ♘f6 12 ♕c4 winning at least a pawn) 11 ♗b3 and White's advantage was already decisive in V.Iordachescu-I.Efimov, Castellaneta 1999.

c) 6...♗d7 7 ♗xc6 ♗xc6 8 dxe5 dxe5 (opening the e-file is dangerous: 8...♗xe4 9 ♖e1 d5 10 ♘g5 ♗f5 11 ♘c3 c6 12 e6 ♗xe6 13 ♘xe6 fxe6 14 ♕g4 with a strong attack, or if 12...fxe6 13 g4 h6 14 gxf5 hxg5 15 ♖xe6+ and White is much better) 9 ♘xe5 ♗xe4 10 ♕e2 ♕d5 11 ♗f4 f6 12 ♘c3 ♕e6 13 ♕xe4 fxe5 14 ♗xe5 (but this finally turned out to be even worse, as now Black had to resign!) 1-0 K.Szabo-J.Brustkern, Budapest 2007.

d) 6...b5 7 ♗b3 ♗g7 looks like it holds for a second, but as the late Robert B.Parker would have said, "We'd be fools not to launch an immediate attack!": 8 dxe5! ♘xe5 (after 8...dxe5 9 ♘g5 ♘h6 10 ♕xd8+ ♘xd8 11 ♘c3 White's lead in development is virtually decisive; e.g. 11...c6 12 ♖d1 ♔h7 13 ♗e3 a5 14 a3 f6 15 ♖xd8+! ♖xd8 16 ♘e6 and White wins material) 9 ♗g5 ♘xf3+ 10 ♕xf3! with a tremendous attack.

What a setback that would have been for Alekhine! But the good player is, as ever, lucky.

6...♗g7 7 d4 ♗d7 8 ♗g5

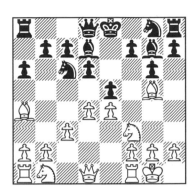

On 8 ♗e3 Black should play 8...♘f6 as in Chapter Three with a quite reasonable position: here's a typical example of this line: 9 dxe5 ♘xe5 10 ♘xe5 dxe5 11 ♘d2 0-0 12 ♗c2 ♕e7 13 h3 ♘e8 14 ♕e2 and now, instead of the quiet 14...♘d6 with equality of I.Kashdan-S.Flohr, Bled 1931 (though one must note that Flohr did grind out the win in 65 moves), Black can take over the initiative immediately with 14...f5, the King's Indian type break that is typical of this MS variation.

8...♘ge7

Black would rather have his knight on f6, but tactically it doesn't work well now because of his wrong move order: 8...♘f6 9 ♗xc6 ♗xc6 10 dxe5 dxe5 11 ♘xe5 ♕xd1 12 ♖xd1 ♘xe4 13 ♗f4 with some advantage to White, as Black's c6-bishop, knight and c7-pawn are all targets, and he won't be able to avoid making some concessions.

9 dxe5 dxe5 10 ♕d3 h6 11 ♗e3 ♗g4 12 ♕e2 0-0

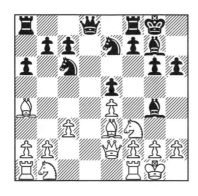

13 ♘bd2

This move reminds me of the DDT acronym I coined for *True Combat Chess*: Dubious Development Traumatizes! Yates misses a second chance to turn the game sharply in his favour—misses it because he *routinely* develops a fresh piece, rather than moving an already developed piece for the third time!

As Alekhine points out, 13 ♗c5! is much stronger and gives White a plus; e.g. 13...f5 14 ♘bd2 fxe4 15 ♘xe4! ♗xf3 16 gxf3 ♔h7 17 ♖fd1 ♕e8 18 ♖d3 and Black has one of those dreadful "no counterplay" positions: he's pinned this way and that, his knights are tied to each other and have no activity, and White can just build up on the d-file with ever increasing pressure.

But White missed this because he followed the "rules" of development!
13...f5 14 h3 ♗h5 15 ♗b3+ ♔h8 16 exf5?

White must hold the e4-square, and can still get the advantage with 16 ♖ad1! fxe4 17 ♘xe4 ♗xf3 18 gxf3 ♕c8

19 ♔h2 ♕f5 20 ♘g3! ♕xf3 21 ♕xf3 ♖xf3 22 ♖d7. This position shows the strength of White's game, even a pawn down, as the light squares are all White owned! A typical continuation would be 22...♖c8 23 ♖g1 ♔h7 24 ♗c5 ♘f5 25 ♘xf5 ♖xf5 26 ♗e6 ♖f6 27 ♖xg7+! and the light-squared bishop wins the game.

Evidently Yates was afraid of the doubled kingside pawns, but by avoiding that, he lost his advantage and then the game.
16...gxf5

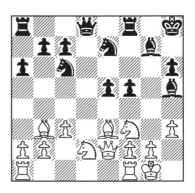

Just like that, Black is better with mobile pawns and kingside attacking chances.
17 g4 fxg4 18 ♘e1

No better is 18 ♘h2 ♗g6 19 ♕xg4 (not 19 hxg4 ♗d3 winning the exchange) 19...♗f5 20 ♕h5 ♕e8 21 ♕xe8 ♖axe8 22 ♔g2 ♖d8 23 ♖ad1 ♘d5 and Black is attacking in the queenless middlegame.
18...♘d5 19 hxg4 ♘xe3 20 fxe3 ♕g5!

A "closely calculated combination" with a "little surprise" says Alekhine.

21 &e6 &xg4!

There's the surprise!

22 ♕xg4

22 &xg4 h5 is good for Black too.

22...♕xe3+ 23 ♔h1 ♕xd2 24 ♖g1 ♕g5

Alekhine points out that 24...&f6 is more accurate.

25 ♕h3 ♕f6 26 &d5 ♘e7 27 &e4 ♘f5

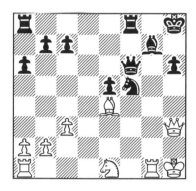

28 ♘f3

28 ♘d3! would set Black a difficult problem, as White has real compensation on the light squares and g-file; e.g. 28...♖ad8 29 ♖g4 and White is still playing.

Whereas now White's bishop is tied to his knight and the game is over, except for the final tactical flourish.

28...♘d6 29 &d5

Not 29 ♖g6? ♘xe4 30 ♖xf6 ♘f2+ and wins.

29...c6

Actually better is 29...♕f5 with a clean extra pawn, as...

30 ♖xg7

...instead of the text, 30 ♘h4! cxd5 31 ♖af1! gives White surprising counterplay!

30...♔xg7

But now it's all over except for the final tactical flourish.

31 ♖g1+ ♔h8 32 ♘xe5 cxd5 33 ♕h5 ♘e4 34 ♘g6+ ♔h7 35 ♕xd5 ♘g3+! 0-1

One can count on Alekhine to win stylishly! After the forced acceptance of the piece, 36 ♖xg3, Black wins with 36...♕f1+ 37 ♔h2 (37 ♖g1 ♕h3 mate is only slightly worse) 37...♖f2+ 38 ♖g2 ♕xg2+ 39 ♕xg2 ♖xg2+ 40 ♔xg2 ♔xg6 and the extra rook is good enough.

While Alekhine's opening play was certainly inaccurate, the fundamental idea of Black's structure—kingside fianchetto followed eventually by ...f7-f5—is positionally sound as we will see in Chapter Three.

Game 7
A.Trott-M.Euwe
Beverwijk 1953

---

1 e4 e5 2 ♘f3 ♘c6 3 &b5 a6 4 &a4 d6 5 &xc6+

This third move of the bishop is recommended by Andrew Greet in his Worrall repertoire book, *Play the Ruy Lopez*, but I can't feel too much terror here given White's loss of time.

5...bxc6 6 d4 f6

Although played by Euwe and also Capablanca (which would seem enough endorsement for practically anyone) I don't recommend this move at all, as I think that only after this does White have chances for advantage.

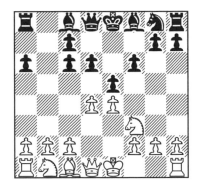

Black now gets a cramped and usually closed game where the white knights can be effective. Keres usually played the more logical 6...exd4, opening the game for the two bishops, and this was also Nigel Short's method in his world championship match vs. Kasparov, where he drew quickly with Black. I will give full coverage of 6...exd4 in Chapter Six, plus one more game with 6...f6 where the master of the white position, Jacob Yukhtman, shows how White can get an edge in this line.

7 c4

This leads to a blocked position that White shouldn't lose, but he has more chances of advantage with Yukhtman's simple 7 ♘c3 (see Game 59).

7...♘e7 8 ♘c3 c5

The dark side of 7 c4 is the weakness at d4, which Euwe the mathematician precisely exploits. He almost completely equalizes this way, but a win for Black does not seem likely!

9 dxc5 dxc5 10 ♕xd8+

White accomplishes nothing with

10 ♗e3 ♘c6 11 ♕d5 ♕d6 12 0-0-0 ♖b8 and Black is fine.

10...♔xd8 11 b3 ♘c6 12 0-0 ♘d4 13 ♘e1 ♗d6 14 ♘d3 ♗d7 15 ♖b1 a5 16 ♗a3 ♘e6 17 ♖fd1 ♔e7

18 ♘b2

White evidently overestimates his position: instead he should nail down a marginal edge with 18 ♘a4! which forces the exchange of Black's better bishop. After 18...♗xa4 19 bxa4 White has a slight plus due to his own good bishop. However, the position is so blocked that a draw would be the most likely result—but one can't even *imagine* Black winning this position.

In the game the experienced World Champion keeps some activity, and finally outplays his opponent.

18...♖a6 19 ♖d2 ♖b8 20 ♘ba4 ♖c6 21 f3 ♘d4!

This good knight makes up for a lot of passive pieces: Black has full equality, and White is still a long way from a clear draw.

22 ♖e1 ♔f7 23 ♖f2 g5 24 g4 h5 25 h3 ♖h8 26 ♔g2 ♘e6 27 ♘e2 ♖a6 28 ♖d1

♗c6 29 ♗c1 ♗xa4 30 bxa4 ♖b6 31 ♗a3 ♖bb8 32 ♖ff1 ♖h6 33 ♖b1 ♖bh8 34 ♖h1 ♘f4+ 35 ♘xf4 exf4 36 ♖bf1 ♔e6 37 ♖d1 ♗e5!

I give the exclam for fighting spirit: though the position is dead even, Euwe nonetheless makes a spirited attempt to win—which shouldn't succeed, but...

38 ♗xc5 hxg4 39 hxg4 ♖xh1 40 ♖xh1 ♖d8 41 a3??

This looks like a "first move after the time control" relaxation move. Instead, the zielbewußt 41 ♖h7!, threatening mate, draws easily as can be seen: 41...♖d2+ 42 ♔f1 ♗d6 (not 42...♖d7? 43 ♖xd7 ♔xd7 44 ♔e2 and the ending is better for White, in view of Black's fixed pawns on the colour of his bishop) 43 ♗xd6 cxd6 (or 43...♔xd6 44 ♖f7 ♔e5 45 ♖xc7 ♖xa2 46 ♖d7 ♖xa4 47 ♖d5+ ♔e6 48 c5 ♖a3 49 ♔e2 a4 50 c6 ♖c3 51 ♖a5 ♖xc6 52 ♖xa4 and draws) 44 ♖a7 ♖xa2 45 ♖xa5 ♖c2 46 ♖d5 ♖xc4 47 a5 ♖a4 and the position is a dead draw.

41...♖d2+ 42 ♔f1 ♗d6! 43 ♗xd6

43 ♗f2 ♖d3 is also good for Black.

43...♖d1+

The surprising point: though nominally a pawn down, Black's better king position means that a potential pawn ending is winning for him. Therefore White tries to fight on an exchange down, but to no avail. The failure to play actively (a2-a3 instead of ♖h7) cost him dearly!

44 ♔g2 ♖xh1

45 ♗xc7

Black's point is seen in this easy king and pawn ending: 45 ♔xh1 ♔xd6 46 ♔g2 ♔c5 47 ♔f2 ♔xc4 48 ♔e2 ♔b3 49 ♔d2 ♔xa3 50 ♔c3 ♔xa4 51 ♔c4 c6 52 ♔c5 ♔b3 and queens.

45...♖a1 46 ♗xa5 ♖xa3 47 c5 ♖xa4 48 ♗c7 ♖a6 49 ♔f2 ♔d7 50 ♗d6 ♔c6 51 ♔e2 ♖a2+ 52 ♔e1 ♔b5 53 ♗e7 ♖a6 54 ♔e2 ♔c4 55 ♗d6 ♖a2+ 56 ♔e1 ♔d3 57 ♗e7

Black also wins after 57 c6 ♔e3 58 ♗c5+ ♔xf3 59 c7 ♖a8 60 ♗a7 ♖c8 61 ♗b8 ♔xe4.

57...♔e3 58 ♗xf6 ♖c2 59 ♔d1 ♖xc5 0-1

White resigns in view of 60 e5 ♔xf3 61 ♗xg5 (or 61 e6 ♖c6 62 e7 ♖e6 63 ♗xg5 ♔xg4 64 ♗f6 f3 and wins as the white king is cut off) 61...♖xe5 62 ♗f6 ♖d5+ 63 ♔e1 ♔xg4 64 ♔f2 ♖d2+ 65 ♔e1 ♖a2 66 ♔f1 ♔f3 67 ♗h4 ♖a1+ etc.

Returning to the opening, note that the blocking 6...f6 led to a closed game where Black had no legitimate winning chances until after the first time control! While I admire Euwe's endgame perseverance, I think Black would have had much more chances with the natural 6...exd4.

I was struck by the tremendous (pre-computer!) annotations to the following game in the *Soviet Absolute Championship* book by Botvinnik. One wishes our modern champions wrote so incisively!

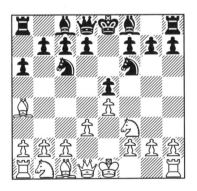

Game 8
V.Smyslov-M.Botvinnik
USSR Championship,
Leningrad/Moscow 1941

1 e4 e5 2 ♘f3 ♘c6 3 ♗b5 a6 4 ♗a4 ♘f6 5 d3

"An old move, which holds out no possibility of any sort of advantage," writes Smyslov of his own move. Botvinnik writes: "An ancient continuation, White declines to fight in the opening, reckoning on a favourable middlegame."

But I ask: How can one reach a favourable middlegame when you get nothing out of the opening? I've never understood these passive variations (which is why I play things like the Four Pawns Attack against the King's Indian!) but they've always been popular—and are even more so now, with thousands of games in the database. Of course I've run into this one in practice, which I don't mind. It's nice to have a free hand with Black (see the note to White's tenth move).

5...d6

Again, 4...d6 5 d3 ♘f6 reaches the game position by the MS order.

6 c3 ♗e7

One recalls that in Game 3 Lasker played 6...b5 here and won with a *modern* double fianchetto, while Botvinnik chooses to play very classically. In either case Black has no problems.

7 0-0 0-0 8 ♖e1 b5 9 ♗c2 d5 10 ♘bd2

I'm not sure if White's e-pawn has enough protection (bishop/knight/rook and the pawn at d3!). Amusingly enough, I also ran into this sort of over-protection in a recent game: 1 ♘f3 ♘c6 2 e4 e5 3 ♗b5 a6 4 ♗a4 d6 5 c3 ♗d7 6 0-0 ♘f6 7 d3 g6 8 ♖e1 ♗g7 9 ♘bd2 (with the e-pawn protected in only three ways, this is not quite as secure as Smyslov—White needs ♗c2 to complete the picture!) 9...0-0 10 ♘f1 and since White had not undertaken anything, I gladly seized the initiative with 10...♔h8 followed soon by ...♘g8 and ...f7-f5, and won with a kingside attack in S.Kitagami-I.Taylor, Los Angeles (rapid) 2010.

10...dxe4 11 dxe4 ♗e6

It's worth comparing this position to the Rauzer Attack in the Chigorin Variation of the Ruy, which occurs after 4...♘f6 5 0-0 ♗e7 6 ♖e1 b5 7 ♗b3 d6 8 c3 0-0 9 h3 ♘a5 10 ♗c2 c5 11 d4 ♕c7 12 ♘bd2 ♘c6 13 dxc5 dxc5

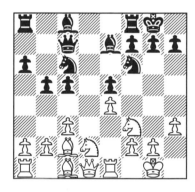

and a position is reached from which Fischer had tremendous success; one important factor is the hole at d5 which often, as in the following game, attracts a white knight: 14 ♘f1 ♗e6 15 ♘e3 ♖ad8 16 ♕e2 g6 17 ♘g5 ♗c8 18 a4 c4 19 axb5 axb5 20 b3 b4 21 ♕xc4 h6 (Black is counting on 22 ♘f3?! ♗e6 when he is better, but he gets a surprise) 22 ♘d5! (White's advantage is decisive) 22...♘xd5 23 exd5 hxg5 24

♕xc6 ♕xc6 25 dxc6 bxc3 26 ♖xe5 ♗f6 27 ♖ea5 ♖fe8 28 ♗xg5 ♗xg5 29 ♖xg5 ♖d2 30 ♖c1 ♖ee2 31 ♗xg6 fxg6 32 ♖xc3 ♔h7 33 b4 ♖e1+ 34 ♔h2 ♖xf2 35 b5 ♖b2 36 ♔g3 ♔h6 37 ♖cc5 ♖e3+ 38 ♔f4 ♖eb3 39 ♖gd5 ♖xg2 40 ♖d8 ♗e6 41 ♔e5 ♗xh3 42 ♖h8+ ♔g7 43 ♖xh3 ♖xh3 44 c7 ♖h8 45 ♖d5 ♖e2+ 46 ♔d6 ♔f6 47 b6 ♖b2 48 ♔c6 ♖c8 49 ♖d8 ♖c2+ 50 ♔b7 ♖8xc7+ 51 bxc7 ♔f5 52 c8♕+ ♖xc8 53 ♖xc8 g5 54 ♔c6 g4 55 ♔d5 ♔f4 56 ♔d4 ♔f3 57 ♔d3 1-0 R.J.Fischer-C.Kalme, New York 1958.

Now look at the main game:

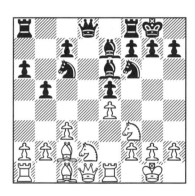

While White's position superficially resembles the Rauzer/Fischer weapon, a closer look reveals that Black has d5 covered, and there is no hole on this square, as the c-pawn is still back at c7. In other words, even if White should eventually land a knight on d5, it could be driven back post haste with ...c7-c6.

The bottom line is that Black is already slightly better.

12 h3

12 ♘g5 is met easily by 12...♗g4.

12...h6 13 ♘h2 ♘h7 14 ♘g4 ♗g5 15

♕e2 ♛d6 16 ♘e3 ♖fd8 17 ♘f3 ♗xe3 18 ♕xe3

As Botvinnik points out, 18 ♗xe3 ♗c4 is good for Black as the white queen is embarrassed.

18...♕e7 19 ♘h2

Botvinnik correctly evaluates the position as still better for Black, but in the game he now loses his way.

19...♘f8?!

Best is 19...♘f6 20 ♕f3 b4 with a queenside initiative.

20 ♕f3 ♖d7 21 ♘f1

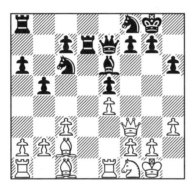

White has finally generated real kingside threats (♘g3-f5) and the struggle shifts in his favour—but it's so complex that Smyslov in turn will go wrong.

21...♘h7 22 ♘g3 ♖ad8 23 ♘f5 ♕f6 24 g4 ♘e7 25 ♕g3 ♗c4 26 f3 ♗d3 27 ♗b3 c5 28 ♗e3 c4 29 ♗d1 ♘g5 30 h4 ♘e6 31 a4 b4!

Smyslov's methodical play over the last several moves fails to unnerve Botvinnik, who shocks the positional master with a "confusion" pawn sac! White can no longer play mechanically.

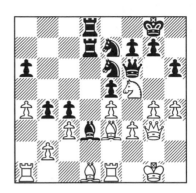

32 cxb4 ♘f4 33 ♔h1 g5 34 b5 a5 35 ♗c5?!

Confused! This forces Black to make an exchange he will make anyway, and puts the bishop on an insecure square. Correct is 35 ♖c1! which brings the rook into play and prevents the tactical blow ...♗c2 seen in the notes to move 37—in this way White could have maintained an edge.

35...♘xf5 36 gxf5 ♔h7 37 ♕g4

On 37 hxg5 hxg5 the h-file becomes an attacking avenue for Black, while if 37 ♕h2 ♗c2!! 38 hxg5 (White has no good way to take the piece: 38 ♗xc2 ♖d2 recovers material with advantage, and even worse is 38 ♕xc2 ♖d2 39 ♕c1 g4! with a winning attack for Black) 38...♕xg5 39 ♗e2 ♘xe2 40 ♖xe2 ♖d1+ 41 ♖xd1 ♗xd1 42 ♗e3 ♕f6 43 ♖f2 ♖d3 44 ♖f1 ♖xe3 45 ♖xd1 ♖xf3 White's situation is grave (Botvinnik).

37...gxh4

Suddenly Black has a winning attack!

38 ♖g1 h5

As Botvinnik points out, he missed a quick win here with 38...♗f1! 39 ♖xf1 (or 39 ♗f2 ♗g2+ 40 ♖xg2 ♘xg2 and Black wins material) 39...♖g8 and the white queen goes.

39 ♕g5 ♕xg5 40 ♖xg5 f6 41 ♖g1 ♘h3 42 ♖e1 ♖g8 43 ♖a2!

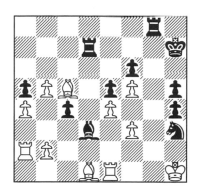

An heroic defence! He avoids the following queenless mating attack: 43 ♖c1 ♖g3 44 ♗e3 ♖dg7 45 ♔h2 (45 b3 ♘f2+! 46 ♗xf2 ♖h3 mate is Botvinnik's key point) 45...♘f4! 46 ♗xf4 exf4 and White has no defence; e.g. 47 b3 ♖g2+ 48 ♔h1 ♖f2 49 bxc4 ♖gg2 and mates.

43...♗b1 44 ♖a1 ♗d3 45 ♖a2 ♘f4 46 b4 ♖c8 47 b6 ♖b7 48 ♗e3 axb4 49 a5 b3 50 ♖a3?!

A critical inaccuracy: 50 ♖b2! may draw; e.g. 50...♖a8 (or 50...c3 51 ♖xb3 c2 52 ♗xc2 ♗xc2 53 ♖a3 and the passed pawns give compensation for the piece) 51 ♗d2 and White holds, at least for the moment!

50...b2 51 ♗a4 c3 52 ♖b3 ♘e2 53 ♗b5 ♗xb5 54 ♖xb5 ♘d4! 55 ♗xd4

White has to take, in view of 55 ♖b4 ♘c2 forking.

55...exd4

Now the three connected passed

pawns are decisive, though Smyslov continues his heroic resistance.

56 a6 ♖xb6! 57 ♖xb6 d3 58 ♖g1 d2 59 ♖xf6 ♖c7 60 ♖fg6!

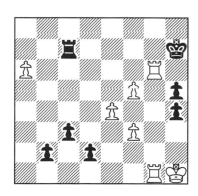

A fantastic resource: now if 60...c2? 61 ♖6g5! and White draws despite three black pawns on the seventh rank!

60...d1♕!! 0-1

But Botvinnik trumps that resource with this diversion! After 61 ♖xd1 c2 62 ♖dg1 c1♕ 63 ♖6g5 ♕xg5 (Black sacrifices a second queen, but he has one more coming!) 64 ♖xg5 b1♕+ Black mates in six—therefore Smyslov resigns.

This was truly a titanic struggle between two future World Champions—though it's interesting that they both agreed that White played a "nothing" opening.

1 e4 e5 2 ♘f3 ♘c6 3 ♗b5 a6 4 ♗a4 d6 5

0-0

It might seem strange that the late, great Vassily Smyslov is represented only by two losses in this section, and no wins—but while Smyslov did play the MS on occasion, he did not seem to have the feel for this opening. He made an uncharacteristic minus score with Black—the following game is typical: 5 c3 ♗d7 6 d4 ♘f6 7 0-0 ♗e7 (I recommend the more active 7...g6 in Chapter Three) 8 ♖e1 0-0 9 ♘bd2 exd4 10 cxd4 ♘b4 11 ♗xd7 ♕xd7 12 ♘f1 c5 (Black's plan makes no sense to me) 13 a3 ♘c6 14 d5 ♘e5 15 ♘xe5 dxe5 16 ♘g3

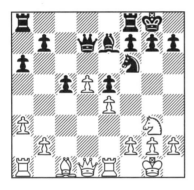

(White is simply clearly better with the good bishop and protected passed pawn, and Averbakh wasn't showing the pre-champion Smyslov any courtesies!) 16...♘e8 17 f4! (White plays for the attack!) 17...♗d6 18 ♘f5 f6 19 g3 g6 20 ♘h6+ ♔h8 21 f5 c4 22 h4 ♗c5+ 23 ♔g2 gxf5 24 ♘xf5 ♘d6 25 ♘xd6 ♗xd6 26 ♖f1 f5 27 ♗h6 ♖f7 28 exf5 ♖xf5 29 ♕c2 ♖xf1 30 ♖xf1 ♖g8 31 ♕f5 ♕xf5 32 ♖xf5 (and now Averbakh, who literally wrote the book on endings, brings his

advantage home) 32...♖g6 33 ♗g5 ♔g8 34 h5 ♖g7 35 ♔f3 b5 36 ♗h6 e4+ 37 ♔xe4 ♖xg3 38 ♖f6 ♗c5 39 d6 ♔h8 40 ♔d5 1-0 Y.Averbakh-V.Smyslov, USSR Championship, Moscow 1951.

As White he suffered as well, and not just against Botvinnik. Smyslov often played with excessive passivity against the MS, which led to draws and losses against those beneath his station—here's another example: 5 c3 ♘f6 6 d3 (of course 6 d4 is the only hope for advantage, when 6...♗d7 7 0-0 g6 transposes to various games in Chapter Three) 6...g6 7 ♘bd2 ♗g7 8 ♘f1 0-0 9 ♗g5 h6 10 ♗h4 ♘e7 11 ♘e3 c6 12 ♗c2 ♕c7 13 d4 ♘h5 14 dxe5 dxe5 15 ♘d2 ♘f4 16 g3 ♘e6 17 ♗xe7 (White's retrograde play is capped by giving up the two bishops) 17...♕xe7 18 h4 h5 19 ♕e2 b5 20 a3 a5 21 0-0 a4 (Black has the advantage all across the board) 22 ♖fd1 ♘c5 23 ♘f3 ♗h6 24 ♘e1 ♗e6 25 ♘d3 ♘xd3 26 ♖xd3 ♖fd8 27 ♖ad1 ♖xd3 28 ♖xd3 ♖d8 29 ♔f1 (Black's bishops are dominant, and Gligo has a clear advantage on both flanks—but of course, the World Champion has his "get out of jail free" card ready—a draw offer!) ½-½ V.Smyslov-S.Gligoric, Kiev 1959.

5...♗g4 6 h3 h5!

Best! I haven't found any name for this gambit in chess literature, but I think it should be called the Yandemirov Gambit, after the hero of this game. He has played this line—often giving up a whole piece—at least 38 times in high-level play, defeating many GMs and here a world champion!

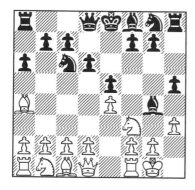

As a side note, one recalls that Geller tried the weaker 6...♗h5 against the young Bobby Fischer and achieved "Memorable Game" status by being crushed in 22 moves: 7 c3 ♕f6 8 g4! (so much for the pin; the key idea of the Yandemirov Gambit is that Black maintains the pin as long as possible—and if White at some point takes the g4-bishop, then Black gets the open h-file for attack) 8...♗g6 9 d4! ♗xe4 10 ♘bd2 ♗g6 11 ♗xc6+ bxc6 12 dxe5 dxe5 13 ♘xe5! ♗d6 14 ♘xg6 ♕xg6 15 ♖e1+ ♔f8 16 ♘c4 h5 17 ♘xd6 cxd6 18 ♗f4 d5 19 ♕b3 hxg4 20 ♕b7! gxh3+ 21 ♗g3 ♖d8 22 ♕b4+ 1-0 R.J.Fischer-E.Geller, Bled 1961.

7 ♗xc6+

This and the other critical move (7 d4) are fully analysed in Chapter Five.

7...bxc6 8 d3

Smyslov tries his typical early d2-d3, gets nothing, and goes down in flames to a specialist in this line! Good opening preparation can go a long way towards defeating a higher-rated player.

8...♕f6

Yandemirov has had this position three times and scored 3-0 with Black, beating Smyslov in the main game as well as IM Zheliandinov (Game 46) and master Bukavshin.

9 ♘bd2

Bukavshin tried 9 ♖e1 here without success, while Zheliandinov (see Game 46) didn't deviate until move 11. All of this will be covered in Chapter Five, but it's worth mentioning here that the immediate capture of the daring bishop gives Black a very dangerous attack: 9 hxg4 hxg4 10 ♘g5—because d2-d3 has been played, White can speculate with this move which prevents the immediate ...♕h4. However, according to the *Mega*, no one has been bold (or foolhardy) enough to try this, so Mr. *Fritz* and I are left on our own—but we like Black! First let's note that White has to play ♘g5, since 10 ♘fd2? ♕h4 11 f4 g3 mates at once. But even after the correct knight block Black gets a strong attack with 10...♕h6 and then:

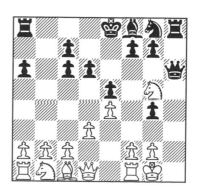

a) 11 f4 ♕h4 12 fxe5 dxe5 (12...g3 is

premature in view of 13 ♘h3) 13 ♗e3 (defending against ...♗c5+) 13...f6 14 ♘f3 (now if 14 ♘e6? g3 wins, as the white knight has been diverted from its defensive duties) 14...gxf3 15 ♕xf3 ♖h5! (15...♘h6 16 ♗f2 and White holds) 16 ♘d2 ♘h6 with advantage to Black, who has maintained his attack while recovering material.

b) 11 f3 ♕h2+ 12 ♔f2 ♗e7! (the trapped white knight on g5 is a recurring feature in this gambit) 13 fxg4 (13 ♖g1 is no better, as 13...f6 14 ♘e6 ♔f7 15 ♘xc7 ♖a7 terminates the white knight, and after 16 ♘xa6 ♖xa6 Black's attack outweighs the pawn) 13...♕h4+ 14 g3 ♕h2+ 15 ♔f3 ♖h6 16 ♕e2 ♖f6+ 17 ♔e3 (or 17 ♗f4 ♖xf4+ 18 gxf4 ♕xf4+ 19 ♔g2 ♕xg5 20 ♘c3 ♖b8 21 ♖f5 ♕g6 22 ♖h5 ♘h6 23 b3 ♔d7 24 ♖h3 f5 25 exf5 ♘xf5 and Black is at least equal) 17...♕h6 and one sees why this line does not entice White players: the prospect of a king on e3, and losing the piece back after all, is not something most would enjoy.

9...♘e7 10 ♖e1 ♗d7

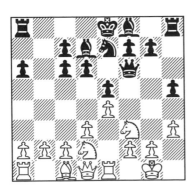

Now it's finally time to save the bishop, for if 10...♘g6? 11 hxg4 hxg4, then 12 ♘h2 ♕h4 13 ♘df1 and White defends the attack on the h-file.

11 ♘f1

Zheli deviated here with 11 ♘c4.

11...♘g6 12 ♗g5 ♕e6 13 d4 f6

Black has a solid position and can attack the white king.

14 ♗e3 ♘e7

Slower but safer is 14...h4!? which prevents ♘g3, and the black king can find a relatively safe home on f7.

15 ♕d2 g5 16 dxe5 dxe5 17 ♕a5

Smyslov is concerned about Black's weak pawns on the queenside—but Yandemirov is not!

17...♘g6 18 ♕xc7 g4

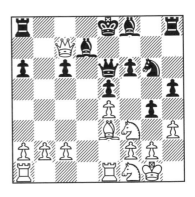

A "king attack" pawn sacrifice—obviously!

19 hxg4 hxg4 20 ♘3h2 ♗d6 21 ♕a5 ♖b8 22 ♖ed1!?

Having said "A" (18 ♕xc7) I think White should say "B" (22 ♕xa6) and speculate on the strength of his passed a-pawn after 22...♖xb2 23 a4.

22...♖xb2 23 ♕xa6 ♘f4 24 ♖d2

Stronger is 24 ♘g3 when White might beat off the attack, but Smyslov must still be suffering from sacrificial shock!

24...♗b4! 25 c3

White should probably try 25 ♖xd7 with some compensation for the exchange.

25...♖xd2!

The "king attacking" diagonal a7-g1 is more important to Black than a mere pawn.

26 ♗xd2 ♗c5

It looks like Black is just winning here, but Smyslov has one more chance...

27 ♖b1

...which was 27 ♗xf4 exf4 28 ♘xg4 ♕xg4 29 ♕a8+ ♗c8 30 ♕xc6+ ♗d7 31 ♕a8+ (but not 31 ♕xc5? ♕h4 with a winning attack) 31...♗c8 32 ♕c6+ and amazingly enough, it looks like White draws.

27...♗c8! 28 ♖b8 ♔f7

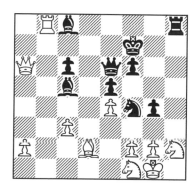

Now one sees that the white queen and rook are not playing, and Yandemirov, with a material superiority on

the king's flank, finishes efficiently.

29 ♕a5 ♘e2+ 30 ♔h1 ♗xf2

There are no more miracle draws!

31 g3

Necessary to prevent Black's pawn advance...

31...♘xg3+ 32 ♔g2 ♘xf1 33 ♘xf1 g3

...but the pawn gets through anyway!

34 ♘xg3 ♗xg3

This is completely winning, of course, but the reader might enjoy finding the quick mate that occurs after 34...♖h2+!.

35 ♕a7+ ♔g6

Only the black king is safe.

36 ♔xg3 ♕g4+ 0-1

Smyslov resigns, as it's mate in three.

This was a wonderful attack by Yandemirov, and it shows the dangers of passive play in the opening, even by World Champions!

1 e4 e5 2 ♘f3 ♘c6 3 ♗b5 g6

I have played this myself to disconcert Exchange players, but the problem is that I don't see an equalizer after the theoretical and strong 4 d4!. Therefore I don't recommend this move order—except as a psychological surprise!

4 c3

The surprise works on Tal! Now

Black gets back into the MS.

4...a6 5 ♗a4 d6 6 d4 ♗d7 7 0-0

Another reason I don't like Muk-hametov's move order is the Capablanca finesse 7 ♗g5! which disorganizes Black's game—see Game 29 for the conclusion.

Once again, my preferred move order when Black wants a kingside fianchetto is 3...a6 4 ♗a4 d6 5 c3 ♗d7 6 d4 ♘f6 7 0-0 g6 which reaches Parma-Keres (Game 25).

7...♗g7 8 dxe5 ♘xe5 9 ♘xe5 dxe5 10 f4

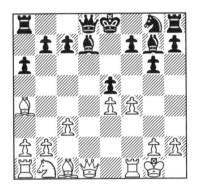

Tal tries to blow his much lower-rated opponent off the board, but the MS is resilient! A more restrained approach was tried in the following encounter between two strong American GMs, though White also got nothing: 10 ♗e3 ♘f6 11 ♘d2 ♗xa4 12 ♕xa4+ ♕d7 13 ♕b3 ♕b5 14 f3 ♕xb3 15 ♘xb3 0-0-0 (once again we see long castling for Black!) 16 ♔f2 ♘e8 17 c4 f5! and Black had good counterplay and made an eventual draw in N.De Firmian-R.Byrne, Reykjavik 1986.

10...♗xa4 11 ♕xa4+ b5 12 ♕b3 exf4 13

♗xf4

At this point Tal probably didn't mind the isolated e-pawn, but it soon becomes a serious weakness.

13...♘f6 14 ♘d2

Tal has to stop to complete his development as 14 e5 ♘d5 15 ♖d1 c6 favours Black—White can't exploit the pin and the isolani is weaker than ever.

14...0-0 15 ♖ae1 ♘g4 16 ♘f3 ♕e7 17 e5

If 17 h3? ♕c5+ 18 ♔h1 ♘f2+ 19 ♔h2 (or 19 ♖xf2 ♕xf2 20 ♗e3 ♕g3 and the queen escapes!) 19...♘d3 wins material.

17...♕c5+ 18 ♔h1 ♖ae8

But 18...♘f2+? 19 ♖xf2 ♕xf2 20 ♗e3 now wins for White as there is no bolt hole on g3!

19 e6

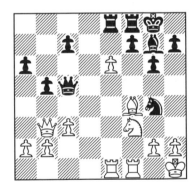

White must play for equality, as otherwise the e-pawn is a permanent weakness.

19...fxe6 20 ♖xe6 ♔h8 21 ♗g3 ♖xe6?

This allows a fork, whereas after the obvious 21...a5 Black has good play; e.g. 22 ♖xe8 ♖xe8 23 ♘d4 b4 softening up the long diagonal.

22 ♕xe6 ♘e5 23 ♕xa6 ♘d3 24 a4
♘xb2 25 axb5?

Back to back errors! Correct is 25
♕xb5 ♕xc3 26 ♗e5 ♗xe5 27 ♘xe5 and
White is just a good pawn up.

25...♕xc3 26 ♕b7 ♕c4 27 ♖a1 ♘a4 28
♖e1 ♘c3 29 b6 cxb6 30 ♗d6 ♕c8 31
♕xb6 ♖e8 32 ♘e5 ♘d5 33 ♕a7 ♕f5 34
h3 ♘f6 35 ♕a2 h5 36 ♕f7 ♔h7 37 ♔g1
♘e4!

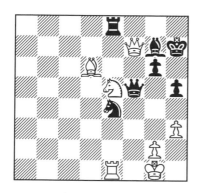

Black finds a drawing combination.

38 ♖xe4 ♖xe5 39 ♕xf5 ½-½

Since 39...♖xf5 is equal, Tal and
Mukh leave this messy game behind
them—one sees that both players need
to keep their move order straight!

Game 11
A.Matanovic-T.V.Petrosian
USSR-Yugoslavia match,
Leningrad 1957

1 e4 e5 2 ♘f3 ♘c6 3 ♗b5 a6 4 ♗a4 d6 5
c3 ♗d7 6 d4 ♘ge7 7 0-0 ♘g6 8 ♖e1
♗e7 9 ♘bd2

9 d5 ♘b8 10 ♗xd7+ ♘xd7 11 c4 to

develop the knight to c3 might be better.

9...0-0

I think ...h7-h6 and ...♗g5 before
castling is best (see Games 21-22), but
Petrosian conjures up kingside counterplay anyway!

10 ♘f1

10 d5 ♘b8 11 ♗xd7 ♘xd7 12 ♘f1
♘h4 transposes to Game 24 where
Black had no problems—but at least
the struggle would continue. Now a
draw arises almost by force.

10...♗g4 11 ♗xc6

It looks like everything draws: 11 d5
♘h4 12 dxc6 ♗xf3 13 gxf3 ♕c8 14 cxb7
♕h3 15 ♘e3 ♖ab8 16 ♔h1 ♘xf3 17 ♘f1
♘h4 18 ♘e3 with a repetition.

11...♘h4 12 ♘1d2

12 ♗xb7 ♗xf3 13 gxf3 ♕d7 is our
basic draw again.

12...bxc6 13 h3 ♘xf3+ 14 ♘xf3 ♗xf3 15
♕xf3 ♗f6

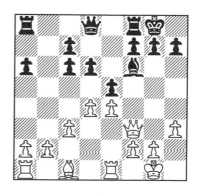

Thirteen years later, Smyslov, who
always seemed to have trouble vs. the
MS, followed this same path to no advantage for White: 16 ♗e3 ♕b8 17 ♖e2

♕b5 18 dxe5 ♗xe5 19 ♗d4 ½-½ V.Smyslov-A.Medina Garcia, European Team Championship, Kapfenberg 1970. **16 dxe5 ♗xe5 17 ♕d3 ♖e8 18 ♗e3 ½-½**

With equality on the board, the players take a rest.

This looks like lesson 73 in the unwritten Petrosian book, "How to Draw with Black!"

Game 12
J.Timman-B.Spassky
Linares 1983

1 e4 e5 2 ♘f3 ♘c6 3 ♗b5 a6 4 ♗a4 d6 5 ♗xc6+ bxc6 6 d4 exd4

As mentioned previously, I think this is more logical than Euwe's 6...f6 from Game 7. Since Black has the two bishops, why not open the game?

7 ♕xd4 c5 8 ♕d3 g6

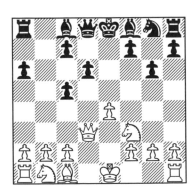

Keres' 8...♘e7 (Game 53) is safer, as with the present game's move order White can try a dangerous pawn sacrifice.

9 ♘c3

More enterprising is 9 0-0 ♗g7 10 e5! (a "pawn cracker" sacrifice!) 10...♘e7 (if Black captures 10...dxe5 White can get the pawn back immediately with 11 ♕c3 or just play positionally, as the pawns at c5 and c7 are inoffensive and weak; Black has also tried 10...♗f5, but after 11 ♕e2 d5 12 ♘c3 ♘e7 13 ♘a4! c4 14 ♘d4 White saddled him with weak squares—not much better than weak pawns—and went on to win in M.Wahls-J.Piket, Hamburg 1991) 11 ♖e1 0-0 12 ♗g5 ♖e8 13 ♘c3 ♗f5 14 ♕e3 dxe5 15 ♖ad1 ♕c8 16 ♗xe7 ♖xe7 17 ♘d5! when White doesn't care about the fact that he is momentarily a pawn down: as Wahls did above, he occupies the weak squares with his knight and then after 17...♖e6 18 ♘g5 ♖e8 19 ♕xc5 regains the material. Following 19...h6 20 ♘f3 ♗f8? 21 ♕c3 ♗g7 22 ♘xc7 even more material fell and White converted in J.Friedel-J.Curdo, Manchester, New Hampshire 2003.

9...♗g7 10 ♗f4 ♘e7 11 0-0-0

Here 11 e5 does nothing as Black doesn't have to make the capture: 11...♗f5 12 ♕e2 0-0 13 ♖d1 ♖e8 with good counterplay.

11...0-0 12 ♕d2

12 e5 ♗f5 13 ♕e3 ♖e8 is similar: it's clear that even if White picks off the d-pawn, Black will have more than enough compensation with his raking bishops and the b-file open towards White's king.

12...Ee8 13 Âh6 Âh8

Black preserves the powerful bishop.

14 h4 Eb8

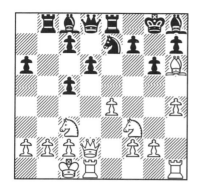

An Alekhine annotation comes to mind, also of an MS from this variation: "Black comes first: not surprising considering the open file."

15 a3 Âe6 16 Äg5 ₩c8 17 Äxe6 ₩xe6

One sees the advantage shifting to Black.

18 ☗b1?

Imperative is 18 h5 to get at least an open line for counterplay (this would have been even better on move 15). Instead, walking into Black's open b-file is a disaster.

18...Âb7! 19 ☗a1 Eeb8 20 Eb1 Äc6 21 f4 Âd4!

Spassky makes sure that his attacking bishop is not blocked off by the white e-pawn.

22 ₩d3 a5 23 ₩h3 f5 24 Ehe1

Relatively better is 24 exf5 gxf5 25 ₩g3+ ☗f7 26 Âg5 ₩c4, though Black's attack is still very strong.

24...Äb4!!

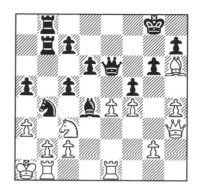

25 axb4

If White thinks that only he is attacking and plays 25 h5, then 25...Äxc2 mate would be a rude awakening; or if he thought defending that mate would work, 25 Ee2 Âxc3 26 bxc3 ₩a2 mate would disabuse him of that notion too.

25...axb4

But now the newly opened a-file is decisive.

26 Äa4 Ea7 27 ₩b3 c4 28 ₩a2 Eba8 29 exf5 Exa4 0-1

This pretty queen sac ends the game. How often did Timman lose so quickly on the white side of the Ruy?

Game 13
E.Lobron-B.Spassky
Hamburg 1982

1 e4 e5 2 Äf3 Äc6 3 Âb5 a6 4 Âa4 d6 5 d4

This variation is covered in Chapter Eight. Unlike Steinitz (Game 2), Spassky immediately punishes White for his move order (the premature d2-d4) and might even win a piece if White is not careful (see Game 65).

5...b5 6 ♗b3 ♘xd4 7 ♘xd4 exd4 8 c3

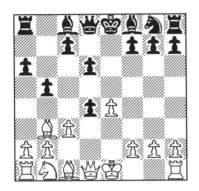

"A gambit of doubtful value," says Alekhine, but at least better than 8 ♕xd4 as seen in the above-mentioned piece-losing game.

8...dxc3

So if there's a doubtful gambit pawn on the board, take it!

9 ♘xc3

White ambitiously tries to win. After 9 ♕h5 ♕d7 White got nothing for the pawn and was essentially lost by move 14 in Game 67, but he can play for a draw with 9 ♕d5 (see Game 66).

9...♘f6 10 e5

Clearly if Black is allowed to develop and castle, White has no compensation, as the following game shows: 10 0-0 ♗e7 11 a4 ♖b8 12 axb5 axb5 13 ♗e3 ♗d7 14 ♖a7 0-0 (Black has a safe king and an extra pawn) 15 ♗d4 ♖a8 16 ♕a1 ♕b8 17 ♕a2 ♖xa7 18 ♗xa7 ♕b7 19 ♗d5 c6 20 ♗b3 c5 21 ♖a1 c4 22 ♗d1 ♗c6 23 ♕a6 b4 24 ♕xb7 ♗xb7 25 ♘a2 b3 26 ♘c3 ♘xe4 27 ♗f3 and

White resigned in P.Cramling-G.Iskov, Copenhagen 1982, as after the simple 27...f5 she has nothing for the two pawns.

So Lobron mixes it up—but Boris is ready.

10...dxe5

But not 10...♘g4? 11 ♕f3, attacking a8, f7 and g4, with a quick win for White in V.Dobrov-S.Silivanov, St Petersburg 2004.

11 ♗xf7+ ♔e7

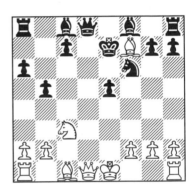

White carries out his idea, but Boris is unfazed.

12 ♕xd8+

White must trade queens, not usually auspicious in a gambit, but characteristic of doubtful ones! Even worse is 12 ♕b3 c5 13 ♗d5 c4 14 ♕d1 ♘xd5 15 ♕f3 (15 ♘xd5+ ♔e6 16 ♘f4+ exf4 17 ♕xd8 ♗b4+ also wins for Black) and now, instead of 15...♖b8 as in L.Kerkhoff-M.Yeo, London Lloyds Bank 1979, Black could have simply developed with 15...♗e6 when White has no compensation for the piece.

12...♔xd8 13 ♗g5 ♗b7 14 0-0-0+

After 14 0-0 ♗d6 White has nothing for the pawn.

14...♗d6 15 f4

If 15 ♘d5 Black holds the material with 15...h6.

15...exf4

Boris takes everything on offer!

16 ♘d5 ♔c8

17 ♘b6+

Perhaps a mistake, but White hardly has compensation anyway for two pawns. If 17 ♗xf6 gxf6 18 ♖hf1 ♖d8.

17...cxb6 18 ♖xd6 ♘e4 19 ♗e6+ ♔b8 20 ♖xb6 ♘xg5 21 ♗d5 ♖c8+ 22 ♔b1 ♖c7 23 ♖e1 ♔a7!

Boris finds a clear win.

24 ♖xb7+ ♖xb7 25 h4 ♘h3!

To create a passed pawn.

26 ♗xb7 ♔xb7 27 gxh3 ♖f8

When all is said and done, one sees that the World Champion has retained the gambit pawn, and has set up a classically winning ending with his rook behind the passed pawn.

28 ♖e7+

If 28 ♖f1 ♔c6 29 ♔c2 ♔d5 30 ♔d3 f3 31 ♖f2 ♔e5 32 ♔e3 ♖f6! and White is

in zugzwang; i.e. 33 ♔d3 ♔f4, or 33 ♖f1 f2, or 33 b4 ♔d5. That only leaves the pawn ending after 33 ♖xf3 ♖xf3+ 34 ♔xf3 ♔d4, but this is won for Black too; e.g. 35 ♔e2 (the other race also loses: 35 ♔f4 ♔d3 36 ♔f5 ♔c2 37 b4 ♔c3 38 h5 ♔xb4 39 ♔e6 ♔a3 40 ♔f7 ♔xa2 41 ♔xg7 b4 42 ♔xh7 b3 43 h6 b2 44 ♔g7 b1♕ 45 h7 ♕h2+ 46 ♔g8 ♕b3+ 47 ♔g7 ♕xh3 and Black will have the only queen) 35...♔e4 36 a3 (36 h5 h6 doesn't change anything) 36...h5 37 b4 ♔d4 38 ♔d2 ♔c4 39 ♔c2 g6 40 ♔b2 ♔d3 41 ♔b3 ♔e4 42 a4 ♔f3 43 axb5 axb5 44 ♔c3 ♔g3 45 ♔d4 ♔xh4 46 ♔c5 g5 47 ♔xb5 g4 48 hxg4 hxg4 49 ♔c4 g3 50 ♔d3 g2 and queens.

28...♔c6 29 ♖xg7 f3 30 ♖g1 f2 31 ♖f1 ♔d5 32 ♔c2 ♔e4 0-1

It's safe to say that Spassky agrees with Alekhine: this gambit is still doubtful, at least if White wants to win.

Game 14
R.J.Fischer-L.Pachman
Mar del Plata 1959

1 e4 e5 2 ♘f3 ♘c6 3 ♗b5 a6 4 ♗a4 d6 5 c3 ♗d7 6 d4 ♘ge7

I recommend 6...♘f6.

7 ♗b3

As previously pointed out, Black should not have played the ...♘e7-g6 line before White castled, since White could get the edge here with 7 ♗e3 (see Game 20).

7...h6 8 0-0

Also ineffective is 8 ♕e2 ♘g6 9 ♕c4 ♕f6 10 d5 b5 and now... what can one say? I would call White's next four moves nonsensical. I could imagine telling a student: "What is this? You play four non-developing moves in a row in order to leave your kingside full of holes and your pieces helpless on the back rank, all because you *hope* that after all your nonsense your opponent—a strong master, mind you—will overlook a one move trap! That is the worst example of 'hope chess' I've ever seen!" And if one of my students did try this, he would not succeed, he would lose the game—except... Yes, the "student" who did play this way was in fact the young Bobby Fischer in another game against the MS—*and his nonsense worked.* Hypnosis seems to be the only explanation.

Here's how the game continued: 11 ♕e2 ♘a5 12 ♗d1 ♗e7 13 g3 0-0 14 h4 and there you have it!

White has no development and an absurdly posted queen and bishop

"battery" that attacks nothing. It will be an age before White can connect his rooks, and Black is ready to open the game. All White has going for him is a one move threat which any master (or less!) should spot, a threat that is easily met by the logical 14...♗d8 with advantage to Black; e.g. 15 ♕f1 (trying to get to the h-file; 15 ♘bd2 is better, but 15...c6 still gives Black a plus) 15...c6! (Black opens the game against White's lack of development and prepares to activate the d8-bishop) 16 ♕g2 cxd5 17 exd5 ♗b6 and Black has a dominating game—indeed Mr. *Fritz* goes all the way to decisive advantage here.

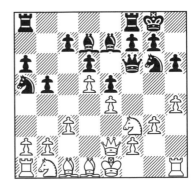

But of course, as any Fischer fan knows, this did not happen. His opponent played 14...♖fc8?? and lost his queen to the one-mover: 15 ♗g5 hxg5 16 hxg5 and White won in R.J.Fischer-V.Ciocaltea, Varna Olympiad 1962.

8...♘g6 9 ♘bd2 ♗e7 10 ♘c4 ♗g5

The key idea—see more in Chapter Two (Games 21-23). Because of White's early castling, Black can often get a strong attack down the h-file if the bishop is taken (as for example in Game 23, where the white king is driven down the board to e7!), but otherwise Black exchanges this sometimes problematic piece and frees his game.

11 ♘e3 ♗xe3 12 ♗xe3 0-0 13 h3 ♖e8 14 ♘h2 ♕e7

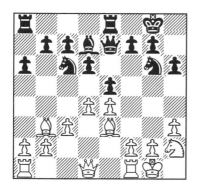

White has nothing, as Black's rock solid centre repels the bishops—but the young Fischer reckoned the bishop pair was a "half point advantage" and so no doubt thought he was better.

15 dxe5

Fischer tries to open the position, to no avail—but 15 d5 ♘a5 16 ♗c2 ♗b5 17 ♖e1 ♘c4 is also equal.

15...dxe5 16 ♕h5 ♘a5

I suppose 16...b5?? 17 ♕xg6 was White's one move "trap".

17 ♗c2

And now 17 ♕xg6?? ♘xb3 is *Black's* one move trap. Though neither trap catches anyone, we can see that Black is improving his position whereas the white queen is just misplaced—on an 'attacking' outpost when there is no attack. White should go for 17 ♗d5 c6

18 ♕xg6 cxd5 19 ♕b6 ♘c4 20 ♕xb7 dxe4 when Black is just slightly better.

17...♘c4 18 ♗c1 ♘f4 19 ♕f3 ♖ad8

Pachman pushes the white bishops back and installs his knights on the fifth rank—Black has the edge.

20 ♗xf4

This knight must have really annoyed Bobby—he gave up one of his bishops for it!

20...exf4 21 ♕xf4 ♗c6

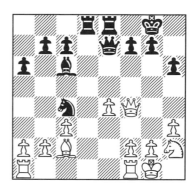

Black's temporary pawn sac has given him an excellent position; and White can hardly hold the pawn, as the next note shows.

22 ♘g4

Black maintains his edge against other moves as well: 22 b3 (22 ♖ab1 ♘d2 and 22 ♖fb1 ♖d2 are both clearly better for Black) 22...♘a3 23 ♗b1 ♘xb1 24 ♖axb1 ♗xe4 25 ♖be1 g5 26 ♕g3 f5 27 f3 ♕c5+ and ironically enough, Black ends up with the sole bishop and a Fischeresque superiority!

22...h5 23 ♘e3 ♘xb2 24 ♘f5 ♕f6 25 ♕xc7 ♖xc3 26 ♖ac1 ♕f6 27 ♖fe1 ♘d3 28 ♗xd3 ♖xd3 29 ♕f4??

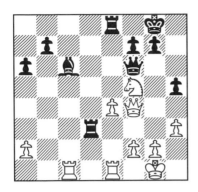

Blundering or sacrificing a piece. Better is 29 f3 g6 30 ♘e3 ♕g5 when Black has attacking chances and the superior minor piece, but White is still in the game.

29...g6 30 ♖c5 ♖e6 31 ♕b8+ ♖d8 32 ♕f4 gxf5 33 ♖xf5 ♕g7 34 ♖xh5 ♖de8 35 f3 ♖e5 36 ♖h4 ♖g5

White only has two pawns for the piece and now must exchange to halt Black's attack.

37 ♖g4 ♖xg4 38 hxg4 ♕d4+ 39 ♖e3 ♕e5 40 ♕f5 ♕xf5 41 gxf5 ♖d8 42 ♔f2 ♗b5 43 ♔e1 ♔g7 44 e5 ♖d4 45 g4 ♔h6 46 e6 f6 47 ♔f2 ♖d2+ 48 ♔g3 ♔g7 49 ♖c3 ♗c6 50 a3 ♖e2 51 ♔f4 a5 52 ♖d3 a4!

The key to the ending: Black will win with his queenside pawn majority.

53 ♖d8 ♖f2 54 ♖d3 b5 55 ♖c3 ♖xf3+! 56 ♖xf3 ♗xf3 0-1

It's the black bishop (not the white ones that Fischer tried to keep) that wins the game. As 57 ♔xf3 b4 wins easily, Fischer resigned.

Black's system (when handled correctly) is so solid that it's an excellent line against attacking players like Fischer, who are liable to beat their heads against the wall of Black's well-defended centre.

Game 15
A.Karpov-G.Ravinsky
Leningrad 1966

1 e4 e5 2 ♘f3 ♘c6 3 ♗b5 a6 4 ♗a4 ♘f6 5 d3 d6

Again 4...d6 5 d3 ♘f6 is the MS route to this "no hope for advantage" line.

6 c3

Again this ineffective set-up!

6...♗d7 7 0-0 g6

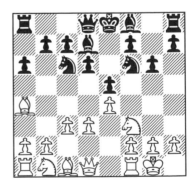

Black follows a simple MS recipe that's worked since Lasker's time, and we'll see the same type of logical development in a recent Mamedyarov game from 2006 (Game 75).

8 b4 ♗g7 9 ♗b3 0-0 10 ♖e1 h6 11 ♘bd2 ♔h7 12 ♗b2 ♘h5 13 a3 f5

Black has achieved this thematic break "for nothing" and it's clear he is better. Karpov starts to defend, since there is nothing active he can do.

14 ♕c2 fxe4 15 ♘xe4 ♘f4 16 ♔h1 ♗g4 17 ♘g1!

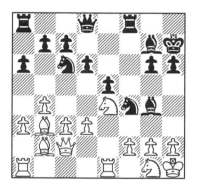

Karpov digs in for defence! As my *Fritz* or yours will tell you, Black is clearly better here—but you don't beat Karpov by being "clearly better". At some point you have to go all Kasparov on him and crash through, something Ravinsky doesn't manage.

17...d5 18 ♘g3 h5

18...e4 19 dxe4 d4 20 cxd4 ♘xd4 21 ♗xd4 ♗xd4 22 ♖ad1 ♗xd1 23 ♖xd1 ♕f6 24 ♘f3 ♖ad8 25 ♖xd4 ♖xd4 26 ♕xc7+ ♔h8 27 ♘xd4 ♕xd4 28 h3 ♘xg2 29 ♕e7 ♕xf2 30 ♘f5 ♕f1+ 31 ♔h2 ♕f4+ is a long *Fritz* variation leading to

a draw by perpetual check.

The game move also turns out to be ineffective, so I offer 18...♗e6! which frees up the queen. After 19 f3 ♕f6 Black's kingside pressure is very alarming if not yet decisive.

19 f3 ♗e6 20 ♘3e2 ♕d7 21 ♖ad1 h4 22 ♘xf4 ♖xf4 23 ♗c1 ♖f7 24 ♗g5 ♗f6

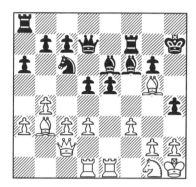

Black's last chance to attack was 24...h3!?—after the text Karpov chops wood and makes his draw.

25 ♗xf6 ♖xf6 26 ♕f2 g5 27 d4 exd4 28 cxd4 ♗f5 29 ♗a4 ♖e8 30 ♗xc6 ♖xc6 31 ♕d2 ♕g6 32 ♖xe8 ♕xe8 33 ♖e1 ♖e6 34 ♖xe6+ ♕xe6 35 g4 hxg3 36 hxg3 g4 37 ♔g2 gxf3+ 38 ♘xf3 ♗e4 39 ♕g5+ ♔f7 40 ♕f4+ ½-½

Yes, Karpov held this—but the passive d2-d3 is proven once again to have no effect, and Black easily obtains equality or more, as here. The combination of kingside fianchetto and ...f7-f5 break is noteworthy; Black gets King's Indian play, whereas White has nothing on the other wing because his pawn is at d3, rather than the King's Indian style d5.

Game 16
G.Kasparov-N.Short
World Championship
(19th matchgame),
London 1993

1 e4 e5 2 ♘f3 ♘c6 3 ♗b5 a6 4 ♗a4 d6

In three previous games of this match, the challenger Short played the fashionable 4...♘f6—and ended up losing all three! Finally, he went to the Modern Steinitz and made a short draw—a big success against the Kasparov of 1993!

5 ♗xc6+

Undoubtedly surprised, Kasparov plays a less critical line than he usually does—for a more "Kasparov-like" treatment of the MS, see note to move 9 in Game 23; and an even more aggressive, though this time somewhat misguided effort, can be found in the notes to Game 34.

5...bxc6 6 d4 exd4 7 ♕xd4 ♘f6

I think the immediate 7...c5 as played by Spassky and Keres (Games 12 and 53) is more accurate, since the knight on f6 invites an e4-e5 break—though as we'll see, that doesn't seem to faze Short a bit!

8 0-0 ♗e7 9 e5 c5 10 ♕d3 dxe5 11 ♕xd8+ ♗xd8 12 ♘xe5

White has inflicted doubled isolated pawns on his opponent, but the board has also opened more for the bishop pair and Short equalizes against the World Champion.

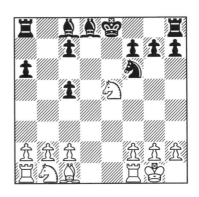

12...♗e7 13 ♖e1!?

If 13 ♘c3 ♗f5 targets c2 and shows the strength of the unopposed light-squared bishop.

13...0-0 14 ♗g5 ♗e6 15 ♘d2

Short points out that 15 ♘g4 ♖ab8 16 b3 ♘xg4 17 ♗xe7 ♖fe8 18 ♗xc5 ♗xb3! exploits White's weak back rank.

15...♖fe8 16 h3!? h6 17 ♗h4 ♖ad8 18 ♘df3! g5 19 ♗g3 ♗d5 20 ♖ad1

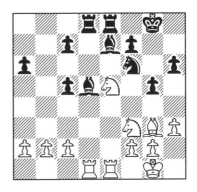

20...♔g7?!

Better is 20...♗d6, activating both bishops with equality.

21 c4 ♗b7 22 ♖xd8! ♖xd8 23 ♘c6!

Finally Kasparov makes something of the position: he trades a knight for a bishop and gets a small plus.

23...♗xc6 24 ♖xe7 ♖d1+ 25 ♔h2 ♘e4 26 ♖xc7 ½-½

Makarichev gives the following drawing line in the *Informator* and indeed the players agreed to a draw here: 26 ♖xc7 ♗d7 27 ♖a7 h5 28 ♗e5+ ♔g6 29 ♖xa6+ ♔f5 30 ♗c3 g4 31 hxg4+ hxg4 32 ♘e5 ♘xc3 33 ♘xd7 ♘e4 34 ♘xc5 g3+! 35 fxg3 ♘f2 36 g4+ ♔xg4 37 g3 ♖d2 and Black has sufficient counterplay.

But then Kasparov points out the move he missed: 26 ♘e5! ♘d2 27 h4 g4 28 ♘xg4 ♘f1+ (not 28...♘f3+? 29 gxf3 ♗xf3 30 ♔h3 when White both avoids mate and emerges with an extra piece) 29 ♔h3 ♗d7 30 h5 ♔f8 31 ♖xd7! (this exchange sac is the key to the variation) 31...♖xd7 32 ♗f4! and one can see that White comes out with two pawns for the exchange and some real winning chances.

However, this was a tough line to find (so tough that Kasparov missed it at the board!) and was only possible at all because of Black's inaccuracy on the 20th move. Furthermore, if Black plays more actively in the beginning (7...c5, which will be fully analysed in Chapter Six) there doesn't seem to be any way for White to get an advantage.

It's too bad Short didn't go to the MS at the beginning of the match! When he finally did, after the aforementioned three losses, it was too late to save the situation.

One reason the next game is interesting is that it features the two recent contenders for the world championship—and as in that match, we see in this individual game Anand's great imagination and fighting spirit.

Note that we skip Vladimir Kramnik in this book—not due to lack of respect, but because, according to the database, he has never played a Modern Steinitz in his life, whether with White or Black!

Game 17
V.Topalov-V.Anand
Bastia (rapid) 2003

1 e4 e5 2 ♘f3 ♘c6 3 ♗b5 a6 4 ♗a4 ♘f6 5 d3 d6

Our favourite transposition; as always, the MS order is 4...d6 5 d3 ♘f6.

6 c3 ♗d7 7 0-0 g6

This Lasker style move seems to be simplest.

8 ♖e1

With this move, the most popular choice, White scores only 50% according to the *Mega*, confirming once again Smyslov's comment about the d2-d3 line giving "no possibility of any sort of advantage". It's not clear to me why White, given the gift of the first move, should play so passively, but I have seen this type of play consistently at the highest levels: for example, in my book *Alekhine Alert*, I noted that a line often played against World Champions was 1 e4 ♘f6 2 e5 ♘d5 3 ♘c3 which, like 5 d3 here, gives White *no advantage whatsoever*! Yet the line was played over and over with a conspicuous lack of success.

In this particular case, one sees that Anand had enjoyed this position before. Again, White got nothing, while Anand created Shirovian fire and won stylishly: 8 ♘bd2 ♗g7 9 ♖e1 0-0 10 d4 ♖e8 11 a3 ♗h6 12 ♗c2 a5 13 ♖b1 ♗g7 14 b4 axb4 15 axb4 exd4 16 cxd4 ♘h5 17 d5 ♘a7 18 ♘c4 ♘b5 19 ♕d3 b6 20 h3 ♘f6 21 ♗g5 h6 22 ♗h4 ♕c8 23 g4 ♘xe4! (a very imaginative sacrifice!)

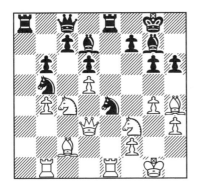

24 ♖xe4 ♖xe4 25 ♕xe4 ♘c3 26 ♕d3 ♘xb1 27 ♗xb1 ♖a1 (Black has only a rook against two knights, but it's quite a rook!—besides that, Black has kingside play, and White proves unable to put out the fires on both sides of the board) 28 ♘cd2 h5 29 gxh5 ♗f5 30 ♘e4 c6 31 ♘fd2 cxd5 32 ♕xd5 ♕e6 33 ♕xe6 fxe6 34 ♔h2 ♖xb1 35 ♘xb1 ♗xe4 36 ♘d2 ♗d5 37 hxg6 ♗c3 38 ♘f1 ♗e4 39 b5 ♗xg6 40 ♘e3 ♗d4 41 ♘c4 d5 42 ♘d6 ♔f8 43 ♔g2 ♗c5 44 ♘b7 ♗e7 45 ♗g3 ♔e8 46 ♗c7 d4 47 ♔f3 d3 48 ♔e3

♗b4 49 f3 d2 50 ♔e2 ♗c2 0-1 V.Kupreichik-V.Anand, Belgrade 1988.

8...♗g7 9 ♗g5 h6 10 ♗h4 g5!?

Anand signals his aggressive intentions with Black but allows White some positional advantage. Simpler is 10...0-0 11 ♘bd2 ♕e8 as played by Alekhine which looks already better for Black, who has the only good break (the coming ...f7-f5) and can meet 12 d4 with the clever 12...♘xd4!. In the game A.Ilyin Zhenevsky-A.Alekhine, USSR Championship, Moscow 1920, White resorted to 12 ♘f1 (à la Karpov) and finally held a difficult draw, but this is no advertisement for White's opening play.

11 ♗g3 ♘h5

11...♕e7 intending ...0-0-0 is interesting.

12 ♘xe5 ♘xe5 13 ♗xd7+ ♕xd7 14 ♗xe5 dxe5 15 ♕xh5 ♕xd3

Evidently Anand's idea, though his weak light squares will cause him trouble for a while.

16 ♘a3 ♕d6 17 ♘c4

17 ♖ed1 is better, when Black must

work to castle and put his bishop on an ineffective square (d6, instead of the game's f6 where it doesn't interfere with the black rooks). After the plausible continuation 17...♕e6 18 ♘c2 ♗f8 19 ♘e3 ♗d6 20 ♘f5 0-0-0 21 ♖d5 c6 22 ♖xd6 ♖xd6 23 ♕xf7 ♖hd8 24 ♘xd6+ ♕xd6 25 h3 Black has compensation due to his control of the open d-file, but it's probably not quite enough for the pawn.

17...♕e6 18 ♘e3 0-0-0 19 ♘f5 ♗f6 20 g3 ♖d7 21 ♖e2 ♖hd8

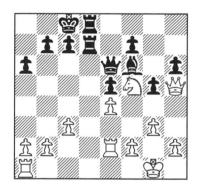

22 ♔g2

White's nominally superior minor piece means nothing now in view of Black's control of the d-file. Also note that the black h-pawn is poisoned: both 22 ♕xh6? and 22 ♘xh6? would be met by a decisive 22...♖h8.

22...a5 23 b3 ♔b8 24 ♖ae1 c6 25 ♖e3 ♖h8 26 ♖1e2 ♗d8 27 ♖f3 ♗b6

Now the "bad bishop" has become such a great piece that White offers to exchange it!

28 ♘e3 ♗xe3 29 ♖exe3 f6 30 ♕g6 ♖d6 31 ♖f5 h5 32 h3 h4 33 ♖ef3 hxg3

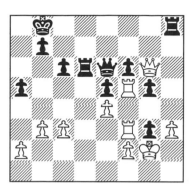

34 fxg3

White's position has slipped downhill, so Topalov should seize the moment to run for a difficult draw with 34 ♕xf6! ♕xf6 35 ♖xf6 ♖xf6 36 ♖xf6 gxf2 37 ♖xf2 ♖h4 38 ♖e2 ♔c7 39 ♖e3 ♔d6 40 ♔f2 g4 41 hxg4 ♖xg4 42 ♖e1 ♔c5 43 ♔f3 ♖f4+ 44 ♔e3 ♖h4 45 ♖f1 and White should draw even though both Black's king and rook are slightly more active. A sample continuation is 45...b5 46 a3 ♖h3+ 47 ♔f3 ♖xf3+ 48 ♔xf3 a4 (but not 48...b4? 49 cxb4+ axb4 50 a4 ♔d4 51 ♔e2 c5 52 a5 c4 53 a6 cxb3 54 ♔d2 and White wins!) 49 bxa4 bxa4 50 ♔g4 ♔c4 51 ♔f5 c5 52 ♔xe5 ♔xc3 53 ♔d5 c4 54 e5 ♔b3 55 e6 c3 56 e7 c2 57 e8♕ c1♕ 58 ♕e4 ♔xa3 and the Tablebase says "draw", though this still wouldn't be too easy for a human.

34...♖d2+ 35 ♖f2 ♖xf2+ 36 ♔xf2

Not 36 ♖xf2? ♕xh3+ winning.

36...♖xh3 37 ♔g2 g4 38 ♕xf6 ♕xf6 39 ♖xf6 ♖h7 40 ♖g6 ♖d7 41 ♖xg4 ♖d2+ 42 ♔h3 ♖xa2 43 ♖g5 ♖b2

Black has the active rook and more pawns to take.

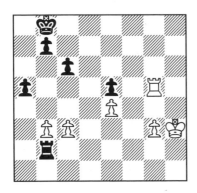

44 ⌶xe5 b5 45 ⌶e8+

Running with the g-pawn looks like a better try, but it seems Black wins anyway after 45 g4 ⌶xb3 46 g5 ⌶xc3+ 47 ⌷g4 ⌶c1 48 g6 ⌶g1+ 49 ⌷f5 a4 50 ⌶e8+ ⌷a7 51 ⌶e7+ ⌷b6 52 ⌶e8 b4 etc.

45...⌷c7 46 e5 ⌶xb3 47 ⌶e7+ ⌷b6 48 ⌷g4 ⌶xc3 49 e6 ⌶e3 50 ⌷f4 ⌶e1 51 ⌷f5 a4 52 ⌶e8 a3 53 ⌶a8 b4 54 g4 ⌷c7 55 g5 b3 56 ⌶a7+ ⌷d6 57 ⌶xa3 b2 58 ⌶d3+ ⌷e7 59 ⌶d7+ ⌷e8 60 ⌶b7 b1♕+ 61 ⌶xb1 ⌶xb1 0-1

An excellent win from Anand!

From the opening point of view, as usual 5 d3 does nothing. Note that Anand could have continued less aggressively, like Alekhine (now there's an odd phrase!), and been comfortably if slightly better, though his risk-taking ...g6-g5 was ultimately rewarded.

> ### Game 18
> ### G.Kamsky-V.Anand
> Sofia 2006

1 e4 e5 2 ♘f3 ♘c6 3 ♗b5 a6 4 ♗xc6

Rather than retaining the tension with 4 ♗a4, White can try to deaden the position with this capture. I give full coverage of this necessary—the MS player *must* be prepared to meet it—line in Chapters Ten and Eleven.

4...dxc6

This rather boring line is fully analysed in Chapter Ten; instead, Chapter Eleven features Larsen's take on the Exchange Ruy, namely the sharper 4...bxc6 as played in Andersson-Larsen (Game 82).

5 0-0 ♗g4

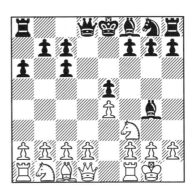

If you must play 4...dxc6, I recommend this follow-up, which dovetails neatly with the Yandemirov Gambit of Chapter Five.

6 h3 h5 7 d3

7 hxg4? hxg4 8 ♘e1 ♕h4 and wins is the obvious tactical point.

7...♕f6

And the positional point is this: Black threatens to damage the white pawn structure by giving back the bishop pair. White often accepts this, as Kamsky does in a few moves, and a very drawish position results.

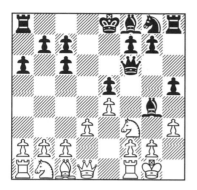

8 ♘bd2

8 ♗e3 ♗xf3 is similar: Black gives his opponent doubled pawns to compensate for his own.

8...♘e7

8...♗d6 is also possible, and on the next move White could keep the position slightly more complicated with 9 ♖e1—all this will be covered in Chapter Ten.

9 ♘c4

The US champion essentially forces an equal ending.

9...♗xf3

Black must make the equalizing exchange, as can be seen: Black loses quickly after both 9...♘g6? 10 hxg4 hxg4 11 ♗g5 ♕e6 12 ♘h2 and 9...0-0-0? 10 hxg4 hxg4 11 ♘fxe5 ♕h4 12 ♕xg4+.

10 ♕xf3 ♕xf3 11 gxf3 ♘g6

A typical position, often seen in the 5...♗g4 line: Black blockades the doubled f-pawns, while of course he has his own defective queenside pawns. As the weaknesses balance themselves out

two good players will make a draw every time. Yes, this is a theoretical success for Black, but very annoying if you want to win!

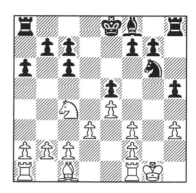

12 ♖d1

In the following note one sees how Spassky and other luminaries collect their draws, with the games given in order of number of moves played before both sides accept the inevitable! Note that the young and talented IM Jacek Stopa achieves a better position and even an extra pawn with Black, but the drawish nature of the position is finally too much for him!

a) 12 ♗e3 ♗e7 13 ♖fd1 0-0-0 14 ♔f1 f6 15 ♔e2 ♘f8 16 f4 exf4 17 ♗xf4 ♘e6 ½-½ S.Kindermann-J.Dorfman, Austrian Team Championship 2003.

b) 12 ♗e3 ♗e7 13 ♖fb1 c5 14 ♔f1 f6 15 ♔e2 ♔f7 16 a3 a5 17 a4 b6 18 ♖g1 ♗d6 19 ♖g3 ♘f8 20 f4 exf4 21 ♘xd6+ cxd6 22 ♗xf4 ♘e6 23 ♗e3 g6 24 ♖ag1 ♖hg8 25 ♔d2 ♖ad8 26 f4 ♘c7 27 c4 ½-½ S.Erenburg-L.Fressinet, Andorra 2004.

c) 12 ♗e3 ♗d6 13 ♖fd1 f6 14 ♔f1

0-0-0 15 ♔e2 ♖d7 16 ♖g1 ♘h4 17 f4
exf4 18 ♘xd6+ cxd6 19 ♗xf4 g5 20 ♗e3
d5 21 f3 ♖e8 22 ♔f2 ♘g6 23 a4 ♘e5 24
b4 g4 25 hxg4 dxe4 26 fxe4 ♘xg4+ 27
♔e2 f5 28 b5 fxe4 29 d4 ♖f7 30 bxc6
bxc6 31 ♖gf1 ♖f3 32 ♗f4 ♖xf1 33 ♖xf1
♔d7 34 ♗g3 ♔e6 35 c3 ♖g8 36 ♖f4 e3
37 c4 ♖d8 38 ♔f3 ♖d7 39 ♗h4 ♖f7 40
♖xf7 ♔xf7 41 a5 ♔e6 42 ♗g5 e2 43
♔xe2 ♔f5 44 ♗d8 ♔e4 45 d5 cxd5 46
cxd5 ♔xd5 47 ♔f3 ♔e5 48 ♔g3 ♔f5 49
♔h4 ♔g6 50 ♔g3 ♘e5 51 ♔f4 ♘c6 52
♗c7 ♔f6 53 ♔e4 ♔e6 54 ♔f4 ♔d5 55
♔g5 ♔c5 56 ♔xh5 ♔b5 57 ♔g4 ♘xa5 58
♔f3 (after all that effort the extra pawn
doesn't win!) ½-½ M.Rutkowski-J.Stopa,
Polish Team Championship 2005.

d) There's an interesting story about
the final example: this was the last
game of the Hort-Spassky Candidates
Match in 1977 (in the cycle to deter-
mine a challenger to World Champion
Anatoly Karpov). Spassky, a point
ahead, needed only a draw, whereas
Hort absolutely had to win—so Hort
chose the most drawish line at his dis-
posal!? It's true that he had won an
earlier game of the match with the Exchange Ruy, but there Boris played the
less classical 5...♕d6 and did not fare
well; here he is prepared and equalizes
with ease. But then Hort plays on for
ages to no avail when he should have
played, much earlier, 4 ♗a4!.

The game continued from our opening tabiya as follows: 12 ♗e3 ♗e7 13
♔h1 ♗f6 14 a4 0-0-0 15 a5 ♘h4 16
♘d2 ♘g6 17 ♖ad1 ♘f4 18 ♗xf4 exf4 19

♘c4 g5 20 ♔g2 ♖h6 21 ♖fe1 c5 22 c3
♗g7 23 ♖g1 ♖g6 24 ♔f1 b5 25 axb6
cxb6 26 ♔e2 b5 27 ♘a5 ♔c7 28 ♘b3
♔b6 29 ♖a1 ♗f8 30 ♖a2 ♗e7

(one sees clear equality on the
board, and the same signified by Mr.
Fritz—and no winning chances for either side; but Hort perseveres for *another* thirty moves!) 31 ♖ga1 ♖a8 32
♖a5 ♖c6 33 ♔d2 ♗f6 34 ♔c2 c4 35 ♘c1
cxd3+ 36 ♘xd3 ♗e7 37 e5 h4 38 b4
♔b7 39 ♖5a3 ♖d8 40 ♖d1 ♖dc8 41 ♔b2
♖e6 42 ♖aa1 ♔b6 43 ♖ac1 ♖c7 44 ♔b3
♖ec6 45 ♘b2 a5 46 bxa5+ ♔xa5 47 ♖d5
♔b6 48 c4 ♖c5 49 ♖xc5 ♖xc5 50 ♘d3
bxc4+ 51 ♖xc4 ♖d5 52 ♔c3 ♗c5 53 ♖a4
♔b5 54 ♖e4 ♖d7 55 e6 fxe6 56 ♖e5 ♖d5
57 ♖xe6 ♗d4+ 58 ♔c2 ♖d8 59 ♘e5
♗xe5 60 ♖xe5+ ♔c4 61 ♖xg5 ♖d3 62
♖c5+ (since 62 ♖g4 ♖xf3 63 ♖xh4
♖xf2+ is even better for Black, Hort finally forces the draw) 62...♔xc5 63
♔xd3 ½-½ V.Hort-B.Spassky, Reykjavik
(16th matchgame) 1977. After 63...♔d5
there's no win there.

Is this variation drawish enough for
you?

12...c5 13 ⌂f1 ♗d6 14 ⌂e2 f6 15 c3 ⌂f7 16 ♗e3 ♖hd8 17 a3 a5

18 a4 b6 19 ♖dc1 ♖d7 20 b4 cxb4 21 ♘xd6+ cxd6 22 cxb4 axb4 23 ♖cb1 d5

Anand gets some activity but, as usual in this variation, it's not enough.

24 ♖xb4 d4 25 ♗d2 ♖da7

Black has gotten rid of his doubled pawns, while White still has his—but now Kamsky solves that problem and essentially forces the draw.

26 f4! ♘xf4+ 27 ♗xf4 exf4 28 ⌂f3 b5

If 28...g5 29 h4 ♖a5 30 hxg5 fxg5 31 ♖xb6 ♖xa4 32 ♖xa4 ♖xa4 33 ♖b7+ ⌂g6 (White forces the draw by perpetual check, as avoidance is worse: 33...⌂e6?! 34 ♖b6+ ⌂d7 35 ♖b5) 34 ♖b6+ ⌂g7 35 ♖b7+ and draws.

29 ♖xb5 ♖xa4 30 ♖b7+ ⌂f8 31 ♖g1 g5 32 h4 ♖a1 33 ♖xa1 ♖xa1 34 ♖b5 gxh4 35 ♖xh5 ♖a3 36 ♖xh4 ♖xd3+ 37 ⌂e2 ♖a3 38 ♖xf4 ⌂e7 39 ♖f5 ⌂e6 ½-½

The drawish reputation of this line is upheld: if White tries to somehow take the attacking bishop, exciting games can occur—but they usually favour Black. So White players usually try something like this, and very exciting ...snooze... games occur.

I say follow Larsen and take back with 4...bxc6—see full coverage in Chapter Eleven.

Now, as Anand still reigns as I write, we have run out of World Champions—so let's follow the great Keres into the specific analysis of the opening.

We start with the solid line that defeated Fischer!

Chapter Two
Solid Line 1:
The Knight Defence

The fundamental quality of this first solid line, the Knight Defence, is seen after the moves **1 e4 e5 2 ♘f3 ♘c6 3 ♗b5 a6 4 ♗a4 d6 5 0-0 ♗d7 6 c3 ♘ge7 7 d4 ♘g6**.

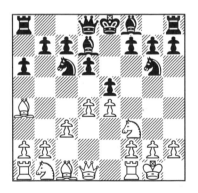

Black has unpinned the knight and uses the king's knight to create a rock-solid defence of e5. One recalls that the young and impatient Fischer of 1959 bashed his head against the wall of this defence (Game 14). Black usually continues with the manoeuvre ...♗e7/...h7-

h6/...♗g5 which exchanges a minor piece to ease his slightly cramped position, and might also open the h-file (see Game 23). In general, Black has excellent chances to equalize in this variation, and can pursue counter-attacking chances later—*if* (and this is a very important "if"!) he follows the above move order.

However, in the MS White's most popular move after 4...d6 is 5 c3, beating out 5 0-0 by an extra ten percent or so. But I gave 5 0-0 in my sample line above—thus the obvious question is: "Can we play this knight manoeuvre against the more popular 5 c3 - ?" I answer, "*No!*", since if White is not castled, he can shake Black's entire formation by attacking the g6-knight with h2-h4 (something that is obviously impossible after castling). We will see White get an advantage after this pawn thrust in Game 20. White even has a secondary attacking system involving a pawn sacrifice with ♘h4, as in the first game of this chapter where Keres somewhat fortuitously beats off the attack.

In short, the Knight Defence variation is *not* a universal system, but is really only effective against lines where White castles early.

Meanwhile, what of our Solid Line II: the Bishop Defence, where Black plans a kingside fianchetto? This can indeed be played against both of White's fundamental continuations 5 c3 and 5 0-0, as 5 c3 ♗d7 6 d4 ♘f6 7 0-0 g6 or 5 0-0 ♗d7 6 c3 ♘f6 7 d4 g6 is a simple transposition. So one solid line is a universal system and the other is not: why do we have to learn both of them?

Well, you don't! The highest rated exponent of the MS today, GM Shak Mamedyarov, only plays the Bishop Defence—and with success (drawing with Anand in this line, for example). However, let's not forget our mentor Keres, who played both variations.

My feeling is that there are at least three advantages to playing both lines:

1. In the age of databases, it's good to keep your opponents guessing!

2. This knight defence is so unfashionable now that when I wheeled it out twice recently (Games 23 and 24) my opponents did not know what to do, which helped me set up early attacking positions in both games.

3. Play the opponent, not the position: If your opponent is an attacking

player and opts for 5 0-0, play the Knight Defence and frustrate him. If your opponent plays passively, use the Bishop Defence. If your opponent is an attacking player and ventures 5 c3, choose neither: force him onto the defensive with the Siesta 5...f5!?.

Now let's expand our minds and begin the real study of this opening—with, of course, Paul Keres.

Game 19
E.Geller-P.Keres
USSR Championship,
Moscow 1950

1 e4 e5 2 ♘f3 ♘c6 3 ♗b5 a6 4 ♗a4 d6 5 c3 ♗d7

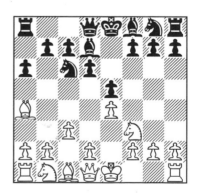

Both of Black's solid systems start with this pin-breaking move but Black can also go wild with 5...f5!? (see Chapter Four).

6 d4 ♘ge7

Keres played this inaccuracy many times in his career and was never punished for it—as the strongest reply, 7

♗e3 (see the next game), was never played against him! But even here Geller finds an attacking scheme that throws a scare into our Estonian hero.

Best is 6...♘f6, heading for the Bishop Defence with a coming ...g7-g6, seen in the next chapter. Note that generally I will not cover lines with ...♘f6 and ...♗e7 as this is more of Main Line Ruy than a Modern Steinitz, though I've made a few exceptions (such as Game 8, for the fabulous middlegame play; and Game 30, where White's opening play left Black no other option).

7 ♗b3

Fischer's primitive attack, but Geller has a stronger continuation in mind.

7...h6 8 ♘h4!?

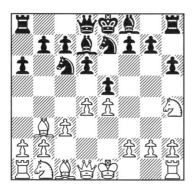

White tries to radically "prevent" Black's plan of ...♘g6 (though as we'll see, not everyone is deterred!), offers an at least temporary pawn sacrifice, and announces his intention to blow Black off the board! One recalls that Fischer got nowhere with the quieter 8 0-0 in Game 14, though Bronstein's more flexible 8 ♘bd2 of Game 1 gave

White a slight edge.

8...♘c8

There are three reasonable alternatives:

a) 8...♘g6 (Black is undeterred, but also I think unwise!) 9 ♘xg6 fxg6 (I doubt the f-file is worth the doubled pawns) 10 0-0 ♕h4 11 f4 0-0-0 12 ♗e3 g5 13 d5 ♘a5 14 g3 ♕h3 15 fxe5 dxe5 16 ♘d2 ♗d6 17 ♕e2 ♗g4 18 ♕d3 ♘xb3 19 axb3 ♕h5 20 ♖fe1 ♖df8 21 b4 ♖f6 22 b5 ♖hf8 23 bxa6 bxa6 24 ♖xa6 ♔d7, and now 25 ♖a7 would give White a very strong attack. Instead, in V.Kotronias-S.Cvetkovic, Athens 1998, 25 ♕b5+ was played, which drove the black king where he wanted to go (away from the white attack on the queenside!) and Black eventually made a draw.

b) 8...exd4 (Black can snatch a pawn) 9 cxd4 ♘xd4 10 ♕xd4 ♘c6 11 ♗xf7+ (Tal wins with a magical or some might say irrational attack—much more reasonable but less fun is 11 ♕d5 ♕xh4 12 ♕xf7+ ♔d8 when White exploited Black's bad king position as follows: 13 ♘c3 ♘e5 14 ♕d5 g5 15 ♗e3 ♕g4 16 h3 ♕xg2 17 0-0-0 ♕f3 18 ♖hg1 ♔c8 19 ♖g3 ♕h5 20 f4 gxf4 21 ♗xf4 ♗e7 22 ♖g8+ ♖xg8 23 ♕xg8+ ♕e8 24 ♘d5 ♗g5 25 ♕h7 ♗xf4+ 26 ♘xf4 ♔b8 27 ♖g1 ♔a7? 28 ♖g8 1-0 A.Suetin-V.Ciocaltea, Debrecen 1961) 11...♗xf7 12 ♕d5+ ♗e6 13 ♕h5+ ♔g8 14 0-0 ♘e5 15 ♘f5 (Tal offers a piece...) 15...g6 16 ♕h3 gxf5 17 exf5 ♗c4 18 f4 ♘d7 19 ♖f3 ♗g7 20 ♘c3 ♘f6 21 ♗e3 c5

22 ♗f2 b5 23 ♗h4 b4 24 ♘e4 ♗d5 25 ♗xf6 ♗xf6 26 ♖e1 ♗d4+ 27 ♔h1 ♖h7 28 ♖g3+ ♔g7 29 ♖g6 (calmly advances...) 29...♖xg6 30 fxg6 ♕f8 31 ♕d7 ♗g7 32 ♘g3 ♖d8 33 ♕g4 ♖e8 34 ♖d1 ♗xa2 35 f5 c4 36 h4 d5 37 ♖f1 ♗f6 38 ♕d1! (finds an attacking square for his queen...) 38...d4 39 ♕a4 ♗b3 40 ♕c6 ♕e7 41 ♘h5 ♖f8 42 ♕d5+ ♔h8 43 ♘xf6 ♕xf6 44 ♕b7 ♕g7 45 ♕xb4 ♔g8 46 h5 ♕d7? 47 f6 ♕g4 48 f7+ ♔g7 49 ♕c5 ♕h4+ 50 ♔g1 (...and wins with this king move! Black has been a piece up for 35 moves but must resign in view of the dual threats ♕e5+ and ♕xf8+!) 1-0 M.Tal-A.Bannik, USSR Championship, Leningrad 1956.

c) After barely surviving the main game, Keres tried the other side and faced 8...♘a5 9 ♗c2 g5 10 ♘f5 ♘xf5 11 exf5 ♕f6 12 d5 ♗g7 13 ♘d2 b5—but Mr. K brushed aside Black's impetuous advances with 14 a4 bxa4 15 ♗xa4 and Black could already be pronounced dead in P.Keres-A.Arulaid, Parnu 1955.

In short, 9...♘c8, seems best.

9 ♘f5 g6 10 ♘g3 ♗g7 11 0-0

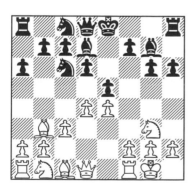

11...exd4

Keres can no longer resist the centre pawn, but taking it is extremely risky. I would prefer the solid 11...0-0.

12 f4 dxc3

12...♕h4 seems to be more in the spirit of Black's wild play, rather than this second capture which develops White.

13 ♘xc3 ♘b6

Now Black won't be able to castle—13...0-0, then 14 f5 with a strong attack.

14 f5 ♘e5

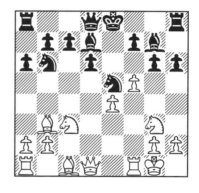

15 ♗e3?

DDT! What are these Grandmasters doing developing their pieces!

Best is 15 fxg6! fxg6 16 ♘h5! which was evidently missed by Geller. The knight blow opens lines, secures the two bishops and prevents castling—not bad for a single combination.

Since the knight can't be taken (16...gxh5? 17 ♕xh5+ ♔e7 18 ♖f7+ and mates), Black has to play 16...♕e7 17 ♘xg7+ ♕xg7 18 ♗e3, when White's positional pluses give him a clear advantage despite the missing pawn.

15...♘bc4 16 ♗d4 ♗b5 17 fxg6 fxg6 18 ♗xc4?!

White commences a series of exchanges that only helps Black. The centralizing 18 ♘d5 is better, still with good compensation, as Black can't go kingside and so must prepare queenside castling where White has the c-file and fresh attacking chances.

18...♗xc4 19 ♗xe5

It is too late for 19 ♘h5 gxh5 20 ♕xh5+ ♔d7 and Black escapes.

19...♗xe5 20 ♕a4+?

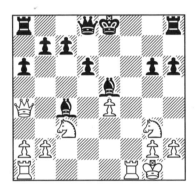

The game has turned—now White blunders an exchange, but at this point there was no compensation for the pawn anyway.

20...b5 21 ♕c2 ♗xf1 22 ♖xf1 ♖f8 23 ♘d5 ♖xf1+ 24 ♘xf1 ♔d7 25 ♕d3 ♕h4 26 a4 ♖f8 27 g3 ♕h3 28 ♘de3 c6 29 axb5 axb5 30 ♘g2 ♕e6 0-1

While this line is somewhat playable for Black after the improvement 11...0-0, the white attack seen in the next game is seemingly quieter, but in fact is even more dangerous.

1 e4 e5 2 ♘f3 ♘c6 3 ♗b5 a6 4 ♗a4 d6 5 c3 ♗d7 6 d4 ♘ge7 7 ♗e3!

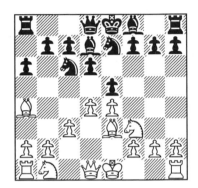

Stronger than Geller and Fischer's primitive 7 ♗b3. Here White makes a healthy developing move, without committing his king. This simple and powerful move has also been played by Anand, and is recommended by my editor John Emms in *Easy Guide to the Ruy Lopez*.

7...♘g6

In an earlier Candidates game, Yusupov tried 7...h6 8 ♘bd2 g5, but this radical plan was well handled by future world champion Anand: 9 dxe5 dxe5 10 h4 g4 11 ♘h2 h5 12 ♘hf1 ♘g6 13 g3 ♗e7 14 ♗c2 ♗e6 15 ♗b3 ♕d7 16 ♗xe6 ♕xe6 17 ♕b3! (now one sees that Black's impetuous pawn advances have only left him with long-term weaknesses; Anand won in the endgame...) 17...♕xb3 18 axb3 0-0 19 b4 b5 20 ♘b3 a5 (Black tries to break the bind with this pawn sacrifice, but never quite finds compensation) 21 ♘xa5 ♘xa5 22 bxa5 c5 23 ♘d2 ♖a6 24 ♘b3 ♖c8 25 ♔e2 c4 26 ♘c1 b4 27 ♖d1 bxc3 28 bxc3 ♗d8 29 ♖a4 ♘f8 30 ♖d5 f6 31 ♘a2 ♖ca8 32 ♖xd8 ♖xd8 33 ♘b4 and White converted in V.Anand-A.Yusupov, Wijk aan Zee (3rd matchgame) 1994.

8 h4!

The point of not castling is revealed: White gains space and threatens to push back the black knight; furthermore ....♗e7-g5 is prevented. In short, Black is forced onto the defensive, with no active plan in sight. In my opinion this attack refutes the knight defence in the 5 c3 variation.

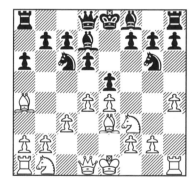

8...h5

If Black allows the h-pawn to move forward, he will be seriously cramped even into the ending, and can only hope for good fortune (as seen in the following game) to reach an eventual draw: 8...♗e7 9 h5 ♘h4 10 ♘xh4 ♗xh4 11 d5 ♘b8 12 ♗xd7+ ♘xd7 13 ♕g4 ♗f6 14 ♘d2 h6 15 ♘f3 ♘c5 16 0-0-0 ♕d7 17

♕xd7+ (the grinding begins!) 17...♔xd7 18 ♘d2 ♗g5 19 ♖h3 ♘d3+ 20 ♔c2 ♗xe3 21 ♔xd3 ♗xd2 22 ♔xd2 a5 23 ♖g3 ♖hg8 24 ♖h1 ♔e7 25 c4 b6 26 b3 ♖af8 27 ♖f3 ♖h8 28 a3! (while Black's kingside is cramped and passive, a legacy of allowing h4-h5, White starts operations on the queenside) 28...g5 29 hxg6 fxg6 30 ♖xf8 ♔xf8 31 b4 axb4 32 axb4 ♔g7 33 ♖a1 ♖f8 34 ♔e3 h5 35 ♖a7 ♖f7 36 c5 bxc5 37 bxc5 dxc5 38 ♖a5 g5 39 ♖xc5 h4 40 f3 ♖e7 41 ♖c6 ♔f8 42 ♔f2 ♖g7 43 ♖h6 ♖f7 44 ♖h5 ♖g7 45 g3 hxg3+ 46 ♔xg3 ♔e7 47 ♔g4 ♔d7 48 ♖xg5 (White picks up a pawn for absolutely nothing) 48...♖e7 49 ♖g6 ♖f7 50 ♖e6 ♖g7+ 51 ♔h4 ♖f7 52 ♔g3 ♖g7+ and now White strangely took the draw by repetition (53 ♔h3? ♖f7 ½-½ O.Korneev-D.Lobzhanidze, Krasnodar 1998), instead of playing the obvious 53 ♔f2 with good winning chances. But who would want to defend that position with the only the faint hope that your opponent would eventually show mercy?

9 g3

9 ♘g5 ♗e7 10 ♗b3 is an untried suggestion of Dolmatov, and this seems like an easy way to a slight plus: evidently Black must give up the two bishops and then attempt to defend; e.g. 10...♗xg5 11 ♗xg5 f6 12 ♗e3 ♕e7 13 ♘d2 and I certainly wouldn't want this defensive chore! White can play on both sides of the board (targets from h5 to a6) and the bishops will be a long-term asset.

9...♗e7 10 d5 ♘b8

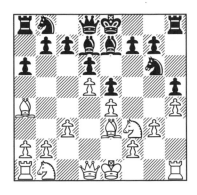

11 ♗xd7+

White trades off Black's good bishop, but in closed positions that's not a huge deal. I'd prefer 11 ♗c2 here, when Black's cramp is exceptionally painful: 11...c6 12 c4 cxd5 13 cxd5 ♗g4 14 ♘bd2 ♘d7 15 ♕b1 ♘f6 16 ♘g5 ♖c8 17 ♗d3 b5 18 a4 ♗d7 19 axb5 axb5 20 f3 0-0 21 ♔e2 ♕c7 22 ♖a7 ♕b8 23 ♕a2 ♖c7 24 ♖a1 ♖fc8 25 ♖a6 ♘e8 26 ♖b6 ♖b7 27 ♖xb7 ♕xb7 28 ♕a7 (White sets his game on grind mode, while Black has no play whatsoever) 28...♖c7 29 ♕xb7 ♖xb7 30 ♘b3 ♗d8 31 ♖a8 ♗b6 32 ♗xb6 ♖xb6 33 ♘a5 ♘f8 34 ♔e3 g6 35 f4 ♔g7 36 ♖a7 ♘f6 37 ♘c6 exf4+ 38 gxf4 ♔g8 39 ♔d4 ♗xc6 40 dxc6 ♖xc6 41 ♗xb5 ♖b6 42 ♗c4 d5 43 ♗xd5 ♘xd5 44 exd5 ♖xb2 45 ♖xf7 ♖h2 46 ♔e5 ♖xh4 47 ♖a7 ♖g4 48 d6 1-0 R.Tischbierek-S.Sale, Budapest 1996. Horrific! Sometimes resignation can be a relief!

11...♘xd7 12 ♘fd2

Black has more room than in the last example, but a dead bishop.

12...♘f6 13 f3 0-0 14 c4 c5 15 ♘c3 ♕d7 16 a4

Probably 16...b6 is better than Black's next, holding out a faint hope of counterplay with a later ...b6-b5, but clearly the whole line can't be recommended, as White gets a clear plus both with Tischbierek's grind and Topalov's more academic light square exploitation (not to mention Dolmatov's knight thrust!).

16...a5 17 ♕e2 ♔h7 18 0-0-0!

This is still legal! Now that the queenside is closed, White safely castles long and launches an attack on the opposite wing.

18...♖h8 19 ♘f1!

The knight aims for f5.

19...♔g8 20 ♗d2 ♘e8 21 ♘e3 ♘f8 22 b3 g6

Keeping the knight out, but weakening the kingside.

23 f4

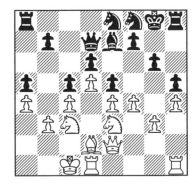

As White levers open a file, it might be time to see what the black rooks are doing—

Oh.

23...♗f6 24 ♖df1 ♕e7 25 f5! ♘g7 26 ♘b5 b6 27 fxg6 fxg6 28 g4 ♗xh4 29 ♘xd6!

White finishes nicely, but it must be said that Black never put up any serious resistance in this game.

29...♕xd6 30 ♖xh4 ♘d7 31 gxh5 ♖xh5 32 ♖xh5 ♘xh5 33 ♘f5! 1-0

White finally reaches the magic f5-square, and Black immediately resigns—and with good reason! If 33...♕c7 (or 33...gxf5 34 ♕xh5 and White wins on the open files) 34 ♘e7+ ♔g7 35 ♕g4 ♘f8 36 d6! ♕d7 37 ♕g5 and there is no rational defence to ♕h6 mate.

I trust Tischbierek's appalling grind and Topalov's technical walkover have convinced you that this is *not* the way to play!

Black has to accept reality and switch to the Bishop Defence against the 5 c3 move order. While I like the Knight Defence myself, I would never play it unless White has castled early. In the game, after 8 h4, Black was already doomed to thankless defence.

1 e4 e5 2 ♘f3 ♘c6 3 ♗b5 a6 4 ♗a4 d6 5 0-0

Now that White has castled, the ...♘e7-g6 line is fine: Black doesn't have to fear h2-h4, as in the previous game, and can try to open the h-file himself.

5...♗d7 6 c3 ♘ge7 7 d4 ♘g6 8 ♖e1

White keeps the tension in the centre. Another possibility is to lock things up and exchange Black's "good" bishop with 8 d5, for which see Games 23 and 24. A simplifying line that helps Black is 8 ♗g5 ♗e7 9 ♗xe7 ♕xe7 10 ♘bd2 0-0 11 ♖e1 ♘f4 and in view of the weak dark squares Black was slightly better in Fesad_kolpaoglu-Taylor, playchess.com (blitz) 2010—we'll see something similar in the note to White's eleventh.

8...♗e7 9 ♘bd2 h6!

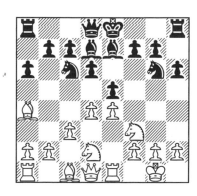

The key point: one recalls the similar line from Game 14 where Fischer crashed and burned. Black wants to open the h-file, and if White doesn't take, Black forces an exchange of minor pieces that eases his position.

10 ♘f1 ♗g5 11 ♘e3

Usual: White at least gets the two bishops. Instead, 11 ♘xg5 hxg5 gives Black what he wants: the open h-file for attack; e.g. 12 g3 ♕f6 13 d5 ♘b8 14 ♗xd7+ ♘xd7 15 ♕g4 ♘f4! (a typical sacrifice in this sort of position) 16 gxf4 exf4! and Black has more than enough for the piece: he will bring his knight to e5, castle long, then launch an h-file and pawn storm attack on the white king!

The "standard Lopez move" 11 ♘g3 is probably weaker, after which White only scores 34%! Here's a GM game that illustrates what one could see already from my blitz game above: the ex-change of dark-squared bishops favours Black due to the fixed central pawns, and Black gets good attacking chances with ideas of ...♘f4 and ...♗h3. Let's take a look: 11...♗xc1 12 ♖xc1 0-0 13 dxe5 dxe5 14 ♘f5 b5 15 ♗b3 ♘a5 16 ♗d5 c6 17 ♗b3 ♘xb3 18 ♕xb3 ♕f6 19 ♕b4 ♘f4 20 ♘e7+? ♔h7 21 ♖cd1 ♘xg2!!

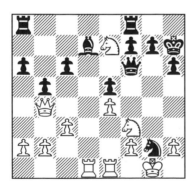

(the Spanish GM crashes through!— the combination shows the difference between the white and black minor pieces: the former are inoffensive, but the latter can dismember the white king position!) 22 ♘xe5 (22 ♔xg2 ♗h3+ forces mate) 22...♗h3 23 ♘d7 ♕g5 (with no opposing bishop, the black queen is invulnerable on this dominating attack-ing post, the minor pieces aiding the mating attack—meanwhile the white knights can only capture trivial mate-rial) 24 ♕c5 f5 25 ♘xf8+ ♖xf8 26 f3 ♘xe1+ 27 ♔f2 ♘xf3! 28 ♘xf5 ♖f6 29 ♔e2 ♗xf5 0-1 J.Cuadras Avellana-O.Rodriguez Vargas, Barcelona 2001.

11...♗xe3 12 ♗xe3 0-0

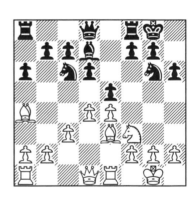

The position is now quite similar to Fischer-Pachman (Game 14). The white bishops can't do much with the fixed centre, while the black knight eyes f4. I would say it's about even, but far from drawish.

13 ♘d2

For 13 h3 see the next game. In-stead, 13 ♕d2?! ♘xd4 is a typical MS trick that exploits the undefended bishop at a4: sometimes this trick wins a pawn; here White can desperado it back, though Black is certainly at least equal after 14 ♘xe5 ♘xe5 15 ♕xd4 ♗xa4 16 ♕xa4 ♕h4.

13...♖e8 14 ♗c2 ♘f4 15 ♗xf4 exf4 16 ♕f3

This too obvious move doesn't help White at all, and only encourages Black to bring his pieces to the kingside. Better is 16 e5 with the idea of obtaining positional compensation for the pawn after 16...dxe5 17 d5!.

16...♕g5 17 ♕d3 ♘e7 18 e5?!

Walking into a pin. 18 ♘f3 is better.

18...♗f5

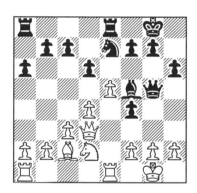

Black's last three moves have efficiently transferred three pieces to White's poorly defended kingside.

19 ♘e4 ♕g6 20 exd6 cxd6 21 d5 ♖ad8!

A "discreet use of the rook" that Nimzowitsch would admire: by securing his centre pawn, Black frees every other piece to attack.

22 ♖ad1?

22 f3 is necessary, despite the weakening of e3.

22...f3!

Keres alertly exploits the potential skewer that White inadvertently set up with his last move: now 23 ♕xf3 ♗g4 24 ♘f6+ (or just 24 ♕d3 ♗xd1) 24...gxf6 wins for Black.

23 g3 ♕h5 24 ♖e3 ♗g6! 25 c4

The f-pawn is still taboo: 25 ♖xf3 ♘xd5 26 ♖e1 (or 26 ♕xd5 ♕xf3) 26...♘c7 27 c4 f5 and Black wins by pin.

25...♘f5! 26 ♖ee1

26 ♖xf3 ♘d4 wins material.

26...♘d4!! 0-1

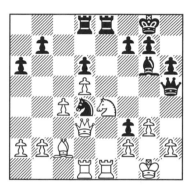

Suddenly it's all over:

a) 27 ♕f1 ♘xc2 wins a piece.

b) 27 ♔h1 ♕h3 28 ♖g1 ♖xe4 wins a piece.

c) 27 ♗b1 ♘e2+ 28 ♔h1 ♗xe4 wins a piece.

d) 27 ♕xd4 ♕h3 wins a king!

White resigns just in time.

Although White didn't have to lose in 26 moves, one sees that, unlike in Topalov-Yusupov (Game 20), Black had full counterplay in this position with real possibilities of attack on the castled white king.

Game 22
M.Sagafos-T.Gareev
Cappelle la Grande 2007

1 e4 e5 2 ♘f3 ♘c6 3 ♗b5 a6 4 ♗a4 d6 5 c3 ♗d7 6 0-0

An interesting point: if White plays the more logical 6 d4, Black should answer 6...♘f6 and head for Chapter Three. However, since White commits to castling here, Black can play an effective Knight Defence.

6...♘ge7 7 d4 ♘g6 8 ♖e1 ♗e7 9 ♘bd2 h6 10 ♘f1 ♗g5 11 ♘e3 ♗xe3 12 ♗xe3 0-0 13 h3

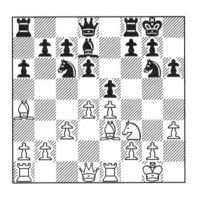

White tries to improve on the previous game, but the pawn on h3 can be a target in some lines.

White does have another alternative, seen in the following nail-biting Keres encounter: 13 dxe5 ♘cxe5 14 ♘xe5 and the players couldn't stand the tension any more, so... ½-½ B.Ivkov-P.Keres, Amsterdam 1971. Not every Keres game is a great struggle!

13...♖e8 14 ♗c2 ♕f6

The "target problem" with 13 h3 can now be seen: White would like to play 15 g3 to deny the black knight the f4-square, but then h3 hangs.

15 dxe5 ♘cxe5 16 ♘xe5 ♕xe5 17 ♕d2 ♗c6 18 ♗d4 ♕g5 19 ♗e3

White should just exchange queens with equality—but he underestimates Black's play.

19...♕h5 20 f3 ♖e7 21 ♕f2 ♖ae8

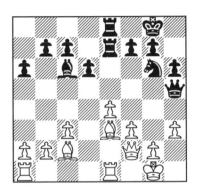

Now the white centre is under Nimzowitschian restraint—note that when White finally gets his kingside pawns going, he is left with serious weaknesses behind the advancing foot soldiers.

22 ♖ad1 ♘e5 23 b3 ♖e6 24 f4 ♘d7 25 f5 ♖e5 26 ♗d4

The tricky 26 ♖xd6!? is possible, with the idea 26...cxd6? 27 ♗d1 winning the queen for too little, but Black equalizes with 26...♗xe4! 27 ♖xd7 ♗xc2 28 ♕xc2 ♖xe3.

26...♖5e7 27 g4?!

Pawns can't move backwards; now the white king is seriously exposed. The plus side is that the black queen is also exposed, but this is only good for a possible repetition. Better is 27 ♖e3! f6 with equality due to the lock on e5, but not 27...♗xe4? 28 ♖de1 d5 29 ♗d1 ♕g5 30 h4 and White cleverly wins material.

27...♕g5

Certainly not 27...♕xh3? 28 ♖d3 ♕xg4+ 29 ♖g3 and White breaks through to g7.

28 ♖e3

White should chase the queen and the draw by 28 ♗e3 ♕f6 29 ♗d4 ♕g5 (Black can avoid the draw with 29...♘e5, but then White is okay after 30 ♕g3) 30 ♗e3 with a repetition.

28...♗xe4 29 h4

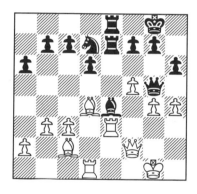

After 29 ♖de1 ♗xc2 30 ♖xe7 ♖xe7 31 ♖xe7 ♕xe7 32 ♕xc2 Black is a good pawn up. White is trying to trap Black's queen, but the young Uzbek GM doesn't care!

29...♕xe3!

White was probably counting on 29...♕xg4+? 30 ♖g3 with the g-file attack again, but Gareev's surprise queen sacrifice knocks the pins from under White's position.

30 ♗xe3 ♗xc2 31 ♕xc2 ♖xe3

Now the terribly exposed white king tells: meanwhile Black owns the only open file and has a secured knight outpost in the centre.

32 ♕g2

Or 32 ♖d3 ♖e1+ 33 ♔f2 ♖h1 with attack.

32...♖8e4

Decisive! The white rook is a spectator as the three attacking black pieces run amok.

33 ♖f1 ♘e5 34 ♔h1 ♖xg4 35 ♕xb7

White could drag the game out by 35 ♕h2 ♘f3 36 ♖xf3 (or 36 ♕h3 ♖xh4 and Black ends up with an extra piece) 36...♖e1+ and Black will emerge with an extra rook, but mate could be avoided for a few moves.

35...♖h3 mate!

A quick end!

In this case exchanging queens was the better course for White—instead of "winning" Black's queen and facing a horde of revenge-seeking pieces!

As far as the opening goes, one could see by move 14 that Black had an equal game and active counterplay—so White must try to gain the advantage earlier... if he can!

The last two games of this chapter will feature a different strategy on White's part (since normal Lopez methods don't seem to be getting anywhere, as the previous two games attest). Here White will block the centre with an early d4-d5, reaching a King's

Indian type structure—pawn chain of e4/d5 vs. e5/d6—but without the fianchettoed black king's bishop. This line was played against me both times that I tried the Knight Defence; and even though it has also been played by Kasparov, I think Black has sufficient counterplay.

1 e4 e5 2 ♘f3 ♘c6 3 ♗b5 a6 4 ♗a4 d6

This was my first "post study" game with the Modern Steinitz—at least I had some idea what I was doing!

5 0-0 ♗d7 6 c3 ♘ge7 7 d4 ♘g6 8 d5

This was Kasparov's choice in his only win against the Modern Steinitz—he drew against both Lautier (see the notes to Game 34) and Short (Game 16). Generally, White soon reaches a pawn structure similar to the Petrosian Variation of the King's Indian (1 d4 ♘f6 2 c4 g6 3 ♘c3 ♗g7 4 e4 d6 5 ♘f3 0-0 6

♗e2 e5 7 d5); note the central pawn chain which is identical to the present game position.

In the very un-Lopez scenario that arises, White's play is on the queenside, Black's on the kingside. White gets rid of Black's theoretically good bishop, but Black can often exchange his bad bishop on g5. Black does have a disadvantage in space, but if he can engineer the required ...f7-f5 break, he should be fine.

8...♘b8 9 ♗xd7+

White can also play the positionally necessary 9 c4 at once. Let's look at two sample games featuring two of the biggest guns in our chess main street, Kasparov and Keres. Play continues 9...♗e7 10 ♘c3 and then:

a) 10...0-0 (I think ...h7-h6 and ...♗g5 before castling is best, as in note 'b', since Black might need the open h-file—but it's interesting that even as played Black had good equalizing chances) 11 ♗xd7 ♘xd7 12 ♗e3 ♘h4 13 ♘xh4 ♗xh4 14 ♕g4 ♗f6 (Black should prepare ...f7-f5, so 14...g6 is correct; e.g. 15 g3 ♗f6 16 b4 ♗g7 17 c5 f5 18 exf5 gxf5 with good counterplay) 15 b4 ♘b6? (Black's play is too slow and the knight is misplaced: now Kasparov gains two tempi with his advancing c-pawn and wins in his patented style) 16 ♕e2 ♗g5 17 c5 ♗xe3 18 ♕xe3 ♘d7 19 a4 f5 20 c6! f4 21 ♕d3 bxc6 22 dxc6 ♘f6 23 f3 ♕b8 24 ♕c4+ ♔h8 25 ♔h1 ♕e8 26 b5 a5 27 b6! (White creates a passed pawn before Black can get a kingside attack going) 27...cxb6 28 ♘b5 ♖c8 29 ♖ac1 ♕e7 30 ♖fd1 ♘e8 31 c7 ♖f6 32 ♕c6 ♖h6 33 ♕b7 ♕h4 34 h3 1-0 G.Kasparov-Vasalomidze, Tbilisi 1976.

b) 10...h6

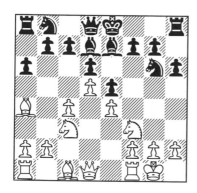

11 ♗e3 ♗g5 (Keres logically exchanges the bad bishop first and offers to open the h-file) 12 ♖e1 ♗xe3 13 ♖xe3 0-0 14 ♖c1 a5 15 ♘e1 ♘a6 16 ♗xd7 ♕xd7 17 ♕a4 ♕xa4 18 ♘xa4 (Black has equalized; now instead of the following simplifying move and draw offer, the positional 18...f5 was possible when Black can make an endgame fight of it) 18...♘c5 19 ♘xc5 dxc5 ½-½ P.Trifunovic-P.Keres, Belgrade

1956.

I wonder what Kasparov had in mind against Keres' smooth equalizing play? I don't see any major difficulties for Black if he follows Keres and plays accurately.

9...♘xd7 10 c4

For 10 ♘bd2 see the next game.

10...♗e7 11 ♘c3 h6 12 ♗d2

White has tried numerous moves at this juncture but hasn't proved an advantage with any of them:

a) 12 ♗e3 ♗g5 and then:

a1) 13 ♘xg5 hxg5 14 g3 ♘f4 (the thematic sac when White opens the h-file—see the note to White's 11th move in Game 21 for a similar blow) 15 gxf4 gxf4 16 ♕g4 (Black gets the piece back immediately, for if 16 ♗d2? ♕g5+ 17 ♔h1 ♕h4 mates) 16...♘f6 17 ♕g2 fxe3 18 fxe3 ♕d7 19 ♖f3 0-0-0 20 ♖af1 ♖h7 and with the h-file and his kingside attack Black was clearly better in W.Pietzsch-O.Troianescu, Bucharest 1951.

a2) 13 b4 ♗xe3 14 fxe3 0-0 15 ♘d2 ♘h4 16 ♕g4 and now, instead of the premature queen exchange 16...♕g5?! of H.Nakamura-R.Hess, New York (rapid) 2004, Black should prefer 16...a5 17 a3 axb4 18 axb4 ♖xa1 19 ♖xa1 f5 with active counterplay and kingside attacking chances.

a3) 13 ♕d2 ♗xe3 14 ♕xe3 ♘f4 15 ♘e2 ♘xe2+ 16 ♕xe2 0-0 17 b4 f5! (Hess shows that he has learned the lesson from his earlier game with Nakamura) 18 exf5 ♖xf5 and Black had active play and went on to win in N.Yap-R.Hess, Philadelphia 2007.

b) 12 g3 ♗g5 13 ♘xg5 hxg5 14 ♕g4 (White is trying to save a tempo with his queen's bishop, but I don't think the position has changed significantly) 14...♘f4! (anyway!—and rather than 14...♘f6 15 ♕xg5 ♖h5 16 ♕d2 with a safe extra pawn in M.Kozakov-G.Emodi, Sarospatak 1995) 15 gxf4 exf4 and Black's attack with the coming ...♘e5 is still extremely strong.

c) 12 a3 ♗g5 13 ♘xg5 hxg5 14 g3 ♕f6 15 b4 ♘f4 16 ♖a2 (not 16 gxf4? ♕h6 with a winning attack) 16...♕g6 17 f3 ♘h3+ 18 ♔h1 g4 19 fxg4 ♘f6 20 ♕f3 ♘xg4 21 c5 ♘f6 22 ♖c2 ♖h5 23 ♗e3 and in this very sharp, exciting, double-edged position—the GMs agreed to a draw! ½-½ J.Van der Wiel-V.Tkachiev, Cannes (1st matchgame) 1999.

12...♗g5 13 ♘xg5

It's risky to open the h-file, but after the cautious 13 ♖e1 ♗xd2 14 ♕xd2 0-0 Black has easy equality and can look forward to active play with ...f7-f5.

13...hxg5 14 g3 ♘f6

This works like a charm in the game, but only because White misses a zwischenzug on the next move (which I noticed, to my horror, right after playing the knight to f6!). With that proverbial 20-20 hindsight, I realize 14...♕f6 was best, intending ...0-0-0 and a kingside attack, while if White goes after my g-pawn, there is the thematic sacrifice we have seen in previous notes; i.e.

15 ♕g4 ♘f4! and then:

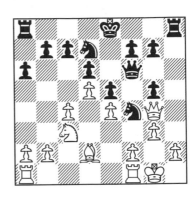

a) 16 gxf4 exf4 (Black's position is so strong that both captures are possible: also good is 16...gxf4 17 f3 ♖h4 18 ♕g2 0-0-0 19 a4 ♖dh8 20 ♖f2 ♘c5 with a long-term bind for the piece) 17 b4 (the desperate 17 e5 still favours Black after 17...♘xe5 18 ♖fe1 ♖h4 and ...0-0-0 cannot be prevented) 17...♘e5 18 ♕g2 g4 and Black has a tremendous attack; e.g. 19 f3 gxf3 20 ♖xf3 ♘xf3+ 21 ♕xf3 ♕d4+ 22 ♕f2 ♕xf2+ 23 ♔xf2 ♖xh2+ 24 ♔e1 ♖h1+ and wins.

b) Rather than accepting the piece, 16 h4 ♕g6 17 ♗xf4 (after 17 gxf4 ♖xh4 18 ♕g2 exf4 19 f3 ♘e5 Black has the familiar excellent attack) 17...gxf4 18 ♕xg6 fxg6 19 ♔g2 may be relatively best, when White may equalize.

15 ♗xg5

Better is 15 ♕a4+! which throws a spanner in the works! Black has three unappetizing choices: exchange queens, retreat his just moved knight, or give up the castling privilege:

a) 15...♕d7 16 ♕xd7+ ♔xd7 17 ♗xg5 ♖h3 18 ♗xf6 gxf6 19 ♔g2 ♖ah8

20 ♖h1 and while Black has some compensation I doubt it's enough for the pawn.

b) 15...♘d7 16 f3 ♕e7 17 ♗e3 0-0-0 18 b4 and White's attack looks stronger than Black's.

c) During the game I was more or less intending 15...♔f8, but after 16 ♗xg5 it's hard to find real compensation with the queen's rook out of play.

15...♕d7

Now Black just castles long with good practical compensation, as the h-file will always be an important factor in the position—though Mr. *Fritz* weighs in with an "unapproved!".

16 f3

There is nothing better. 16 ♗xf6 has the idea of ♕a4 and a good queen exchange—but Black doesn't have to retake: 16...♕h3! 17 ♗h4 ♖xh4! wins. Or if 16 ♕a4 ♕xa4 17 ♘xa4 ♘xe4 and Black recovers his pawn—a centre pawn at that—with the better game.

16...0-0-0 17 ♖f2 ♖h5 18 ♗e3 ♖dh8 19 b4 ♕h3 20 ♘e2

One could say that White has a good chance for advantage by combining defence with attack—20 ♖g2 ♘e8 21 b5!—but a second opinion is that *Black* has a good chance of advantage due to sacrificial shock!

20...♘e8 21 c5 f5

22 ♕f1?

My human opponent couldn't resist the opportunity to exchange queens, not realizing that Black's attack will grow even stronger without the ladies!

22 exf5! is Mr. *Fritz*'s suggestion and it looks right: White should not allow the exchange on e4 when, as we will see, he is left with weak pawns and weak squares. After 22...♖xf5 (not 22...♘e7 23 g4) 23 ♘c3 Black probably doesn't have enough; e.g. 23...♖fh5 24 ♘e4 ♘f6 25 cxd6 (but not 25 ♘g5? ♕xg3+! and her majesty is immune due to mate in two) 25...♘xe4 26 fxe4 cxd6 27 ♖c1+ ♔b8 28 ♕c2 and White has the more dangerous attack, *and* an extra pawn.

22...fxe4

22...♕xh2+!? looks exciting, but doesn't come to anything after 23

♖xh2 ♖xh2 24 ♕g2 ♖xg2+ 25 ♔xg2 with equality.

23 fxe4 ♘f6

Now both e4 and g4 are weak, and White is fighting for survival.

24 cxd6 ♕xf1+

Black has a draw if he wants it with 24...cxd6 25 ♖c1+ ♔b8 26 ♕xh3 ♖xh3 27 ♖g2 ♘h4 28 ♖f2 ♘g6 29 ♖g2 etc.

25 ♖axf1

Not 25 ♖fxf1 ♖xh2 with an immediate Black advantage.

25...♘xe4

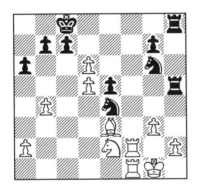

26 ♖f7?

An error, as Black's rooks break through. Instead, White can try an unclear ox sacrifice with 26 dxc7 ♘xf2 27 ♖xf2 (though Black looks better here anyway), or play for equality (best) and probably get it after 26 ♖g2 ♘xd6.

26...♘xd6 27 ♖xg7 ♖xh2 28 ♖c1

White could still avoid serious trauma with 28 ♖g8+ to exchange one of the attacking rooks: after 28...♖xg8 29 ♔xh2 ♘e7 Black is better in view of White's scattered pawns, but this is far preferable to the game continuation!

28...♖h1+

A 19th century king hunt begins!

29 ♔g2 ♖8h2+ 30 ♔f3 e4+!

The white king must go to the fourth rank, and won't be able to stop there!

31 ♔g4 ♘e5+ 32 ♔g5

If 32 ♔f4 ♘d3+ wins.

32...♖h5+ 33 ♔f6 ♘e8+!

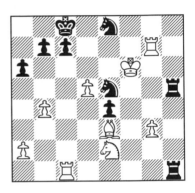

This amazing final blow wins a full rook! It's rare to see a white king being driven to e7 in a Ruy Lopez—in Game 44 I was only able to drive my opponent's king to e5!

34 ♔e7 ♘xg7 35 ♖c2 ♘f5+ 36 ♔f6 ♘xe3 37 ♖c3 ♘3c4 38 ♘f4 ♖h6+ 39 ♔g5 e3 40 d6

White sheds even more material and then...

40...♖xd6 0-1

...wisely resigns.

Note that the carnage has been so absolute that Black can even win by tossing a rook: 41 ♔f5 ♖h5+! 42 ♘xh5 (or 42 ♔e4 ♘d2+ 43 ♔xe3 ♘g4+ 44 ♔e2 ♖h2+ 45 ♔e1 ♘e5 and mates) 42...e2 43 ♖c1 ♖d1 and queens.

With the improvement 14...♕f6 (remember that thematic knight sac on f4!) in hand, one sees that Black has excellent chances of not just equalizing, but of playing for a win in this line.

Yes, White can go for equality by refusing to take the bishop on g5, but then Black should have no problems.

Game 24
C.Glawe-T.Taylor
Los Angeles (rapid) 2010

1 e4 e5 2 ♘f3 ♘c6 3 ♗b5 a6 4 ♗a4 d6 5 0-0 ♗d7 6 c3 ♘ge7 7 d4 ♘g6 8 d5 ♘b8 9 ♗xd7+ ♘xd7 10 ♘bd2

10 c4 is the positional move, as played in the previous game. Glawe continues as in a regular Lopez, failing to realize he is on the wrong track.

The light dawned afterwards: as he related in an excellent article for *Chess Life Online*, he showed the game to his coach, IM Jeremy Silman, and Mr. Silman pointed out that the new pawn structure—the e4/d5 vs. e5/d6 chain—had so changed the nature of the position that White should look for King's Indian ideas (queenside expansion) rather than typical Ruy ideas of a slow kingside build-up.

10...♗e7 11 ♖e1 0-0

Of course 11...h6 12 ♘f1 ♗g5 is possible, but I thought—correctly—that I could also play more slowly against my opponent's quiet moves. There is no need to rush: with White castled on the kingside (Black's strong side) the long-term positional factors favour Black, especially since White has nothing going on the queenside.

12 ♘f1 ♘h4

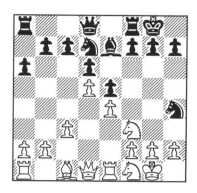

Another thematic move: Black removes a kingside defender and prepares ...♗g5.

13 ♘g3

White can try to play like Kasparov (see the note to White's 9th move in the previous game) with 13 ♘xh4 ♗xh4 14 ♕g4—but here this gives nothing, since Black gets his "base of the chain" attack in first: 14...g6 15 ♗h6 f5! 16 exf5 ♖xf5 and Black has good kingside play.

13...♘xf3+ 14 ♕xf3 ♗g5 15 ♘f5 ♗xc1 16 ♖axc1 g6 17 ♘g3

Or 17 ♕g3 ♘f6 and Black has many positive ideas such as ...♘h5-f4 and ...♔h8, followed eventually by ...f7-f5. Note that White, trying to play on the wrong side of the pawn chain, can only make superficial threats, whereas Black has long-term play.

17...♕g5

Now Black is clearly better as White has nothing against the ...f7-f5 break.

18 b4 f5 19 exf5

19 c4 is too late in view of 19...f4 20 ♘e2 a5! (Black's position is so strong that he, unlike White, can play on both sides of the board) 21 a3 (or 21 b5 ♘c5 with a permanently annoying knight; Black would then continue his kingside pawn storm, planning ...♕h4, ...g5-g4 etc) 21...axb4 22 axb4 ♖a4 23 ♕b3 ♖fa8 with a full board attack.

19...gxf5 20 ♕h5

Otherwise the black pawns roll through—but now the famed "dim knight on rim" appears.

20...♕xh5 21 ♘xh5 f4

Paging Sartre! (No Exit!)

22 g3

22 g4 is relatively best, when the white knight will not be lost, but after 22...a5 23 b5 ♔f7 it is totally out of play.

22...a5 23 a3

23 gxf4 also saves the knight, but then 23...♖f5 24 ♘g3 ♖xf4 gives Black a decisive positional advantage.

23...♘b6 24 gxf4 exf4 25 ♖e7

If 25 ♖e4 axb4 26 axb4 ♘xd5 and Black pockets an extra pawn...

25...♖f5

...but now that last variation looks good, since this move wins a piece!

26 ♘xf4

As 26 ♘g7 fails to 26...♖g5+, the unfortunate knight perishes with only two pawns for compensation.

26...♖xf4 27 ♖xc7 ♖f7 28 ♖xf7 ♔xf7 29 ♖d1 axb4 30 axb4 ♖g8+ 31 ♔f1 ♖g5 32 ♖d4 ♖xd5 33 ♖f4+ ♔e6 34 ♖h4 h5 35 ♖h3 ♘c4 36 ♖h4 b5 37 ♖e4+ ♖e5 38 ♖d4 d5 39 f4 ♖e4 40 f5+ ♔f6 0-1

After 41 ♖d3 (or 41 ♖xd5 ♘e3+ forking) 41...♖f4+ 42 ♔e2 ♖xf5 Black has regained both his pawns and can calmly evaluate his extra piece.

This is an instructive game because it shows that certain lines of the MS reach pawn structures that are more King's Indian than Ruy Lopez, and must be treated accordingly. If White plays in normal Ruy fashion, as here, Black can easily get the advantage—which can be quite baffling to the opponent!

Conclusion

The Knight Defence is very solid and Black has excellent chances to equalize—*if* White has castled early, which allows the key ...h7-h6/...♗g5 counter. I don't recommend this line at all (remember Game 20) if White has *not* castled and can play h2-h4.

To face that move order, Black must also be prepared with the Bishop Defence—for which see the next chapter.

Chapter Three
Solid Line 2:
The Bishop Defence

This is the most difficult *move order* chapter in the book, and GMs, and even Keres himself, go astray. The basic motif of the Bishop Defence is that Black intends to fianchetto his king's bishop. Black can play this against almost any move order by White, but must adapt himself to whatever White plays. There are innumerable ways for either side to go wrong. Furthermore, the key word above is "intends"—in a few lines the kingside fianchetto is not advisable (e.g. Game 30). Despite the complexity and difficulty of this variation, it's necessary to learn if you want to play the MS (and don't want to venture the razor-sharp gambit lines)—for as we have already seen, if White adopts the 5 c3 move order, reserving castling, then the ...♘e7-g6 line *does not work*.

Also, as noted previously, if you do get the Bishop Defence down, you actually don't need the Knight Defence, as the former is a universal system while the latter only works against a specific move order. Another good point is that, as Keres has repeatedly shown, the Bishop Defence also works against some important early d2-d4 variations (independent lines of this type, without the kingside fianchetto, will be seen in Chapter Eight).

One further point: this is my first book on a really theory heavy mainstream opening like the Ruy Lopez and it is *absolutely impossible* to cover every subvariation and transpositional possibility. All the ones that I *am* covering are already straining the length of this book! So I am basically following a combination of what Keres played with success and what I believe to be best, and letting the rest go. For example, I believe that when Black fianchettoes the dark-squared bishop, the king's knight belongs on f6 (King's Indian style) where it is most active. I simply have no space to cover the secondary ...♘e7 (beyond the brief look we had in Game 6), which I think is significantly weaker—one recalls Alekhine got a bad game with it before his inevitable comeback—and it's hard enough to cover all the twists and turns of the lines with ...♘f6. So let's focus on the best and I will try to explain the move order contortions!

Game 25
B.Parma-P.Keres
USSR-Yugoslavia match,
Yerevan 1971

---

1 e4 e5 2 ♘f3 ♘c6 3 ♗b5 a6 4 ♗a4 d6 5 0-0

Transposition one: 5 c3 ♗d7 6 d4 ♘f6 7 0-0 g6 reaches the same position as the game.

5...♗d7 6 d4

Transposition two: 6 c3 ♘f6 7 d4 g6 reaches the same position as the game.

6...♘f6!

Best: Black develops and counter-attacks. Weaker is 6...b5 7 ♗b3 ♘xd4 8 ♘xd4 exd4 as White can offer the strong pawn sacrifice 9 c3—see analysis in Game 69.

7 c3

White reverts back to the main line which, as we saw from the transpositions above, is usually reached via c2-c3 and then d2-d4. Other moves (where White plays an early d2-d4 but not c2-

c3) are covered in Chapter Eight.

7...g6

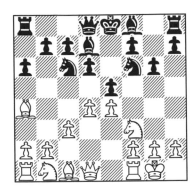

This is the basic position Black is aiming for, though as one sees, it can be reached by a variety of move orders. On the kingside, Black is playing a King's Indian, complete with fianchet-toed bishop and latent ...f7-f5 break; and on the queenside, Black is defending a Ruy! This schizophrenic board division leads to interesting and very complex play—to put it mildly!

In this and the following two games White retains the Ruy character by either keeping the tension in the centre or exchanging on e5. Then Games 28-29 show inaccurate move orders that Black should avoid; Games 30-32 see White creating a full King's Indian type position by advancing d4-d5; and Game 33 features an attempt at outright refutation of Black's plan, which is fortunately not successful!

Returning to the position in front of us, note that 7...♘xe4?! is anti-positional and should be avoided. In the Open Lopez Black needs to play

...d7-d5, and here the black d-pawn is committed to ...d7-d6. So, as Black is not winning a pawn, it's clear that White easily obtains the advantage; e.g. 8 ♖e1 ♘f6 9 dxe5 ♘xe5 (no better is 9...dxe5 10 ♗xc6 ♗xc6 11 ♕xd8+ ♔xd8 12 ♘xe5 ♗d5 13 ♗g5 ♗e6 14 ♘d2 h6 15 ♗xf6+ gxf6 16 ♘g6 ♖g8 17 ♘xf8 ♖xf8, when it's evident that the shattered kingside pawns give White a considerable plus; therefore Alekhine employed his World Champion "get out of jail free" card—a draw offer—and escaped to never play this variation again! ½-½ A.Lilienthal-A.Alekhine, Paris 1933) 10 ♗f4 ♗e7 11 ♘xe5 dxe5 12 ♗xe5 ♗xa4 13 ♕xa4+ b5 14 ♕f4 (Black can't defend the c-pawn in view of the threat to f6, so...) 14...0-0 15 ♗xc7 ♕d7 16 ♗e5 ♘g4 17 ♕d2! ♕f5 18 ♗d4 ♗g5 19 ♕e2 ♕f4 20 g3 ♕f5 21 ♘d2 ♗xd2 22 ♕xd2 ♖fe8 23 ♖e2 and White consolidated and won easily in A.Petrushin-Y.Shabanov, Russian Championship, Orel 1992.

8 ♖e1

Natural, though there are alternatives:

a) 8 ♗g5 doesn't cause trouble here, as it did in Yates-Alekhine (that game's very inaccurate move order was 5 0-0 g6 6 c3 ♗g7 7 d4 ♗d7 8 ♗g5 and now Alekhine had to resort to the inferior ...♘ge7, as 8...♘f6 would have been bad in view of 9 ♗xc6 going after the e5-pawn), since Black has 8...b5! (instead of the casual and inferior 8...♗g7, transposing into the aforementioned

problems) 9 ♗b3 ♗g7 when his e-pawn is secure and he will castle and soon dodge the pin. By then it will be clear that the white bishop is not well placed on g5 (does it really want to take the f6-knight?) and will be driven back by Black's kingside pawns. A good example, from an IM vs. IM encounter, continued 10 ♖e1 0-0 11 ♘bd2 ♖e8 12 ♖c1 h6 13 ♗h4 ♕b8—now there's no pin, and what does the white bishop accomplish over on the kingside? Meanwhile Black has activated his queen on the opposite flank and has good play. This was finally drawn after a fighting game in L.Day-C.Coudari, Canadian Championship, Calgary 1975.

b) The direct but failed attempt at refutation, 8 ♗xc6, will be seen in Game 33.

Returning to the text, 8 ♖e1,

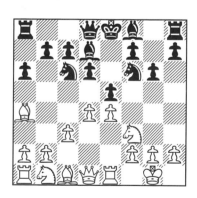

one notices that White has defended e4, which means there is a real threat to take on c6 and pirate the black e-pawn. Keres (here!) plays the best answer, driving off the a4-bishop with gain of time. In a previous game he chose the inaccurate 8...♕e7 (for which see Game 28).

The third path is to ignore the "threat" with 8...♗g7, when 9 ♗xc6 ♗xc6 10 dxe5 ♘xe4 11 exd6 0-0 12 dxc7 ♕xc7 is a sound gambit where Black's two bishops and lead in development give him compensation for the pawn—note that this transposes to the note to White's tenth move in the above-mentioned Game 33.

However, from the point of view of simplicity, Keres' next 8...b5 is best, and I recommend it as a repertoire move since it can be played in many similar situations to completely secure the e5-pawn.

8...b5 9 ♗c2

Khalifman, in *Opening for White according to Anand, Vol. 2*, claims that 9 ♗b3 ♗g7 10 dxe5 ♘xe5 11 ♘xe5 dxe5 12 ♗g5 0-0 13 ♘d2 gives White the advantage, but I can't see any justification for that opinion—see the note to White's 12th move in Game 27.

9...♗g7

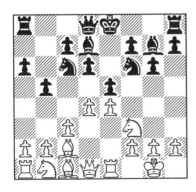

10 dxe5

If 10 ♗e3 0-0 11 dxe5 ♘xe5 (also possible is 11...dxe5 12 ♗c5 ♖e8 13 ♘bd2 ♘a5, preparing to eject the c5-bishop with ...♘b7, when Black is a shade better if anything) 12 ♘xe5 dxe5 and Black has equality. A recent high-level game reached this position by transposition back in the 20th century, and continued as follows: 13 ♘d2 (if 13 ♗c5 ♖e8 14 ♘bd2 ♗f8 and Black is fine) 13...♕e7 14 b4 ♖fd8 (Black gets his rook to the d-file with speed; this file is key to the final drawing combination) 15 ♕e2 a5 16 ♘b3 axb4 17 ♗c5 ♕e8 18 cxb4 ♘h5 19 g3 ♗h6 20 ♗e3 ♗xe3 21 ♕xe3 ♕e7 22 ♕c3 ♗e8 23 ♘a5 ♖d4 24 a3 ♖ad8 25 ♖ac1 ♕f6 26 ♕xc7 ♖d2 27 ♖f1 ♘f4 28 gxf4 ♕xf4 29 ♕c3 ♖2d3! 30 ♗xd3 ½-½ S.Tiviakov-G.Giorgadze, Kropotkin 1995.

I will refer to this game in the note to move 12—yes, these numerous transpositions are tricky!

Another 10th move should not give Black any trouble: 10 ♘bd2 0-0 11 h3 ♘h5 12 dxe5 ♘xe5 13 ♘xe5 dxe5 14 ♘b3 ♕e7 15 ♗e3 ♘f4 and Black was at least equal and went on to win in A.Goloshchapov-V.Malaniuk, Pardubice 1998—we'll see another fine Malaniuk win in Game 31.

10...♘xe5

Keres often took back on e5 with the knight (see also Game 72) as he recognized the Nimzowitschian truth that one does not always need a pawn in the centre to control these squares—active piece play that restrains the centre will also do the trick. If White does not take again (as here) and fix the pawn structure, Black will castle and play ...♖e8 with good pressure against the e4-pawn.

11 ♘xe5 dxe5

The position looks dead even—and it is, as the following game attests: 12 ♗g5 h6 13 ♗h4 ♕e7 14 ♘d2 ♖d8 15 ♘f1 ♗c8 16 ♕e2 0-0 17 ♘e3 c6 18 ♖ed1 ½-½ L.Shamkovich-P.Keres, USSR Team Championship 1968.

12 ♗e3

Yet now, after this unwary move, Black has amazing attacking chances! It's hard to believe (but also a testament to the richness of the royal game) what a huge difference there is between Shamkovich's and Parma's natural bishop developments!

12...♘g4!

It's interesting that two young GMs of the present day (Karjakin and Mamedyarov) apparently did not know this famous Keres victory! A recent game between them went as follows: 12...0-0 (not a mistake, but neither is it

as strong and sharp as Keres' great attacking move; by playing this way, the position should be equal—in fact this is the same position as the Tiviakov-Giorgadze game given in the note to White's tenth move above!) 13 ♘d2 ♗e6?! (but this is a slight error; correct is Giorgadze's 13...♕e7, preparing to quickly bring a rook to the only open file) 14 ♘f3 ♘g4 15 ♗c5 ♖e8 16 h3 ♘h6 17 ♗b3 f6 18 a4 ♕xd1 19 ♗xe6+ ♖xe6 20 ♖exd1 (now White owns the d-file, and gradually increases this advantage until he wins a pawn and, simultaneously, the game) 20...♖c6 21 ♖d5 bxa4 22 ♖xa4 ♗f8 23 ♗e3 ♖b8 24 ♖a2 ♘f7 25 ♘d2 ♘d6 26 ♖c5 ♖xc5 27 ♗xc5 f5 28 ♗xd6 cxd6 29 f3 ♔f7 30 ♔f2 ♔e6 31 ♘c4 ♖c8 32 ♘e3 ♘h6 33 ♘d5 ♗g5 34 g3 and Black resigned in S.Karjakin-S.Mamedyarov, Wijk aan Zee 2006, in view of 34...♖c6 35 ♖xa6! with a technically won ending.

This was a good positional grind by Karjakin—but what would he have done if Mamedyarov had attacked like Keres?

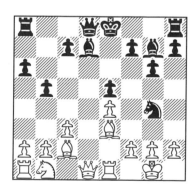

13 ♗c5

After 13 ♘d2 ♘xe3 14 ♖xe3 0-0 Black is just better because of his two bishops, much as will be seen in the main game; and 13 ♗c1? loses at once to 13...♕h4.

13...♕h4!

Now we see why the white bishop had to go to g5 on move 12: to keep the black queen from attacking!

14 h3 ♗f8!!

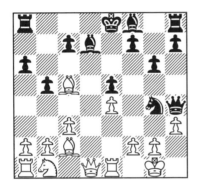

The stunning point: the bishop has no safe square on the a7-g1 diagonal.

15 ♗e3

Now White is just a little worse.

It's almost impossible, even with computer assistance, to give a definite evaluation of the attack Black gets if White takes the piece, but it looks to me like White *might* draw if he makes a ton of correct moves, but Black has excellent practical winning chances. Here's a quick view of this amazingly beautiful sacrificial assault: 15 ♗xf8 ♕xf2+ 16 ♔h1 h5! 17 ♗g7 (weaker is 17 ♗a3? ♕g3 18 hxg4 hxg4+ 19 ♔g1 ♕h2+ 20 ♔f2 g3+ 21 ♔e3 ♕h6+ 22 ♔d3

0-0-0 with a winning attack; note again that the possibility of queenside castling in the MS is an attacking plus!), when a critical position is reached.

My first thought was to continue in 19th century style by sacrificing a rook with 17...0-0-0!?, which gave rise to some amazingly beautiful variations: 18 ♗xh8 ♖xh8 (Black is a full rook down, but all four of his pieces are attacking White's denuded king!) 19 ♕d2 ♕g3 20 hxg4 (make that a rook and a piece down) 20...hxg4+ 21 ♔g1 ♕h4 and then:

a) If White dares to make a threat, Black comes back by activating his bishop and the attack never stops: 22 ♖d1 ♗e6 23 ♕e3 ♗c4 24 ♖d3 (not 24 ♘d2? g3 and the trapped white king perishes) 24...♕h2+ 25 ♔f1 ♖h3 26 gxh3 g3 27 ♕g1 ♕xc2 28 ♔e1 ♕xd3 29 ♕g2 ♕e3+ 30 ♔d1 ♗d3 31 ♘d2 ♕f2 32 ♕xf2 gxf2 33 ♖c1 (Black is too fast in the line 33 a4 f5 34 axb5 fxe4 35 bxa6 e3 and queens) 33...f5! and Black can justifiably play for a win, a rook down in the ending!

b) 22 ♕e3 g3 23 ♔f1 ♕g4 24 ♕f3 (if 24 ♔g1 ♖h2 and as far as I can see Black has a winning attack: there doesn't seem to be any reasonable defence to ...♕h4) 24...♕g5 25 ♗b3 ♗g4 26 ♕xg3 ♖h1+ 27 ♔f2 ♕f6+ 28 ♔e3 ♕g5+ 29 ♔d3 (29 ♔f2 ♕f6+ is a draw, and this might be White's best) 29...♗e2+ 30 ♔c2 ♕xg3 31 ♖xh1 c5 32 ♘d2 c4 33 ♖ae1 ♗d3+ 34 ♔c1 cxb3 35 ♘xb3 ♕xg2 and Black is better with queen and pawn for two rooks, and a continuing attack.

Unfortunately, a computer with no sense of beauty refuted the rook sacrifice with 19 ♖e2! (instead of the 19 ♕d2?! that I gave above) 19...♕g3 20 ♕g1 and Black doesn't have enough for the rook.

So it was back to the drawing board! On reflection, I could see that the rook sac was too extravagant for our silicon age—but Keres' sacrifice is nonetheless correct, if he stops at one piece. After 17 ♗g7 Black should continue with 17...♖h7! 18 ♖e2 (if 18 ♕e2 ♕g3 19 hxg4 hxg4+ 20 ♔g1 ♕h2+ 21 ♔f1 ♖xg7 22 ♕e3 0-0-0 with a terrific attack for the piece; e.g. 23 ♘d2 f5 and the pawn storm is very dangerous for White, or worse 23 ♕a7 ♗c6 24 ♕xa6+ ♗b7 25 ♕xb5 ♕h1+ 26 ♔f2 g3+ 27 ♔f3 ♕xe1 and Black wins) 18...♖xg7! (in view of the fork the black queen doesn't need to move) 19 hxg4 ♕h4+ 20 ♔g1 hxg4 21 ♕e1 g3 22 ♖e3 ♕h2+ 23 ♔f1 ♕h1+ 24 ♔e2 ♕xg2+ 25 ♔d1 ♗g4+ 26 ♔c1 ♕f2! 27 ♘d2 ♖h7 and

Black is better, as his three pawns outweigh White's piece.

No wonder Parma avoided this mess, but chess fans would have enjoyed the mêlée!

15...♘xe3 16 ♖xe3 ♖d8

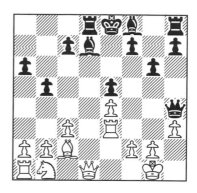

Now Black's two bishops give him a somewhat better game.

17 ♘d2 ♗e6 18 b4

If 18 ♖d3 ♖xd3 19 ♗xd3 ♗c5 with a plus for Black.

18...c5!

Now Black opens the game for his bishops and stands clearly better.

19 ♖d3

A mistake under pressure that loses a pawn. He should continue to defend the joyless position with 19 ♕e1.

19...♖xd3 20 ♗xd3 cxb4 21 ♘f3 ♕d8 22 ♕d2 ♗c4 23 ♖d1

If 23 ♘xe5 ♗g7 and White has no good defence for his hanging pieces.

23...♕xd3 24 ♕xd3 ♗xd3 25 ♖xd3 f6 26 g4 bxc3 27 ♖xc3 ♔d7

Despite the "bad" bishop, Keres makes the technical task of winning the pawn up ending look easy.

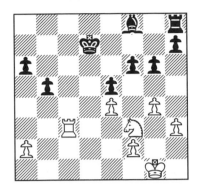

28 g5

Although this splits Black's pawns, the bishop now gets a little more room—but I doubt anything would have held for White.

28...♗e7 29 gxf6 ♗xf6 30 ♖d3+ ♔c6 31 ♔f1 ♖e8 32 ♔e2 ♖e6 33 ♖d5 ♔b6 34 ♔d2 h5 35 ♔c2 ♔c7 36 ♘e1 ♖d6 37 ♖xd6 ♔xd6 38 ♘d3 ♗e7 39 ♘b4 a5 40 ♘d5 ♗h4 41 f3 ♔c5 42 ♔d3 a4 0-1

White resigns, as the win is now straightforward; e.g. 43 ♔c3 ♗f2 44 ♔d3 b4 45 ♘e7 g5 46 ♘f5 ♗d4 47 ♔c2 h4 48 ♘h6 (White can't block the black king, for if 48 ♔d3 b3! 49 axb3 a3 wins) 48...♔c4 49 ♘f7 b3+ 50 axb3+ axb3+ 51 ♔b1 ♔d3 52 ♘xg5 ♔d2! (Black waits and forces the white knight to move) 53 ♘e6 ♔e3 54 ♘g5 ♔f4 55 ♘h7 ♔xf3 56 ♘f6 (56 ♘g5+ ♔f4 is just as bad) 56...♔g3 etc.

This was a tremendous game by Keres, which shows that even a "routine developing move" like 11 ♗e3 can allow an awesome attack! One sees the counter-attacking resources of this opening, and once again the many in-

stances of long castling that occur in the main games or, as here, in the notes.

Game 26
T.Fogarasi-N.Davies
Budapest 1993

1 e4 e5 2 ♘f3 ♘c6 3 ♗b5 a6 4 ♗a4 d6 5 0-0 ♘f6

Just to keep your transposition finder on alert, note that Black usually plays 5...♗d7 here, which transposes to the game after 6 c3 ♘f6.

6 c3 ♗d7 7 ♖e1

Another transposition that gets us to the main game by a more common route is 7 d4 g6 8 ♖e1 b5 9 ♗b3 ♗g7.

7...g6 8 d4 b5

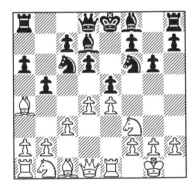

If you're learning this opening for the first time, just remember that just because you played ...g7-g6 on the last move, you don't have to (and you shouldn't!) automatically follow ...♗g7. First Black must relieve the threat to his e-pawn, without losing time.

9 ♗b3

9 ♗c2 transposes back to Parma-Keres (Game 25).

9...♗g7 10 ♘bd2 0-0 11 h3

Preventing ...♗g4. The immediate 11 ♘f1 allows 11...exd4 12 cxd4 ♗g4 when it's difficult to see how White can avoid kingside pawn damage.

11...♖e8 12 ♘f1?!

A "normal Lopez move" but not very good now. I think people have been so trained by the Main Line Ruy positions they get all the time that they forget the MS is really a different animal, and independent thought is required rather than rote moves.

Correct is 12 dxe5 ♘xe5 13 ♘xe5 dxe5 with equality, which is all White can expect here. Note how easily Black equalized: he just made reasonable moves in the correct order.

12...exd4

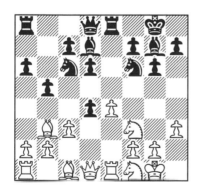

13 cxd4?

Davies points out an amazing drawing combination: 13 ♘g5! d5! (not 13...♖e7 14 cxd4 h6 15 ♘xf7 ♖xf7 16 ♗xf7+ ♔xf7 17 e5 which is good for White) 14 cxd4 ♘xe4 15 ♘xf7 ♕h4 16 ♖xe4 ♕xe4 17 ♘g5 ♕xd4 18 ♗xd5+ ♔h8 19 ♘f7+ ♔g8 20 ♘g5+ with what he calls an "unlikely looking draw by perpetual check"—indeed! But if White is reduced to all this just to equalize in the opening, I am very happy!

13...♘xe4

Black has taken a centre pawn, and White must jump through hoops to maintain material equality.

14 ♗xf7+ ♔xf7 15 ♖xe4 ♖xe4 16 ♘g5+ ♔g8 17 ♕b3+ ♗e6 18 ♘xe6 ♖xe6 19 ♕xe6+ ♔h8 20 d5 ♘e5

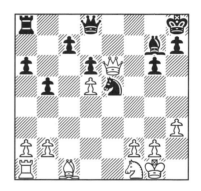

White got his pawn back, but it's clear that both of Black's minor pieces are stronger than their opposite numbers.

21 a4 b4 22 ♗d2 a5 23 ♖b1 ♕f8 24 h4

If 24 b3 the reply 24...♖e8 traps White's queen!

24...♘d3

The scattered white pawns (a4/b2/d5/h4) are all vulnerable: Davies finishes efficiently.

25 ♕e3 ♕f5 26 ♘g3 ♕xd5 27 ♕e7 ♘xf2! 28 ♗g5 ♘g4 29 ♖f1 ♕e5 0-1

The queens come off, leaving Black with a decisive material advantage.

Black had a surprisingly easy win in this game (despite the trick draw at move 13) in that White got no advantage at all in the opening, then continued with a "normal Lopez move" (one recalls that I was the beneficiary of a similar error in Game 24) and was in great difficulties—with White—by move 14.

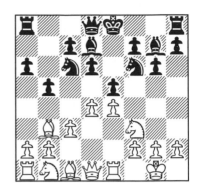

Game 27
T.Luther-S.Conquest
European Championship,
Liverpool 2006

1 e4 e5 2 ♘f3 ♘c6 3 ♗b5 a6 4 ♗a4 d6 5 c3 ♗d7 6 0-0 g6

Still another move order to reach our basic position. There's nothing wrong with this, but there is with Black's next!

7 d4 ♗g7

The continuation 7...♘f6 is correct, when we find ourselves back in our main line.

8 ♖e1

White could get some advantage with 8 ♗g5, as we already saw when Alekhine also played this inaccurate move order (Game 6). Capablanca takes advantage of a similar move order inaccuracy in Game 29.

8...b5 9 ♗b3 ♘f6

Black finally reaches the main line unscathed.

10 dxe5

Instead, 10 h3 might cause Black (in this case our mentor Keres!) to think about sac'ing a bishop against this pawn; e.g. 10...0-0 11 ♗g5 h6 12 ♗h4 ♕c8!? 13 a4 ♘h5 (clearly the sac will be on if Black gets the knight to f4) 14 axb5 (White has to rush to chop wood!) 14...axb5 15 ♖xa8 ♕xa8 16 dxe5 ♘xe5 17 ♘xe5 ♗xe5 18 ♘d2 ♗c6 ½-½ M.Matulovic-P.Keres, Sarajevo 1972—another case where Black was pushing and White was working hard to draw.

10...♘xe5 11 ♘xe5 dxe5 12 a4

So far we have seen an *Opening for White according to Anand*, and now Khalifman gives 12 ♗g5 0-0 13 ♘d2 h6 14 ♗h4 "and White's pieces are obviously more active", but neither I nor Mr. *Fritz* can find any advantage for White, obvious or not!

Practice tells the same story: instead of the immediate 13...h6, Black could first play 13...♗c6 and White has nothing; e.g. 14 ♕e2 h6 15 ♗h4 ♕e8 16 ♖ad1 ♔h7 17 ♗xf6 ♗xf6 18 ♘f1 ♗e7 19 ♗d5 ½-½ D.Maxion-S.Loeffler, German League 1990. But I would play on with Black: 19...♗xd5 20 exd5 (or 20 ♖xd5 c6 21 ♖d2 ♖d8, similar to the main game where Black has no weaknesses and the bishop may yet outperform the knight) 20...♗d6 followed by ...f7-f5 with an active, and attacking, kingside pawn majority.

12...0-0 13 ♗g5

If 13 ♗e3 ♕e7 14 axb5 axb5 15 ♘d2 ♘g4 16 ♘f1 ♘xe3 17 ♘xe3 c6 and Black was slightly better with his two bishops (rather similar to Parma-Keres) in S.Marjanovic-V.Smyslov, Subotica Interzonal 1987.

13...♕e7 14 ♘d2 h6 15 ♗h4 ♗e6

The English GM plays well in the equal position.

16 ♗xe6 ♕xe6 17 ♕b3 ♕c6 18 ♗xf6

White chops before the unpinned knight activates itself via ...♘h5-f4.

18...♗xf6 19 g3 ♗e7 20 axb5 axb5 21 ♖xa8 ♖xa8 22 ♘f3 ♗f6

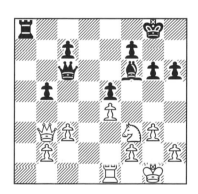

The computer says Black is marginally better and I agree: the bishop has prospects, and ...f7-f5 may come later.

23 h4 h5 24 ♔g2 ♖d8 25 ♖e3 ♔g7 26

♘g5 ♖d7 27 ♘f3

White offers a repetition and the GMs call it a day. Black could try for a win by organizing an invasion on the d-file, though this would admittedly be difficult.

27...♕c5 28 ♘g5 ♕c6 ½-½

If Black gets to the ideal Keres set-up, he has no serious problems. However, inaccurate move orders are rife, as we saw in this game. Continuing the theme, the next two games will feature common move order mistakes.

> ## Game 28
> ## V.Jansa-P.Keres
> ## Luhacovice 1969

1 e4 ♘c6 2 ♘f3

Maybe White should have played 2 d4 !

2...e5 3 ♗b5 a6 4 ♗a4 d6 5 0-0 ♗d7 6 d4 ♘f6 7 c3 g6 8 ♘bd2 ♕e7

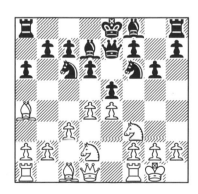

As we already know, Keres will later switch to the correct 8...b5 9 ♗b3 ♗g7 10 ♖e1 0-0 when Black should equalize, as the last three games show.

The use of the queen to bolster the e-pawn is flawed simply because the queen is too important to take on such a menial job as pawn defence. Her Majesty is also somewhat vulnerable to a ♘f1-e3-d5 attack and a ♗g5 pin.

Nonetheless, showing commendable chutzpah, Keres adopts this move despite the fact that he himself had defeated it seventeen years earlier! However, he no doubt saw that Black's play could be improved, and even if this line is not objectively best, it's hard to refute—and there is one advantage of the queen move, so obvious you might not notice it—Black is ready to castle long!

9 ♖e1 ♗g7

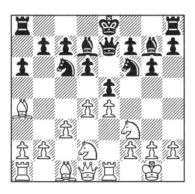

10 dxe5

This is no way to get an advantage with White! The coming exchanges ease Black's game and even give him chances to play for a win. Instead, White should follow Keres himself and play 10 ♘f1!, planning to exploit the black queen position as mentioned

above. Now if 10...exd4?! 11 e5 dxe5 (not 11...♘xe5? 12 cxd4 winning a piece) 12 ♗xc6 bxc6 (not 12...♗xc6? 13 ♖xe5 winning the queen) 13 ♘xe5 and White has a big advantage due to the e-file attack—so Black usually plays 10...0-0.

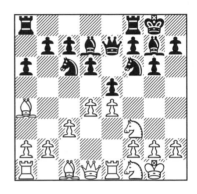

Following are three sample games—three White wins—and potential improvements for Black:

a) 11 ♘g3 (I think 11 ♗g5 as played by Keres and Botvinnik—see line 'b'—is objectively stronger, though the exposed black queen invites tactics even here: check out move 19!) 11...b5 12 ♗c2 ♘a5 (this looks like the wrong plan: Black starts playing as in a Main Line Ruy but only succeeds in weakening the d6-square; I think the more Steinitzian 12...h6, which denies White's pieces access to the kingside, is stronger, and if White has anything at all it's only a marginal advantage) 13 b3 c5 14 h3 cxd4 15 cxd4 ♘c6 16 ♗b2 ♖ac8 17 ♕d2 ♖c7? (fatal—better is 17...exd4, when d6 is weak but Black's open lines offer some counterplay) 18 d5 ♘b8 19 ♗xe5! (based on the d5-d6 fork) 19...♖fc8 20 ♗b1 ♘xe4 21 ♗xe4 1-0 E.Perelshteyn-E.Akhmilovskaya, US Championship, Seattle 2002.

b) 11 ♗g5 and now:

b1) 11...b5 (for the superior 11...h6 see 'b2') 12 ♗c2 ♘a5 13 ♘e3 c6 (Keres' opponent finds a way to meet the ♘e3-d5 threat, but weakens his queenside pawns in the process) 14 a4 ♘c4 15 ♘xc4 bxc4 16 ♕e2 exd4 17 ♘xd4 c5 18 ♘f3 h6 19 ♗h4 ♗g4 20 ♖ad1 ♗xf3 21 gxf3! (this surprising recapture actually consolidates White's centre, while leaving Black with weak targets at c4 and d6) 21...♕e6 22 ♗g3 ♖fd8 23 f4 ♘h5 24 ♗b1 ♖e8 25 ♗a2 (White must win material) 25...♕f6 26 ♕d2 d5 27 exd5 ♗f8 28 ♖xe8 ♖xe8 29 d6 ♖d8 30 d7 ♕e6 31 f5! ♕xf5 (if 31...gxf5 32 ♗c7 f4 33 ♗xd8 ♕g4+ 34 ♔f1 f3 35 ♕d5 and the white king escapes) 32 ♗xc4 ♘f6 33 ♕f4 (Keres wins technically, not giving Black the slightest chance) 33...♕xf4 34 ♗xf4 ♖xd7 35 ♖xd7 ♘xd7 36 ♗xa6 g5 37 ♗c7 ♗g7 38 ♗b5 ♘f6 39 ♗c6 ♗f8 40 a5 c4 41 a6 ♗c5 42 ♗e5 1-0 P.Keres-H.Pilnik, Budapest 1952. Black was savagely slammed here, but as we see, Pilnik erred early and could never recover—following is a tougher struggle:

b2) 11...h6! 12 ♗h4 ♕e8 (Black has to do something about the aforementioned ♘e3-d5, and this is best, even though it's not as smooth as the ...♖e8/...♕b8 unpinning of Day-Coudari in the notes to Game 25—yes, ...♕e7-e8

loses time and disconnects the rooks, but Black's position is still very solid, and he will have a good chance at counterplay or equalization soon) 13 ♗c2 ♘h5 14 ♘e3 ♘e7 15 dxe5 dxe5 16 ♗g3 ♘xg3 17 hxg3 ♖d8 18 ♕e2 ♘c8 19 ♖ad1

19...c6? (too slow: Black's hesitation allows White to take over the d-file—which is enough for Botvinnik, who now wins scientifically) 20 ♖d2 ♕e7 21 ♖ed1 ♘b6 22 b4 ♗e6 23 ♗b3 ♖xd2 24 ♕xd2 24...♗xb3 25 axb3 ♕e6 26 c4 ♗f6 27 c5 ♘c8 28 ♕d7 ♕xb3 29 ♕xb7 ♗g5 30 ♘xg5 hxg5 31 ♕xa6 ♘e7 32 ♕b7 ♖e8 33 ♕d7 ♔f8 34 ♕d6 ♕xb4 35 ♘g4 ♖a8 36 ♕xe5 ♕b3 37 ♖d7 ♘g8 38 ♕d6+ ♔g7 39 ♕d4+ ♔h7 40 ♘f6+ ♘xf6 41 ♕xf6 ♔g8 42 ♔h2 ♖f8 43 ♕xc6 ♔g7 44 ♕d5 ♕b1 45 ♕d4+ ♔h7 46 c6 1-0 M.Botvinnik-I.Boleslavsky, USSR Championship, Moscow 1945.

Returning to move 19, evidently critical is 19...♗c6 20 ♘d5 (otherwise Black equalizes with d-file exchanges) 20...♗xd5 21 exd5 ♕e7 22 ♘xe5 ♖fe8 23 f4 f6 24 ♗xg6 fxe5 25 ♗xe8 ♖xe8 26 fxe5 ♗xe5 and Black's two pieces may well be the equal of White's rook + two pawns. In any case, Black is fighting back here, and I suspect this would have been Keres' choice had his opponent used his own line on him—but this didn't happen!

10...♘xe5

Once again the typical Keres recapture, simplifying the game.

11 ♘xe5 dxe5 12 ♗xd7+ ♘xd7

Now there will be no pin with ♗g5, and the knight shields the d-file so Black can castle long.

13 ♘f3 0-0-0!

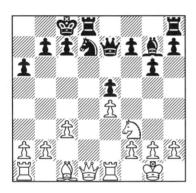

The MS Defence has turned into an attacking position in 13 moves! Is it possible Keres' 8...♕e7 was a psychological trap and he predicted White's passive follow-up?

14 ♗e3?!

This invites Black's f-pawn to rush forward with gain of time. Correct is 14 b4, trying to open a queenside file as soon as possible.

14...f5!

Keres, on the other hand, wastes no time and it's already difficult to find a good plan for White—while Black has an easy to play, straightforward attack.

15 exf5

Or 15 ♗g5 ♗f6 16 ♕c1 f4 and Black has a massive attack.

15...gxf5 16 ♕d5 ♖he8 17 ♖ad1 f4 18 ♗c1

So much for development! Black is clearly better.

18...♘c5 19 ♕c4 ♖xd1 20 ♖xd1 e4

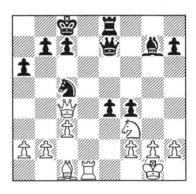

Black re-establishes his pawn duo on the fifth rank. White is already in desperate shape.

21 ♘e1 ♗h6 22 b4 ♘d7 23 b5 ♘b6 24 ♕e2 f3!

It's all over, as the attack breaks through on both the g-file and the h6-c1 diagonal.

25 ♘xf3

If 25 gxf3 ♗xc1 26 ♖xc1 ♕g5+ wins—ouch!

25...♗xc1 26 ♘d4

26 ♖xc1 exf3 is even easier.

26...♗a3 27 bxa6 ♔b8 28 axb7 ♔xb7 29 ♕b5 e3 30 ♕c6+ ♔c8 31 ♕f3 exf2+ 32 ♕xf2 ♕e3

pointless on g5.

7 ♗g5!

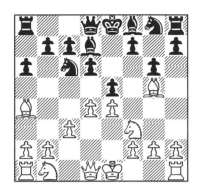

Ruthless! White should resign now.

33 ♕xe3 ♖xe3 34 ♘b5 ♗c5 35 ♔f1 ♘a4 36 ♖d5 c6 37 ♘a7+ ♔c7 38 ♖h5 ♖e7 0-1

A second piece goes. This was an absolute crush.

Apparently Keres counted on his opponent exchanging in the centre, but the 8...♕e7 line can't be recommended wholeheartedly in view of the Botvinnik/Keres ♘f1/♗g5 manoeuvre, when Black must still struggle to equalize.

Game 29
J.R.Capablanca-G.A.Thomas
Margate 1939

1 e4 e5 2 ♘f3 ♘c6 3 ♗b5 a6 4 ♗a4 d6 5 c3 ♗d7 6 d4 g6?!

Inaccurate, as it allows the following attack. 6...♘f6 is correct, when Black can probably follow with ...g7-g6 and ...♗g7 as we have seen—or if 7 ♗g5 Black has the good option 7...♗e7 (one mustn't be a slave to the fianchetto) and the white bishop is

7...f6

Ugly, but what else? If 7...♘f6? 8 ♗xc6 ♗xc6 (8...bxc6 is slightly better but still hopeless) 9 dxe5 wins a piece. Also poor is 7...♗e7 8 h4 which gives White attacking chances due to the weakness of Black's dark squares, while the failed fianchetto would be psychologically difficult to play.

8 ♗e3

I have to agree with *Fritz*'s clear plus already—don't mess with Capablanca, and learn your move order! Note that in Chapter Six, Game 59 (which starts 4 ♗a4 d6 5 ♗xc6+ bxc6 6 d4 f6), Black gets this kingside pawn structure with the compensation of the two bishops—but even then I don't like his game!

8...♘h6 9 h3 ♗g7

9...♘f7 is also possible, but there's a big difference between this passive knight and an active steed one square up the board on f6—and it gets to f6 in one move, too, instead of this two move shuffle! White obtained a big advantage after 10 0-0 ♗g7 11 dxe5 fxe5 12 c4 0-0 13 ♘c3 b6 14 ♘d5 h6 15 ♖c1 ♔h7 16 b4 in Y.Grünfeld-B.Spassky, Brussels 1985—even though Spassky eventually turned the tables and won in the endgame!

10 ♘bd2 ♘f7

Another world champion—poor Smyslov—was less fortunate than Boris: 10...♕e7 11 b4 exd4 12 cxd4 0-0 13 0-0 f5 14 ♗g5 ♕e8 15 ♗b3+ ♔h8 16 ♖e1 (Black has no play at all; note again the unfortunate position of his king's knight) 16...♕c8 17 e5 dxe5 18 dxe5 ♗e6 19 ♗xe6 ♕xe6 20 ♘b3 ♘f7 21 ♘c5 ♕c4 22 ♖c1 ♕xb4 23 ♗d2 ♕a3 24 ♖e3 ♕xa2 25 ♖c2 and Black resigned in A.Sokolov-V.Smyslov, Montpellier Candidates 1985, as his queen is caught after 25...♕d5 26 ♖d3.

11 g4

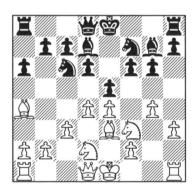

Capablanca exploits the fact that he hasn't castled to bind his opponent's kingside.

11...♕e7

11...exd4 12 cxd4 0-0 would be Black's relatively best chance to get some counterplay.

12 d5 ♘b8 13 ♗c2

Now one can sit back and watch the master of manoeuvre gradually take over the board, square by square.

13...c5 14 a4 ♗c8 15 ♘c4 ♘d7 16 a5 ♗h6 17 ♗xh6 ♘xh6 18 ♕d2 ♘f7 19 ♖g1 0-0 20 h4 ♖b8 21 g5 fxg5 22 hxg5 ♘d8 23 ♖g3 ♖f4 24 ♘e3 ♘f8 25 ♗d3 ♗d7 26 ♔e2 b5 27 axb6 ♖xb6 28 ♕c2 ♗c8 29 ♖a4 ♘f7 30 b3

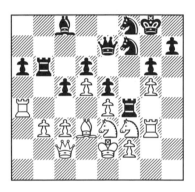

30...h5?!

Black can't stand it anymore, lashes out, and loses quickly—though I think passive defence would also lose in the long run, as Black just doesn't have the space to defend both wings continually, and h7 or a6 will finally fall.

31 gxh6 ♘xh6 32 ♖a1 ♘g4 33 ♖ag1 ♘xe3 34 fxe3 ♖f7 35 ♘g5 ♖g7 36 ♗c4 ♘h7 37 ♔d3 ♘xg5 38 ♖xg5 ♗d7

If 38...♕f7 39 ♕g2 ♔h7 40 ♕h2+ ♔g8 41 ♕h6 wins the g-pawn anyway.

39 ♖xg6 1-0

White has a decisive attack after 39...♖xg6 40 ♖xg6+ ♔f7 (or 40...♔h7 41 ♖g1) 41 ♕g2.

This is one of Capa's famous "chess-machine" wins, where Black never seemed to be in the game—but note that even Capa could not have gotten that bind had Black played correctly on move six!

Note that fellow world champions Spassky and Smyslov likewise got terrible positions with this move order—Keres may have been "forever second" but he knew better!

As we saw in the previous chapter, Kasparov's choice against the ...♘e7-g6 line was to close the centre with d4-d5, create a pawn chain and play on the queenside. Naturally this is a possibility here too—when Black has fianchettoed the dark-squared bishop, the position is even more like a King's Indian, with similar long-term assaults on opposite wings. This pawn chain battle will be the subject of the next three games.

1 e4 e5 2 ♘f3 ♘c6 3 ♗b5 a6 4 ♗a4 d6 5 c3 ♗d7 6 d4 ♘f6

Best!

7 ♕e2

Unusual—7 0-0 g6 is the Keres main line.

Another rarely played line is 7 ♘bd2 g6, but Keres has faced this like every-

thing else—and played inaccurately on his way to a fifteen move draw, no doubt due to the fact that this was the last round of a very tough and exhausting tournament.

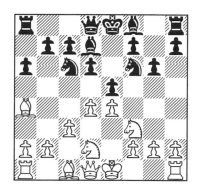

a) 8 ♗xc6 gives nothing after White's quiet previous move; e.g. 8...♗xc6 9 dxe5 ♘xe4 10 ♕e2 (if 10 ♘xe4 ♗xe4 11 ♕e2 d5 and Black stands well) 10...♘xd2 11 ♗xd2 ♕e7 12 ♗g5 (or 12 ♗f4 ♗g7 13 exd6 ♕xe2+ 14 ♔xe2 0-0-0 15 dxc7 ♗b5+ 16 ♔e1 ♖he8+ 17 ♗e3 ♔xc7 with compensation) 12...♗xf3 13 ♗xe7 ♗xe2 14 ♗f6 ♖g8 15 ♔xe2 dxe5 16 ♗xe5 0-0-0 with dead equality.

b) 8 0-0 b5 9 ♗c2 ♗g7 10 ♘b3 (instead of 10 ♖e1, which would transpose to equalizing lines we have already covered, Kaplan tries an interesting positional idea: the white knight wants the c5-square, though this shouldn't give anything against correct play) 10...0-0 11 dxe5 dxe5? (was Keres asleep or was this a last round fingerfehler? Mr. K normally plays 11...♘xe5 in this sort of position, as we have already seen a few times in this book, and the knight capture is correct once again as it frees Black's game and gives the c6-square to the light-squared bishop: after 12 ♘xe5 dxe5 13 ♘c5 ♗c6 14 ♗e3 ♘d7 White has absolutely nothing—but look at the game!) 12 ♘c5 ♗g4 (this poor bishop now has nowhere to go, so White can force its exchange) 13 h3 ♕e7 (if 13...♗xf3 14 ♕xf3 ♕e7 15 ♗e3 and White has the two bishops and the c5-square) and now the game concluded 14 b4 ♖fd8 15 ♗d3 ½-½ J.Kaplan-P.Keres, San Antonio 1972, and presumably both players went back to bed! However, as Kaplan later pointed out, he could have obtained a very large advantage with 14 hxg4! ♕xc5 15 g5 when White not only has the two bishops but also a bind on Black's kingside.

Although it doesn't seem like either contestant was playing seriously, the reader should remember to take back on e5 in such positions with the knight—as Keres *usually* did!

7...♗e7!

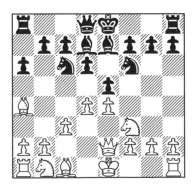

Black, as I have already noted, must not be a slave to the fianchetto. With the queen on the e-file, protecting e4 and indirectly aiming at the black king, White is threatening to take the pawn on e5, and it's unreasonable to ask so much of the position to try and make 7...g6 work with tactical tricks.

The problem with 7...g6 is that Black is still two moves from castling, which is fine if White himself has just made a non-threatening move (7 0-0 or 7 ♘bd2), but rather less so when White is ready to attack. In other words, I have no faith in 7...g6 8 ♗xc6 ♗xc6 9 dxe5 dxe5 10 ♘xe5 ♗b5 11 c4 ♕d4 12 ♘c3 which is way too artsy crafty for me and is probably good for White anyway.

On the other hand, after the simple 7...♗e7, the white queen gives "more inconveniences than advantages", as Alekhine points out in his classic collection of best games.

8 0-0

Now 8 ♗xc6 ♗xc6 9 dxe5 dxe5 10 ♘xe5 ♗xe4 is at least equal for Black, who has no worries on the e-file.

8...0-0 9 d5

Since Black was threatening ...♘xd4 (an *inconvenience* of ♕e2) White has nothing better than closing the centre, as Alekhine comments.

9...♘b8 10 ♗c2

Later on White must have regretted not exchanging the theoretically bad bishop here, even though it would re-develop Black's queen's knight.

10...a5

A solid positional move typical of King's Indian positions: the b8-knight aims for c5. However, 10...c6 is even more "dynamical" (to use Alekhine's word), with the idea of opening a file before White has completed development.

11 c4 ♘a6 12 ♘c3 ♘c5 13 ♗e3 b6 14 h3 g6

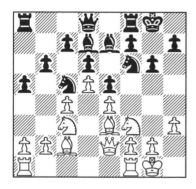

Black threatens ...♘h5-f4. White's strenuous efforts to prevent this only make the position worse.

15 ♗h6

I think White should just live with the knight incursion and create some play on the queenside; e.g. 15 b3 ♘h5 16 a3 with a double-edged game.

15...♖e8 16 g4 ♗f8 17 ♗xf8

17 ♗e3 is better; White will pay dearly for being left with the bad bishop. Yes, I know, Capablanca exchanged his "good bishop" in the previous game, but given his overwhelming space advantage and attacking chances, there the exchange just weakened Black's kingside—here it just

weakens White! Yes, chess is a difficult game!

17...♖xf8 18 ♘h2 ♕e7 19 ♕e3 h5 20 f4

This looks bad, since White is attacking on the wrong side of the pawn chain (the positional plan would be to advance eventually with b2-b4 and c4-c5, attacking the base of Black's chain. Unfortunately for Kashdan and his ally, if White plays slowly in *this* position, Black will build up a winning attack much faster with ...♔g7/...♖h8 etc. So while f2-f4 is not "good" there may be nothing better; e.g. 20 f3 ♔g7 21 ♔f2 hxg4 22 hxg4 ♖h8 23 ♖h1 ♖h3 24 ♖ag1 ♖ah8 25 ♖g2 ♘xg4+! would be a potential White disaster.

20...hxg4 21 hxg4 exf4 22 ♕xf4 ♔g7 23 ♖ae1 ♖ae8 24 ♔g2 ♖h8 25 ♖e2 ♖h4 26 ♖ef2 ♖eh8!

Black beats back White's f-file demonstration with some inspired tactical and strategical play; first the h-file balances the f-, then the e5-square decisively tips the balance.

27 ♔g1

If 27 ♕xf6+?, Black surprisingly wins a clean piece as follows: 27...♕xf6 28 ♖xf6 ♖xh2+ 29 ♔g1 (29 ♔g3 ♖8h3+ 30 ♔f4 ♔xf6 is shorter) 29...♖h1+ 30 ♔g2 ♖8h2+ 31 ♔g3 ♖xf1 32 ♖xf1 ♖xc2 and there goes the bad bishop!

27...♗e8 28 ♕g5 ♔f8 29 ♖g2 ♘cd7 30 ♘b5 ♘e5!

The strategical decision: Black occupies the key central square, while also covering the vulnerable points (c7 and f7).

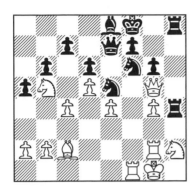

31 ♕xf6

White has two other tries that also fail in interesting ways:

a) 31 ♘xc7 is a desperate diversion, but Black can just take it as the knight on f6 is magically protected!—31...♕xc7! and then:

a1) 32 ♖xf6 ♕c5+ and there is no good answer to the check: 33 ♔h1 (33 ♖gf2 ♖xh2 snaps off a piece, while 33 ♖ff2 ♘f3+! catches the white queen) 33...♘xg4 34 ♕xh4 (forced but fatal) 34...♖xh4 35 ♖xg4 ♖xg4 36 ♘xg4 ♗d7 37 ♘h2 ♕xc4 and the black queen rules.

a2) 32 ♕xf6 ♕c5+ and once again the check crushes White in all variations: 33 ♕f2 (if 33 ♔h1 ♖xh2+ 34 ♖xh2 ♖xh2+ 35 ♔xh2 ♘xg4+ and the queen goes once more; or 33 ♖gf2 ♖xh2 and Black is a piece up with a winning attack; or if 33 ♖ff2 ♖xh2 34 ♖xh2 ♖xh2 35 ♔xh2 ♘xg4+ etc) 33...♘f3+ 34 ♔h1 (forced) 34...♖xh2+ 35 ♖xh2 ♖xh2+ 36 ♕xh2 ♘xh2 and as so often in these lines, Black wins the queen.

b) 31 ♖xf6 ♖xh2 32 ♖xh2 ♖xh2 33 ♔xh2 ♘f3+ and again the queen goes—so White has nothing better than to go into the bad ending seen in the game.

31...♕xf6 32 ♖xf6 ♗xb5

An important zwischenzug: Black wants the pure knight vs. bishop ending.

33 cxb5 ♖xh2 34 ♖xh2 ♖xh2 35 ♖xf7+

If 35 ♔xh2 ♘xg4+ with an extra pawn.

35...♔xf7 36 ♔xh2 ♘xg4+ 37 ♔g3 ♘e5 38 b3

Now that's a bad bishop! The ending is hopeless as all five white pawns are on the same colour as the bishop.

38...♔f6 39 ♗d1 ♘d3 40 ♔f3 ♔e5 41 ♔e3 ♘c5 42 ♗f3 g5 43 ♗h1 ♘d7 44 ♗g2 ♘f6 45 ♗f3 g4 46 ♗e2

If 46 ♗g2 ♘h5 47 ♗h1 ♘f4 48 ♔f2 ♘d3+ 49 ♔e3 ♘c1 and the white queenside collapses.

46...♘xe4 47 ♗xg4 ♘c3 48 ♗f3 ♘xd5+ 49 ♔d2 ♔d4 50 a3 ♘c3 51 ♗c6 a4! 52 ♔c2 d5 53 bxa4

53 ♔b2 axb3 54 ♔xb3 ♔d3 55 a4 d4

56 ♔b4 ♔e3 57 ♗g2 (57 a5 bxa5+ 58 ♔xa5 d3 shows just how bad the white bishop is—the luckless cleric can't even sacrifice itself for Black's passed pawn!) 57...♘e2 58 ♗h3 d3 59 ♗f5 d2 60 ♗c2 ♔d4 61 a5 bxa5+ 62 ♔xa5 ♔c5 63 ♔a4 ♘c3+ and Black wins the bishop.

53...♗c4 0-1

White resigns in view of 54 ♗d7 ♘xa4 55 ♗c6 ♘c3 56 ♗d7 ♘xb5 etc.

This was a great win by Alekhine (and Wahrburg)—from the unprejudiced opening play, to the tactical underpinnings of his kingside strategy, all capped by precise endgame play.

From the opening point of view, we see that White gained nothing by preventing the kingside fianchetto with 7 ♕e2.

Game 31
I.Yagupov-V.Malaniuk
Tula 2000

1 e4 e5 2 ♘f3 ♘c6 3 ♗b5 a6 4 ♗a4 d6 5 c3 ♗d7 6 d4 g6

6...♘f6!.

7 0-0

As we know, White can exploit this move order with Capablanca's 7 ♗g5!.

7...♘f6

Black reverts to Keres' main line—and White immediately decides to close the centre.

8 d5 ♘e7 9 ♗xd7+

Unlike the previous game, here White exchanges his bad bishop right away—but it must be said that this also eases Black's slight space cramp and helps his development. And is the "King's Indian" bishop so bad?

9...♕xd7 10 ♕e2 ♗g7 11 c4

White loses a tempo compared to the King's Indian as his c-pawn takes two steps to get to c4. Perhaps this is not so important in a closed position, but one can see that Black is ahead in development and has no real strategic disadvantage.

11...0-0 12 ♘c3 ♘h5 13 g3 h6

With no queen's bishop, Black does have to careful about his light squares. 13...f5 would be premature in view of 14 ♘g5 and the white knight parachutes into e6.

14 ♘e1 f5

"In closed positions, there are no good bishops" is a Larsen quote I've always liked. Here I think the most important factor is Black's kingside attack.

15 f3

15 exf5 ♘xf5 only activates the black knights, and there is no good

fork: if 16 g4? ♘d4 and the other black knight comes to f4 with a huge advantage.

15...♖f7 16 ♗d2 ♖af8 17 ♘d3 c6!

As the direct attack doesn't break through (17...fxe4 18 fxe4 ♕h3 19 ♘f2) Black creates sharp play on the queenside as well, gradually overloading White's defensive capabilities.

18 a4

Black's basic idea is seen after 18 dxc6 ♘xc6!—if Black can get a knight to d4 he generally takes over the advantage. Furthermore, 18 c5 cxd5 19 exd5 e4 is a strong pawn sacrifice that activates all of Black's pieces: 20 fxe4 ♗d4+ 21 ♔g2 dxc5 22 ♗xh6 ♖e8.

18...a5 19 c5 b6!?

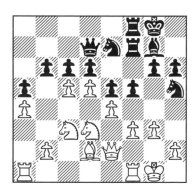

Extravagant! The good thing about this move is that it creates such massive confusion on the board that White will soon go astray, and Black will win with an attack—but objectively correct is to continue as in the previous note with 19...cxd5 20 exd5 e4 21 fxe4 ♗d4+ 22 ♔g2 (or 22 ♗e3 ♗xc3 23 bxc3 fxe4 24 ♘f2 ♘xd5 25 ♗xh6 ♖e8, when Black

has destroyed the white centre and has good counterplay) 22...dxc5 23 ♗xh6 ♖e8 with great activity for the pawn.

20 cxb6

If 20 dxc6 ♘xc6 21 cxb6 ♘d4 and Black's strong knight gives him excellent compensation for the pawn.

20...♕b7 21 dxc6

Or 21 ♗e3 cxd5 22 exd5 ♘xd5 again with central counterplay.

21...♕xb6+ 22 ♔g2 ♘xc6 23 ♘b5

White has to put his knight out of play to prevent ...♘d4.

23...♕d8 24 ♖ac1 ♕d7 25 ♖fd1 fxe4 26 ♕xe4

If 26 fxe4 ♘d4! and Black attacks down the f-file as well as towards a4/b5. One can imagine that dealing with all Black's threats cost White a lot of time—but objectively he is better through this sequence that started with 19...b6.

26...♘e7

Black offers a deflecting pawn sacrifice which White can decline with advantage—but no better is 26...♖xf3 27 ♕xc6 ♕xc6 28 ♖xc6 ♖xd3 29 ♖xd6 ♖d8 30 ♖xd8+ ♖xd8 31 ♔f3 and White will break the pin with an advantageous endgame.

27 ♗xa5?!

A bit greedy. Best is 27 ♕g4! which highlights Black's weakness on the light squares. White is evidently better after this, since Black must either exchange queens (when there is no attack) or retreat with loss of time—note that Black's pawn weaknesses are more significant if he loses the initiative.

27...d5

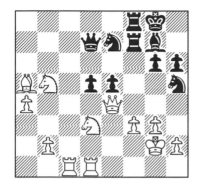

Now Black has compensation.

28 ♕g4

White can enter tactical complications with 28 ♘xe5, but Black can follow a narrow path to advantage: 28...♕e6 29 ♖xd5 ♖xf3! (but not 29...♘xd5 30 ♘xf7 ♕xf7 31 ♘d6 which miraculously favours White) 30 ♖d2 ♗xe5 31 ♗c7 ♘xg3! (this thematic sac works in many variations and will be seen in the main game: the fundamental idea is to destroy the white king's cover) 32 ♕xe5 (of course 32 hxg3? allows a quick mate after 32...♖xg3+) 32...♕xe5 33 ♗xe5 ♘f1! 34 ♖e2 (or 34 ♖xf1 ♖xf1 and White doesn't have enough for the exchange) 34...♘e3+ and again White must give up the exchange—though the ending won't be as easy for Black to win as the similar one (without the white b-pawn) that occurs in the main game.

28...♘f5 29 ♖e1 e4! 30 ♕xg6?

Not 30 fxe4? ♘e3+, winning the queen. But White can play 30 ♖c7!,

when Black's best is 30...♘e3+ (30...exf3+ 31 ♔f2 favours White, as the black queen is short of squares) 31 ♖xe3 exf3+ 32 ♔h3 ♕xg4+ 33 ♔xg4 f2 34 ♖xf7 ♖xf7 35 ♘xf2 ♖xf2 and Black can struggle, perhaps successfully, for a draw.

30...exf3+ 31 ♔g1

31 ♔f2 ♘fxg3 also wins for Black, while if 31 ♔xf3 ♘h4+ is an immediate winner.

31...♘fxg3!

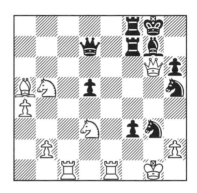

This decisive blow is *finally* landed on the board rather than in a variation! One only has to count pieces to see the soundness of the sacrifice: Black has six attacking pieces going after the enemy king; White is defending only with his queen!

32 ♖e6

If 32 hxg3 ♕h3 33 ♖c2 ♖f6 traps the queen, when 34 ♖h2 ♕xh2+ 35 ♔xh2 ♖xg6 gives Black an exchange up ending similar to the game.

32...f2+ 33 ♘xf2

White has no choice but to allow the decisive knight fork, as otherwise the pawn simply queens.

33...♘f4

Of course this wins, but the slightly fancier 33...♘e2+!, clearing the f-file, is quicker; e.g. 34 ♖xe2 ♘f4 35 ♕c2 (after 35 ♖c7 ♘xe2+ 36 ♔h1 ♖xf2 37 ♖xd7 Black has a forced mate by 37...♖f1+ 38 ♔g2 ♖g1+ 39 ♔h3 ♘f4+ etc) 35...♘xe2+ 36 ♕xe2 ♖xf2 with a winning attack.

34 ♖c7

34 ♕xg3 ♕xe6 is no better.

34...♘ge2+

Here 34...♘fe2+! is quicker.

35 ♔f1 ♕xe6 36 ♕xe6 ♘xe6 37 ♖xf7 ♔xf7 38 ♔xe2 ♗xb2!

The revenge of the bad bishop!

39 ♘d3 ♘d4+ 40 ♔e3 ♘xb5 41 ♘xb2 ♘d6

Now, it's true, Black has to play the ending instead of deciding in the middlegame as in the notes to moves 32 and 34, but on the other hand this ending is clearly winning: thanks to Black's bishop capture on b2, White no longer has connected passed pawns, and in fact has *no* pawns for the exchange, while Black already has a passed pawn.

Malaniuk handles the technical side convincingly.

42 ♔d4 ♔e6 43 ♘d3 ♘f5+ 44 ♔c5 ♖c8+ 45 ♔b6 ♖b8+ 46 ♔a7 ♖b1 47 ♗c7 ♔d7 48 ♗e5 ♘e7 49 ♗b2 ♘c6+ 50 ♔b6 ♔d6 0-1

A plausible finish would be 51 ♔a6 (if 51 a5 ♘e5! wins at once, exploiting the pin) 51...d4 52 a5 ♘b4+ 53 ♘xb4 ♖xb2 54 ♘d3 ♖d2 55 ♘f4 d3 56 ♔b6 ♔e5 57 ♘xd3+ ♖xd3 58 a6 h5 59 a7 ♖a3 60 ♔b7 h4 61 a8♕ ♖xa8 62 ♔xa8 h3 63 ♔b7 ♔f4 64 ♔c6 ♔f3 65 ♔d5 ♔g2 66 ♔e4 ♔xh2 67 ♔f3 ♔g1 and queens.

This was a bold game on Black's part—even if he got a bit extravagant in the middlegame, I still like it!

As for the opening, one sees that the exchange of Black's "good" bishop is compensated for by his kingside initiative.

> ## Game 32
> ### D.Sharma-M.Sorokin
> ### Calcutta 1999

1 e4 e5 2 ♘f3 ♘c6 3 ♗b5 a6 4 ♗a4 ♘f6 5 ♕e2

This game reaches an MS by way of the Worrall Attack!

5...d6 6 c3 g6

This could lead to typical move order problems. Correct, as we have already seen, is 6...♗d7 7 d4 ♗e7 which is Alekhine's set-up from Game 30.

7 d4 ♗d7 8 0-0

As pointed out previously, 8 ♗xc6 ♗xc6 9 dxe5 is dangerous for Black.

8...♕e7

We've also seen this move before, which is at best a loss of tempo, and at worst the black queen can get into serious trouble after ♘f1 and ♗g5. I recommend the simpler, Keres style 8...b5; e.g. 9 ♗b3 ♗g7 10 a4 0-0 11 ♖d1 ♖e8 12 ♘g5 ♖e7 13 d5 ♘a5 14 ♗c2 h6 15 ♘f3 c6 16 b4 ♘c4 17 ♘fd2 ♘xd2 18 ♕xd2 cxd5 19 exd5 and now, instead of the defensive 19...♗e8 of V.Sikula-K.Valko, Nyiregyhaza 2004, correct is 19...e4! when Black is better as he dominates the centre and controls the long dark diagonal.

9 d5

But White just closes the centre, after which the black queen is well placed. One could say that Black has no difficulties now. Despite the slightly inaccurate opening on both sides, I wanted to include this game because of Black's enterprising and creative middlegame play. It seems that the MS is that rare mainstream opening that

has not been played out, so there is much scope for individual ideas.

9...♘b8 10 ♗xd7+ ♘bxd7 11 c4 h5!

Black suddenly finds a way to exchange his bad bishop while gaining space on the side where the white king lives! White can hardly avoid the trade, since 12 ♗g5 ♗h6 13 ♗h4 ♖g8 only helps Black, who now threatens to win a piece.

12 ♘c3 ♗h6 13 h4 ♘g4

But here Black should not hesitate and just take on c1 with equal chances, whereas White in turn should take advantage of this hesitation and play 14 ♘g5 with an edge.

14 g3 f6 15 ♗xh6 ♘xh6 16 ♕d2 ♘f7 17 ♔g2 ♖g8 18 ♖ae1 0-0-0

Once again, long castling! We should be used to this by now in the MS, but in this case Black deliberately castles on the "wrong side" of the pawn chain, confident that his kingside play will at least offset White's potential attack.

19 b4 f5 20 ♘g5

Possible is 20 b5 ♘c5 with double-edged play and most likely a decisive result—but White has a different aim. **20...♞xg5 21 hxg5 ♜gf8 22 f4 ♜de8 23 a4 exf4 24 gxf4 fxe4 25 ♜xe4 ♛f7 26 ♜fe1 ♜xe4 27 ♜xe4 ♜e8 ½-½**

Instead of just acquiescing to the draw with this standard move, I suggest 27...a5!, when Black gains the c5-square and can use his passed h-pawn for attack. I'd rate Black's chances as slightly favourable after this—but by now he had played enough enterprising moves and took the draw!

As for the opening: inaccuracies abound, but if White steers the game towards the closed, pawn chain positions, Black seems to have no theoretical problems.

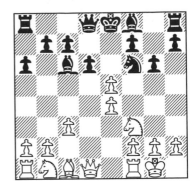

This is Geller's idea: he hopes to win a pawn or gain a positional advantage with forcing moves right in the opening! However, given Black's sound system, there is no real chess basis for this to work.

Note that if White now changes course he can only equalize at best: 9 ♞bd2 exd4 10 cxd4 (better is 10 ♞xd4 ♝g7 11 ♞xc6 bxc6 12 ♛a4 ♛d7 13 ♜e1 0-0 with equality) 10...♝g7 (Black has a good open two bishops position) 11 e5 (trying to force matters, but the attempt backfires; instead White should settle for 11 ♜e1 0-0 with a slight edge for Black) 11...dxe5 12 dxe5 ♞g4 13 h3 ♞xe5 14 ♞xe5 ♝xe5 15 ♜e1 ♛d5 16 ♞f3 ♛xd1 17 ♜xd1 ♝xf3 18 ♜e1 f6 19 gxf3 0-0-0 and Black is much better with his good extra pawn—and note again that queenside castling option! **9...♞xe4**

Worse is 9...dxe5 10 ♞xe5 ♝xe4 11 ♝g5 ♝e7 (Black clearly doesn't want to play this move, as the "extra" ...g7-g6 is then just a waste of a tempo and weakening of the dark squares; but if

Game 33
E.Geller-S.Zhukhovitsky
USSR Championship,
Moscow 1969

1 e4 e5 2 ♞f3 ♞c6 3 ♝b5 a6 4 ♝a4 d6 5 c3 ♝d7 6 d4 ♞f6 7 0-0 g6

Here's our good Keres move order—which Geller, in this last game of the chapter, tries to refute outright!

But even though he wins the game, this rare attempt should not lead anywhere as there are two strong improvements possible on move ten—one my suggestion, and the other courtesy of GM Nigel Davies. Either of these should solve Black's opening problems. **8 ♝xc6 ♝xc6 9 dxe5**

11...♗g7 12 ♕e2 and Black doesn't seem to have anything better than losing a pawn for doubtful compensation with 12...h6 13 ♗xf6 ♕xf6 14 ♘xf7 ♔xf7 15 ♕xe4) 12 ♕e2 (White has a clear plus) 12...♕d5 13 ♗xf6 ♗xf6 14 ♘g4 ♗e7 15 ♘d2 f5 16 ♘xe4 ♕xe4 17 ♕xe4 fxe4 18 ♖ad1 ♖f8 19 g3 ♗d6 20 ♖fe1 0-0-0 21 ♖xe4 and White won a pawn and eventually the game in Y.Razuvaev-R.Knaak, Polanica Zdroj 1979.

10 ♘bd2

Black's trump in this line is the two bishops that White voluntarily gave up: if 10 ♖e1 ♗g7 11 exd6 (not 11 ♘bd2?! dxe5! 12 ♘xe4 ♕xd1 13 ♖xd1 ♗xe4 and it's not clear whether White can even get his pawn back; 12 ♕e2 f5 is also good for Black) 11...0-0 12 dxc7 ♕xc7 and the bishop pair provides more than enough compensation for the pawn.

10...♗e7?

Just looking at this move could make you sick! Black gives up on the fianchetto and settles for: "I hope I can draw this slightly worse ending against Geller." What fun!

The aforementioned two strong improvements come here—but this line is so rare I could find only one example of my line, and none at all of Davies' suggestion:

a) 10...♘xd2 (Taylor) 11 ♗xd2 ♗g7 12 exd6 0-0 13 dxc7 (or 13 ♗f4 cxd6 14 ♘d4 d5 15 ♖e1 ½-½ K.Leenhouts-L.Winants, Belgian Team Championship 2007; while after 14 ♕xd6 ♕b6 Black has more than enough for the pawn) 13...♕xc7 14 ♘d4 ♗d5 and we see a typical two bishops pawn sacrifice: Black's active clerics should be good for at least a draw.

b) 10...♘c5 (Davies); Black threatens to attack with ...♘d3 or block the e-file with ...♘e6, so if White is going to get something, he has to do it now: 11 ♘c4 (this looks like the only reasonable try for advantage; 11 ♖e1 ♘e6 clearly doesn't trouble Black) 11...dxe5 12 ♘fxe5 ♕xd1 13 ♖xd1 ♗b5 14 ♗g5 ♗g7 15 ♖e1 ♘e6 (the Davies block puts an end to White's ambitions) 16 a4 (White must eliminate one of Black's bishops before the pair becomes too strong) 16...♗xc4 (but not 16...♘xg5?! 17 axb5 and Black's pawn structure cracks) 17 ♘xc4 0-0 with complete equality.

Evidently the Modern Steinitz is not yet refuted!

11 ♘xe4 ♗xe4 12 exd6 ♕xd6 13 ♕xd6 cxd6

Black must take on the isolani and defend, since 13...♗xd6? 14 ♖e1 f5 15

♘g5 ♚d7 16 ♘xe4 fxe4 17 ♖xe4 ♖he8
18 ♖xe8 ♖xe8 19 ♗e3 just gives White
a solid extra pawn.

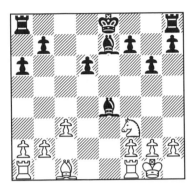

**14 ♖e1 ♗d5 15 ♗g5 ♗e6 16 ♖e3 h6 17
♗xe7 ♚xe7 18 ♘d4 ♚f6 19 ♖f3+ ♚e7
20 ♖e1 ♖ae8 21 a3 ♖hf8 22 h4 h5 23
♚h2 ♚d7 24 ♖fe3 ♗d5 25 ♖xe8 ♖xe8
26 ♖xe8 ♚xe8 27 f3 f6 28 ♚g3**

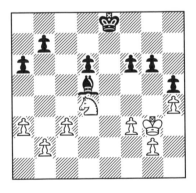

White has a marginally superior
ending which, given that Black has only
one weakness (at d6) should be
drawable, though of course difficult
against a world-class foe like Geller. If
one thing is clear, it is that passive defence will never hold in the long run, as
we will see in the game.

Black should play actively here with
28...g5, gaining kingside space and preventing the entrance of the white king.
Black will still have a difficult task, but I
think the position is objectively drawn
after the g-pawn advance.

**28...♗c4 29 ♚f4 ♚f7 30 ♚e4 ♗f1 31 g3
♗g2 32 a4 ♗h3 33 a5 ♚e7 34 ♚f4 ♗f1
35 ♚e3 ♚f7 36 ♚e4 ♚e7 37 g4 hxg4 38
fxg4 ♚f7**

Geller has made headway against
his opponent's passive play and now
has, in addition to the original weakness at d6, a potential outside passed
pawn on the h-file and a fixed weakness at b7. Having three trumps rather
than one means Geller can now grind
to victory.

**39 b3 ♗g2+ 40 ♚f4 ♗f1 41 ♚e3 ♗h3 42
♚f3 ♗f1 43 ♘e2 ♗xe2+ 44 ♚xe2 ♚e6
45 ♚f3 f5 46 c4 ♚e5 47 gxf5 ♚xf5 48
♚g3 ♚e6 49 ♚f4 ♚f7 50 ♚g5 ♚g7 51
b4!**

Zugzwang.
**51...♚f7 52 ♚h6 ♚f6 53 b5 ♚f7 54 ♚h7
1-0**

After the forced 54...♚f6 White wins

the pawn ending as follows: 55 bxa6 bxa6 56 ♔g8 ♔f5 (56...♔e5 57 ♔g7 ♔f5 58 ♔f7 comes to the same thing, or if 56...g5 57 h5 g4 58 h6 and White queens with check) 57 ♔f7 ♔g4 58 ♔xg6 ♔xh4 59 ♔f5 and White gets to the queenside first.

This was a superb endgame grind, but choose either Davies or my improvement on move 10 and White has nothing. This is undoubtedly why Geller's "refutation" has not been played since at that high level.

Conclusion

Double-edged fighting games are the rule in the Bishop Defence with Black having plenty of play, while White has no clear path to advantage, if indeed any exists. However, move order is crucial and quite difficult, as Black must react to White's order in turn (note Alekhine's 7...♗e7 in Game 30—the fianchetto can't always be forced). Generally speaking Black should develop his king's knight to f6 before fianchettoing the bishop, though great alertness is required throughout. This line is more strategically complicated than the set-up with ...♘e7-g6 (note Malaniuk's board-wide play in Game 31), but also more flexible—and very rewarding for the player who studies it deeply.

This chapter may be the most important in the book: remember, the Bishop Defence is the only universal line against White's main moves of 5 c3 and 5 0-0. So unless you choose a steady diet of gambits, you will find yourself in this territory!

But speaking of gambits, the next two chapters are devoted to just that—next up, the Siesta!

Chapter Four
The Siesta

The Siesta occurs after the specific move order **1 e4 e5 2 ♘f3 ♘c6 3 ♗b5 a6 4 ♗a4 d6 5 c3** (but does not work against the developing 5 0-0, so again, this is not a universal system), when Black decides to play in reversed King's Gambit style with **5...f5!?**.

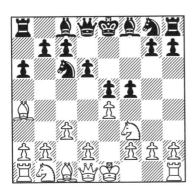

While it's possible to enter the solid Bishop Defence with 5...♗d7 6 d4 ♘f6 7 0-0 g6 as in the previous chapter, you will—if you play 5...f5—immediately get your opponent's attention!

Is the Siesta sound? In my opinion, *yes*. I have done a ton of research (for example, going through David Levy's *The Siesta Variation*, which is an entire book devoted just to this variation) and I have checked everything with the fearless *Fritz*, and basically what I find is this: in the critical line, the "true gambit" variation that continues 6 exf5 ♗xf5 7 d4 e4 8 ♘g5 d5 9 f3 e3! (Games 34-35; 9...h6 is weaker—see Game 36) Black has compensation for the pawn. No more, no less: the sac doesn't win, but White has no way to clearly consolidate his material either. Ultra-sharp and critical positions occur on practically every move, and very exciting and nerve-wracking chess ensues!

On the other hand, quite *non-critical* is what seems to be the main line now, the extremely boring 6 exf5 ♗xf5 7 0-0 ♗d3 8 ♖e1 ♗e7 9 ♗c2 ♗xc2 10 ♕xc2 ♘f6 11 d4 e4 12 ♘g5 d5 13 f3 h6 14 ♘h3 0-0 15 ♘d2 exf3 16 ♘xf3 ♖f7 which is often played at a high level, but gives White absolutely nothing—and from the fighting gambiteer point of view of Black Siesta players, an unconscionably high percentage of draws! Try to stay awake as I cover this line in Games 37-38.

Various tactical lines where White tries to refute the Siesta are seen in Games 39-41—although none of these work, Black must know the answers.

Game 42 shows an attempt by White to force a draw right in the opening, while in Game 43 White tries to revive Réti's line against Capablanca which we saw in Game 4. Once again, these tries prove unsuccessful.

Finally, Game 44 shows the only move I've faced when I've played the Siesta, 6 d3?!, when Black gets the edge right away—which is fun, but hardly challenging. Now let's jump right in, with Keres of course, and face the critical line at once.

Game 34
M.Euwe-P.Keres
World Championship,
The Hague/Moscow 1948

1 e4 e5 2 ♘f3 ♘c6 3 ♗b5 a6 4 ♗a4 d6 5 c3 f5

I wondered how the Siesta fared at the highest level, so I clicked on "Elo White" on *ChessBase*—and it turns out that the top ten by rating didn't make much of a dent in this opening. White scored one win and there were nine draws! White was higher rated in nine of the ten games, often by as much as 200 points (and was only two points lower in the other game), but the only win came courtesy of the young Anand, whereas Shirov and Kasparov could do no damage! This seems quite encouraging—with all the databases and super-core machines, there is no known refutation!

Keres played the Siesta three times, the main game's big win, then a short draw (see the notes to Game 42), and then fell victim to a prepared line (see the note to White's 11th move below). While this was a painful loss, Black's play can be improved, as I will show.

Nevertheless, the reader is warned: sharp lines like this are vulnerable to prepared lines in specific variations (as our first two solid lines were not), especially in this computer age!

6 exf5

Best!

6...♗xf5 7 d4!

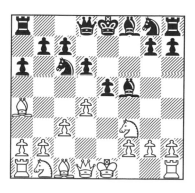

And best again! As already mentioned, this sharp counterblow is the critical test of the Siesta.

7...e4

Clearly there is no other move: the die was cast by Black's bold ...f7-f5, and now it's attack at all costs!

8 ♘g5

One recalls that Capablanca's 8 ♕e2 was quite ineffective against Marshall's Siesta—Black was better after 8...♗e7 9 ♘fd2 ♘f6 10 h3 d5, as I pointed out in a note to Game 4.

Another great world champion got nothing with 8 d5 exf3 9 ♕xf3 (not 9 dxc6 b5 10 ♗b3 fxg2 with a clear advantage for Black, or 10 ♕xf3 ♗xb1 11 ♗b3 ♗g6 12 0-0 ♘f6 13 ♖e1+ ♗e7 14 ♗g5 ♔f8 and Black keeps his extra piece, though White has some pressure) 9...♕e7+ 10 ♔d1 ♗e4 11 ♕h3 ♕f7 (Black returns the piece to avoid problems on the e-file) 12 dxc6 ♗xc6 13 ♖e1+ ♗e7 14 ♗xc6+ bxc6 15 ♘d2 ♘f6 16 ♘f3 (White can't keep the black king in the centre, as 16 ♕e3 fails to 16...♘g4) 16...0-0 17 ♘g5 ♕d5+ 18 ♗d2 h6 19 ♕e6+ ♔h8 20 ♘h3 ♕xe6 21 ♖xe6 ♖fe8 and Black equalized and eventually drew in G.Kasparov-J.Lautier, Lyon 1994.

8...d5

Black gains space and gives the king's bishop the d6-square. 8...♗e7 is worse, as this move has no threat: White can just castle with some advantage; e.g. 9 0-0 ♗xg5 10 ♕h5+ g6 11 ♕xg5 and Black has a dreary, slightly worse position—not what the Siesta gambiteer wants!

9 f3

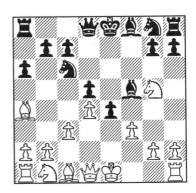

The first critical moment: Black must note that calm moves fail.

a) 9...exf3? only helps White, who responds with 10 0-0! ♗d6 (and not 10...♗xb1 11 ♖xb1 fxg2 12 ♖xf8+ with an immediate win by fork) 11 ♕xf3 and White has the superior development and an attack.

b) 9...♘f6? 10 0-0 ♕d7 11 fxe4 ♘xe4 12 ♘xe4 ♗xe4 13 ♘d2 ♗g6 14 ♘f3 and Black will have to compromise his position still more to meet the threat of 15 ♘e5.

Since White's play is so easy in these lines, it's obvious that strong measures are required: in short, gambit play! When you play 5...f5, you *must* be ready to sacrifice a pawn, and this is the moment—but which pawn? There are two legitimate contenders: Keres' 9...e3, seen here, and Lautier's 9...h6, seen in Game 36. I prefer Keres more complex move, but we're going into the jungle here, and there is no completely certain evaluation of the complex and unclear variations to come.

9...e3! 10 f4

10 ♗xe3 allows Black to damage the white kingside—which means another case of Black castling queenside: 10...h6 11 ♘h3 ♗xh3 12 gxh3 ♕f6 13 ♕d3 0-0-0 14 0-0 ♘ge7 15 ♗c2 g6! (well played—Black establishes a knight on a square, f5, that White can't attack due to his shattered pawns) 16 ♘d2 ♘f5 (White's extra pawn is meaningless, but his breezy king is not! Black gradually outplays his opponent and finally forces a win—note that White's doubled h-pawns never have a role in the game) 17 f4 ♗d6 18 ♖f3 ♖hf8 19 ♗f2 ♘h4 20 ♗xh4 ♕xh4 21 f5 ♘e7 22 ♕e2 ♘xf5 23 ♔h1 ♖de8 24 ♗xf5+ gxf5 25 ♕f2 ♕h5 26 ♖e1 ♖xe1+ 27 ♕xe1 f4 28 ♕e6+ ♔b8 29 ♕g4 ♕e8 30 ♕g2 ♖g8 31 ♕f1 ♕a4 32 ♕b1 ♖e8 33 b3 ♕b5 34 ♕f1 ♕d7 35 ♕d3 ♖e1+ 36 ♘f1 ♕e6 37 c4 c6 38 c5 ♗c7 39 ♔g1 ♖e2 40 ♔h1 ♖xa2 41 ♘d2 ♗a5 42 ♘b1 ♕e4! 0-1 V.Baturinsky-I.Bondarevsky, Moscow 1946; White resigns in view of 43 ♕xe4 dxe4 44 ♖xf4 e3 45 ♖e4 e2 and queens.

10...♗d6

I think that 10...♘f6, which in some lines transposes to variations from this game, is more accurate, as it avoids the white queen check on h5—see next game for this alternative.

11 ♕f3

The position is razor sharp and, facing a new attack, it's understandable that Euwe falters. Indeed, it's not easy

to elucidate what the positional aims of White and Black should be in this chaotic position—but after some study, I believe I have at least that part down.

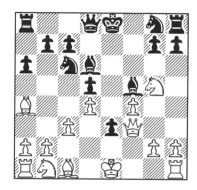

White needs to capture the pawn on e3 (if he delays too long it will become a dangerous passed pawn, as seen in the next game) *and* has to establish a knight on e5 to block the e-file, which is otherwise full of weak squares due to the pawn advances d2-d4 and f2-f3-f4. If White can do both (as for example in the Marciniak game given in variation 'b' below) then he gets the better game and usually wins.

From the other side, Black can't hold the e-pawn—though he should watch for White taking too long to take it, when he may have interesting tactical opportunities. However, let's say White takes the pawn off early. Then Black has to prevent the white knight manoeuvre to e5, usually by putting pressure on f4, and so forcing g2-g3. Then Black must prepare a breakthrough piece sac on the kingside—there really isn't any other way through. In my note to the ninth move above, I said how Black has to be ready to sac a pawn in the opening—but really one must be ready and eager to sac more if you want to play this gambit successfully!

Keres succeeds in carrying out Black's positional aims in the game, whereas Euwe never gets his knight to e5, and finally perishes due to Keres' strategically sound piece sac on f4. Likewise in the next game, Black will have the opportunity for a decisive piece sac on g2.

The sharp play and duelling aims make this an extremely exciting opening (at least this variation of it!).

Again, one can easily forgive Euwe his inaccurate play while facing this mess for the first time! With the benefit of hindsight, Keres' annotations and my faithful *Fritz*, it becomes clear that White had two better tries at this point, namely castling immediately and the opportunistic check on h5. Let's see where these take us:

a) 11 0-0

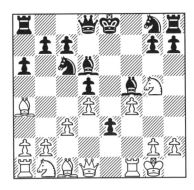

Keres dismissed this move in his annotations to the main game, saying that Black is fine after 11...♗xf4 12 ♖xf4 ♕g5. Unfortunately, while most of his notes in general, and indeed for this game, are of a very high order, this particular note is casual and flawed—and a relatively unknown player spotted it and played his improvement against Keres 18 years later! That game continued (after 11...♗xf4) not with 12 ♖xf4, but the surprising 12 ♘h3! (skewering both black bishops!)

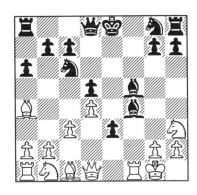

12...♗xh3 (there is nothing better: if 12...b5 13 ♘xf4 bxa4 14 ♘h5! and a4, e3, g7 and f5—three black pawns and a bishop—are all hanging, which simply means White is winning) 13 ♕h5+! (the point of the novelty: White gets the two bishops and multiple attacking possibilities) 13...g6 14 ♕xh3 e2 (trying to mix it up, as after 14...♗d6 15 ♗xe3 White's positional advantage is practically decisive) 15 ♕e6+ ♕e7 16 ♗xc6+ ♔d8 (the complicated 16...bxc6 comes down to a simple pawn up position for White: 17 ♕xc6+ ♔f7 18 ♖xf4+ ♔g7 19 ♗d2 ♕e3+ 20 ♖f2 e1♕+ 21 ♗xe1

♕xe1+ 22 ♖f1 ♕e3+ 23 ♔h1 and White can finally develop while maintaining at least a one pawn advantage) 17 ♕xd5+ ♗d6 18 ♖e1 and as Black's last trump, the e-pawn, is now doomed, Keres went down to a rare MS defeat in K.Skold-P.Keres, Stockholm 1966—and never played the Siesta again!

I understand Keres' aversion to prepared variations, but there is a simple improvement available: Black could have played 11...♘f6, which is recommended by Levy in his Siesta book. This transposes to critical lines in the next game, and will be analysed there.

b) 11 ♕h5+! is probably the real test of Keres' move order. In the main game Black carried out his piece sac idea as follows: he developed his king's knight to g6 (forcing g2-g3 by White), and eventually sac'ed a bishop on f4, when the g6-knight recaptured with a decisive attack. Whereas after the white queen check, Black has to block the g6-square with another piece, thus derailing the smooth progress of his attack. In the following game he never gets full compensation, and if 10...♗d6 is to be revived, Black needs an improvement before move 20: 11...g6 (Keres rejects 11...♗g6 because of 12 ♕f3 ♕f6 13 ♕xe3+ ♘e7 and the "disagreeable" 14 ♕e6—but I'm not so sure: after 14...♗f5 15 ♕xf6 gxf6 Black has certain compensation in the queenless middlegame, as he prevents the e-file blocking ♘e5 because of his new f-pawn; nevertheless, it's not clear if Black's positional pluses

are really enough for the pawn) 12 ♕f3 ♕f6 13 0-0 ♘e7 14 ♗xe3 h6 15 ♘h3 ♗e4 16 ♕e2 0-0 17 ♘d2 ♗f5 18 ♘f2 h5 19 ♘f3 ♘d8 20 ♘e5

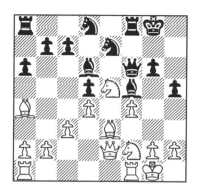

(if White achieves this knight journey with no side effects in this variation, he gets the better game) 20...b5 21 ♗c2 ♗xc2 22 ♕xc2 ♘f5 23 ♗d2 ♗xe5 24 fxe5 ♕c6 25 ♕d3 ♘e6 26 ♘h3 ♖ab8 27 ♘g5 and it's now obvious that Black doesn't have a shred of compensation for the pawn, and White duly converted in A.Marciniak-W.Swiecicki, Poland 1957. Where can Black improve? I haven't been able to find anything after 11...g6, so I'd recommend 11...♗g6, when Black might hold the ensuing pawn down—though it all seems rather cheerless.

This last variation (11 ♕h5+) is why I prefer 10...♘f6 to Keres' 10...♗d6.

11...♕f6 12 ♕xe3+?!

This develops Black while blocking the queen's bishop—not exactly a world champion move.

Evidently correct is 12 ♗xe3 h6 13 ♘h3 ♕f7 (not 13...♕g6 14 0-0 ♗e4 15 f5 ♕f7 16 ♕e2 ♘f6 17 ♘d2 and White eliminates the strong light-squared bishop with a clear advantage) 14 ♘d2 ♘f6 15 ♘f2, reaching a typical Siesta where Black has some compensation due to the hole at e4 and the unblocked e-file, but is it enough? Black must evidently throw caution to the winds and play 15...0-0-0 16 ♗xc6 bxc6 when his king position is compromised, but his centre is strong and he has the two bishops. Risky for Black, dangerous for White is all I can say!

12...♘e7 13 ♗xc6+!?

Although Keres cites this as a serious mistake for three reasons—the exchange strengthens Black's centre, gives him the bishops, and weakens the light squares—it's not clear that White had anything better; e.g. 13 ♘f3 0-0 14 ♘e5 ♗xb1 15 ♖xb1 ♗xe5 16 dxe5 ♕g6 and Black recovers his pawn with the advantage; or if 13 0-0 0-0 14 ♘d2 ♘g6 15 g3 h6 16 ♘gf3 ♗h3 "with a decisive attack" according to Keres—but, amusingly enough, with a "clear advantage to White" according to Mr. *Fritz*!

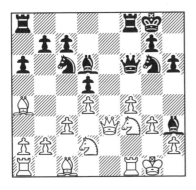

The Siesta is definitely not a line to play if you suffer from "fear of *Fritz*"! Not afflicted with this malady, I put in a few "human" attacking moves, and soon the machine admitted the great Keres was right (but still no "sorry" feature!): 17 ♖f2 ♘xf4! (the thematic sacrifice) 18 ♗xc6 bxc6 19 ♘e5 (or 19 gxf4 ♕g6+ 20 ♔h1 ♖xf4 with excellent compensation) 19...♘g2!! 20 ♖xg2 (if 20 ♖xf6 ♘e3 21 ♖xf8+ ♖xf8 22 ♘df3 ♘c2 23 ♖b1 ♗xe5 24 dxe5 ♖xf3 snaps off a piece) 20...♗xg2 21 ♔xg2 ♖ae8 (White's lack of development is painful) 22 ♘df3 ♗xe5 23 dxe5 ♖xe5! 24 ♕xe5 ♕xf3+ 25 ♔h3 ♖f5 26 ♕e8+ ♔h7 27 ♔h4 ♕g2 (Kotovian creep!) 28 a4 (28 h3 g5+ 29 ♗xg5 hxg5+ 30 ♔h5 ♕xh3 is a nice mate; and 28 ♗f4 g5+ 29 ♔g4 ♖xf4+ 30 ♔h5 ♕xh2 mate is similar) 28...♕xh2+ 29 ♔g4 h5+! 30 ♔xf5 ♕h3+ 31 ♔f4 (if 31 ♔e5 ♕g4 32 ♕a8 ♕e4 mate, or White can settle for losing his queen with 32 ♗f4 ♕e2+ 33 ♔d4 ♕xe8) 31...♕f1+ 32 ♔g5 ♕f6+ 33 ♔xh5 g6+ 34 ♔g4 ♕f5+ 35 ♔h4 ♕h5 mate.

Now that's a winning attack! Black mates with his last piece! One sees again that only bold sacrificial play can justify the Siesta.

13...bxc6 14 0-0 0-0 15 ♘d2?

This is the real mistake: 15 ♘f3! may equalize; e.g. 15...♗e4 (if 15...♗xb1 16 ♖xb1 ♕g6 17 ♗d2 ♖xf4 Black recovers his pawn, but only with an equal game) 16 ♘g5! (16 ♘e5 is positionally good, but here it fails tactically to 16...♗xe5! 17 dxe5 ♕g6 with a fatal fork) 16...♗f5 17 ♘f3 with a Sofia draw looks like best play.

15...♘g6 16 g3 ♖ae8

Black gets a rook to the e-file and White can't block with ♘e5, which means that Black's plan has worked—and White is in big trouble!

17 ♕f2 ♗d3!

Simple but very strong: Black eliminates a defender (the f1-rook) while the other white rook is not playing. My study of this game paid off when I used a similar manoeuvre in Game 44.

18 ♖e1 ♖xe1+ 19 ♕xe1 ♗xf4!!

Breakthrough! Now Black has a winning attack, but note that this was the only way—on virtually any quiet continuation White would soon get a knight to e5 and Black would have nothing for the pawn. Instead, by sacrificing a piece, Black decisively opens the enemy king position.

20 gxf4

If 20 ♕e6+ ♕xe6 21 ♘xe6 ♗e3+ 22 ♔g2 (22 ♔h1 ♖f1+! 23 ♘xf1 ♗e4 mate is amusing!) 22...♖f2+ and Black wins a piece.

20...♘xf4 21 ♘df3

Or 21 ♘gf3 ♕g6+ 22 ♔f2 (not 22 ♕g3 ♘e2+) 22...♘h3+ 23 ♔e3 ♗c2! and this beautiful blow, exploiting the weak light squares, forces White to give up the queen to avoid mate; e.g. 24 ♕f1 (if 24 ♕e2 ♕h6+ 25 ♘g5 ♕xg5 mate) 24...♕e6+ 25 ♘e5 ♖xf1 etc.

21...♘e2+ 22 ♔g2 h6

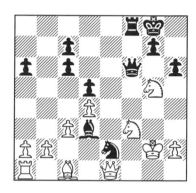

Black recovers his piece with a winning attack.

23 ♕d2 ♕f5 24 ♕e3 hxg5 25 ♗d2 ♗e4 0-1

After 26 ♖f1 ♕g4+ wins everything.

A fantastic attacking game by Keres—he defeats a World Champion in 25 moves with Black!—but the improvement 11 ♕h5+ casts serious doubts on his move order. This issue is addressed in the next game.

Game 35
O.Kinnmark-V.Ciocaltea
Halle 1967

1 e4 e5 2 ♘f3 ♘c6 3 ♗b5 a6 4 ♗a4 d6 5

c3 f5 6 exf5 ♗xf5 7 d4 e4 8 ♘g5 d5 9 f3 e3 10 f4 ♘f6!

No queen check!

11 0-0

11 ♗xe3 ♗d6 12 0-0 is just a transposition to the critical next note.

11...♗d6 12 ♘f3

The soundness of the entire Siesta may rest on the evaluation of the obvious 12 ♗xe3—which has never occurred in a high-level game. If White gets a knight to e5 with nothing bad happening, he will win. However, White has a hole at e4, while g4 invites the opposing pieces too. Black has plenty of tactical play and, in my opinion, good compensation for the material after 12...0-0, when White can try:

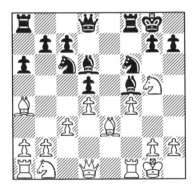

a) 13 ♗c2 (tempting but weak— White won't have time to use the e6-square) 13...♗xc2 14 ♕xc2 h6 15 ♘e6 ♕e7 16 f5 (not 16 ♘xf8? ♕xe3+ and wins) 16...♗xh2+! 17 ♔f2 (17 ♔xh2 ♘g4+ is also good for Black) 17...♘e4+ 18 ♔e1 ♕h4+ 19 ♔d1 ♕g4+ 20 ♖f3 ♖xf5 21 ♘d2 ♖e8 22 ♘c5 ♗f4 23 ♘f1 ♘g5! 24 ♘h2 ♗xh2 25 ♕xf5 ♕xf5 26

♖xf5 ♖xe3 and Black's combination netted two pieces for a rook, which was good enough to win in J.Leon Barreto-W.Simonsen, correspondence 1975.

b) 13 ♘d2 ♘g4 14 ♕f3 ♔h8! and again Black has compensation for the pawn, with tricks such as 15 ♖ae1 ♘xh2! 16 ♔xh2 ♕xg5 with equality.

c) 13 ♘f3 ♘g4 and then:

c1) 14 ♕d2 ♘a5 15 ♗b3 ♗e4 and Black's extremely active pieces give him compensation for the pawn.

c2) 14 ♗d2 ♘a5 15 ♘e5 ♘c4! 16 ♘xg4 ♘xb2 17 ♕b3 ♘xa4 18 ♕xd5+ ♖f7 19 ♘e5 ♗xe5 20 ♕xd8+ ♖xd8 21 fxe5 b5! and Black's bind on the light squares is worth a small unit; e.g. 22 ♗g5 (22 ♖c1 h6 23 ♗e3 c5 24 ♘d2? ♘xc3! shows how difficult it is for White to develop; also if 22 ♘a3 c5 with counterplay) 22...♖df8 23 ♖c1 ♗e6 24 ♘d2 ♖f2 and Black's compensation is obvious.

c3) 14 ♗c1 (this retrograde move is no better) 14...♘a5 15 h3 ♘f6 16 ♘e5 c5! (yes, White got his knight to e5, but not for free, as Black speedily undermines and takes advantage of his superior development) 17 ♗e3 cxd4 18 ♗xd4 ♕c7 19 ♘d2 ♘c6 20 g4 (amazingly enough, Mr. *Fritz* calls it as plus equals here, when the attacking player can clearly see the weakness of the white king position; better is 20 ♘df3 with the possible continuation 20...♘xd4 21 cxd4 ♖ac8 22 ♖c1 ♕xc1 23 ♕xc1 ♖xc1 24 ♖xc1 ♘h5 and Black recovers his pawn with a slight edge;

and not 21 ♕xd4? ♗c5) 20...♘xe5 21 fxe5 ♗xe5 22 gxf5 ♗xd4+ 23 cxd4? ♕g3+ 24 ♔h1 ♕xh3+ 25 ♔g1 ♕g3+ 26 ♔h1 ♘g4 27 ♕e2 ♖f6 with a winning attack.

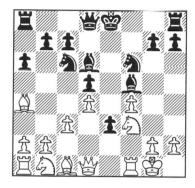

12...0-0

Black misses his chance—he still has equality after this, but he could have the advantage!

a) 12...♗xf4?! fails to 13 ♘e5! g5 14 ♕e2! when Black's e-pawn and position both fall (but not 14 g3 ♕d6 15 gxf4 ♖g8! with a strong sacrificial attack, which just shows how play is balanced on a knife edge).

But Black has a vital Steinitzian zwischenzug:

b) 12...b5! (Levy—this key MS resource breaks the pin and so activates the queen's knight) 13 ♗b3 ♗xf4 14 ♘e5 ♗xh2+! 15 ♔xh2 ♘xe5 16 ♖xf5 (or 16 dxe5 ♘g4+ 17 ♔g3 ♗e6! and Black's mighty passed pawn holds White at bay while the decisive ...♕g5 is coming) 16...♘eg4+ with a winning attack, as the student can work out for himself!

13 ♘e5?

White lets the e-pawn live. The simple 13 ♗xe3 transposes back to note 'c' above (to White's 12th move), where Black's compensation was approximately equal to White's extra pawn.

13...♗xe5!

Black takes advantage of White's hesitation and saves his passed pawn—and even advances it to the seventh! Now Black is better.

14 dxe5 ♗g4 15 ♕d3 e2!

Nimzowitsch's "dangerous criminal" can barely be contained. This is a good illustration of White's failed goals. As I said in the previous game, for success White needs both to capture the e-pawn and get a knight to e5 (as in the note with 13 ♗xe3 above). Here he has only accomplished the knight jump, which is trumped by Black's passer.

However, both sides still play inaccurately in this complex position!

16 ♖e1 ♘h5 17 ♘a3 ♘xf4! 18 ♕g3

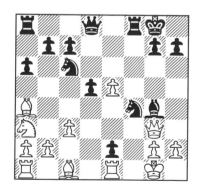

18...♕g5?

Black misses the win! In tactical positions in general, and particularly in the Siesta, it's necessary to see the shots, as you rarely get a second chance like Black does in this game. Correct is 18...♘xg2!!, demolishing the white king position while attacking the blockading rook at e1. Black must always watch for these thematic Siesta blows, as there is usually no other way to break through than with a piece sacrifice.

After this shot the knight must be taken (of course 19 ♗xc6 ♘xe1 20 ♕xe1 ♖f1+ is hopeless), but Black wins against either capture:

a) 19 ♔xg2 ♘xe5! 20 ♕xe5 ♕h4 21 ♗f4 ♗h3+ 22 ♔h1 ♕xf4 23 ♕xe2 (after 23 ♕xf4 ♖xf4 24 ♗b3 ♖f1+ 25 ♖xf1 exf1♕+ 26 ♖xf1 ♗xf1 Black emerges with an extra exchange—note the strength of the passed pawn in these variations) 23...♕xa4 and wins: although White finally got the e-pawn, Black is now two good pawns up.

b) 19 ♕xg2 ♘xe5 20 ♖xe2 ♗xe2 21 ♕xe2 ♕h4 (again we see the important tempo gain off the Lopez bishop!) 22 b4 ♘f3+ 23 ♔h1 b5 24 ♗b3 ♖ae8 25 ♗xd5+ ♔h8 with a mating attack.

19 ♗xc6!

Removing the attacking piece which came to e5 with great effect in the previous note—now White is better!

19...bxc6 20 h3 h5 21 hxg4 h4 22 ♕f3?

White misses his chance in turn! After 22 ♗xf4! ♖xf4 23 ♕d3 Black doesn't have adequate compensation for piece; e.g. 23...♖xg4 24 ♖xe2 ♖g3 25 ♕d2 and White should win.

22...♖ae8 23 ♘c2 ♕xe5 24 ♘d4?

24 ♗e3, developing while blocking the e-file, is necessary—the text gives Black that second tactical chance, and this time he finds it!

24...♘h3+! 0-1

White resigns, as 25 ♕xh3 ♖f1+! 26 ♖xf1 exf1♕+ 27 ♔xf1 ♕e1 is mate.

What an amazingly topsy-turvy game for one that lasted only 24 moves! This is the line to take up if you want to sharpen your tactics!

As for the opening, I think Ciocaltea's improvement (10...♘f6!) rehabilitates Keres' 9...e3 pawn sacrifice, but the subsequent play is extremely tense and difficult.

And if this is not enough for you, in the following game the very strong French GM Lautier tries a *different* pawn sacrifice!

Game 36
S.Dvoirys-J.Lautier
Biel Interzonal 1993

1 e4 e5 2 ♘f3 ♘c6 3 ♗b5 a6 4 ♗a4 d6 5

c3 f5 6 exf5 ♗xf5 7 d4 e4 8 ♘g5 d5 9 f3 h6

Instead of Keres' 9...e3, Lautier gives himself an exclam for this alternative sacrifice, but I am not quite as enthusiastic.

10 fxe4

Correct, since 10 ♘h3 ♗xh3 11 gxh3 ♕h4+ turns the white king into a nomad.

10...hxg5 11 exf5 ♗d6

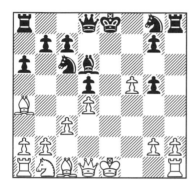

The crucial position of Lautier's line: White is up a pawn and Black has doubled g-pawns. However, Black has compensation in the open files (e- and h- now, and maybe f- soon) that he can occupy and so discourage White from castling kingside. White's problem is, how does he go queenside with so many pieces to clear out?

In practice the white king usually ends up floating around on the d-file, which gives Black practical chances—but is this enough given that his pawns are so weak?

12 ♘d2

In two later games, GM Dvoirys improved with 12 ♕f3! which is critical. No clear equalizer has been found: Dvoirys won one game in crushing style, and drew the other, but should actually have won both as he failed to convert a pawn up ending. Following are some sample games with this improvement:

a) 12...♗xh2 (stepping into a dangerous pin, but 12...♖xh2? 13 ♖xh2 ♗xh2 14 ♕h5+ is even worse) 13 ♔d1 ♖h4 14 ♗b3 ♔f8 (if 14...g4 15 ♕xd5 and White exchanges queens with an extra pawn) 15 g4 ♘h6 16 ♗d2 ♘xg4 17 ♗e1 and wins, as the black rook is overloaded.

b) 12...g4!? (as played by the wild and crazy Yandemirov, hero of the next gambit chapter of this book!) 13 ♕xg4 ♘f6 and now:

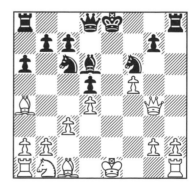

b1) 14 ♕e2+ ♘e4 15 ♘d2 ♕f6 16 ♘xe4 dxe4 17 ♗xc6+ bxc6 18 ♗e3 ♕xf5 19 0-0-0 (with a safe king and an extra pawn, White is much better) 19...0-0 20 ♔b1 a5 21 h4 ♖ab8 22 h5 ♗a3 23 ♗c1 e3+ 24 ♔a1 ♕e4 25 ♖de1 c5 26 h6 ♖fe8 27 ♕c4+ ♖e6 28 ♖h4

♕xh4 29 ♕xe6+ ♔h7 30 ♖xe3 1-0 A.Ingerslev-Cl.Norregaard, correspondence 1979.

b2) 14 ♕f3 ♘e4 15 ♔d1 ♕h4 16 ♗e3 0-0-0 17 ♗xc6 bxc6 18 ♘d2 ♘g3 19 ♗f2 ♕g5 20 ♗xg3 ♗xg3 21 h4 ♖xh4 22 ♖xh4 ♕xh4 23 ♔c2 (White is a good pawn up...) 23...♖e8 24 ♖f1 ♗d6 25 ♕d3 ♕g4 26 ♕xa6+ ♔d7 27 ♖f2 ♖e1 28 ♘f3 ♕e4+ 29 ♔b3 ♖e3 (...and with 30 a4! he would be winning, but wait—Siesta turbulence is coming!) 30 ♘d2? ♕xd4 31 ♖e2? ♕g4!!—surprise! White resigned in Z.Almasi-L.Winants, Calvia Olympiad 2004, since 32 ♖xe3 (or 32 ♘f3 ♕c4+ wins a rook) 32...♕d1 is mate! Break out that tactics book before you try the Siesta!

b3) 14 ♗xc6+ bxc6 15 ♕g6+ ♔f8 16 ♔d1 ♘e4 17 ♖f1 ♕h4 18 f6 gxf6 19 ♘d2 ♖g8 20 ♘f3 ♕h8 21 ♕h6+ ♔e7 22 g3 ♕xh6 23 ♗xh6 ♖g4 24 ♔c2 ♖h8 25 ♗e3 f5 26 ♖ae1 f4 27 gxf4 ♗xf4 28 ♗xf4 ♖xf4 29 ♘d2 ♖xf1 30 ♘xf1 ♔d6 31 ♖e2 ♖h3 32 ♘d2?! (Black is just a pawn down, but his active rook gives him some hopes of a draw—therefore White is exchanging the wrong piece! 32 ♖e3 is correct with real winning chances) 32...♘xd2 33 ♔xd2 c5 34 dxc5+ ♔xc5 35 ♔e1 ♔c4 36 ♔d2 c5 37 b3+ ♔b5 38 a4+ ♔c6 39 b4 cxb4 40 cxb4 ♖b3 41 ♖e6+ ♔c7 42 ♖xa6 ♖xb4 43 ♖a7+ ♔b6 44 ♖a8 ♖h4 45 ♔d3 ♖xh2 ½-½ A.Kosteniuk-V.Yandemirov, Moscow 2001.

c) 12...♔f8 13 ♔d1 ♕f6 14 ♕xd5 ♘ge7 15 ♕e6 ♘d8 16 ♕d7 b5 17 ♗c2

♖h4 18 ♘d2 ♘d5 (White has completely outplayed his foe and now 19 ♖e1 wins easily—instead he makes one mistake and we see another astonishing turnabout courtesy of a Siesta tactic!) 19 ♘e4?? ♖xe4! 20 ♗xe4 ♘b6 and the white queen is trapped! 0-1 R.Veselinov-P.Kamenov, correspondence 1989.

d) 12...♖h4 13 ♔d1 ♔f8 14 ♗b3 ♘h6 15 g3 ♖h3 16 ♕xd5 ♕f6 17 ♘d2 ♘e7 18 ♕g2 ♘g4 19 ♘e4! (Dvoirys gets his revenge with this perfectly timed attack) 19...♕h6 20 ♘xg5 ♖xh2 21 ♖xh2 ♕xh2 22 ♘e6+ ♔e8 23 ♘xg7+ ♔d7 24 ♗e6+ ♔d8 25 ♕xh2 ♘xh2 26 f6 and that's hammer time! 1-0 S.Dvoirys-S.Kravtsov, Moscow 1998.

e) 12...♕e7+ 13 ♔d1 0-0-0 14 ♖e1 ♕f6

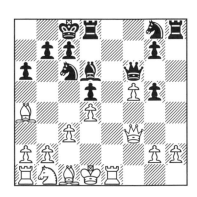

15 ♗xc6 (but not 15 ♖e6?! which overlooks a Siesta tactic: 15...♘xd4!, and if 16 cxd4? ♕xd4+ 17 ♗d2 ♕xa4+ Black wins back his piece with a clear advantage; or 16 ♖xf6 ♘xf3 17 ♖e6 ♘xh2 18 ♗xg5 ♘f6 19 ♘d2 ♖h5 20 ♗xf6 gxf6 21 ♖xf6 d4 22 cxd4 ♗f4 23

d5 ♘g4 24 ♖e6 ♖xf5 25 ♗b3 ♘e3+ 26 ♔e2 ♘xd5 27 ♘e4 ♗e5 28 ♗xd5 ♖xd5 and again Black has recovered all the material and stands slightly better: he eventually squeezed out a win in V.Fedorov-A.Hamatgaleev, Perm 1997) 15...bxc6 16 ♖e6 ♕f7 17 ♗xg5 (Black certainly has no sufficient compensation for two pawns—it looks like Dvoirys is cruising to another revenge victory, but soon made a slight inaccuracy that ended up costing half a point) 17...♖f8 18 h4 ♘h6 19 ♗xh6 gxh6 20 ♘d2 (this is the culprit!—now Black gets counterplay and, as we'll see, hangs on to draw) 21 ♔c2 ♖g3 22 ♕f1 ♕xf5+ 23 ♕xf5 ♖xf5 24 ♖e2 ♖f4 25 ♖ae1 ♖xh4 26 ♖f1 ♖g7 27 ♖ff2 ♖hg4 28 ♘b3 ♖g8 29 ♘c5 ♗xc5 30 dxc5 a5 31 ♖f6 ♖xg2 32 ♖xg2 ♖xg2+ 33 ♔b3 ♔b7 34 ♖xh6 ♖g4 35 a4 ♖c4 36 ♖g6 ♖xc5 37 ♖g4 ½-½ S.Dvoirys-P.Ponkratov, Cheliabinsk 2004. Instead of 20 ♘d2, White needs to reposition his rook behind his pawns with 20 ♖e1! ♖hg8 (not 20...♕xf5? 21 ♖e8+! and wins) 21 g4 ♕f6 22 ♖h1 h5 23 g5 ♕xf5 24 ♕xf5+ ♖xf5 25 ♔c2 ♖f2+ 26 ♘d2 ♗f4 27 ♖ad1 ♖e8 28 ♖hf1 ♖ee2 29 ♖xf2 ♖xf2 30 ♔d3 with good winning chances; e.g. 30...♖h2 31 ♘f3 ♖xb2 32 g6 ♗h6 (if 32...♖g2 33 ♖g1 ♖xg1 34 ♘xg1 ♗h6 35 ♘h3 ♔d7 36 ♘f4 wins prettily) 33 ♖g1 ♖f2 34 g7 ♖xf3+ 35 ♔e2 and wins.

The bottom line is that in none of these games did I see Black get legitimate counterplay. Yes, the Siesta is full of tactics, and Black won some games (from lost positions!) with great tricks—but overall I don't think this variation can be trusted.

Keres' 9...e3 appears to me as having a much sounder positional basis, since (unlike here) Black's pawn structure stays intact, while White is left with weak squares on the e-file.

12...♕e7+ 13 ♕e2 0-0-0

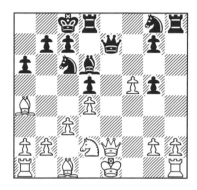

Lautier claims Black is already better, but this is way too optimistic.

14 ♗xc6

White should play his knight to f1 here or the next move—this was Dvoirys' first improvement (though not as strong as his later 12 ♕f3!). After 14 ♘f1! ♖e8 15 ♕xe7 ♖xe7+ 16 ♔f2 ♘f6 17 g3 ♖he8 18 ♘e3 b5 (18...♖xe3? fails to 19 ♗xe3 ♘g4+ 20 ♔f3 ♘xe3 21 ♖ae1 g4+ 22 ♔f2 and White emerges with an extra exchange) 19 ♗d1 ♘a5 20 ♗f3 c6 21 b4 ♘b7 22 a4 ♗b8 23 axb5 axb5 24 ♖a6 ♔c7, then 25 ♘g4 is better for White who is a pawn up, while the black rooks have no invasion squares. Instead, he went haywire with 25 c4??

and after 25...bxc4 26 ♘xc4 dxc4 27 ♖xc6+ ♔d7 28 ♖xc4 ♘d6 29 ♗c6+ ♔d8 30 ♖c2 ♖h8 Black eventually won in S.Dvoirys-E.Frosch, Graz 1994.

14...bxc6 15 ♘f3

15 ♘f1 is Wolff's suggestion, and this is still correct; e.g. 15...♖e8 16 ♕xe7 ♖xe7+ 17 ♔d1 g4 18 ♘e3 and White holds.

15...♖e8! 16 ♕xe7 ♖xe7+ 17 ♔f2 g4 18 ♘g5 ♘h6

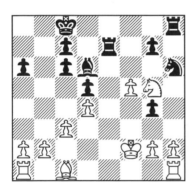

Now one sees that Black is not only recovering his pawn, he also has a serious advantage despite the various doubled pawns. The key factors are Black's open files and lead in development.

19 g3

Lautier gives 19 ♗d2 ♘xf5 20 ♖ae1 with only a slight plus for Black, but this time I think he is underestimating! After 20...♖xh2 21 ♔g1 (not 21 ♖xh2 g3+) 21...♖xe1+ 22 ♗xe1 ♖xh1+ 23 ♔xh1 c5 Black's advantage is close to decisive.

19...♖he8 20 ♖f1 ♖e2+ 21 ♔g1 ♖c2

Black's advantage increases as both his rooks invade the seventh rank.

22 ♖f2

22 ♘e6 fails to close the e-file due to 22...♘xf5!.

22...♖e1+ 23 ♔g2

Or 23 ♖f1 ♖ee2 and the blind pigs run amok.

23...♖cxc1 24 ♖xc1 ♖xc1

Now it's technical, and the French GM is up to the task.

25 ♘e6 ♘g8 26 ♘xg7 ♘f6 27 ♘e6 ♘e4 28 ♖e2 ♔d7 29 a3 a5 30 a4 ♖a1 31 h3 ♘xg3 32 ♘c5+ ♗xc5 33 ♔xg3 ♗d6+ 34 ♔xg4 ♖g1+ 35 ♔h5 ♗e7 36 h4 ♖f1 37 ♔g6 ♗xh4 38 ♖e3 ♖f2 39 b3 ♖g2+ 40 ♔f7 ♖g3 41 ♖e8 ♖f3 42 ♖e5 ♖xc3 43 f6 ♗xf6 44 ♔xf6 ♖f3+! 0-1

This last move diverts the white king or exchanges rooks. After 45 ♖f5 (45 ♔g6 ♖xb3 is just as easy) 45...♖xf5+ 46 ♔xf5 ♔d6 47 ♔f4 c5 Black wins the pawn ending.

Although Lautier won a good game against the surprised Dvoirys, the *prepared* Dvoirys, armed with 12 ♕f3, was another matter!

Again, I think Black has too many

weaknesses in this variation to justify his pawn sacrifice, so Keres' 9...e3! must be preferred.

Game 37
S.Simonov-V.Yandemirov
Kazan 2007

1 e4 e5 2 ♘f3 ♘c6 3 ♗b5 a6 4 ♗a4 d6 5 c3 f5

The Russian GM Yandemirov is a great champion of the sharp gambits available in the MS, the Siesta as here and also the complex line 5 0-0 ♗g4 6 h3 h5 which I have named after him. Many of his games will be seen in this book.

6 exf5 ♗xf5 7 0-0

The choice of the chess establishment (instead of the hard-hitting 7 d4), but this slow move gives Black a good position through the following blockade. Note that Black cannot mindlessly develop here: 7...♘f6? 8 d4 e4 9 d5 exf3 10 dxc6 b5 11 ♖e1+ ♗e7 12 ♗b3 fxg2 13 ♗g5 ♔f8 (the king is caught in the centre...) 14 ♗xf6 ♗xf6 15 ♕d5 ♗g6 16 ♘d2 h5 17 ♘f3 ♗e8 18 ♖e4 g6 19 ♘d4 ♗xd4 20 ♕xd4 (...where it soon perishes!) 1-0 A.Giaccio-C.Perez Pietronave, Mar del Plata 1995.

7...♗d3

Moving the same piece twice is correct and necessary! Since the vital d-pawn is blockaded, White must lose time extracting the "bone in the throat".

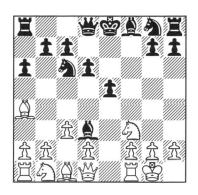

8 ♖e1

Krogius' 8 ♕b3 is the only serious alternative. Then 8....♗xf1?! is too risky due to 9 ♕xb7 ♗b5 10 ♗xb5 axb5 11 ♕xc6+ ♔f7 12 d4 "with a strong attack" (Levy)—note that in the Siesta Black is usually better off gambiting than going for material gain! Keeping this in mind, 8...♖b8!? 9 ♖e1 ♗e7 10 ♕d5 e4 is playable, when Black has transposed into a wild gambit line, usually reached by the move order 7...♗d3 8 ♖e1 ♗e7 9 ♕b3 and then 9...♖b8 10 ♕d5 e4. Full analysis of this variation, with the above move order, is given in the notes to Game 41.

Returning to 8 ♕b3, Black can equalize with 8...b5!. White obviously continues 9 ♕d5, but then 9...♘d4! solves Black's opening problems, though the main line is a draw. 10 cxd4 (White has no choice, for both 10 ♘g5 ♘e2+ 11 ♔h1 ♕xg5 12 ♕xa8+ ♔d7 13 ♕xa6 e4!—note how Black maintains the strangling light-squared bishop!—14 c4 bxa4 15 ♕xa4+ ♔e6 16 ♘c3 ♘f4 0-1 L.Teemae-M.Graefe, correspondence 1964, and 10 ♘xd4 ♘e7 11 ♕f3 e4 12 ♕f4 bxa4! with a continuing bind, are far from appetizing for White) 10...♘e7 11 ♕e6 ♗xf1 and now:

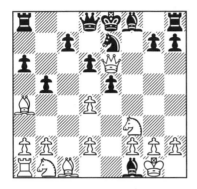

a) 12 ♗b3 ♗c4 13 ♗xc4 bxc4 14 ♘g5 exd4 15 ♕f7+ ♔d7 16 ♕e6+ ♔e8 (16...♔c6 17 ♘f7 is too risky for me!) 17 ♕f7+ (17 ♘a3 d5 is probably too risky for White; e.g. 18 d3 ♕d6 and Black begins to consolidate his extra material) 17...♔d7 18 ♕e6+ ♔e8 ½-½ N.Minev-M.Damjanovic, Bad Lieben-stein 1963.

b) 12 ♔xf1 is also probably a draw, though both sides can riskily play to win: 12...bxa4 13 ♘g5 ♕c8!? (Black bravely goes for the full point—in the game White has a strong attack but never quite gets through; 13...exd4 14 ♕f7+ ♔d7 15 ♕e6+ is our usual draw) 14 ♕f7+ ♔d7 15 dxe5 h6 16 e6+ ♔c6 17 ♕f3+ ♔b6 18 ♕e3+ ♔b7 19 ♘f7 ♖g8 20 ♘c3 g5 21 d4 (21 d3, keeping the e3-a7 diagonal open for the bishop, looks like it gives White excellent attacking chances; whereas now his centre pawns come under fire and Black is

able to use the advantage of the ex-change) 21...♖g6 22 d5 ♖b8 23 ♗d2 ♔a8 24 ♖c1 ♕b7 25 ♕d3 ♗g7 26 ♔g1 a3 27 b3 ♗xc3 28 ♗xc3 ♘xd5 29 e7 ♘f4 30 ♕f1 ♖e8 31 ♗f6 ♖xf6 32 ♘d8 ♕b5 33 ♕xb5 axb5 34 ♖xc7 ♔b8 35 ♖b7+ ♔c8 and fortune favoured the brave! 0-1 L.Mista-V.Ciocaltea, Reggio Emilia 1967/68.

Note how many more or less forced draws there were! Although the Siesta is a fierce gambit (as we saw in the first three games of this chapter), there is another side to the opening as well. As we will see in this main game (and its sidelines, such as those above), if White is both knowledgeable and determined to make a draw, he can almost certainly reach that half point; and as Black, you must accept that reality or take extreme risks.

In Fischer's time, players with the white pieces were ashamed to head straight for the draw—not so today!

8...♗e7

Black needs to develop in anti-Lasker style (the bishop before the knight) so as to unpin the e-pawn. Following the "knights before bishops" rule would allow the calamitous 8...♘f6? 9 ♘d4! ♕d7 10 ♕f3.

9 ♗c2

This is the main (and very boring and very drawish) move. The alternatives 9 ♖e3, 9 ♕b3 and 9 c4 are covered in Games 39-41.

9...♗xc2 10 ♕xc2

White finally breaks the blockade;

meanwhile Black completes his kingside development and stands well with his central pawn majority.

10...♘f6 11 d4 e4

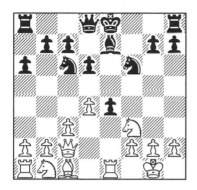

In typical Siesta style, Black blocks the white centre and gains space.

12 ♘g5 d5 13 f3

In an internet blitz game, my opponent thought I'd left something hanging and ventured 13 ♘e6, not realizing that this is all story-booked to a Shirov, and there are no pawns to be found: 13...♕d7 (White realizes that 14 ♘xg7+ ♔f7 would cost him a piece, and retreats, but the loss of two tempi is soon fatal) 14 ♘f4 14...0-0 15 ♕e2 ♗d6 16 ♗e3 ♘g4! 17 h3 (not 17 ♘xd5 ♗xh2+ winning) 17...♘xe3 18 fxe3 ♗xf4 19 exf4 ♖xf4 and I won easily with my extra, protected passed pawn in Wilmonx16-Taylor, playchess.com (blitz) 2009.

13...h6 14 ♘h3

Or 14 ♘e6 ♕d7 (again) 15 ♘f4 exf3, destroying White's kingside while the black king goes for a walk—I prefer Black after, for example, 16 ♕g6+ ♔d8

17 ♘e6+ ♔c8 18 gxf3 ♗d6 19 ♗d2 ♔b8 20 ♘a3 ♔a7 due to his safer king.

14...0-0 15 ♘d2 exf3 16 ♘xf3

It doesn't seem credible that this boring drawish line should be recommended in *Opening for White according to Anand*, or that fighting players like Shirov should voluntarily go in for it!

16...♖f7!

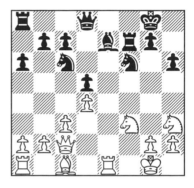

This prevents any tricks with ♕g6 or ♗xh6. White scores a miserable 48% after this move, and nothing is forthcoming but more draws!

The pawn structure reminds me of an Exchange French, but instead of one open e-file we have two (e- and f-). This factor helps Black, for if White takes the e-file (a big deal in the Exchange French), then here Black takes the f-file (note that he is already about to double rooks there) and White has nothing.

17 ♕f5

As just mentioned, Black's last move was specifically directed against ♕g6 and ♗xh6. According to my database, seven White players decided to test this and played 17 ♕g6?! anyway! The result? White managed four draws and lost the other three! Here's how Black can play for a win: 17...♗d6! (the bishop goes to its best square, while eviction proceedings are prepared against the white queen) 18 ♗xh6 (White is still optimistic, when it was really time to look for equalization) 18...♘e7! (since White's last threatened absolutely nothing—due to the prophylactic ♖f7—this counterblow is both possible and very strong) 19 ♕g5 (no matter how he squirms, White must lose material; in L.Abramov-E.Terpugov, Moscow 1949, White accepted the inevitable immediately, but after 19 ♖xe7 ♖xe7 20 ♗g5 ♕e8 21 ♕f5 ♕h5 22 ♖f1 ♕h7 23 ♘e5 ♕xf5 24 ♖xf5 ♖ae8 25 ♗xf6 gxf6 26 ♘g4 ♖e1+ 27 ♔f2 ♖8e2+ 28 ♔f3 ♗e7 29 ♘f4 ♖xb2 30 ♘xd5 ♔f7 31 ♖h5 ♖f1+ Black won the exchange up ending) 19...♘h7 (the immediate 19...♕c8 saves a move, but there's nothing wrong with a two time repetition) 20 ♕g4 ♘f6 21 ♕g5 ♕c8! (Black could take the draw with 21...♘h7, but correctly goes for the win: White's "aggressive" bishop on h6 can't get home again) 22 ♘e5 (if 22 ♗xg7 ♘e4 is crushing) 22...♗xe5 23 ♖xe5 (if 23 dxe5 ♘h7 24 ♕g3 ♘f5 wins a piece) 23...♘e4 24 ♕h5 (Black also comes out a piece up after 24 ♖xe4 dxe4 25 ♘f2 ♕e6 26 ♘g4 ♖af8 27 h3 ♘f5) 24...gxh6 25 ♕xh6 ♖h7 26 ♕e3 ♕g4 (the dust has finally cleared and Black has an extra piece vs. only two pawns—and he

wastes no time in making the material advantage tell) 27 ♘f2 ♕h4 28 ♘xe4 ♕xh2+ 29 ♔f2 ♖f8+ 30 ♔e2 dxe4 31 ♖g5+ ♖g7 32 ♖xg7+ ♔xg7 33 ♕xe4 ♘g6 34 ♕xb7 ♕g3 35 ♖f1 ♖e8+ 36 ♔d2 ♕e3+ 0-1 S.Melia-S.Halkias, Kavala 2007. One sees that 17 ♕g6 is to be welcomed, not feared!

Also ineffective is 17 ♘e5 ♘xe5 18 ♖xe5 (18 dxe5 ♘g4 is a little better for Black, since the white king is vulnerable on the g1-a7 diagonal as well as the f-file) 18...♗d6 and Black is again for choice in view of his superior development, stronger bishop, and kingside attacking chances.

Finally, 17 ♘f2 is the *"according to Anand"* move—and this terrifies me so much I will wait until the next game to cover it!

17...♗d6 18 ♗f4 ♗xf4 19 ♘xf4 ♘h5

Black utilizes the second open file to chop wood—the game is dead even.

20 ♕xh5 ♖xf4 21 ♖e6 ♕d7 22 ♖ae1 ♖af8 ½-½

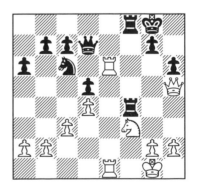

The files balance, as I mentioned above.

Easy equalization for Black equals theoretical success, as all the books including mine say—but what if you needed a win with Black in the last round? If White has studied this game, then he could probably find several ways to draw, from the boring main line to Krogius' 8 ♕b3.

1 e4 e5 2 ♘f3 ♘c6 3 ♗b5 a6 4 ♗a4 d6 5 c3 f5 6 exf5 ♗xf5 7 0-0 ♗d3 8 ♖e1 ♗e7 9 ♗c2 ♗xc2 10 ♕xc2 ♘f6 11 d4 e4 12 ♘g5 d5 13 f3 h6 14 ♘h3 0-0 15 ♘d2 exf3 16 ♘xf3 ♖f7

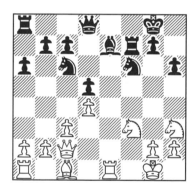

The key position of the BML (boring main line!). It is absolutely critical that one *memorizes* the moves leading here, *and* understands this critical position. Yes, I know it's move sixteen, and I know I have in many books advocated free creative play without too much memorization. But this is the Ruy Lopez, and if you want this theory-heavy opening to work for you—I'm sorry—you will have to put the time in and really learn these lines.

Of course, after all this work, all you will get is a draw!

17 ♘f2

This is the *Opening for White according to Anand* move as recommended by Khalifman, with a supposed advantage to White. The book came out in 2003, and from 2004-present, according to the *Mega* and all other sources I have, this variation has indeed been a hot line, with 11 games played—but the results have not proven the promised White advantage: there is one win for White, two wins for Black, and eight draws. While this is a bit of a statistical plus for Black, in reality the position is dead even—though perhaps easier for Black to play, as he just has to occupy the open files. If White tries to "prove" an advantage here, he will not succeed, which I think explains his negative score.

On the other hand, even if Black really really wants to win, he probably can't overcome the drawish nature of the position, as one sees in the following game: 17 ♘f4 (no more or less drawish than the "Anand" move) 17...♗d6 18 ♕f5 ♗xf4 19 ♗xf4 ♘e4 20 ♕e6 ♕d7 21 ♕xd7 ♖xd7 22 ♘d2 ♘xd2 23 ♗xd2 ♖e7 24 ♖xe7 ♘xe7 25 ♗f4 c6 26 ♖e1 ♘g6 27 ♗g3 ♔f7 28 ♔f2 ♖e8 29 ♖xe8 ♔xe8—many people would agree to a draw here, but not Yandemirov!

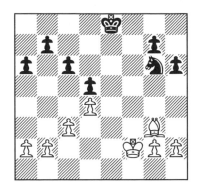

He notes that the white bishop is slightly bad in view of the fixed d-pawn, and attempts to capitalize on that... for the next sixty moves or so! But unfortunately for him, White is obviously content with a draw, and finally gets it by solid defence, not even taking his opponent's risky sacrifice: 30 ♔f3 h5 31 ♗f2 ♔f7 32 g4 hxg4+ 33 ♔xg4 ♘f8 34 ♗h4 g6 35 ♗g5 ♘e6 36 h4 b5 37 b4 ♘f8 38 ♗d8 ♘e6 39 ♗g5 ♔e8 40 ♗f4 ♔d7 41 ♗e5 ♔e7 42 ♗f4 ♘f8 43 ♔g5 ♔f7 44 ♗e5 ♘d7 45 ♔g4 ♔e6 46 ♔g5 ♔f7 47 ♔g4 ♘b6 48 ♗f4 ♘c4 49 ♔g5 ♘b2 50 ♗d2 ♘d1 51 ♗e1 ♔g7 52 ♗d2 ♘f2 53 ♗e1 ♘e4+ 54 ♔g4 ♔f6 55 ♔f4 ♘d6 56 ♗d2 ♘c4 57 ♗c1 ♔f7 58 ♔g4 ♔f6 59 ♗g5+ ♔e6 60 ♗c1 a5 61 a3 a4 62 ♔g5 ♔f7 63 ♔g4 ♘d6 64 ♗d2 ♘e4 65 ♗e1 ♔e6 66 ♔f4 ♔f6 67 ♔g4 ♘d6 68 ♗d2 ♘f5 69 ♗g5+ ♔e6 70 ♗f4 ♘xh4!? (a bold move, with the idea 71 ♔xh4 ♔f5 exploiting the bad white bishop, but the first player sidesteps this and heads for an "all pawns on one side" draw) 71 ♔g5 ♘f3+ 72 ♔xg6 ♘g1 73 ♗d2 ♘e2 74 ♔g5 ♘g3 75 ♔g4 ♘e4 76 ♗e1 ♔f6 77 ♗h4+ ♔g6 78 ♗e1 ♘d6 79 ♗d2 ♔f6 80 ♗g5+ ♔f7 81 ♗d2 ♔e6 82 ♔f4 ♘e8 83 ♔g4 ♘f6+ 84 ♔f4 ♘e4 85 ♗e1 ♘d6 86 ♗d2 ½-½ M.Meszaros-V.Yandemirov, Cappelle la Grande 2003.

17...♗d6

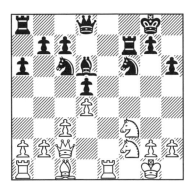

Look at the symmetrical pawn structure—where Black has the better bishop—and it's clear that White has equality at best.

18 ♗d2 ♖e7

Alternatively, if you want "Fire on Board"—here it is: 18...♕f8 19 ♖e2 ♖e8 20 ♖ae1 ♖xe2 21 ♖xe2 ♖e7 22 ♖xe7 ♕xe7 23 ♔f1 ♕e6 24 ♗e1 ♘e7 ½-½ A.Shirov-J.Lautier, Paris 2000. I can practically feel the flames!

19 ♖xe7

Khalifman gives 19 b3 ♕d7 20 c4 and claims a White advantage, but this is clearly dead even too; e.g. 20...♖ae8 (simple chess is best) 21 c5 ♖xe1+ 22 ♖xe1 ♖xe1+ 23 ♗xe1 (but not 23 ♘xe1? ♘xd4 24 ♕d3 ♗xc5 and Black takes two pawns!) 23...♗f4 24 ♕e2 ♕e7 (it is absolutely impossible to see any advantage to White, whereas it is still possible to see that better bishop for Black—but, alas, that can be exchanged) 25 ♕xe7 ♘xe7 (an exciting position is reached) 26 ♘d3 ♗e3+ 27 ♗f2 ♗xf2+ 28 ♔xf2 ♘f5 29 ♘de5 ♘e4+ 30 ♔e1 g5 31 g4 ♘g7 32 a3 ♘e6 33 ♔e2 ♘f4+ 34 ♔e3 ♘g2+ 35 ♔e2 ♘f4+ and now a draw is forced, which is all I could find for either side in my analysis.

Note that Black doesn't even have to follow Khalifman with 19...♕d7, for he has other ways to equalize as well; e.g. 19...a5!? (to attack b3) 20 c4 ♗b4 with another dead equal position.

19...♕xe7 20 ♖e1 ♕f8 21 ♘e5 ♖e8 22 ♕f5

If 22 ♘xc6 ♖xe1+ 23 ♗xe1 bxc6 24 ♕a4 ♕e8 25 ♔f1 ♗xh2 with the idea ...♘h5-g3 mate, or 25 ♗d2 ♕e2 26 ♕d1 ♗xh2+! and Black is better in both cases thanks to his more active bishop.

22...♗xe5 23 dxe5 ♘e4

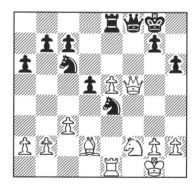

The two open files lead to exchanges, which is characteristic of the variation.

24 ♕xf8+ ♔xf8 25 ♘xe4 dxe4 26 ♖xe4 ♖xe5 27 ♖f4+ ♔e7 28 c4 g5 29 ♖f2 ♖e4 30 b3 b5 31 cxb5 axb5 32 ♔f1 ♘d4

This centralized knight is as good as or better than the bishop. Nonetheless, White, more than 200 points higher rated than Black, is apparently trying to win—though neither side has objective winning chances.

33 h3 c5 34 ♗c3 b4 35 ♗b2 ♔e6 36 ♗c1 ♘f5 37 ♖f3 c4 38 bxc4 ♖xc4 39 ♗b2 ♖c2 40 ♖b3 ♘d6 41 ♖xb4 ♘c4 42 ♗g7 ♘e3+ 43 ♔g1 ♖xg2+ 44 ♔h1 ♖xa2 45 ♗xh6 ♖a1+ 46 ♔h2 ♖a2+ 47 ♔g1 ♖g2+ 48 ♔h1 ♖g3 49 ♗xg5

White finally decides it's time to draw!

49...♖xh3+

49...♖xg5 50 ♖e4+ ♖e5 51 ♖xe5+ ♔xe5 is also a draw.

50 ♔g1 ♖g3+ 51 ♔f2 ♖xg5 52 ♖e4+ ♖e5 53 ♖xe5+ ♔xe5 ½-½

After 54 ♔xe3 the position looks pretty drawish.

The Siesta player must realize that White can *force* these boring positions on the would-be gambiteer. But while death by boredom is possible, the good news is that you shouldn't ever lose in these lines, even against a much higher-rated opponent.

The next three games feature violent attempts by White to refute the Siesta—and consequently, much more exciting play!

Game 39
J.Klavins-V.Mikenas
Riga 1959

---

1 e4 e5 2 ♘f3 ♘c6 3 ♗b5 a6 4 ♗a4 d6 5 c3 f5 6 exf5 ♗xf5 7 0-0 ♗d3 8 ♖e1 ♗e7 9 ♖e3

Besides the equalizing 9 ♗c2 that we saw in the previous two games, White has two other ways to attack the blockading bishop: the text, 9 ♖e3, which will be considered in this and the next game; and 9 ♕b3 followed by ♕d5 or c3-c4, which will be covered in Game 41.

9...e4

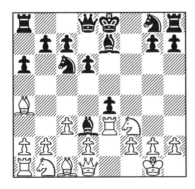

No other move makes sense—Black

must maintain the blockade as long as possible.

10 ♘e1

After 10 ♘d4 ♕d7 White has made no progress towards getting rid of the cramping bishop.

10...♗g5

Correct! Of course giving up the blockade with the wimpish ...♗xb1 makes no logical sense—Black must counter-attack!

11 ♘xd3

White makes a tempting (even Michael Adams played this and lost!) but faulty exchange sacrifice. The non-sacrificing alternatives 11 ♖g3 and 11 ♖h3 will be covered in the next game.

11...♗xe3 12 ♘b4

12 dxe3 is a new try to rehabilitate the line, which was successful in the one game played, but can't be recommended: 12...exd3 13 ♕xd3 ♕h4 14 ♕d4 ♕xd4 15 cxd4 ♘f6 16 ♘c3, and now Black played 16...0-0, continued passively, and eventually lost in A.Cherniaev-M.Yeo, Jersey 1998. Instead, correct is active play with 16...b5! 17 ♗d1 (or 17 ♗c2 ♘b4 18 ♗b1 c5 again with great activity) 17...0-0-0 and Black is better with his extra exchange and potential queenside expansion.

12...♗xf2+!!

This was first played by the creative attacking IM Vladas Mikenas in the main game—and we now see there are seven games that feature this sacrifice in the *Mega*, and Black wins them all! Mikenas' idea is that the white king does not have a single defender, while Black can quickly bring up the queen, king's knight and both rooks.

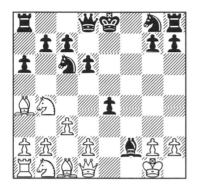

13 ♔xf2 ♛h4+ 14 ♔g1

This was played in all seven games, and in each one we see the white king trapped between Black's powerful queen and the rook coming soon to the f-file.

I think the untried 14 ♔e2 is White's last hope, though Black is still much better; e.g. 14...♞e7 15 ♞xc6 ♞xc6 16 ♗xc6+ bxc6 17 ♛a4 ♛g4+ 18 ♔e1 0-0 19 ♛c4+ d5 20 ♛e2 and White has some drawing chances.

14...♞h6

The reason for the rim development is to leave the f-file clear for the rook, and so Black quickly threatens a back rank mate as we'll see in the following note.

15 g3

White has also found other ways to lose:

a) 15 ♞xc6 0-0 16 g3 ♛h3 17 ♞e7+ ♔h8 18 ♛e2 ♞g4.

This is the basic picture of the at-

tack: White has brought up his queen to defend, but Black has a queen, knight and rook already attacking, with the other rook coming fast if he needs it.

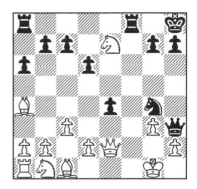

With that kingside material superiority, it means absolutely nothing that White has, overall, a material advantage of three pieces for a rook—those pieces are sleeping! One possible finish is 19 ♛g2 ♛h5 20 h3 ♖f2 21 ♛h1 ♖e2! 22 ♔f1 (or 22 hxg4 ♖e1+ and mates) 22...♞h2+ 23 ♔g1 ♛c5+ 24 d4 exd3+ 25 ♗e3 ♛xe3 mate!

A quicker demise is 16 d4? ♛f2+ 17 ♔h1 ♛f1+ 18 ♛xf1 ♖xf1 (which is the aforementioned back rank mate), while Tiviakov made it to move 25 with 16 h3 ♖f2! 17 ♞e7+ ♔h8 18 ♞d5 ♖af8 19 ♞e3 ♖8f3 20 ♗d7 ♛g3 21 ♛e1 ♞f7 22 d4 (or 22 ♞a3 ♞e5 23 ♞ac2 ♞d3 24 ♛d1 ♞f4 25 d4 ♖xg2+ 26 ♞xg2 ♛xg2 mate) 22...♖xe3 23 ♛xf2 ♖e1+ 24 ♛f1 e3 25 ♞d2 ♛f2+ 0-1 S.Tiviakov-B.Adhiban, Bhubaneswar 2009; White resigns in view of 26 ♔h2 ♖xf1 27 ♞xf1 e2 and the pawn promotes to something, e.g. 28 ♗e3 exf1N+ 29 ♖xf1 ♕xf1 etc.

b) 15 ♕f1 ♘g4 16 ♕f4 ♖f8 17 ♕g3 ♖f1+! 18 ♔xf1 ♘xh2+ 19 ♔xh2 (19 ♔f2 ♘g4+ doesn't help) 19...♕xh2 0-1 M.Adams-J.Piket, Wijk aan Zee 1991. It's not often one sees a 2600 player defeated in 19 moves—White resigned in view of 20 ♘xc6 b5 21 ♘a3 bxa4 22 d3 ♔d7 23 ♘d4 ♖f8+ and mates.

c) 15 ♕e2 0-0 16 ♗b3+ ♔h8 17 ♘xc6 ♘g4 (again we see our basic attacking pattern) 18 h3 ♘f2 19 ♗e6 (if 19 ♘b4 ♘xh3+! 20 gxh3 ♕g3+ wins the queen, with mate coming soon) 19...bxc6 20 ♕e3 ♘d3 21 ♘a3 ♖f2 22 ♗c4 ♖af8 23 ♗xd3 exd3 24 ♘h2 ♖f1 25 b3 ♖e1 26 g3 ♖h1+! (a pretty finale) 0-1 A.Olsson-B.Soderborg, Swedish Championship, Ornskoldsvik 1962.

d) 15 d4 lasted longest in A.Zapata-W.Arencibia Rodriguez, Cienfuegos 1996, but I believe Black could have shortened things quite a bit.

♗b3 ♔h8 23 ♖f1 ♘xe3 24 ♘xe3 ♖xf1+ 25 ♘dxf1 ♘e7 and Black outplayed his opponent and finally won this rook + pawn vs. two minor pieces ending after 60 moves, though Arencibia didn't really have any advantage when that basic ending began.

However, I don't think he needed to play the endgame at all! Much stronger is 15...♘g4! 16 h3 ♕f2+ 17 ♔h1 h5!—we saw this motif in the notes to Parma-Keres (Game 25), and will see it again in the Yandemirov Gambit which I will cover in the next chapter: Black uses a piece sacrifice to (eventually) open the h-file for attack; e.g. 18 ♘xc6 ♕g3! 19 ♘e5+ c6 20 ♘xg4 hxg4 21 ♔g1 gxh3 22 ♕e2 hxg2 23 ♕xe4+ ♔d8 and White has no defence to ...♖h1 mate other than 24 ♕xg2, but then Black wins with 24...♕e1+ 25 ♕f1 ♖h1+. This would have been a lot quicker than the game!

15...♕h3

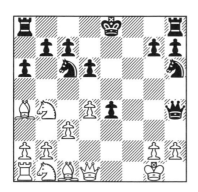

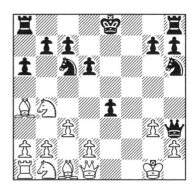

The game continued 15...0-0 16 ♕e2 e3 17 ♗xe3 ♖ae8 18 ♘d2 ♘g4 19 g3 ♕xh2+ 20 ♕xh2 ♘xh2 21 ♘d5 ♘g4 22

16 d4

Exchanging queens doesn't stop Black's attack: 16 ♕f1 ♕xf1+ 17 ♔xf1

0-0+ 18 ♔g1 ♘e5 19 d4 ♘f3+ 20 ♔g2 ♘e1+ 21 ♔g1 ♘g4 22 h3 ♘f2 23 ♘a3 ♘xh3+ 24 ♔h2 ♖f1 25 ♘ac2 (accepting the piece sacrifice with 25 ♔xh3 allows 25...♖af8 with a winning attack; e.g. 26 ♔g4 ♘f3 27 ♗d7 ♖h1! threatening a hard to stop mate in one!) 25...♘g1 26 ♘xe1 ♖xe1 27 ♘c2 ♘f3+ 28 ♔g2 ♖e2+ 29 ♔f1 ♖h2 30 ♗e3 ♖f8 31 ♖c1 ♘xd4+ 32 ♔g1 ♘f3+ 33 ♔f1 d5 34 b4 c6 35 ♗b3 ♖f5 36 ♗f4? (making it quick, though White had no chances to hold in the long run, given Black's material superiority and bind on the position) 36...♖xf4 0-1 A.Bangiev-V.Zhuravliov, Liepaia 1971.

16...♘g4 17 ♕e2 0-0

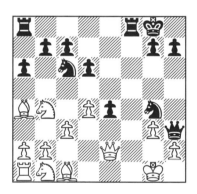

The basic attacking picture is seen one more time.

18 ♗f4 g5!

The f-file is the main highway of Black's attack, so he can't let White obstruct it.

19 ♗b3+ ♔h8 20 ♗e6

20 ♗xg5? is suicidal due to 20...♖f1+ 21 ♕xf1 ♕xh2 mate.

20...gxf4 21 ♗xg4 ♕h6 22 ♘d2

No better is 22 gxf4 ♖xf4 23 h3 ♖g8 24 ♕g2 (or 24 ♘d2 ♕xh3) 24...♖f3 25 ♔h2 ♕f4+ 26 ♔h1 ♖f1+, winning the white queen.

22...f3 23 ♕d1 ♘xb4 24 cxb4 ♕e3+ 25 ♔h1 ♕f2 26 ♗h3 ♖ae8 27 ♖c1 e3

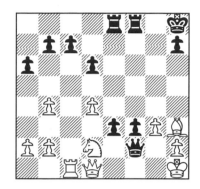

28 ♖xc7

White can also try 28 ♘xf3, after which I amused myself by working out the following pretty endgame win: 28...e2 29 ♕g1 ♕xf3+ 30 ♗g2 ♕d3 31 ♖e1 ♕d2 32 a3 ♖f1 33 ♖xf1 (not 33 ♗xf1 ♕xe1) 33...e1♕ 34 ♖xe1 ♖xe1 35 ♗f1 ♕xb2 36 ♕g2 ♕a1 37 ♔g1 ♕xd4+ 38 ♔h1 ♕d1 39 ♔g1 c5 40 ♕f2 ♖xf1+! (this was my point; now the connected pawns win) 41 ♕xf1 ♕xf1+ 42 ♔xf1 c4 43 ♔e2 d5 44 ♔d2 d4 45 ♔c2 c3 46 ♔d3 ♔g7 47 ♔c2 ♔g6 48 ♔d3 ♔g5 49 h3 h5 50 a4 b5 51 axb5 axb5 52 ♔c2 ♔f5 53 ♔d3 h4! (Black forces king entry—the passed white g-pawn is meaningless) 54 g4+ ♔f4 55 ♔c2 ♔e3 56 g5 d3+ 57 ♔xc3 d2 etc.

28...exd2 0-1

Mate is inevitable.

Attempts to improve for White have

failed, so the exchange sac 11 ♘xd3 appears to be refuted by Mikenas' great counter-sacrifice 12...♗xf2+!.

1 e4 e5 2 ♘f3 ♘c6 3 ♗b5 a6 4 ♗a4 d6 5 c3 f5 6 exf5 ♗xf5 7 0-0 ♗d3 8 ♖e1 ♗e7 9 ♖e3 e4 10 ♘e1 ♗g5 11 ♖h3

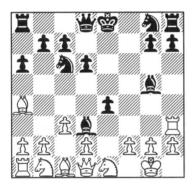

This is the only way White can play for a win. 11 ♖g3 lets the rook get hit again, which is to Black's advantage unless White wants a draw: 11...♗h4 12 ♖h3 (12 ♘xd3 ♗xg3 13 ♘b4 ♗xf2+! returns to Game 39, while 12 ♖e3 ♗g5 is yet another Siesta draw—this gambit has more forced draws than any sharp opening I know!) 12...♗xf2+ 13 ♔xf2 ♕f6+ 14 ♘f3 (or 14 ♔g3 ♘e7 with a fierce attack) 14...♘e7 15 ♘a3 0-0 16 ♘c2 ♘e5 17 ♘ce1 exf3 18 gxf3 ♘7g6 19 ♕b3+ ♔h8 20 ♕xb7 ♘f4 (Black's attack is overwhelming, while White has no development at all) 21 ♖g3 ♕h4

22 ♔g1 ♘e2+ 23 ♔g2 ♘xg3 24 hxg3 ♕xa4 and Yandemirov scores again! 0-1 S.Voitsekhovsky-V.Yandemirov, Moscow 1996.

11...♕e7

Also good is 11...♘f6 which confused Smyslov: 12 ♘xd3 exd3 13 ♖xd3 0-0 14 ♖h3 ♕e7 15 ♘a3 ♖ae8 16 ♘c2 ♘e4 17 ♗b3+ ♔h8 18 f3 ♘c5 19 d4 ♗xc1 20 dxc5 ♗e3+ 21 ♘xe3 ♕xe3+ 22 ♔h1 dxc5 23 ♗c2 h6 24 ♗e4 ♘e5 25 ♕g1 ♕xg1+ 26 ♔xg1 c6 27 ♖h5 c4 28 ♖d1 ♘d3 29 ♗xd3 cxd3 30 ♖xd3 ♖e2 31 b4 ♖fe8 (Black's compensation for the pawn persists into the endgame and is soon translated into material gain) 32 ♖h4 ♖e1+ 33 ♔f2 ♖8e2+ 34 ♔g3 ♖g1 35 ♖d8+ ♔h7 36 ♖d7 ♖gxg2+ 37 ♔f4 b5 38 ♖g4 ♖xg4+ 39 fxg4 ♖xh2 40 ♖d6 ♖xa2 41 ♖xc6 ♖a4 ½-½ V.Smyslov-A.Lutikov, USSR Championship, Moscow 1961—Smyslov could never find the handle against the MS, but he still got the World Champion courtesy draw a pawn down.

12 ♘xd3 exd3 13 ♖xd3 ♘f6

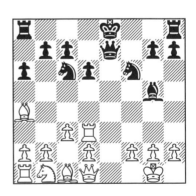

Finally a true gambit instead of a

draw! White has removed the bone and chowed down on an extra pawn as well but, while doing all this, has fallen far behind in development—a double-edged game is in prospect.

14 ♗xc6+

The *Fritz* suggestion of 14 g3 is met by 14...0-0-0! when Black has excellent compensation, with his lead in development and the light square holes around the white king.

14...bxc6 15 ♖g3 0-0!

An insouciant piece offer.

16 d3

If White takes the piece with 16 ♖xg5, Black completes his development with a small threat (of mate!)—16...♖ae8 and now 17 ♕f1 (or 17 f3 ♕e1+ 18 ♕xe1 ♖xe1+ 19 ♔f2 ♖xc1 and Black is obviously better with the back rank pin) 17...♘e4 and Black, attacking with every piece, easily breaks through against White's sleeping army; e.g. 18 d3 (18 ♖g3 ♖xf2 19 ♕e1 ♖ef8 20 d3 ♘xg3! 21 ♕xe7 ♖f1 is a nice mate) 18...♘xf2 19 ♗d2 ♘h3+ wins the queen.

16...♖ae8!

The bishop remains immune in view of White's weak back rank.

17 ♗e3?

A mistake, since Black can leave his bishop en prise even one more move! Correct is 17 ♗d2, which guards the back rank and so actually threatens ♖xg5. Black can play 17...♗xd2 18 ♘xd2 ♕e2 with obvious compensation for the pawn, but a win for Black looks like a lot to ask—about even I'd say.

17...♘d5! 18 ♘d2

It's easy to see the black bishop is still immune; note also that 18 ♗d2 is now too late because of 18...♗h4 19 ♖f3 ♗xf3 20 gxf3 (forced) 20...♕f6 with a powerful attack against White's weakened kingside.

18...♘xe3 19 fxe3 ♗xe3+ 20 ♔h1 ♗xd2 21 ♕xd2 ♕e2

Black has a pawn's worth of play—as in the note to move 17—but here is not even a pawn down! Evidently Black is clearly better.

22 ♕xe2 ♖xe2 23 b4 ♖xa2

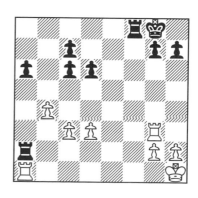

Black picks off a clean pawn.

24 ♖g1 ♖a3 25 d4 ♖f2 26 ♖e3 h6 27 h3

♖c2 28 ♖e8+ ♔h7 29 ♖e7 ♖axc3 30
♖xc7 ♖d3 31 ♖e1 d5 32 ♖a7 ♖dd2 33
♖xa6 ♖xg2 34 ♖xc6 ♖h2+ 35 ♔g1
♖cg2+ 36 ♔f1 ♖b2 37 ♔g1 ♖xh3 38 ♖c5
♖g3+ 39 ♔f1 ♖f3+ 40 ♔g1 ♖g3+ 41 ♔f1
♖gg2 42 ♖b1 ♖bf2+ 43 ♔e1 ♖f4 44 ♖b3
♖xd4 45 ♔f1 ♖a2 46 ♖c1 ♖f4+ 47 ♔g1
♖g4+ 48 ♔f1 ♖h4 49 ♔g1 ♖g4+ 50 ♔f1
♖h2 51 ♖cb1 ♖g6 52 b5 ♖b6 53 ♖d1
♖h1+ 54 ♔e2 ♖h2+ 55 ♔f1 ♖h1+ 56
♔e2 ♖xd1 57 ♔xd1 ♔g6 58 ♔d2 ♔f5 59
♔c3 g5 60 ♔d4 g4!

The kingside pawns will be worth
more than a rook.

**61 ♔c5 ♖b8 62 ♔xd5 ♖d8+ 63 ♔c6 h5
64 b6 h4 65 ♔c7 ♖g8 66 b7 g3 67 ♖b5+**

If 67 b8♕ ♖xb8 68 ♖xb8 g2 69 ♖g8
h3 and queens.

67...♔f6 68 ♖b6+ ♔f7 69 ♖b4 g2 0-1

White loses after both 70 ♖b1 h3
and 70 ♖g4 ♖xg4 71 b8♕ g1♕.

I think the 9 ♖e3/10 ♘e1 plan is too
slow, provided of course that he plays
energetically in gambit style—though
one must note again that there is a
more or less forced draw in this line,
with the rook repetition on move 11.

In the next game, the same opponents meet again two years later.
Bashkov tries a slightly different variation, but Yandemirov is ready!

Game 41
V.Bashkov-V.Yandemirov
Minsk 1993

1 e4 e5 2 ♘f3 ♘c6 3 ♗b5 a6 4 ♗a4 d6 5
c3 f5 6 exf5 ♗xf5 7 0-0 ♗d3 8 ♖e1 ♗e7

Now, instead of rehashing 9 ♖e3,
which didn't bring him anything in the
previous game, White tries...

9 ♕b3!?

We saw that this move brought
White nothing on the previous turn
(recall the analysis in Game 37—
another Yandemirov game—where I
showed that Black can meet 8 ♕b3
with 8...b5 9 ♕d5 ♘d4!). Here the situation is a bit different in view of the interpolation of ♖e1 and ...♗e7, but Black
has the same choices of ...b7-b5 and
...♖b8.

White has one further try that's
worth mentioning as it was recently
played by Topalov, namely 9 c4.

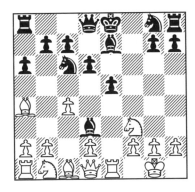

The idea is to follow with ♕b3 when
the queen directly attacks the d3-
bishop. Black answers 9...♖b8 (this
move of Radchenko's is considered
best—giving up the bind with 9...♗xc4
is worse, as White gets attacking
chances after 10 d4 b5 11 ♗b3 ♗xb3 12
axb3 ♘xd4 13 ♘xd4 exd4 14 ♗g5 and
won in V.Lepeshkin-Y.Estrin, Moscow

1964) 10 ♕b3 e4 11 ♘g5 (11 ♘d4 ♘f6 12 ♘xc6 bxc6 13 ♗xc6+ ♔f7 reveals Radchenko's point: the black rook gains a tempo on the queen, while the white position is blockaded by the mighty bishop at d3; Black can castle by hand with ...♖f8 and ...♔g8, and has an excellent attack for only one pawn) 11...♘f6 12 ♘c3 0-0 13 ♘cxe4 ♘xe4 14 ♘xe4 ♘e5 15 ♖e3 b5!? (15...♗xc4 would give Black a simple advantage, but the remainder of this crazy game is worth quoting, as Topalov's beloved bishops hold against a queen!) 16 cxb5+ d5 17 ♖xd3 ♘xd3 18 ♕xd3 dxe4 19 ♕xe4 ♗f6 20 bxa6 ♗d4 21 d3 ♖xf2 22 ♗e3 ♖bxb2 23 ♗b3+ ♔h8 24 ♖e1 ♖xg2+ 25 ♕xg2 ♖xg2+ 26 ♔xg2 ♕a8+ 27 ♔f2 ♗c3 28 a7 ♗xe1+ 29 ♔xe1 ♕h1+ 30 ♔d2 ♕xh2+ 31 ♔c3 ♕g2 32 ♔d4 ♕a8 (one would think the queen should somehow win against the two bishops, but perhaps not in view of White's passed a-pawn—in any case Lautier can't find a way to both advance his kingside pawns and hold back the white a-pawn on the seventh) 33 ♔e5 ♕e8+ 34 ♔f4 c6 35 ♗c5 h5 36 ♗d6 ♕d8 37 ♗b8 ♕d4+ 38 ♔f5 ♕xd3+ 39 ♔e6 ♕a6 40 ♔d7 g5 41 ♔c7 g4 42 ♗c4 ♕a4 43 ♗b3 ♕a6 44 ♗c4 ♕a4 ½-½ V.Topalov-J.Lautier, Linares 1995.

In my opinion, 9 c4 (which weakens d4 as well as the already weak and occupied d3) is too anti-positional to gain an advantage—yes, in some lines White can get a pawn, but Black's bind is worth more.

9...b5

Simplest, though 9...♖b8 is also playable: 10 ♕d5 e4 (transposition alert!—this can also arise via a different move order as noted in Game 37: 8 ♕b3 ♖b8 9 ♖e1 ♗e7 10 ♕d5 c4 and we're back to the present position) and now:

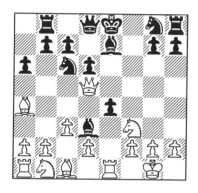

a) 11 ♘d4 ♘f6 12 ♕e6 (if White goes for material with 12 ♗xc6+ bxc6 13 ♕xc6+, then after 13...♔f7 14 ♘a3 ♖b6 15 ♕a4 ♕d7 16 ♕xd7 ♘xd7 17 f3 d5 Black has a terrific bind) 12...♕d7 13 ♗b3 ♘d8 14 ♕xd7+ ♔xd7 15 ♗c2 ♗xc2 16 ♘xc2 ♘c6 17 ♖e3 ♘e5 18 ♘e1 ♖hf8 19 d4 ♘c4 20 ♖e2 d5 and Black has the much superior centre and went on to win in Bernh.Schneider-E.Freise, Brakel 1967.

b) 11 ♘g5 ♗xg5 12 ♕xd3 ♘f6 13 ♗xc6+ bxc6 14 ♕xa6 (White picks up a pawn, but Black has good play) 14...♕d7 15 d4 ♗xc1 16 ♖xc1 ♖xb2!? (16...0-0 with excellent compensation is more rational—whereas the insane text finally leads to a "quiet" draw) 17 ♕a8+ ♔f7 18 ♕xh8 ♕f5 19 ♖f1 e3 20

♕d8 exf2+ 21 ♔h1 ♕f4 22 ♕xc7+ ♔g6 23 ♕xc6 ♘g4 24 g3 ♕f5 25 ♕xd6+ ♘f6 26 ♕c6 ♔g5 27 ♔g2 ♘d5 28 ♕e8 ♔h6 29 h3 ♕g5 30 ♖xf2 ♘f4+ 31 ♔f3 ♕d5+ 32 ♔e3 ♘g2+ 33 ♖xg2 ♕xg2 34 ♕e6+ g6 35 ♕g4 ♕f2+ 36 ♔d3 ♕f1+ 37 ♔e3 ♕f2+ 38 ♔d3 ♕f1+ 39 ♔e3 ♕f2+ 40 ♔d3 ½-½ G.Secheli-L.Vajda, Eger 1994—Black draws a knight and three pawns down!

10 ♕d5 ♕d7 11 ♕xd3 bxa4 12 ♕c2

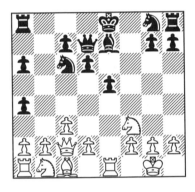

White is winning a pawn while falling behind in development—a typical Siesta situation.

12...♘f6 13 ♕xa4 0-0 14 d3 ♘d4

This is the only move to have been played here, according to the *Mega*.

In a blitz game I tried out 14...d5!?, taking over the centre and giving the bishop a path to d6 or c5. Black has some compensation here, and in fact I soon had more as my opponent immediately blundered: 15 ♘xe5? ♘xe5 16 ♕xd7 ♘fxd7 17 f4 ♘g6 and Black was a piece up in NN-Taylor, blitz game 2009. Obviously 15 ♗g5 is better, when 15...h6 16 ♗xf6 16...♖xf6 17 ♘xe5 ♕f5

18 ♘f3 ♕xd3 19 ♘bd2 ♖af8 is a typical line where Black has compensation for the pawn with his doubled rooks on the f-file.

15 ♕xd7

Geller tried 15 ♕d1 here, and after 15...♘xf3+ 16 ♕xf3 ♘g4 17 ♕d5+ ♔h8 18 f3 ♘f6 19 ♕b3 he beat off the attack and won in E.Geller-A.Lutikov, USSR Championship, Moscow 1961—but Black can improve with the more subtle 16...♖ab8!, when I think he has adequate compensation for the pawn.

½-½

After the game's 15 ♕xd7 the players unexpectedly agreed to a draw! The usually pugnacious "play to the last pawn" Yandemirov must have been tired! Otherwise 15...♘xf3+ 16 gxf3 ♘xd7 is at least equal for Black, who has excellent compensation for the missing pawn in view of White's shattered kingside.

All the lines with 7 0-0 ♗d3 (except the BML of Games 37-38) feature sharp gambit play, where Black is often material down but blockades White's position with the cramping bishop at d3. As far as I can see, Black gets at least equal chances in all these variations, provided of course that he plays actively and is not afraid to sacrifice.

The last three games of the chapter feature playable but non-challenging ideas for White.

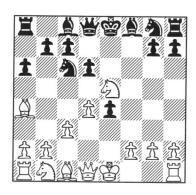

Game 42
K.Honfi-V.Ciocaltea
Reggio Emilia 1966/67

1 e4 e5 2 ♘f3 ♘c6 3 ♗b5 a6 4 ♗a4 d6 5 c3 f5 6 d4 fxe4 7 ♘xe5

This is a blunt attempt by White to force the draw right in the opening—but as it turns out, the draw is not forced! Given the many other less difficult drawing chances for White (such as the ♖e3-g3-e3 shuttle in Game 40, or the draws by boredom of Games 37-38) one must rate this as an outmoded variation.

7...dxe5 8 ♕h5+ ♔e7 9 ♗xc6

After 9 dxe5 White doesn't get enough for the piece: 9...g6 10 ♕h4+ (10 ♗g5+ ♔f7 is also winning for Black) 10...♔f7 11 ♕xe4 ♗f5 and Black develops while his king is relatively safe—it took 40 moves, but Black successfully evaluated the extra piece in A.Matikozian-A.Nadanian, Pasanauri 1997.

9...bxc6 10 ♗g5+ ♘f6 11 dxe5 ♕d5!

Capablanca's great defensive move, planning to pin along the rank, makes White struggle to draw.

12 ♗h4

Hopeless is 12 f4 exf3 13 0-0 ♔d7 14 e6+ ♔xe6 15 ♖e1+ ♔d7 16 ♕h3+ ♔d8 17 ♕xf3 ♕xg5 18 ♘d2 ♗g4 when Black was two pieces up in V.Zaitsev-V.Yandemirov, Krasnoyarsk 1998—though the database states "½-½"! I'm sure White resigned here and the result was entered wrong.

12...♔d7!

After 12...♔e6 White gets the draw he desires (though why *White* should desire a draw is another question): 13 ♗xf6 gxf6 14 ♕e8+ ♔f5 15 ♕h5+ ♔e6

16 ♕e8+ ♚f5 ½-½ E.Geller-P.Keres, Szczawno Zdroj 1950, and many other games as well.

However, as Ciocaltea shows with the text move, Black does not have to make it so easy for White.

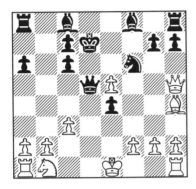

13 ♕g5 ♚e6!

Also good is 13...h6 14 ♕f5+ ♚e8 15 ♕g6+ ♕f7 16 ♕xf7+ ♚xf7 17 exf6 gxf6 which has an interesting evaluation history: Capablanca said it was equal, whereas Levy thought Black's bishops actually gave him the edge—so I paged Mr. *Fritz*. Interestingly enough, the machine agrees with Levy (equals plus) rather than Capa! Of course Levy did win his famous bet against the machines (for those of us old enough to recall such ancient history when people used to beat computers!) so perhaps he was more attuned to the future silicon monster.

14 exf6 ♕xg5 15 ♗xg5 gxf6

Black has reached an ending similar to Capablanca's analysis, and again the machine, and this author, favours Black. This is very important, as it

shows the "forced Siesta draw" *is in fact not there.*

16 ♗e3 ♖g8 17 g3 ♖b8

The open files compensate for the doubled pawns.

18 ♘d2

This allows Black to open the game for his bishops. Better is 18 b3 ♗b7 19 ♘d2 c5 when White is only slightly worse.

18...♖xb2 19 ♘xe4 ♚f7 20 0-0 ♗e6 21 ♖fb1 ♖c2! 22 ♖c1 ♖xc1+ 23 ♖xc1 ♗e7

If 23...♗xa2 24 ♖a1 ♗c4 25 ♘d2 ♗e2 26 c4 ♗b4 27 ♖xa6 ♖d8 28 ♖a2 ♗xd2 29 ♖xd2 ♖xd2 30 ♗xd2 ♗xc4 31 ♗f4 and White should be able to make a draw.

24 c4 ♖b8 25 ♘c5 ♗xc5

Black finally gives up the bishop pair but in compensation gets a rook to the seventh: White's defence is not easy.

26 ♗xc5 ♖b2

27 ♚g2?

White should not give up the pawn since Black has real winning chances with rooks on. Better is 27 a3 ♖e2 28

♗b4 ♖e4 29 c5 ♖e2 30 ♗a5 ♖a2 31 ♗b4 ♗d5 which is unpleasant but probably defensible for White.

27...♖xa2

Now this game reminds me very much of an Alekhine's Defence (Meekins-Taylor, analysed in *Alekhine Alert*) where I also won a rook + opposite-coloured bishop ending after prolonged manoeuvres!

28 ♗e3 ♖a4 29 c5 ♗d5+ 30 ♔f1 a5 31 ♔e2 ♖a2+ 32 ♔d3 a4 33 ♗d4 ♖a3+ 34 ♔d2 ♖b3 35 ♖c3 ♗b4 36 ♔d3 ♗b3 37 ♖c1 a3 38 ♖a1 ♖a4 39 ♖c1 ♗d5 40 h4 h5 41 ♗a1 ♔e6 42 ♖c3 ♗e4+ 43 ♔e3 a2 44 ♖b3 ♗d5 45 ♖c3 f5 46 ♔d2 f4 47 ♖d3 f3 48 ♖e3+ ♗e4 49 ♖c3 ♔d5 50 ♔e3 ♖a5 51 ♔f4 ♖a4 52 ♖e3 ♖b4 53 ♗g7 ♗d3+ 54 ♔xf3 ♗c4 55 ♖e8 ♖a4 56 ♗a1 ♔b3 57 ♖b8+ ♗b5 58 ♔e3 ♔c2 59 ♖d8 ♔c1 60 f3 ♖a3+ 61 ♔f2 ♗c4 62 ♖e8 ♔d2 63 g4 hxg4 64 fxg4 ♖h3 65 h5 ♖h1 66 ♗g7 a1♛ 67 ♗xa1 ♖xa1 68 h6 ♖h1 69 g5 ♔c3 70 ♔g3 ♔d4 71 ♔f4 ♔xc5 72 ♖d8 ♗a2 73 ♔e5 ♗b1 74 ♖b8 ♗d3 75 ♖d8 ♔c4 76 ♖d7 c5 77 ♖xc7 ♔b4 78 ♔f6 c4

79 ♔g7

It seems that Black wins even against the best try, though it's very close: 79 ♖b7+ ♔c5 80 ♖c7+ ♔d4 81 ♖d7+ ♔e3 82 ♖c7 ♖h5 83 ♔f7 ♔d4 84 ♖d7+ ♔e5 85 g6 ♖xh6 86 g7 ♗h7 87 g8♛ ♗xg8+ 88 ♔xg8 ♖c6 and the black rook gets behind his last pawn and forces the win.

79...♖g1?!

This is a bobble right at the end: Black wins cleanly with 79...c3! 80 g6 ♗c4 81 h7 c2 etc.

80 ♔f6 c3 81 h7 ♖h1 82 g6 ♖h6 83 ♖b7+?!

In view of Black's late game inaccuracy above, White has the chance for a miracle draw here: 83 ♖xc3! ♔xc3 84 ♔g5 ♖h1 (84...♖xg6+ 85 ♔h5 ♖h6+ 86 ♔xh6 ♗xh7 is another draw) 85 ♔f6 and it seems that Black cannot improve his position.

83...♗a5 84 ♖c7 c2 85 ♔g5 ♖xg6+ 86 ♔h5 ♖g1! 0-1

Ciocaltea deserves credit for a tremendous endgame struggle and triumph, though I think White would have had good drawing chances with either 18 b3 or 27 a3—and there was that lucky drawing possibility at the end.

Nevertheless, sac'ing a piece in the opening for an illusory draw—then struggling for hours—is not, presumably, what White wants! Meanwhile Black only needs to know Capablanca's precise defensive move (11...♛d5!) and the sac will hold no terrors.

1 e4 e5 2 ♘f3 ♘c6 3 ♗b5 a6 4 ♗a4 d6 5 c3 f5 6 d4 fxe4 7 ♘g5 exd4 8 ♘xe4 ♗f5

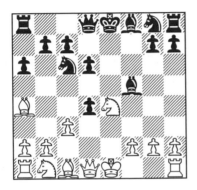

We already saw this variation in Game 4, Réti-Capablanca—and there's nothing wrong with following the great Cuban with 8...♘f6—but the esteemed theoretician Suetin's move might be even better!

9 ♕xd4

It's hard to find another move: if 9 ♘g3 ♕e7+ 10 ♔f1 ♗d7 and White won't castle in this game, or 9 ♕f3 ♗xe4 10 ♕xe4+ ♕e7 11 ♗xc6+ (forced, for if 11 ♕xe7+ ♘gxe7 12 cxd4 b5 and Black wins a pawn with the typical Steinitzian pin break) 11...bxc6 12 ♕xe7+ ♘xe7 13 cxd4 ♘f5 and Black has the better ending.

9...♕e7 10 f3 b5 11 ♕d5 ♗d7 12 ♗b3 ♘f6 13 ♕g5 ♘xe4 14 ♕xe7+ ♗xe7 15 fxe4 ♖f8

The opening has led straight to an

ending that favours Black. White's e-pawn is isolated and weak, while Black has play down the f-file and indeed across the whole board.

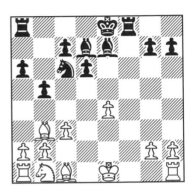

16 ♖f1 ♗h4+ 17 g3 ♗f6 18 ♗f4 b4 19 ♗c4 ♖b8 20 ♖f2 bxc3 21 bxc3 a5 22 ♖c2 g5 23 ♗e3 ♘e5 24 ♗e2 ♗a4 25 ♖c1 ♖b2

Suetin's impressive play has resulted in this absolute positional domination.

26 ♘a3 ♗c6 27 ♖cb1 ♘f3+! 28 ♔f2

If 28 ♗xf3 ♗xc3+ wins.

28...♗xc3 0-1

The positional advantage has taken solid form. There is no defence to

Black's last move; e.g. 29 ♖c1 ♘d4+ or 29 ♖xb2 ♗xb2 30 ♗xf3 ♗xa1 and wins.

Réti's line has not improved with age—Black still gets the advantage right out of the opening.

Game 44
Dar.Robinson-T.Taylor
US Open, Irvine 2010

1 e4 e5 2 ♘f3 ♘c6

Let's steal a moment from our serious Ruy Lopez study, and imagine that you are White and instead of the normal text move, your opponent plays the surprising 2...d5!? which already creates difficulty, as Tal writes: "I had never previously encountered in tournament practice the position after Black's 2nd move. White's first task was at least to remember the name of the opening. At the board I did not succeed in solving this problem."

Since I have a copy of Tim Harding's book *Counter Gambits*, I was able to look this up and solve Tal's first problem: the opening is the Queen's Pawn Counter-Gambit (I'm not at all sure how many chessplayers could rattle that one off!). The next problem one might face, if you were in Tal's shoes, was what to play—but the great Latvian solved *this* in exemplary fashion. He chose the natural capture 3 exd5 and then, after the counter-gambit idea 3...e4, refused to move the attacked knight and struck back with 4

♕e2!, when it turns out that White has obtained the better game from Morphy's day to our own—which explains why no one can remember "Queen's Pawn Counter-Gambit"—2...d5 is just not a very good move! Mr. *Fritz* gives White a "clear advantage" after 4 ♕e2, and practice verifies this. Here are some examples in historical order:

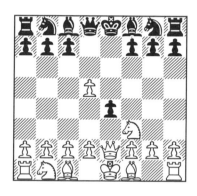

a) 4...♕e7 5 ♘d4 (White is just a pawn ahead) 5...♕e5 6 ♘b5 ♗d6 7 d4 ♕e7 8 c4 ♗b4+ 9 ♗d2 ♗xd2+ 10 ♘xd2 a6 11 ♘c3 f5 12 0-0-0 ♘f6 13 ♖e1 0-0 14 f3 (this central break gives White a decisive advantage) 14...b5 15 fxe4 fxe4 16 ♘dxe4 bxc4 17 ♕xc4 ♔h8 18 ♗d3 ♗b7 19 ♘xf6 ♕xf6 20 ♖hf1 ♕d8 21 ♖xf8+ ♕xf8 22 ♕b4! (Morphy finishes stylishly) 1-0 P.Morphy-A.Mongredien, Paris (6th matchgame) 1859.

b) 4...f5 (this is the Tal game) 5 d3 ♘f6 6 dxe4 fxe4 7 ♘c3 ♗b4 8 ♕b5+ ("Black sank deep into thought" – Tal) 8...c6 9 ♕xb4 exf3 10 ♗g5 cxd5 11 0-0-0 ♘c6 12 ♕a3 ♗e6 13 ♗c4 ♕e7 14 ♘xd5 ♕xa3 15 ♘c7+ ♔e7 16 ♖he1!! (Tal sacs a queen for a development tempo!)

16...♕c5 17 ♖xe6+ ♔f8 18 ♖xf6+ gxf6 19 ♘e6+ ♔e7 20 ♘xc5 fxg5 21 ♖d7+ ♔f6 22 ♖d6+ ♔e7 23 ♖e6+ ♔d8 24 ♘xb7+ ♔c7 25 ♗d5 ♘b4 26 ♗xf3 ♖ae8 27 ♘c5 ♘xa2+ 28 ♔b1 ♖xe6 29 ♘xe6+ ♔d7 30 ♘c5+ ♔d6 31 ♘d3 (after sac'ing everything, Tal ends up with a material advantage—Black resigns the technically lost endgame) 1-0 M.Tal-A.Lutikov, USSR Team Championship 1964.

c) 4...♘f6 5 d3 ♗e7 6 dxe4 0-0 7 ♘c3 ♖e8 8 ♗d2 b5 (wild and crazy, but otherwise no compensation can be seen) 9 ♕xb5 ♘a6 10 ♘d4 ♘xe4 11 ♘xe4 ♗f6 12 ♘e6! (White returns the piece to clarify matters) 12...fxe6 13 ♘xf6+ gxf6 14 0-0-0 exd5 15 ♗c3 c5 (Black suddenly noticed the coming 16 ♖xd5! and resigned before the bomb actually exploded) 1-0 V.Kotronias-P.Pandavos, Peristeri 1993.

All this looks pretty convincing, and it is! After 4 ♕e2 Black doesn't have enough for the pawn, which is why the opening is virtually never played today at the master level. But some masters will play it against a lower-rated opponent...

One day I was giving a lesson to a 1900 rated student. He started to show me a recent tournament game against a master, but he only got four moves in before I stopped him: 1 e4 e5 2 ♘f3 d5 3 exd5 e4 4 ♘d4?? ♕xd5. "Wait, wait!" I cried. "Why not 4 ♕e2?"

My student replied, "I knew that was the book move, but my opponent is a master, and I was sure he was booked up on the opening—so I got him out of his preparation."

I was struggling to remain calm. "But after 4...♕xd5 Black is already better! It's easy to see that Black controls all four central squares—he has more space, and an attack on White's knight—and he's not even a pawn down! If everyone could get this position after four moves with Black, then everyone would play..." but then I ran out of gas, as at that time, like Tal, I didn't know the name of the opening!

In any case, it turned out that my student, after his disastrous fourth move, lost quickly to the master who evidently counted on just this sort of play from a lower-rated opponent.

What does this have to do with the Siesta? Take a look at the note to White's sixth move!

3 ♗b5 a6 4 ♗a4 d6 5 c3 f5

"Black at once exerts such great pressure on the white e-pawn that 6 exf5 is more or less obligatory," writes Levy.

6 d3?!

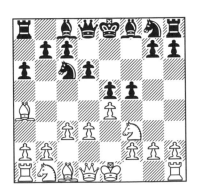

Maybe less, not more!

While I think the Siesta is a sound gambit (as opposed to the very doubtful Queen's Pawn Counter-Gambit), there is no question that if White plays the strongest line (6 exf5 ♗xf5 7 d4), he can force Black to play every move as though his life depended on it—one slip could be fatal!

Furthermore, if White plays the Boring Main Line with 6 exf5 ♗xf5 7 0-0 Black must know sixteen moves of theory—in order to draw.

But what if everyone could get the position after 6 d3 - ? Then the Siesta would be the most popular defence in all of the Ruy Lopez!

And what if everyone could get the position that sly master got against my student: 1 e4 e5 2 ♘f3 d5 3 exd5 e4 4 ♘d4 ♕xd5—then the Queen's Pawn Counter-Gambit would be the number one defence of all the open games!

What I was trying to convey to my student, but probably didn't succeed too well, is that in certain sharp openings, for example gambits like these two—*there is no good move but the main line.* You *can't* get out of book without getting the worse position.

Take this Siesta: Black now gets a central pawn majority, plus the f-file—for free! In other words, Black is already slightly better on move 6, and the ensuing fun was all mine. And this same weak move, 6 d3, was played against me in both of my tournament Siesta games!

Note also that MS gambiteer GM Yandemirov has faced 6 d3 twice, winning both times in under 30 moves, much as I do here.

6...♘f6

Of course this natural developing move can't be bad, but given the complications that White can stir up (with 8 ♘g5 instead of 8 dxc4), even though they probably favour Black, I think it's wiser to get the same kind of favourable position without running the risk of king walking!

Thus 6...fxe4 is simplest, and then 7 dxe4 (7 ♘g5 exd3 8 ♕xd3 ♘f6 doesn't give White anything) 7...♘f6 8 0-0 (8 ♗b3 ♗g4 returns to the main game where White can't even think of attacking) 8...♗g4 (but not 8...♘xe4? 9 ♘xe5 dxe5 10 ♕h5+ and White wins back his piece with advantage; e.g. 10...♔e7 11 ♗xc6 bxc6 12 ♕xe5+) 9 ♗g5 ♗e7 10 ♗b3 (this "preventing castling" move has no effect, as in the MS we can go both ways!) 10...♕d7 11 h3 ♗h5

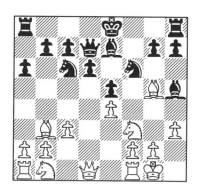

12 ♗xf6?! (White opens the g-file so Black can attack, and provides Black

with a second ...f5 lever—thank you, thank you very much! However, even on other moves Black's plan is simple: castle long and attack with ...h7-h6 and ...g7-g5, etc) 12...gxf6 13 ♕d3 ♗f8 14 ♘bd2 ♗h6 15 ♖fe1 ♘e7 16 ♔h2 ♘g6 17 g3 0-0-0 18 ♗c4 ♖hf8 19 ♗xa6 (a desperation sacrifice in the face of Black's mounting pressure) 19...♗xf3 20 ♘xf3 bxa6 21 ♕xa6+ ♔b8 22 ♖ed1 (or 22 a4 c6 23 ♖a3 ♕b7 and Black evades White's "attack") 22...♘e7 23 c4 ♕c6 24 ♕a3 ♔c8 25 ♖d3 f5 (the well-prepared lever) 26 c5 fxe4 27 cxd6 exd3 28 ♘xe5 ♖xf2+ (mate next is convincing) 0-1 V.Storchak-V.Yandemirov, Tomsk 1997.

7 ♗b3

My other Siesta game saw 7 0-0 ♗e7 8 ♗b3 ♘a5 9 ♗c2 0-0 and Black was already somewhat better and went on to win in J.Landaw-T.Taylor, Los Angeles (rapid) 2008.

Another quick Yandemirov pleasantry went 7 ♕e2 ♗e7 8 a3 0-0 9 ♗b3+ ♔h8 10 ♗g5 fxe4 11 dxe4 ♘h5 12 ♗xe7 ♕xe7 13 g3 ♗g4 14 ♘bd2 ♖xf3! 15 h3 ♘f4 16 gxf4 ♖xh3 17 ♖xh3 (or 17 ♕f1 ♖xh1 18 ♕xh1 exf4 with two extra pawns) 17...♗xe2 18 ♔xe2 exf4 19 ♖hh1 (and White resigned without even making it to move twenty) 0-1 N.Nazarov-V.Yandemirov, Tomsk 2004.

7...fxe4 8 dxe4

White should try 8 ♘g5 ♗g4 9 ♗f7+ ♔e7 10 f3 exf3 11 gxf3 ♗f5 12 ♗b3 (Black wins after 12 f4 h6 13 fxe5 ♘xe5 14 0-0 ♗g4) 12...d5, when Black has a

good centre and extra pawn but must contend with a dodgy king position. Mr. *Fritz* actually calls this a decisive advantage to Black, but I think White has practical chances that she never sees in the game.

8...♗g4

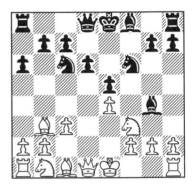

Now White just has a fixed, unpleasant structure, where Black has the f-file and central pawn majority, plus a clear plan of attack, while White essentially has no play at all.

9 ♕d3 ♕d7 10 ♘g5?

Too late, as Black is now developed and the move has no threat. 10 ♘bd2 is relatively better.

10...h6!

Compelling White to carry out her "threat" or retreat with loss of time. White reluctantly does the latter, since if she presses on with 11 ♘f7 ♖h7 the knight is trapped and soon lost, or if 11 ♗f7+ ♔d8 and a piece goes.

11 ♘f3 0-0-0

After eleven moves of one of the strongest openings, the Ruy Lopez, White is left struggling for a plan in a desperate position. That's where moves like 6 d3 will get you!

12 ♗a4 g5 13 h3 ♗h5 14 g4 ♗g6 15 ♘bd2 ♗g7 16 c4 ♔b8

Making ...♘b4 possible in some lines.

17 ♕e3 ♖hf8

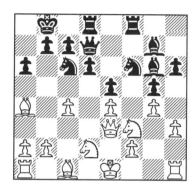

If White continues quietly, I intended simply to double on the f-file and play ...♘xe4!. White's desperate response allows a 19th century king hunt, much like my similar chase in Game 23—and we'll see yet another in the notes to Game 45!

18 0-0 h5!

Now that we know where the white king lives, material no longer matters.

19 ♗xc6 ♕xc6 20 ♕xg5 ♗xe4 21 ♘h4

If 21 ♘xe4 ♘xe4 22 ♕xg7 ♖xf3 with a winning attack.

21...hxg4!

A piece is certainly not too much to sacrifice in such a position.

22 ♕xg7 ♗d3

The bishop is a useful attacking piece, but the white rook may be an even more useful defender—so I would

be willing to exchange, especially in view of White's sleeping queenside pieces. In general, a black rook should defeat two pieces here (as in many Tal games) if two files open on the kingside.

Finally, though I didn't consciously think of this during the game, my move echoes Keres' 17...♗d3! from Game 34.

23 ♖e1 g3!!

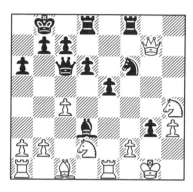

Decisive! The black g-pawn is in the way, either on the g-file, or (after taking on h3) on the h-file. Now an exchange is forced (as the following notes show), the g-file opens, and the white king is driven out to his doom.

24 ♘df3

White can't keep the kingside closed:

a) 24 f3 ♕c5+ 25 ♔h1 ♕f2 26 ♘g2 (if 26 ♘f1 ♗xf1 forces mate) 26...♖h8 27 h4 ♖xh4+ 28 ♘xh4 ♕h2 mate.

b) 24 ♕xg3 ♖g8 wins the queen.

c) 24 fxg3 ♕c5+ 25 ♔h1 (if 25 ♔g2 ♘h5 26 ♕h6 ♕f2+ 27 ♔h1 ♘xg3 mate, or 25 ♔h2 ♕f2+ 26 ♘g2 ♖g8 and wins) 25...♕f2 26 ♖g1 ♖g8 27 ♕f7 (if 27 ♕h6

♖xg3 with a winning attack) 27...♖xg3 (stronger than 27...♖d7 28 ♕e6 ♖e8 29 ♖g2 ♕e1+ 30 ♖g1 ♕xg1+ 31 ♔xg1 ♖xe6, though of course this clear exchange up position also wins for Black) 28 ♖xg3 ♕xg3 29 ♘hf3 (the black knight is taboo: 29 ♕xf6 ♖g8 and mates) 29...♖h8 30 h4 ♘g4 and mates.

24...gxf2+ 25 ♔xf2 ♘e4+ 26 ♔e3

White has to keep moving up, as the g-file is forbidden in view of the pin. Also impossible is 26 ♖xe4 ♗xe4, since Black will win the pinned knight on f3.

26...♗xc4

This quiet move prepares the final mating attack—White has no defence.

27 b3 ♕c5+! 28 ♔xe4 d5+ 29 ♔xe5 ♖de8+ 0-1

And mate next.

The only good sixth move for White is 6 exf5. After 6 d3 in this game—in *both* my Siesta games—I had only to worry about how best to use my central superiority and how best to attack down the f-file! As the notes show, Yandemirov also faced those same "problems"! Sometimes "book" is not just best, but *necessary*.

Conclusion

The Siesta, despite its occasional razor-sharp lines, is emphatically *not* a variation to play when you need to win at all costs. White has innumerable ways to play for a draw, and forced or close-to-forced draws (such as the current main line of Games 37-38) abound. On the other hand, it's deadly against the unprepared player who, like my two opponents, and two of Yandemirov's opponents, will inevitably play 6 d3 and go under quickly. Meanwhile the critical gambit line 6 exf5 ♗xf5 7 d4 e4 8 ♘g5 d5 9 f3 (Games 34-36) is very rarely played, but this is White's only real chance for advantage against the Siesta.

Chapter Five
The Yandemirov Gambit

The gambit that begins with **1 e4 e5 2 ♘f3 ♘c6 3 ♗b5 a6 4 ♗a4 d6 5 0-0 ♗g4 6 h3 h5!?**

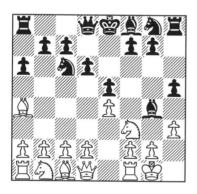

is so risky that our man Keres did not try it even once! This opening doesn't (or didn't) have a name, but I've rectified that by calling it the Yandemirov Gambit after the Russian GM who has played it at least 38 times against top flight opposition—he's made a solid score with Black (10 wins, 17 draws and 11 losses) and we already

know he bagged a World Champion (recall Smyslov-Yandemirov, Game 9).

Like the Siesta, this gambit is move order specific: obviously Black can't play it against 5 c3 since the piece sac shown above doesn't work if White hasn't castled. So once again, it's possible just to play solidly with the Knight Defence or the Bishop Defence.

However, *unlike* the Siesta, there are no boring drawish lines against this gambit! White must fight back immediately, as Fischer said and the first game of this chapter demonstrates, as otherwise Black has easy equality and chances to win.

Then why is this gambit not more popular? Simply this—in the current main line (Games 50-52 which all continue as follows: 7 d4 b5 8 ♗b3 ♘xd4 9 hxg4 ♘xb3 10 axb3 hxg4 11 ♘g5 ♕d7) Black sacrifices a bishop, right in the opening, for two pawns and attack. Not that many people are willing to speculate in this fashion, certainly not our mentor Mr. K!

So whose game can we use to start this chapter? Since five of the eight games will feature Yandemirov, it would seem overkill to put one his games first as well—I know, we can start with some IM for a change!

Game 45
M.Finneran-T.Taylor
US Open, Irvine 2010

1 e4 e5 2 ♘f3 ♘c6 3 ♗b5 a6 4 ♗a4 d6 5 0-0 ♗g4

Obviously Black can play 5...♗d7 here, and then follow with either ...♘e7-g6 (Chapter Two) or ...♘f6 and ...g7-g6 (Chapter Three). The Siesta is *not* possible: as we saw, Black lived or died by the ...♗d3 blockade, which is clearly not on the menu here. But if Black wants sharp play, he can emphatically get it with this straight-ahead attacking move that pins the white knight and immediately puts pressure on the opponent.

Before getting into the morass that is the gambit proper, we'll begin with White's non-challenging replies:

6 c3

In *My 60 Memorable Games* Fischer writes, after his move 6 h3: "It's important to kick immediately, otherwise after ...♕f6 followed by ...♗xf3 White's pawn formation could be smashed."

Exactly right! And yet many players, as here, simply ignore the threat! The text, 6 c3, which does absolutely nothing to stop this f-file doubling, is the second most popular move according to the database, and has been played literally hundreds of times!

Another fairly common move is 6 d3 which also allows Black a quick and easy attack, even if White can keep his pawn structure intact for the moment:

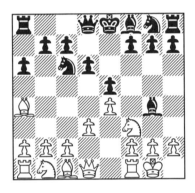

Black follows with 6...♕f6 7 ♘bd2 (defending f3 at the cost of shutting in the queen's bishop) 7...♘e7 8 c3 ♘g6 9 ♗xc6+ bxc6 10 ♕a4 ♗d7 11 ♕a5 ♘f4 12 d4 exd4 13 cxd4 ♗e7 14 ♘c4 ♘xg2! 15 ♗g5 (Black wins material after 15 ♔xg2 ♗h3+ 16 ♔g3 ♗xf1, and not 16 ♔xh3? ♕xf3 mate) 15...♕xf3 16 ♗xe7 ♘f4 0-1 P.Konigova-M.Staif, Czech Team Championship 2001.

Even after 6 h3 h5, White often has a cavalier attitude about the threat to the pinned knight. Once again the careless 7 c3 is common (instead of the sharp and correct 7 d4 or 7 ♗xc6+ bxc6 8 d4), and has even been played by

World Champion Anand (see the notes below). Of course this is no way to get an opening advantage with the white pieces—but Black might feel emboldened already to go for a win! Then 7...♕f6 is similar to the main game:

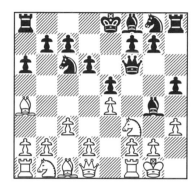

a) 8 d3 (active play from Anand!) 8...♗xf3 9 ♕xf3 ♕xf3 10 gxf3 ♘e7 (this is good but not the only way to play—our friend Yandemirov took a rest day with the following easy draw: 10...f5 11 f4 exf4 12 ♗xf4 fxe4 13 ♖e1 0-0-0 14 ♖xe4 ½-½ M.Saltaev-V.Yandemirov, Volgograd 1994) 11 f4 0-0-0 12 fxe5 dxe5 13 ♖d1 g6 14 ♗b3 f6 15 ♘a3 ♗h6 (White got rid of his doubled pawn, but the second f-pawn is backward) 16 ♘c4 ♗xc1 17 ♖axc1 f5 (Black has the initiative, but White defends well and makes his draw) 18 ♘e3 ♖d6 19 ♔f1 ♖f8 20 ♔e2 fxe4 21 dxe4 ♖df6 22 ♖f1 ♘d8 23 ♖cd1 ♘e6 24 ♗xe6+ ♖xe6 25 ♘d5 ♘xd5 26 ♖xd5 ½-½ V.Anand-J.Piket, Monte Carlo (blindfold rapid) 1993. Wouldn't it be nice if one could always handle the world champion so easily!

b) 8 ♗xc6+ bxc6 9 d4 ♗xf3 (an im-

portant point is that the captures on d4 and f3 have to be played in the correct move order, which is as here, taking on f3 first—if instead 9...exd4?? 10 hxg4 hxg4 11 ♘h2 ♕h4, White has the unexpected defensive move 12 ♗f4! and wins!) 10 ♕xf3 ♕xf3 11 gxf3 exd4 12 cxd4 and now:

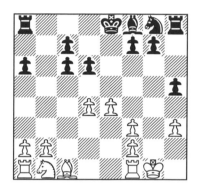

b1) 12...♘e7 (in line 'b2' future GM Vajda, who would grow up to crush me at a First Saturday event, shows his talent by developing his king first!—silly me, I brought out a piece here, and also got the better game—and even though my subsequent play lacked GM precision, the game is still worth seeing as yet another of my Modern Steinitz king hunts!) 13 ♗e3 g5 14 ♘d2 ♗h6 15 ♖fc1 ♔d7 16 ♖c3 f5 17 exf5 ♘xf5 (better is 17...♖hf8 18 ♘e4 ♖xf5 with some advantage) 18 ♖ac1 g4 19 ♗xh6 ♖xh6 20 ♖xc6 ♘xd4 21 ♖xc7+ ♔e6 22 ♖e1+ ♔d5 23 fxg4 (the result of my inaccurate play is that White could seize the advantage with 23 ♖d1, but my opponent wants material...) 23...hxg4 24 hxg4 ♖ah8 (...and now, two pawns up and without queens, falls to a vicious attack!) 25 ♔g2 ♖h2+ 26 ♔g3 ♖8h3+ 27 ♔f4 ♖xf2+ 28 ♔g5 (as in Game 23, the white king is driven up the g-file and finally forked!) 28...♖xd2 29 ♖f1 (White, reeling under the blows, misses the reverse cavalry attack) 29...♘e6+ 0-1 W.Kim-T.Taylor, Los Angeles (rapid) 2010.

b2) 12...♔d7 (now let's see Vajda's technical mastery) 13 ♘c3 g6 14 ♗e3 ♗h6 15 ♗xh6 ♘xh6 16 f4 (the front doubleton advances, but the whole kingside pawn complex is still weak) 16...♖ab8 17 b3 ♖he8 18 f3 h4 19 ♖ac1 ♘g8 20 ♔f2 ♘f6 21 ♔e3 ♖b4 22 ♖g1 ♘d5+ 23 ♘xd5 cxd5 24 ♔d3 c5 25 dxc5 dxe4+ 26 ♔e3 d5 27 c6+ ♔c7 28 ♖gd1 d4+ 29 ♔f2 (Black also wins after 29 ♖xd4 exf3+ 30 ♔d3 ♖xd4+ 31 ♔xd4 f2 32 ♖f1 ♖e2) 29...f5 30 ♖g1 d3 31 ♔e3 exf3+ 32 ♔xf3 ♖be4 33 ♖gd1 ♖e3+ 34 ♔f2 ♖xh3 35 ♖c3 ♖e2+ 36 ♔g1 ♖g3+ 37 ♔f1 ♖ee3 38 ♖d2 ♖ef3+ and White resigned in the face of Black's mating attack: 0-1 G.Bakhtadze-L.Vajda, World Junior Championship, Szeged 1994. Note that in both of these sample games, Black's attack persisted after the exchange of queens, which is not uncommon in this gambit.

6...♕f6

As Fischer warned so long ago, White's pawn structure will now be smashed, and there's nothing he can do about it! Black is already equal.

7 ♗xc6+

It is no better to play à la Anand

with 7 d3 ♗xf3 8 ♕xf3 ♕xf3 9 gxf3 and then:

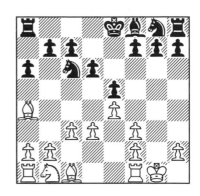

a) 9...f5 10 d4 b5 11 ♗b3 exd4 12 exf5 ♘ge7 13 ♗e6 dxc3 14 ♘xc3 ♘d4 15 ♔g2 ♘exf5 and Black was a pawn up and went on to win in Ismetsan1956-Taylor, playchess.com (blitz) 2010.

b) 9...♘e7 10 f4 0-0-0 (also good is 10...exf4 11 ♗xf4 g5! 12 ♗e3 f5 13 f3 0-0-0 14 d4 d5 15 ♘d2 dxe4 16 fxe4 f4—Black's kingside pawns at least balance White's centre—17 ♗f2 ♘g6 18 ♘f3 ♗e7 19 ♗b3 h5 20 ♗f7 ♖h6 21 d5 ♘ge5 22 ♘xe5 ♘xe5 23 ♗e6+ ♔b8 24 ♗d4 ♘c4 25 ♖f2 c5!—Black takes over the advantage after this fine blow, which forces a favourable minor piece exchange—26 ♗g7 ♖g6 27 b3 ♖xg7 28 bxc4 ♗f6 29 ♖c1 ♗e5 30 h3 g4 31 hxg4 hxg4 32 ♖g2 f3 0-1 M.Duppel-F.Zeller, Willsbach 1997) 11 ♗b3 f6 12 f5 g5 13 fxg6 (better is 13 h4, trying to pry open some lines for the white bishops) 13...hxg6 14 ♘d2 d5 15 ♖d1 ♗h6 16 ♘f1 f5! (again we see a wave of coordinated black pawns marching up the board, while the white kingside infantry is split and weak—future GM Luke McShane is in a very difficult position, and will need all his defensive skills plus luck to hold) 17 ♗xh6 ♖xh6 18 ♘e3 d4 19 ♘d5 ♖dh8 20 ♘xe7+ ♘xe7 21 cxd4 exd4 22 ♔f1 ♖xh2 23 ♔e2 ♖8h3 24 exf5 ♘xf5 25 ♗e6+ ♔d8 26 ♗xf5 gxf5 27 ♖f1 f4 28 ♖ae1 ♔d7 29 ♖g1 f3+ (Black should win with 29...♖e3+ 30 ♔d2 ♖xf2+ or 30 ♔f1 ♖xd3 as he picks off a clean pawn in both variations) 30 ♔f1 ♖h1 31 ♖e5 ♔d6 32 ♖eg5 ♖h6 33 ♖f5 ♖xg1+ 34 ♔xg1 ♖e6 35 ♖xf3 ♖e2 36 ♖f4 c5 37 ♖f6+ ♔c7 38 ♖f7+ ♔c6 39 ♖f6+ ♔b5 40 ♖f7 b6 41 f4 ♖xb2 42 f5 ♖d2 43 f6 ♖xd3 44 ♔g2 ♖d2+ 45 ♔g3 ½-½ L.McShane-T.Upton, Isle of Lewis 1995.

7...bxc6 8 d4 ♗xf3 9 gxf3

If 9 ♕xf3 exd4 10 ♕xf6 (weaker is 10 cxd4 ♕xd4 and White's compensation looks doubtful; e.g. 11 ♘c3 ♕f6 12 ♕d1 ♕e6 13 ♕a4 ♕d7 14 ♗f4 ♘e7 15 ♖fe1 ♘g6 16 ♗g3 ♗e7 and Black maintains his material advantage while completing development) 10...♘xf6 11 cxd4 ♗e7 12 ♘c3 ♔d7 (this set-up, with Black's pawns at c7/c6/d6 and the king neatly sheltered at d7, also occurred in the Vajda game given above—let's call this the "Vajda cluster", often a safe and active endgame arrangement that occurs frequently in the Yandemirov Gambit) 13 f3 ♖ab8 with equality.

9...♘e7 10 ♔h1 ♘g6

Black blockades the doubled pawns

and prepares kingside play.

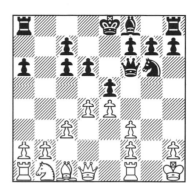

11 ♖g1 ♗e7

As the black queen has adequate squares, there's no reason to panic about ♗g5—in fact, I welcome the exchange, as once the dark-squared bishops are gone, my knight will have free access to the hole at f4.

12 ♗g5 ♕e6 13 ♕a4

Both sides have doubled pawns, but Black's lead in development tips the balance.

13...0-0 14 ♕xc6

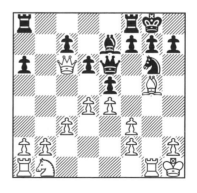

White may as well take, for if 14 ♘d2 ♗xg5 15 ♖xg5 ♖ab8 16 ♘b3 f6 17 ♖gg1 ♖b6 and Black is clearly better, with an advantage stretching from the b-file to the attack squares f4 and h3.

14...♕h3

Black has no less than three ways to recover material here and try to nail down an advantage—perhaps characteristically, I chose the most complicated path. Simpler is 14...♗xg5 15 ♖xg5 ♕f6 (or even 15...exd4 16 cxd4 ♕f6 with a small advantage) 16 ♖g3 ♖ab8! (a key move that weakens the a1-h8 diagonal, where my queen exerts great pressure) 17 b3 exd4 18 cxd4 ♕xd4 19 ♕c3 ♕xf2 20 ♘d2 ♖b5 and White has no real compensation for the pawn.

15 ♘d2 ♗xg5 16 ♖xg5

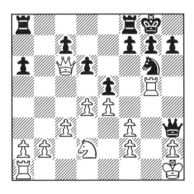

16...♕h6!?

But I liked this third path: an extremely unusual skewer! Strangely enough, neither threatened piece can defend the other, as ♘f3 or ♖g2 is either illegal or ineffectual. White must shed material to stop Black's attack—unfortunately, White does have a good sacrifice, which was missed by both players.

17 f4

White has an extremely unusual rook sacrifice that ultimately retains equality: 17 ♖ag1 f6 18 ♖5g2! ♕xd2 19 ♕d5+ ♔h8 20 ♖xg6! hxg6 21 ♖g3 ♕h6 22 ♔g2 and White emerges with a queen vs. two rooks and about an even game.

17...♘xf4 18 ♖g3 exd4 19 cxd4 ♘h3

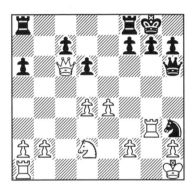

20 ♘b3?!

I expected 20 ♘c4, when I intended to sac a piece: 20...♘xf2+ 21 ♔g2 f5! with a tremendous attack (note that Black should not play 21...♕f4 22 ♖e1 ♘g4 here, as White holds e3 and can play 23 ♖f1 with a counter-attack) 22 ♔xf2 (also losing is 22 exf5 ♖ae8 23 ♕d5+ ♔h8 24 ♔xf2 ♕xh2+ 25 ♖g2 ♕f4+ 26 ♔g1 ♖xf5 27 ♕c6 ♕xd4+ 28 ♔h2 ♖h5+ 29 ♔g3 ♕h4+ 30 ♔f3 ♖f5 mate) 22...♕xh2+ 23 ♖g2 (23 ♔f3 fxe4+ 24 ♔g4 h5+ is a quick death) 23...fxe4+ and wins.

Mr. *Fritz*'s 20 ♕c2 is evidently the only try—but it's a very hard move for a human to play or even contemplate: giving up a pawn with check while retreating his only active piece! Yet White might then survive the attack after 20...♘xf2+ 21 ♔g2 f5 22 exf5 ♖ae8 23 ♔xf2 ♕xh2+ 24 ♖g2 ♕h4+ (not 24...♖e2+ 25 ♔xe2 ♕xg2+ 26 ♔d3 ♕h3+ 27 ♔c4 ♖xf5 28 ♕d3 and White's piece is more important than Black's passed pawns) 25 ♔g1 ♕xd4+ 26 ♔h1 ♖e3 27 ♕c4+ ♕xc4 28 ♘xc4 ♖h3+ 29 ♔g1 ♖xf5 with three pawns for the piece and rough equality. Therefore Black might have nothing better than 20...♖ab8 with about an even game—which (given that White also had the surprising rook sacrifice seen in the note to move 17) is an argument, using computer logic, for the simple 14...♗xg5 and 15...♕f6, when Black could have obtained the advantage without giving the opponent any tactical chances.

But, on the other hand, the mind-bending complications of my line caused my opponent to blunder here with 20 ♘b3—so perhaps, by human logic, my move was best!

20...♘xf2+ 21 ♔g1

At this point my opponent noticed that after 21 ♔g2 the knight is not trapped: Black has 21...♕f4 22 ♖f1 (unlike the similar position with the white knight on c4, here 22 ♖e1 does nothing, since 22...♘g4 23 ♖f1? loses to 23...♘e3+) 22...♕xe4+ and Black cleans up.

21...♘h3+

Black has pirated a pawn.

22 ♔h1 ♖ae8 23 ♖e1 ♕h4 24 e5

Black keeps his pawn after 24 ♘d2 ♖e7 25 ♕xa6 ♘f2+ 26 ♔g2 ♘xe4.

24...dxe5 25 dxe5

If 25 ♕g2 ♘f4! 26 ♖xg7+ ♔h8 and Black wins: both the white queen and e1-rook are attacked, and ...♘g6, entombing the other rook, is a huge threat.

25...♘f2+

Black introduces a new and precisely calculated combination.

26 ♔g1 ♘d3 27 ♖e4 ♘xe5!

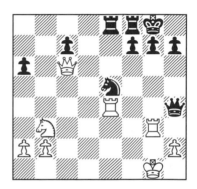

The magic knight destroys White's centre—what's left is purely technical.

28 ♖xh4

28 ♕xe8 ♕xe4 and 28 ♕c2 ♘f3+ 29 ♖xf3 ♕xe4 are even worse.

28...♘xc6 29 ♖c4 ♖e6 30 ♖gc3 ♘e7 31 ♘c5

Not 31 ♖xc7 ♘d5 forking.

31...♖g6+ 32 ♔f2 ♖d8 33 ♖e3 ♘f5 34 ♖e2 ♖c6 35 b4 g6 36 ♖ce4 ♘d6 37 ♖4e3

If 37 ♖e7 a5 38 a3 axb4 39 axb4 ♘f5 repels the invader.

37...a5 38 a3 axb4 39 axb4 ♖b6 0-1

Now that this black rook is activated, White has no compensation whatsoever for two missing pawns.

Note how easy Black's game is in these non-challenging lines, even when your opponent is someone like Anand or McShane!

White *must* enter the complications with 6 h3 (just as 6 exf5 is necessary in the Siesta) and *must* avoid pawn structure destruction on the kingside if he is to play for advantage—but as we'll see in the rest of the games in this chapter, that means "fire on board" and blow for blow on practically every move.

> ### Game 46
> ### V.Zheliandinov-V.Yandemirov
> ### Lvov 1995

1 e4 e5 2 ♘f3 ♘c6 3 ♗b5 a6 4 ♗a4 d6 5 0-0 ♗g4 6 h3 h5

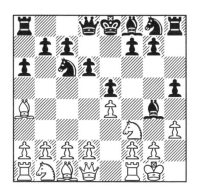

I think that this, the Yandemirov Gambit proper, is the only principled move. Black maintains the pin and threatens pawn structure demolition with ...♕f6, as in the previous game. I will not cover the alternative 6...♗h5,

as we already saw the Fischer-Geller debacle in the notes to Game 9.

White must now try to free himself from the pin—of course Black is sacrificing a piece, even if for the moment it's not advisable to capture.

7 ♗xc6+

One of the two main lines, which will be covered in this and the following two games: White prevents Black from reinforcing the pin with ...b7-b5 and ...♘d4.

7 d4 is the other main line, and absolutely critical: I will examine this in detail in Games 49-52.

Lesser alternatives are:

a) 7 hxg4 is very rare, though it's not quite as bad as one might think: 7...hxg4 8 ♖e1 (but not 8 ♘e1?? ♕h4 9 f4 g3 and mates) 8...gxf3 9 ♕xf3 ♕h4, and now 10 ♕g3?? ♕h1 mate (as in J.Hruska-Jar.Smid, Neratovice 1992) is typical, but in fact White can play 10 ♗xc6 bxc6 11 g3 ♕h2+ 12 ♔f1, avoiding both mate and material loss— though of course after, let's say, 12...♕h3+ 13 ♕g2 ♕e6 Black stands somewhat better in view of his long-term attacking chances on the open h-file.

b) 7 c3 ♕f6 gives Black a good game, as Anand discovered (see the notes to Game 45).

c) 7 c4 is a delayed Duras Variation (see Chapter Seven) which shouldn't cause Black any serious trouble, as long as he switches gears and plays positionally:

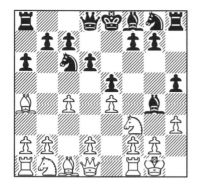

c1) The usual 7...♛f6 is somewhat suspect here, since White's next both unpins and hits b7, introducing even more insane complications than usual; e.g. 8 ♕b3 ♗xf3 9 ♕xb7 ♕g6 10 ♗xc6+ ♔e7 11 g3 ♕g4!? 12 d4! (the queen can't be taken: 12 hxg4 hxg4 and mates) 12...♔f6 (but now if 12...♕xh3 13 ♗g5+ and *White* mates this time!) 13 ♕b3 ♖b8 14 hxg4 hxg4 15 ♕xf3+ (in my opinion this is too many queen sacrifices to have in just 15 moves!) 15...gxf3 16 ♘d2 ♘e7 17 dxe5+ dxe5 18 ♗d7 1-0 S.Khavsky-S.Korolev, Leningrad 1963.

c2) 7...♗xf3 8 ♕xf3 g6 is a more rational system! Now Black has a grip on d4 that White will have to work hard to shake, and the game is approximately even; e.g. 9 ♕b3 ♕c8 (9...♖b8 looks better to me, similar to various previously covered Siesta ♕b3 lines) 10 f4 ♗g7 11 fxe5 ♗xe5 12 c5 ♘f6 13 ♕e3 ♘d7 14 ♗xc6 (not 14 cxd6? ♗d4) 14...bxc6 15 d4 ♗g7 ½-½ S.Azarov-D.Sermek, Turin Olympiad 2006.

7...bxc6 8 d3

Here we'll take one more look at Smyslov's quiet move, previously seen in Game 9; one recalls that Yandemirov scored 3-0 as Black against this (the third game is referenced in the note to move 9).

The next two main games will feature the more challenging 8 d4.

8...♕f6

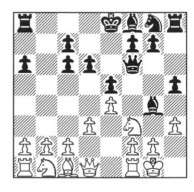

9 ♘bd2

We already saw in the analysis of Smyslov-Yandemirov that taking the bishop was too dangerous for White, but the alternative 9 ♖e1 worked no better against our favourite gambiteer. This move, as we have seen in similar positions before, allows Black to give White doubled f-pawns. Even if White gets rid of them later, the first player will still be left with an unstable kingside that Black can use for attack: 9...♗xf3 10 ♕xf3 ♕xf3 11 gxf3 ♘e7 12 f4 (White gets rid of his doubled pawns, but not for free!) 12...exf4 13 ♗xf4 g5! (Yandemirov strikes with the first, and very typical blow—the pawn is immune in view of 14 ♗xg5 ♖g8 15 h4 f6, so Black takes over the initiative) 14 ♗e3 ♗g7 15 c3 g4 16 hxg4 hxg4 17 ♘d2 ♔d7 (note the Vajda cluster again—the black king is safe throughout the whole game, quite unlike the white king!) 18 ♔g2 ♖ab8 19 ♖ab1 ♘g6 20 d4 f5! (Black opens lines and continues to attack) 21 exf5 ♘h4+ 22 ♔g3 ♘xf5+ 23 ♔xg4 ♖bf8 24 ♖h1 (now all three kingside files open and White's position becomes desperate; there were still reasonable defensive chances with 24 ♗g5, creating a shelter for the white king, though of course Black can at least draw after 24...♘h6+) 24...♘xe3+ 25 fxe3 ♗h6 26 ♘c4?! (26 ♖hf1, giving back the pawn, is the only hope) 26...♖hg8+ 27 ♔h5 ♗f4! (slamming the door) 28 ♖hg1 (there are no saves: 28 exf4 ♖g2 and 28 ♖bf1 ♖g5+ both lead to mate) 28...♖xg1 29 ♖xg1 ♖h8+ 30 ♔g4 ♖g8+ 31 ♔xf4 ♖xg1 0-1 I.Bukavshin-V.Yandemirov, Voronezh 2007. Black will win the exchange up ending by attacking the queenside pawns with his rook and then evicting White's knight with ...d6-d5.

Once again we see that White *must* react to the threat of spoiling the pawns, if he does not want to be in the unpleasant situation of fighting only to draw.

9...♘e7 10 ♖e1 ♗d7

So far, so Smyslov (Game 9) but now, as opposed to Smyslov's 11 ♘f1, Zheli goes his own way.

11 ♘c4 ♘g6 12 d4 ♕e6

Black gains an important tempo to shore up his centre; e.g. 13 b3 f6 with a solid position. White prevents this with his next, but in so doing relieves Black of his doubled pawns and takes the direct pressure off e5—basically, Black has equalized.

13 d5 cxd5 14 exd5 ♕e7 15 ♕d3 ♕d8 16 ♘d4

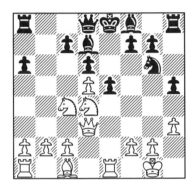

16...♗e7

The computer move 16...♕f6 may be objectively best—this would be the typical "theoretical success" for Black, as White has nothing better than to repeat the position with 17 ♘f3. However, Yandemirov wants to win and is willing to take some risks!

17 ♘e6 ♕c8 18 ♘xg7+

According to our friend Mr. *Fritz*, White can get a slight advantage with the following convoluted variation: 18 f4 ♗f6 19 fxe5 ♘xe5 20 ♘xe5 dxe5 21 ♘g5 ♗f5 22 ♘e4 ♗h4 23 ♖f1 0-0 24 ♘f6+ ♗xf6 25 ♖xf5 and there's the dreaded "plus equals"—but I wouldn't accept this as gospel. For instance, Black might improve at the beginning with 18...♗h4!? 19 ♖f1 ♗f6 20 fxe5

♘xe5 21 ♘xe5 ♗xe5 22 ♕f3 ♗xe6 23 dxe6 f6 24 ♗f4 ♔e7!, when it's not at all clear that White can gain any advantage from Black's centralized king.

Although Yandemirov's play is risky, it's not unsound—and his boldness puts White on the defensive and induces errors.

18...♔f8 19 ♘e6+ ♗xe6 20 dxe6 ♕xe6

Black recovers his material, with great central pawns and the open g-file for attack.

21 f4 ♘h4!

Targeting g2, while the pawn cannot move forward (22 g3? ♕xh3 wins).

22 ♗d2

Relatively best is 22 fxe5 ♖g8 23 ♖e2 d5 24 ♘d2 with defensive chances, though Black still has a strong attack.

22...♖g8 23 ♖e2 e4!

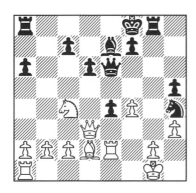

This Falkbeerian blow decides matters: with central domination and the g-file attack, Black now wins in a few moves.

24 ♖xe4

The other capture also fails: 24 ♕xe4 ♕xe4 25 ♖xe4 d5 forks; and if

White dodges, then 24 ♕c3 ♗f6 25 ♕b3 ♘f3+ 26 ♔f1 ♘d4 forks in another way!

24...♖xg2+ 25 ♔h1

25 ♔f1 ♕g6 is also hopeless.

25...♕g6 26 ♖xe7

Since avoiding mate costs a rook (26 ♖e2 ♕xd3 27 cxd3 ♖xe2) White may as well allow the pretty finish.

26...♖h2+! 0-1

Despite Yandemirov's 100% score against this subvariation, one can't describe it as a walkover for Black. Both Smyslov and Zheliandinov had their chances (but not Bukavishin, who could only hope to draw after allowing his kingside to be destroyed), but the fact is that Yand was better prepared for the middlegame positions that can arise. Basically, Black gets violent attacking chances, while White, with exact play, can also try to exploit Black's own dodgy king position and queenside pawn weaknesses. All in all, 8 d3 is not a threat to the Yandemirov Gambit, but it does lead to interesting double-edged play.

In the remainder of the games in this chapter, White goes all out to refute the gambit with an early d2-d4, either after ♗xc6 or straight away—all these lines are razor sharp and critical for both sides.

I mentioned in the introduction that once I started studying the MS in preparation for this book, I succeeded in scoring 7-0 with Black! However, how about *before* I started studying? Then my results were spotty, and one of the spottiest will be seen in the notes to Black's 8th move in the following game, in which I make a fundamental positional error in the opening. The MS *must* be studied before playing, especially the gambit lines as here!

Game 47
S.Sjugirov-V.Yandemirov
St Petersburg 2005

1 e4 e5 2 ♘f3 ♘c6 3 ♗b5 a6 4 ♗a4 d6 5 0-0 ♗g4 6 h3 h5 7 ♗xc6+

Remember the line 7 c3 ♕f6 8 ♗xc6+ bxc6 9 d4 ♗xf3 10 ♕xf3 ♕xf3 11 gxf3 exd4 12 cxd4 ♔d7,

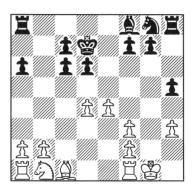

referenced in Game 45, where Black had a good game with his Vajda cluster? Keep this position in mind!

7...bxc6 8 d4

Clearly stronger than 8 d3, this is a real try for advantage: White threatens simply to take on e5.

8...♗xf3

Best. Black must switch from offering his own gambit to accepting White's temporarily sacrificed d-pawn. This move does seem a little illogical (didn't we just play ...h7-h5 to maintain the pin?) and the "natural" (but bad!) move is 8...♕f6. I've talked many times so far in this chapter about the advantages of doubling White's f-pawns, but this is the exception! It's interesting that 8...♕f6 is so natural that Yandemirov himself played it three times early in his career (and scored a miserable one draw and two losses, after which he never played it again). Likewise I, not knowing any better in my pre-study days, also cavalierly played this move—only to find out after the game that I had lost in practically the same way as another unfortunate (that game will also be referenced below). The key factor is that in this particular case Black's queenside pawns are not clustered but rather isolated—and Black has insufficient kingside play to compensate for this weakness, as we will see: so after 8...♕f6?! 9 dxe5! (Yandemirov's opponents all played 9 ♘bd2 which is not bad—but I think the text, forcibly splitting Black's pawns, is even stronger) 9...dxe5 10 ♗e3 ♗xf3 (unless Black takes, White will play ♘bd2 and so consolidate and brush off the pin with no inconveniences) 11 ♕xf3 ♕xf3 12 gxf3, take a look now at this diagram:

Black has three isolated pawns on the queenside, and the c-pawns are particularly weak. Note how Vajda neatly covered his queenside with ...♚d7!, whereas here that would be far too risky in view of the open d-file.

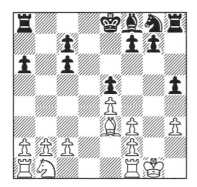

Yes, White's kingside pawns are weak, too, but at least they have a cluster, and the queens are off so a king attack (as I will try) has little chance of success. Meanwhile White can play forever against the weak islands on the queenside. In short, this position offers White a stable advantage, ideal for a Grandmaster grind—with me being on the wrong side of the grind: 12...f5 (12...♗d6 13 ♘d2 ♘e7 14 ♘c4 is also better for White: one can see that Black's position is full of fixed targets) 13 ♖d1! (I think GM Ivanov's move is strongest, though White was also slightly better in the following earlier game: 13 exf5 ♘e7 14 ♘d2 ♘xf5 and White has the useful e4-square, and only three isolated pawns as against Black's four—White went on to win in T.Wessendorf-U.Liley, German League 2007) 13...f4 14 ♗c1 ♗d6 (14...♖h6 15 ♔f1 ♖d6 16 ♔e2 doesn't save Black, since the pawn weaknesses will tell in

the long run) 15 ♘d2 0-0-0 16 ♘c4 g5 17 b3 ♘e7 18 ♗b2 ♘g6 19 ♖d3 (Black is tied down to e5, so my kingside demonstration doesn't work...) 19...g4 (but if Black defends passively, then 19...♖h7 20 ♖ad1 ♖hd7 21 ♔f1 reaches a position where Black is virtually in zugzwang, and I'm sure this could never be held against a master, let alone a GM!) 20 ♖ad1 ♘h4 21 fxg4 hxg4 22 hxg4 ♖hg8 23 ♔f1 ♖xg4 24 ♘xe5 ♖g2 25 ♘f3 ♖g4 26 e5 ♗e7 27 ♘xh4 ♖xh4 28 ♖xd8+ ♗xd8 29 ♔g2 ♗e7 30 ♔f3 ♗g5 31 ♖g1 ♗h6 32 e6 ♖h3+ 33 ♔e4 ♔d8 34 ♗f6+ ♔e8 35 ♖d1 1-0 A.Ivanov-T.Taylor, Asheville 2009.

In general, doubled pawns on the c-file are part and parcel of the Ruy Lopez and are not to be feared—but doubled *isolated* pawns on the c-file can be quite weak and should be avoided *unless* Black has such active play that the pawn weaknesses are not felt; for example if, on the next move, White took back with the pawn: 9 gxf3? ♕h4 10 ♔g2 ♘e7! 11 dxe5 ♘g6 12 exd6 ♗xd6, when Black does have weak, doubled isolated c-pawns—but such a tremendous attack that the position must be assessed clear advantage to Black!

Of course the top players, like the rising young GM Sjugirov (I faced his technical mastery in Hungary, where he convincingly won the First Saturday event in which we both competed) will always take with the queen to avoid pawn disruption—even though White is temporarily sacrificing a pawn.

9 ♕xf3 exd4

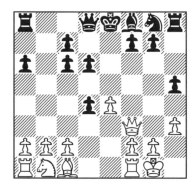

Black is a pawn up, but he won't insist on keeping it—the plan is to make White lose time recovering the material. Most important, Black has kept his queenside c7/c6/d6 cluster together, and so obtains a reasonable game.

10 ♖d1

White tries to get his pawn back directly, but Yandemirov has this covered. The latest try is 10 ♖e1, for which see the next game.

On the direct 10 e5 I like the simple 10...♕d7 (though our hero has played 10...d5, and after 11 c3 dxc3 12 ♘xc3 ♘e7 13 e6 fxe6 14 ♖e1 ♕d7 15 ♗g5 ♘c8 16 ♕f5 ♕f7 17 ♖xe6+ ♗e7 18 ♕e5 ♔d7 actually won this deranged position in S.Zhigalko-V.Yandemirov, Saratov 2006—but I don't recommend such wild play!) 11 ♖e1 ♗e7 transposing to note 'd2' to Black's tenth move in the next game.

10...♕f6 11 ♕b3

White should get nothing from the queen exchange: 11 ♕xf6 ♘xf6 12

♖xd4 g6 13 ♖c4 and now, as we have learned, the obvious move is 13...♔d7 with the Vajda cluster and an equal ending—instead, in P.Mitrovic-D.Sermek, Belgrade 1989, Black played the inexplicable 13...♗g7?? and after 14 ♖xc6 ♘xe4 15 ♖xc7 lost a pawn and eventually the game.

11...♘e7 12 ♕b7

The very high rated Peter Svidler got nowhere with the gambit 12 c3, as Yand, with a "pawn to give", just used the time to reposition his queen: 12...♕e6 13 ♕b7 ♕c8 14 ♕xc8+ ♖xc8 15 cxd4 f5 16 e5 ♘d5, when Black was solid and held the draw in P.Svidler-V.Yandemirov, Russian Team Championship 2003.

12...♖d8

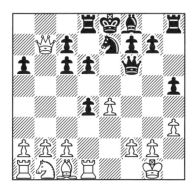

This is Yand's improvement on a previous game, in which White was able to offer a delayed gambit while the black knight was tied to the rook: 12...♖c8 (while the rook is defending a pawn, the black knight is defending the rook—not a lot of mobility there!) 13 c3 ♕e5 14 ♕xa6 ♕xe4 15 cxd4 ♕f5 16

♖e1 ♔d7 17 ♘a3 g6 and now, instead of 18 ♗e3 when White won after a fluctuating struggle in A.Slizhevsky-V.Yandemirov, Moscow 2005, White could have obtained a stable advantage with 18 h4!. The idea is to develop the bishop to the more active g5-square, which will practically force the weakening ...f7-f6—which means White will have targets at e6, e7 and c6.

Thus the present avoidance!

13 c3

Black's last move also functions as a deflecting pawn sac. If White captures 13 ♕xc7, then his queen is far out of play, while Black launches a kingside attack with 13...g5!. Note that in all such positions in the Yandemirov Gambit, Black can open kingside lines because of the ...g5-g4 lever, a legacy of White's necessary 6 h3. Now White rushes to get his queen back in time: 14 ♕b6 ♗g7 15 ♕xa6 g4 16 ♕d3 ♘g6 17 c3 ♘e5 18 ♕g3 h4 (although this finally leads to a drawn ending, I think Black has more winning chances with 18...d3!, intending 19 ♗f4 ♗h6! with sharp counterplay) 19 ♕f4 dxc3 20 ♘xc3 gxh3 21 ♕xf6 ♗xf6 22 gxh3 ♔e7 23 ♖b1 ♖a8 24 ♗e3 ♖hb8 (Black has set up a perfect Benko type position, with full compensation for the pawn) 25 b3 ♘f3+ 26 ♔g2 ♗xc3 27 ♔xf3 ♖xa2 28 ♖dc1 ♖b2 29 ♖xb2 ♗xb2 30 ♖c6 ♖b3 31 ♖b6 ♖xb6 32 ♗xb6 ♗f6 33 ♔g4 ♔e6 34 f3 d5 35 exd5+ ♔xd5 36 ♔f5 ♗e7 37 ♗e3 ♗d8 38 ♗h6 (Black also holds the

pawn ending: 38 ♗g5 ♗xg5 39 ♔xg5 ♔e5 40 ♔xh4 ♔f4 41 ♔h5 ♔xf3 42 h4 ♔g3 43 ♔g5 f6+ and draws) 38...♗d4 39 ♔g4 ♔d3 40 f4 ♔e4 41 ♗g5 f6 42 ♔xh4 ½-½ I.Gerasimov-V.Yandemirov, Kazan 2008.

13...g5!

Again, we see Yand's basic idea: White has three possible pawn captures, but Black plays the same way against any—attack!

14 ♕xa6 g4

This move would also have been played against 14 cxd4 or 14 ♕xc7—that cuts down on the thinking time!

15 ♕d3

15 cxd4 gxh3 16 gxh3 ♕g6+, picking off the e-pawn, obviously favours Black—so White hurries back to defend.

15...dxc3 16 ♘xc3 ♘g6 17 ♘e2 ♗g7 18 ♕b3 ♕e6!

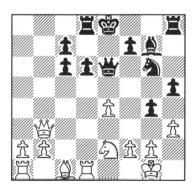

Black's queen is too strong, so White must exchange—but in the coming ending Black has activity on both flanks, while White's queenside is still undeveloped.

19 ♖d3 ♕xb3 20 ♖xb3 ♔d7

The Vajda cluster again!

21 ♖b1 ♖a8 22 a3 ♖a4 23 f3 gxf3 24 gxf3 f5!

Black smashes White's centre and stands clearly better.

25 exf5 ♘h4 26 ♖d3 ♖c4 27 ♗g5 ♘xf5 28 ♖c1 ♖xc1+ 29 ♗xc1 c5 30 ♔f2 ♖b8

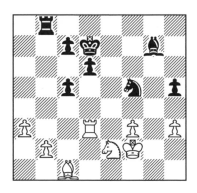

Note that Black has excellent Benko Gambit play (as in the Gerasimov game above), but without being a pawn down!

The young Sjugirov is very strong in positions he understands (as I found out from my game against him in Budapest—he went for the Karpovian positional edge with 3 ♘d2 against my French, and I never got counterplay), but he can't get his bearings in Yandemirov's wild whirlpool!

31 b3 ♗d4+ 32 ♔e1 ♖e8 33 ♔d1 ♖g8 34 b4 ♔c6 35 bxc5 ♗xc5 36 ♖b3 ♖g2 37 ♖b8 ♖h2 38 ♖f8 ♘d4 39 ♘xd4+ ♗xd4 40 ♗d2 ♔d5 41 ♖f4 ♖xh3 42 a4 c5 43 a5 ♖h1+ 44 ♔e2 ♔c4 45 ♗e3 ♖h2+ 46 ♔f1 ♖a2 47 ♗xd4 cxd4

Black's doubled isolated pawns are stronger than White's outside passed pawn.

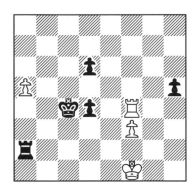

48 ♖f5 d3 49 ♔e1 ♔c3 50 ♖d5 ♖a1+ 51 ♔f2 d2 52 ♔e2 ♖e1+ 0-1

An elegant win by Yandemirov.

The basic ideas of this variation are clearly seen here: Black must not count pawns, but rather count on counterplay with the bayonet attack ...g5-g4.

Game 48
M.Ozolin-V.Yandemirov
Izhevsk 2009

1 e4 e5 2 ♘f3 ♘c6 3 ♗b5 a6 4 ♗a4 d6 5 0-0 ♗g4 6 h3 h5 7 ♗xc6+ bxc6 8 d4 ♗xf3

Note that Black's 8th and 9th moves must be played in the correct order: 8...exd4? 9 hxg4 hxg4 10 ♘h2 ♕h4 11 ♗f4 wins, which is a defensive resource I also noted in a similar position in Game 45. Move order is crucial throughout the MS, especially in the gambit lines!

9 ♕xf3 exd4 10 ♖e1

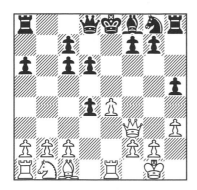

The critical new try: White tries to break with e4-e5, a blow specifically directed against Black's normal ...♕f6. Early results have been encouraging for White, but no one has yet played what I consider Black's strongest reply: 10...♗e7!.

10...♕f6?!

This is a good move after 10 ♖d1, as we saw in the previous game, but the slight change in rook position makes it inaccurate here. The problem is that the queen move *does not stop e4-e5*—in fact it may even make it stronger, as White will advance with tempo. The fact that Black can temporarily win a pawn on e5 will not deter White, as then the advance will often work as a vacating sac (clearing e4 for a knight) and Black's queen will be further harried.

Three more unsuccessful moves—and one good one—are shown in the following variations:

a) 10...g5 11 e5 d5 12 ♘d2 ♕d7 13 e6 fxe6 14 ♘b3 ♕f7 15 ♕e2 ♗d6 16 ♘xd4 ♔d7 (note that in the regular

Vajda cluster, the pawns are at c6/c7/d6, when it's hard to approach the black king; whereas here, with the d-pawn at d5, the c5-square invites a knight—and White finds a brilliant way to make use of this) 17 ♗xg5 e5 18 ♘b3 ♕f5 19 f4 exf4 20 ♗xf4!! (a tremendous speculative sac: Black's king is now firmly caught in the centre, and White has all the play) 20...♗xf4 (not 20...♕xf4?? 21 ♕e6+ ♔d8 22 ♕e8 mate) 21 ♘c5+ ♔d6 22 b4 ♗e5 (and not 22...♖b8?? 23 ♕e6+ ♕xe6 24 ♖xe6 mate!—White is getting a lot of mileage off that strong knight!) 23 ♘b7+ ♔e6 24 ♖f1 ♕g5 25 ♖ae1 ♖b8 26 ♖f3 ♔d7 27 ♘c5+ ♔d6 28 ♕f2 ♖xb4 29 c3 ♖b5 30 h4 ♕g7 31 ♖f7 ♕xf7 (White wins after 31...♕g4 32 ♖d7+ ♕xd7 33 ♘xd7 ♔xd7 34 ♕f5+) 32 ♕xf7 ♖xc5 33 ♕f5 d4 34 ♕g6+ ♔d7 35 ♖xe5 ♖xe5 36 ♕g7+ ♔e6 37 ♕xh8 ♘e7 38 cxd4 ♖d5 and White converted his material advantage in V.Pentzien-M.Schütze, correspondence 2007.

b) 10...♖b8 (too slow to give Black the king safety he needs) 11 ♘d2 ♘e7 (there's no time for 11...g6 12 e5 d5 13 ♘b3 ♗g7 14 ♘xd4 ♘e7 15 ♗g5 with a big White plus) 12 ♘b3 ♘g6 13 ♘xd4 ♘e5 14 ♕c3 c5 15 ♘f5 g6 16 f4 favours White as the black king is caught in the centre.

c) 10...♘e7 11 e5 dxe5 (if 11...♕d7 12 exd6 cxd6 13 c3 dxc3 14 ♘xc3 and Black can't develop) 12 ♖xe5 ♕d6 13 ♗f4 0-0-0 (13...♕g6 14 ♕e2 is also much better for White) 14 ♖xh5 wins.

d) All the above means we are left with the logical but so far unplayed 10...♗e7! which is, in my opinion, the only move.

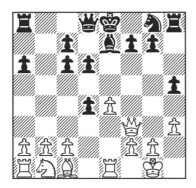

White has two threats that involve e4-e5: obviously this threatens to open the e-file on the black king, but the pawn thrust also opens the diagonal to attack c6. By playing ...♗e7 Black develops and blocks the e-file, thus eliminating one threat, and the threat to c6 can be easily met:

d1) 11 ♘d2 ♗f6 12 ♘c4 (12 e5 dxe5 13 ♕xc6+ ♔f8—another point of the bishop move is that the king has this square; now Black has good central pawns and can develop a tempo with ...♘e7) 12...♘e7 13 ♗f4 0-0! (king safety first—not 13...♘g6 14 e5) 14 e5 (14 ♕xh5 ♘g6 is slightly better for Black—remember, Black started these complications with an extra centre pawn, so giving back a mere rook's pawn is of no great moment, provided his king is safe) 14...dxe5 15 ♗xe5 (15 ♘xe5 ♕d5 is good for Black) 15...♗xe5 16 ♖xe5 ♖b8 17 ♖d1 ♖b5 18 ♕e4 (if 18 ♖xh5

♘g6 19 ♖xb5 cxb5 20 ♘a5 c5 21 ♘c6 ♕c7 and White's knight is in trouble) 18...♘g6 19 ♖xd4 ♕c8 (now White is forced to straighten out Black's pawns) 20 ♖xb5 cxb5 21 ♘e3 ♖e8 22 ♕f3 ♕e6 23 ♕xh5 (or 23 b3 ♕e5) 23...♕xa2 with approximate equality.

d2) 11 e5 ♕d7 (Black refuses to weaken his queenside cluster with ...d6-d5) 12 exd6 cxd6 13 ♘d2 ♘f6 14 ♘b3 0-0 15 ♘xd4 d5 16 ♗g5 ♖ae8 17 ♘f5 (or 17 ♗xf6 ♗xf6 18 c3 ♕b7) 17...♗d8 18 ♗h6 (after 18 ♗xf6 ♗xf6 19 ♕xh5 g6 20 ♘h6+ ♔g7 Black has the superior minor piece and the initiative) 18...♖xe1+ 19 ♖xe1 ♖e8 20 ♖xe8+ ♘xe8 21 ♗c1 g6 and now that the h-pawn is solidly defended, Black has easy equality.

I will definitely try 10...♗e7 as soon as I get a chance!

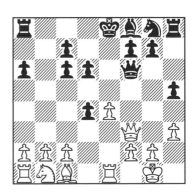

11 ♕b3 ♘e7 12 ♕b7 ♖c8

Here 12...♖d8 (as in the previous game) allows White to show his idea: 13 ♕xc7 g5 14 ♘d2 g4 15 e5! dxe5 16 ♖xe5 ♖d7 17 ♘e4!, highlighting the ill-placed queen on f6—White is better;

e.g. 17...♕xf2+ 18 ♔xf2 ♖xc7 19 ♗f4 ♖a7 20 ♘f6+ ♔d8 21 ♖d1 with a strong attack, even without queens.

13 c3!

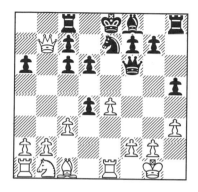

Improving on 13 ♘d2 ♕e5 14 ♕xa6 ♕b5 15 ♕xb5 cxb5 16 ♘f3 c5 17 e5 ♘c6 18 exd6+ ♔d7, when Black consolidated and eventually won in A.Bushkov-V.Yandemirov, Kazan 2009.

13...dxc3

Black would like to play 13...g5, but again the rook on e1 is strong: watch out for 14 e5! dxe5 15 cxd4 exd4 (of course 15...♖d8 16 dxe5 is better, but one can't recommend this position, where White rules the centre and Black has no compensation for the shattered queenside pawns) 16 ♕xc8 mate!

Yand has also tried 13...♕e5 (as in the Bushkov game above), but this turned disastrous after 14 ♕xa6 g6 15 ♗d2 ♗g7 16 cxd4 ♕b5 (not 16...♕xd4? 17 ♗c3 winning a piece) 17 ♕xb5 cxb5 18 ♗c3, when White was a pawn ahead and converted his advantage in S.Azarov-V.Yandemirov, Kazan 2008.

I think these lines make it clear that

the faulty move is 10...♕f6 and no improvements after that can save Black.

14 ♘xc3 g6 15 e5!

Again!

15...dxe5 16 ♘e4

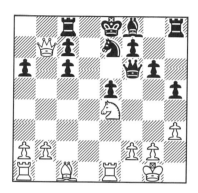

Here's our vacating sac.

16...♕e6 17 ♘c5 ♕f5 18 ♘xa6 ♗g7

No better is 18...♕d7 19 ♗g5 intending ♖ad1.

19 ♘xc7+ ♔f8 20 ♘a6 ♗f6 21 a4 ♔g7 22 ♖a3 ♖hd8 23 ♖f3 ♕d7 24 ♕xd7 ♖xd7 25 ♘c5 ♖d5 26 ♘e4

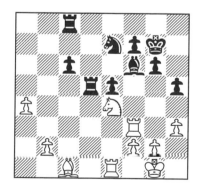

The knight finds its beauty square and this, plus the passed a-pawn, means Black has an uphill battle to draw.

26...♘g8 27 g4 hxg4 28 hxg4 ♗e7 29 ♔g2 ♘f6?

29...♖b8 30 b3 ♖b4 would offer some drawing chances.

30 ♗g5?

Missing 30 ♗h6+! which just wins offhand: 30...♔xh6 31 g5+ ♔h7 (or 31...♔g7 32 gxf6+ winning a piece) 32 gxf6 ♗d8 33 ♖h3+ ♔g8 34 ♖eh1 and White mates or wins massive material.

30...♘xe4 31 ♗xe7 ♖e8 32 ♗h4 ♖d4?

After his lucky break Yand should sense the danger and try to draw with 32...♖h8 33 ♖xe4 ♖xh4 34 ♖a3, though this would still not be easy.

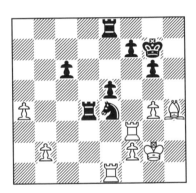

33 ♖xe4!

White sees the mating attack this time!

33...♖xe4 34 ♗f6+ ♔f8 35 ♖h3 ♖xg4+ 36 ♔f1 1-0

Mate is coming.

I don't see an equalizer when Black plays the "traditional" 10...♕f6 as here. However, after my recommendation 10...♗e7 I think Black has good chances to equalize—but we will, as always, have to await practical tests.

Now we proceed to the most critical line of the Yandemirov Gambit—the piece sacrifice that follows 7 d4.

Game 49
N.Short-J.Timman
Pamplona 2000

1 e4 e5 2 ♘f3 ♘c6 3 ♗b5 a6 4 ♗a4 d6 5 0-0 ♗g4 6 h3 h5 7 d4

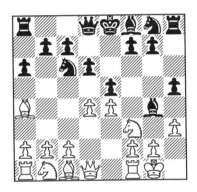

The most critical attempt to refute the Yandemirov Gambit. White threatens simply to take the bishop and then use his newly opened c1-h6 diagonal to park his knight on g5, blocking the potential mating attack with ...♕h4. The only consistent counter is 7...b5 8 ♗b3 ♘xd4!? which gambits a piece! Black gets a centre pawn, a king-protecting pawn, and the open h-file for a bishop. Obviously razor-sharp play ensues.

7...b5

If Black has gone this far, there are few alternatives (probably when Black plays 5...♗g4 he should be psychologically ready to sac the piece), but let's take a quick look at two other moves:

a) 7...♗xf3!? 8 ♕xf3 exd4 is possible, when Black hopes to transpose to the 8 ♗xc6+ bxc6 9 ♕xf3 exd4 line of the previous two games, but White does not have to give up his bishop. Here's one example of this rare line: 9 c3 b5 10 ♗b3 ♘f6 and now, instead of 11 a4 ♖b8 12 axb5 axb5 13 ♗g5 ♗e7 with approximate equality and an eventual draw in Th.Ward-A.Zebrowski, Cleveland 1980, I like 11 ♕d3! dxc3 12 ♘xc3 with two bishops compensation for the pawn, and long-term play, as Black won't know where to put his king. Still, this might be playable if you think a pawn is worth a lot of trouble!

b) 7...♗d7 8 c3 is much less acceptable, as Black has reverted to a "solid line" where the h5-pawn sticks out like the proverbial sore thumb.

8 ♗b3 ♘xd4

8...♗xf3 9 ♕xf3 is even worse here, as 9...♘xd4 allows 10 ♕xf7 mate—and any other 9th move leaves White with material equality and overwhelming positional advantage.

9 hxg4 hxg4?!

The old main line—but as far as I can see, Short refutes it in this game, and no attempts to revive it have succeeded. Black should play Yandemirov's critical and best 9...♘xb3! 10 axb3 hxg4, which is the subject of the final three games of this chapter.

10 ♘g5 ♘h6

Now 10...♘xb3 is too late in view of 11 ♕d5! ♘h6 12 ♕c6+ ♔e7 13 ♘c3!

♔f6 14 axb3 and White is a piece up with a winning attack.

11 f4!

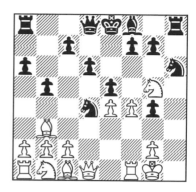

It's difficult if not impossible to see any compensation for Black (beyond the two pawns) for the piece here. The knight on g5 is not trapped since, if attacked by ...f7-f6, it can go to e6, where it will be supported by bishop or pawn.

11...c6

The sharp attempt to rehabilitate the variation with 11...d5 fails tactically: 12 ♗xd5 ♗c5 13 ♗e3 ♕d6 14 ♗xf7+! (the refutation) 14...♘xf7 15 ♘xf7 ♕b6 (if 15...♔xf7? 16 fxe5+ wins the queen and Black doesn't have enough pieces left to mate; e.g. 16...♘f5 17 exd6 ♗xe3+ 18 ♖f2 g3 19 ♕d5+ ♔e8 20 ♕c6+ ♔f7 21 ♕d7+ ♔g8 22 ♕e6+ ♔f8 23 ♕xf5+ ♔g8 24 ♕e6+ ♔h7 25 ♕h3+ ♔g8 26 ♕xg3 and White ends any remaining confusion) 16 ♘xh8 exf4 17 ♕xg4 fxe3 18 ♖f7 (White is a rook up and threatening mate—Black's tricks fail to save the day) 18...♘f5 (or 18...♕d6 19 ♘c3 ♘xc2 20 ♔f1 ♘xa1 21 ♘d5 ♘c2 22 ♘f6+ winning the queen) 19 ♘c3 e2+ 20 ♔h1 0-0-0 21 ♖xf5 ♕e6 22 ♘g6 ♖d1+ 23 ♖xd1 1-0 P.Kruglyakov-A.Solomaha, Kiev 2005.

12 g3

White makes a flight square for his king, and eliminates counterplay on the g1-a7 diagonal.

12...♘xb3

As noted above, 12...f6 13 ♘e6 shows that the knight is not trapped, and it can be supported by the f-pawn (the point of 11 f4!).

13 cxb3 exf4 14 gxf4 ♕d7 15 f5 d5

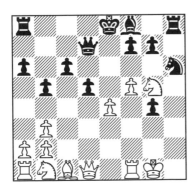

Black's opening has failed, and now, as Short himself points out, White could get a big advantage with 16 ♕d4! 0-0-0 17 ♘c3! ♕c7 (or 17...♕d6 18 ♗f4 ♕c5 19 ♕xc5 ♗xc5+ 20 ♔g2 with a decisive material advantage) 18 ♗f4 dxe4 19 ♕xe4 ♗c5+ 20 ♔g2 and Black doesn't have nearly enough for the piece.

From the opening point of view, such a cheerless position is not what Black wants to get out of a sharp gambit!

While 16 ♕d4 in combination with Short's played 11 f4! knocks out this

particular variation, one must remind ourselves that chess is played by humans—Short's actual 16th move gives Timman some chances—and White only wins after a somewhat rocky trail.

16 ♗f4?! 0-0-0 17 ♘c3 ♗d6 18 ♕d4 ♗xf4 19 ♖xf4 ♕c7 20 ♕f2 d4 21 ♘e2 d3 22 ♘g3 ♔b7 23 ♕e3 d2 24 ♖ff1 ♖d7 25 ♖ad1 ♖hd8 26 ♕f4 ♕b6+ 27 ♖f2 ♖d3 28 ♔g2 ♕d4 29 e5 ♕xb2 30 ♘5e4 ♖8d5 31 f6

Finally decisive.

31...♖f3 32 ♖xf3 gxf3+ 33 ♔xf3 ♕xa2 34 fxg7 ♕xb3+ 35 ♔e2 ♕c4+ 36 ♔f2 ♕d4+ 37 ♔g2 1-0

I can only regard 9...hxg4?! as refuted—so now we go on to the critical 9...♘xb3.

Game 50
K.Aseev-V.Yandemirov
Russian Championship,
Krasnoyarsk 2003

1 e4 e5 2 ♘f3 ♘c6 3 ♗b5 a6 4 ♗a4 d6 5 0-0 ♗g4 6 h3 h5 7 d4 b5 8 ♗b3 ♘xd4 9

hxg4 ♘xb3!

Best! Removing the bishop means White no longer holds the e6-square, which means in many cases Black can recover his piece with a timely ...f7-f6 advance.

10 axb3 hxg4 11 ♘g5 ♕d7

Yandemirov has been amazingly consistent with this variation: he has played it ten times from 2003 to 2008 and has scored a healthy 55% with Black, that is 3 wins, 2 losses, and 5 draws.

12 c4

12 ♘c3 is ineffective as it doesn't open lines, and Black regains the knight with attacking chances: 12...c6 (correct—Black has time for a defensive move since the g5-knight has no escape; after the impatient 12...f6? 13 ♕d5 ♖c8 14 ♘e6 c6 15 ♘xf8 or 14...♗e7 15 ♘xg7+ ♔f8 16 ♘f5 White wins easily with his extra piece) 13 ♗e3 (Short's f2-f4 doesn't work here: 13 f4? ♕a7+ 14 ♖f2 g3 and wins—a typical YG attack) 13...f6 14 f4 exf4 15 ♖xf4 ♘h6 (at this point the simple 15...fxg5 15

♖xg4 ♗e7 is better, when Black stands well with his extra pawn and continued attacking chances; but from now until the end of the game Black continually misses stronger or even outright winning moves—until he finally loses!) 16 ♘e2 (White should try to confuse the issue with 16 ♘d5) 16...fxg5 17 ♖f1 ♗e7 (you must have your attacking game on to win with the YG!—here Black can play 17...♘f7 18 ♘d4 ♘e5 19 ♗xg5 g6 20 ♕d2 ♕h7 when he has an attacking position and an extra pawn) 18 c4 bxc4 19 bxc4 ♗f6 20 ♕b3 g3 21 ♘xg3 ♘g4 22 ♖ad1 ♗e5 23 ♗d4 ♗f4 24 c5 0-0-0 25 ♕a3 ♕b7 (25...♗xg3 26 ♕xg3 dxc5 27 ♗xg7 ♕xd1 28 ♗xh8 ♕e2 is another sharp tactical route to a clear plus) 26 ♖d3 dxc5 (Black wins after 26...♕b5 27 ♖b3 ♗xg3 28 ♖xg3 ♖h1+ 29 ♔xh1 ♕xf1+ 30 ♗g1 ♘f2+ 31 ♔h2 ♖h8+ 32 ♖h3 ♘xh3 and mates or wins the queen; or 28 ♖xb5 ♗h2+ 29 ♔h1 ♗e5+ 30 ♔g1 ♗xd4+ 31 ♖f2 ♗xf2+ 32 ♔f1 axb5 with too many pieces for the queen) 27 ♕xc5 g6 28 ♖fd1 ♗d6?? (the last chance is 28...♖he8 when Black is still better—but now he has run out of wins and there are no draws in such a tactical position) 29 ♕xg5 ♕d7 30 ♗xh8 ♖xh8 31 ♖xd6 ♕a7+ 32 ♖1d4 1-0 D.Hulmes-M.Yeo, British League 2005. I can't stress enough that you must not play the YG unless you are confident in sharp, confused, extremely tactical positions.

Returning to 12 c4—nine of Yandemirov's ten opponents played this just as Aseev does here. However, this might be the case where the one is right and the nine are wrong! The one exception is the very interesting 12 ♕d3 which has the remarkable idea of coordinating with White's rook on the open a-file—Yand had a lot of trouble with this! (see note 'd')

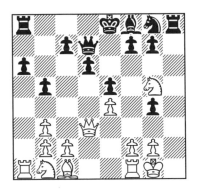

a) 12...f6 fails to 13 ♕d5 c6 14 ♕e6+ ♕e7 15 ♖xa6! (Gashimov).

b) 12...c6 13 c4 b4 14 c5 f6 15 ♘d2! fxg5 16 ♘c4 ♕f7 17 ♖d1! and White's attack is more dangerous than Black's, as Gashimov also points out.

c) 12...♖b8 was tried in another high-level game played a few months earlier (where 12 ♕d3 was introduced), but Black went under quickly: 13 ♖xa6 f6 14 ♘c3 fxg5 15 ♗xg5 ♗e7 16 f4 gxf3 17 ♕xf3 ♘f6 18 ♘d5 ♘xd5 (18...0-0 is better, though after 19 ♗xf6 ♗xf6 20 ♖a7 White has a clear plus anyway) 19 ♕f7+ ♔d8 20 ♕xg7 ♘c8 21 ♕xh8+ ♔b7 22 ♕h7 ♕g4 23 exd5 ♕d4+ 24 ♔h1 ♗xg5 25 ♖fa1 ♗e3 26 ♖a7+ ♕xa7 27 ♖xa7+ ♗xa7 28 g4 ♖f8 29 g5 ♖f2 30 ♕e4 ♖f1+ 31 ♔h2 ♖f4 32 ♕xf4! (a pretty excelsior finish) 32...exf4 33 c3 1-0 V.Gashimov-A.Grischuk, Baku 2008.

d) 12...♘h6 (Yand's move, which I think this is best) 13 c4 b4 14 c5 f6 15 ♖xa6 ♖xa6 16 ♕xa6 fxg5 17 ♕a8+ ♔f7 18 cxd6 cxd6 19 ♗xg5 ♘g8 (19...♔g6 20 ♗e3 ♘f7 looks better to me, when Black unpins his bishop, but White still has the edge) 20 ♘d2 ♖h5 21 ♖a1 ♕e6 22 ♖a7+ ♘e7 23 ♗xe7 ♗xe7 24 ♕b7 and White had an obvious pull in D.Kokarev-V.Yandemirov, Kazan 2008, though Black fought hard and held the draw after 73 moves.

12...♖b8

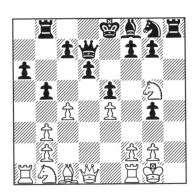

Always played by Yandemirov. The only other move to have been tried here, according to the database, is 12...b4, but the problem with this is that after 13 c5 c6 14 ♕d3 White has transposed into the Gashimov line given above (see note 'b') where Black is struggling for his life!

13 cxb5

For 13 ♕d5 see the next game; and for the logical and absolutely critical pawn grab, 13 ♖xa6, see the game after that, the final game in this chapter.

13...axb5 14 ♘c3 f6 15 ♖a7

If 15 ♘d5 c6 (but not 15...♘e7? 16 ♘e6! winning) 16 ♘e6 cxd5 17 exd5 g6 18 ♕xg4 ♕h7 and Black has the usual YG counterplay.

15...♘e7

And not 15...fxg5? due to 16 ♘d5—as you can easily see, move order has to be exceptionally precise in this variation.

16 ♘d5 ♘xd5 17 exd5 ♕f5

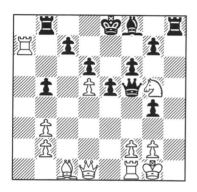

18 f3

Necessary, since if 18 ♘e6? ♕h7 19 ♘xc7+ ♔f7 20 ♘e6+ ♔g8 21 f4 g3 and Black mates with a classic YG attack.

18...fxg5 19 fxg4 ♕h7 20 ♕f3

This is not much of a recommendation for White's opening, but it seems he could draw here with 20 ♗xg5 ♕h2+ 21 ♔f2 ♗e7 (21...♖h3 22 ♖h1 ♕xh1 23 ♕c2 is unnecessarily confusing, though probably also leading to a draw) 22 ♗xe7 ♖h3 23 ♗g5 (now 23 ♖h1?? fails disastrously to 23...♕g3+ 24 ♔g1 ♕e3+ 25 ♔f1 ♖xh1 mate)

23...♕g3+ 24 ♔g1 ♕h2+ with a draw by perpetual check.

20...♕h2+ 21 ♔f2 ♗e7 22 ♕e3

This loses at once. 22 ♔e2 is better, though not good enough to save the game: 22...♖f8 23 ♕h3 ♕xh3 24 gxh3 ♖xf1 25 ♔xf1 ♔d7 and Black has an extra, passed pawn in the ending.

22...0-0+!

Still legal, and probably quite a surprise!

0-1

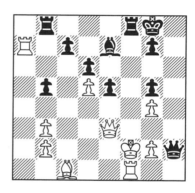

White resigned, for after 23 ♔e2 ♖xf1 24 ♔xf1 ♖f8+ his queen alone cannot defend against Black's onslaught; e.g. 25 ♔e1 ♕h1+ 26 ♔d2 ♕xg2+ and the white queen falls.

Black has real attacking chances here, and this line (13 cxb5) only works if White is both very accurate and content with a draw. On the other hand the new 12 ♕d3 looks extremely dangerous, as does the more traditional 12 c4 ♖b8 13 ♖xa6.

But before we get to that last variation, there is one more quiet—well, relatively quiet—line to discuss.

Game 51
N.De Firmian-I.Sokolov
Selfoss 2003

1 e4 e5 2 ♘f3 ♘c6 3 ♗b5 a6 4 ♗a4 d6 5 0-0 ♗g4 6 h3 h5 7 d4 b5 8 ♗b3 ♘xd4 9 hxg4 ♘xb3 10 axb3 hxg4 11 ♘g5 ♕d7 12 c4 ♖b8 13 ♕d5

The question this high-level game asks is: "Can White simply give the sacrificed piece back, exchange queens, and then count on a draw?"

Of course the truly critical move is 13 ♖xa6 which will be examined in the next game.

13...c6 14 ♕xf7+ ♕xf7 15 ♘xf7 ♔xf7 16 ♖xa6

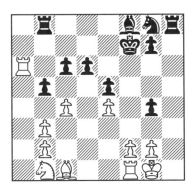

White has restored material equality, but what about the position? Black's rooks are both extremely active, and the g-pawn has a cramping effect—I'd say Black is already for choice.

16...♘f6 17 ♖e1 bxc4 18 bxc4 d5!

Black sacrifices a pawn but takes over the centre and activates his bishop.

19 ♖xc6

If 19 exd5 cxd5 20 cxd5 (or 20 ♖xe5 g3 21 fxg3 ♗c5+ 22 ♗e3 ♖xb2 with attack) 20...♗c5 21 ♗e3 (not 21 ♖xe5? g3 22 ♗e3 ♖xb2! and Black wins due to his back rank threats) 21...♗xe3 22 fxe3 ♖xb2 with some advantage for Black. One sees that the exchange of queens has hardly lessened his attacking chances.

19...♗b4 20 ♖d1 d4

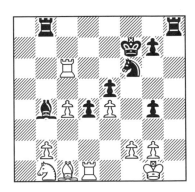

Great play by Sokolov! Black has given up a pawn, but still has threats down the h-file and has added the now protected passed d-pawn to his arsenal.

21 ♖c7+ ♔g6 22 f3 g3 23 ♘d2 ♗xd2!

Eliminating an important defensive piece: note that White has nothing that can control h2 in the near future.

24 ♗xd2 ♖h2!

Excellent! Black threatens to double on the h-file, or double on the seventh rank. Worse is the impatient 24...♖xb2 25 ♖c5 with some counterplay.

25 ♗e1

White has no time for 25 b4, since

25...♖bh8 26 ♔f1 ♖h1+ 27 ♔e2 d3+ wins a rook.

25...♖xb2

26 ♗d2

And White has no time to take on g3 either, while 26 ♖d2 ♖b1 27 ♖e2 d3 28 ♖e3 d2 is another loss.

26...♘h5 27 c5 ♘f4 28 ♗xf4 exf4 29 c6 ♖bxg2+

Blind pigs!

30 ♔f1 ♖c2 31 ♔g1 ♖h5! 0-1

White resigns, since 32 ♖xd4 ♖c1+ 33 ♔g2 ♖h2 is mate, or 32 ♖c8 g2 mates next.

This was a quality game by Sokolov, which shows that after 12 sharp YG moves, White *must* play the challenging 13 ♖xa6 if he wants to win, and indeed if he wants to draw!

There is no safety in exchanges; we see in this game that Black's attack was still extremely strong without queens.

The Yandemirov Gambit is much riskier than the Siesta, but in one way the lines are alike: White must go into the maelstrom to survive or possibly prosper—when White avoids complica-

tions in both gambits, Black usually equalizes or even gets some advantage.

Now on to the critical main line of the present day.

Game 52
P.Smirnov-V.Yandemirov
Zvenigorod 2008

1 e4 e5 2 ♘f3 ♘c6 3 ♗b5 a6 4 ♗a4 d6 5 0-0 ♗g4 6 h3 h5 7 d4 b5 8 ♗b3 ♘xd4 9 hxg4 ♘xb3

Summing up as we go along, recall that the old main line of 9...hxg4 10 ♘g5 ♘h6 fails to Short's 11 f4! of Game 49.

10 axb3 hxg4 11 ♘g5 ♕d7 12 c4

I mentioned Gashimov's 12 ♕d3 in Game 50 which is extremely dangerous, and Yandemirov just barely drew against this.

12...♖b8

Since 12...b4 only transposes to the favourable (for White) Gashimov line, it's hard to find a better move to meet White's threat of c4xb5, when his queenside play would make it nearly impossible to recover the sacrificed piece.

13 ♖xa6!

Obviously critical.

We saw 13 cxb5 in Game 50 and a quick win for Black, though it seems that White should have been able to draw. Game 51 featured 13 ♕d5 with a quick return of the piece, but this led to a position that only Black could win.

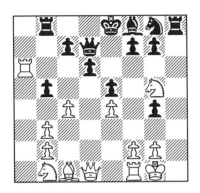

13...f6 14 ♘c3 fxg5

Black must take immediately: 14...bxc4 accounted for one of Yand's three losses in the 9...♘xb3 variation, as White went a good exchange up after 15 ♘d5 fxg5 16 ♖a7 ♖c8 17 ♗xg5 ♘e7 18 ♘b6 and eventually won in V.Popov-V.Yandemirov, Russian Championship, Krasnoyarsk 2003.

15 ♘xb5 ♘f6

In an earlier game, Yand won in 25 moves with the alternative 15...♗e7, but Davies has pointed out two improvements for White, queen moves at 18 and 22: 16 ♖a7 ♗d8 17 ♗xg5! ♘f6 18 f3 (18 ♕d3! looks stronger, when White is a pawn up with a well-coordinated position) 18...g3 19 ♕e1 ♘h5 20 ♗xd8 ♕xd8 21 ♘xc7+ ♔f7 22 ♕a5? (22 ♕e3 was mandatory) 22...♔g6 23 ♖d1 ♕h4 24 ♘b5 ♘f4 25 ♖xg7+ ♔h5 0-1 V.Popov-Yandemirov, Voronezh 2003. That's a nice finish, but had White found 18 ♕d3 it's hard to see any compensation for the pawn.

16 ♖a7

Another win for Yand came after the weak 16 ♕d3, when Black ran straight for the h-file: 16...♕f7 17 ♕g3 ♕h5 18 f3 ♔d7 19 ♗e3 ♗e7 20 ♖a7 ♖bc8 21 ♘c3 gxf3 22 gxf3 ♕h1+ 23 ♔f2 ♕h2+ (as often in this variation, if Black can get his attack going it will usually persist even after the exchange of queens) 24 ♕xh2 ♖xh2+ 25 ♔e1 ♖xb2 26 ♗xg5 ♖xb3 27 ♗xf6 ♗xf6 28 ♘d5 ♗g5 29 ♔e2 ♖h8 30 ♔f2 ♖b2+ 31 ♔g3 ♗h4+ 32 ♔g4 ♖g2+ 33 ♔h3 ♖g6 (Black will mate on the thematic h-file) 0-1 O.Chebotarev-V.Yandemirov, Moscow 2005.

16...♖c8

Black is threatening ...♕f7-h5, or ...g7-g6 and ...♕h7, in both cases getting to the h-file with attack.

17 ♖e1

17 ♗xg5 ♘xe4 18 ♗e3 ♕f5 is of course good for Black, who is again running to the h-file.

17...♕f7 18 ♗e3 ♕h5 19 ♔f1

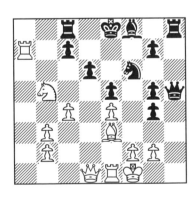

19...♕h1+

Yand improves on an earlier game against the same opponent, where he had a difficult position and only heroic defence and a bit of luck (see move 42) got him a draw in 97 moves: 19...♔d7 20 b4 ♕h1+ 21 ♔e2 ♕xg2 22 ♕a4 ♔d8 23 ♘xc7 ♖xc7 24 ♕a5 ♘e8 25 ♔d2 ♔d7 26 ♕b5+ ♔e7 27 ♖xc7+ ♘xc7 28 ♕b7 ♔d7 29 ♗b6 ♗e7 30 ♕xc7+ ♔e6 31 ♕b7 g3 32 ♖e2 ♖h2 33 ♕c8+ ♔f7 34 ♕g4 ♕g1 35 ♕xg3 ♕b1 36 ♔c3 ♖h1 37 ♕d3 ♖c1+ 38 ♖c2 ♖d1 39 ♖d2 ♖c1+ 40 ♔b3 ♕a1 41 c5 dxc5 42 bxc5 (Maxim Notkin pointed out that 42 ♗xc5! wins by force, as Black's king has no shelter from the queen and rook attack; I checked it, and he's right—it's a good exercise to see how the queen and rook win on the open board!) 42...♔g6 43 ♖c2 ♖d1 44 ♕f3 ♖d4 45 ♖c4 ♖d2 46 ♕c3 ♖xf2 47 c6 ♖f6 48 c7 ♖xb6+ 49 ♔c2 ♖d6 50 ♕f3 ♖b6 51 ♕f5+ ♔h6 52 ♕xe5 ♗f6 53 c8♕ ♖xb2+ 54 ♕xb2 ♕xb2+ 55 ♔d1 ♕b3+ 56 ♔d2 g4 57 ♕e6 ♕f3 58 e5 ♕f2+ 59 ♔d3 ♕f3+ 60 ♔d4 ♕d1+ 61 ♔c5 ♕e2 62 ♔d6 ♔g5 63 exf6 ♕xe6+ 64 ♔xe6 gxf6 65 ♔d5 g3 66 ♔e4 g2 67 ♖c8 f5+ 68 ♔f3 g1♘+! (heroic!—Black makes his draw) 69 ♔e3 ♘h3 70 ♖c6 ♘f4 71 ♔d4 ♘g6 72 ♖c1 ♔f6 73 ♔e3 ♔g5 74 ♔d4 ♔f6 75 ♔d5 ♘f4+ 76 ♔d6 ♘g6 77 ♖e1 ♘f4 78 ♖e8 ♘g6 79 ♖a8 ♔f7 80 ♔d5 ♔f6 81 ♖a6+ ♔g5 82 ♔e6 ♘f4+ 83 ♔f7 ♘d5 84 ♖g6+ ♔h4 85 ♖h6+ ♔g5 86 ♖h1 ♘e3 87 ♔e6 f4 88 ♖g1+ ♘g4 89 ♖f1 ♘e3 90 ♖f2 ♘g4 91 ♖f1 ♘e3 92 ♖g1+ ♘g4 93 ♖f1 ♘e3 94 ♖g1+ ♘g4 95 ♔d5 ♔f5 96 ♔d4 f3 97 ♖f1 ½-½ P.Smirnov-V.Yandemirov, European Club Cup, Izmir 2004.

Yandemirov understandably did not want to endure that long defence again—but got something quite similar in this game nonetheless: a worse ending that he only manages to draw after many moves.

20 ♔e2 ♕xg2 21 ♘xc7+ ♔f7 22 ♘d5+ ♔g6 23 ♘xf6 ♕f3+ 24 ♔d3 gxf6 25 ♖b7 f5

If 25...♕xd1+ 26 ♖xd1 f5 27 exf5+ ♔xf5 28 b4 and White's doubled knight pawns look stronger than Black's doubled knight pawns!

26 ♕xf3 gxf3 27 exf5+ ♔xf5 28 ♖f7+ ♔e6 29 ♖xf3 ♗e7 30 ♖g3 d5

31 ♗xg5

A good alternative is 31 cxd5+ ♔xd5 32 ♗xg5 with real winning chances.

31...e4+ 32 ♔c2 ♖hf8 33 ♗xe7

White should win with 33 f3!, when Black's centre collapses and White is, after all, up two pawns: 33...♖g8 (or 33...♗xg5 34 ♖xg5 ♖xf3 35 ♖xd5 and White's material advantage should decide) 34 ♗f4 ♖xg3 (34...♖gf8 35 ♖g4 ♗b4 36 ♖e2 ♔f5 fails to the tactical sequence 37 ♗h6 exf3 38 ♖f4+ ♔g6 39 ♖e6+ ♔h5 40 ♗xf8) 35 ♗xg3 dxc4 36

♖xe4+ is routine.

33...♖xf2+ 34 ♔c3 ♖xe7 35 ♖d3 ♖f5 36 ♔d4 ♖d8 37 ♖de3 dxc4+ 38 ♔xc4 ♖c8+ 39 ♔d4 ♔d6 40 ♖xe4 ♖d5+ 41 ♔e3 ♖h8 42 ♖f1 ♖h3+ 43 ♖f3 ♖xf3+ 44 ♔xf3 ♔c5 45 ♔e3 ♔b5 46 ♖e8 ♖d1

Now the doubled b-pawns are blockaded and weak.

47 ♖b8+ ♔c5 48 b4+ ♔c4 49 b5 ♖d3+ 50 ♔e4 ♖d4+ 51 ♔e3 ♖d3+ 52 ♔e2 ½-½

After 52...♖b3 Black (heroically!) holds the draw.

Is this what Black wants out of this bold opening?

Conclusion

The Yandemirov Gambit is clearly under a cloud right now, but in such sharp positions improvements are always possible. We'll see if Yandemirov comes back with new variations. As we saw, in the recent games against well-prepared opponents (Smirnov here and Kokarev—recall the note in Game 50) it was all he could do to make desperate draws from worse positions. An improvement must be found if the gambit is to survive at the highest level.

On the other hand, at a somewhat lower level, and with the advantage of surprise, then the opening is absolutely deadly, as can be seen in my win in Game 45, when my opponent made a serious but extremely common error on move 6!

Summing up, one can see why Keres never played this: it's almost beyond risky at the 2600 level, and the critical line 6 h3 h5 7 d4 comes close to refuting the whole opening. However, all other lines give Black reasonable counterplay (for example, 7 ♗xc6+) and not every opponent will be prepared to a Gashimov level against you!

You'll have to decide for yourself whether to risk this gambit—or maybe you can find a key improvement in one of the multitude of razor-sharp lines!

Chapter Six
Delayed Exchange Variation

When facing the Modern Steinitz, White can force Black into a type of Exchange Variation with the somewhat more unusual ...b7xc6 by losing a tempo as follows: **1 e4 e5 2 ♘f3 ♘c6 3 ♗b5 a6 4 ♗a4 d6 5 ♗xc6+ bxc6**

which is the subject of this chapter. To me this is one of the easiest variations to deal with in the whole MS—as I don't think that taking with the b-pawn is bad even in the regular Exchange Variation (4 ♗xc6), indeed it

might be best (see Chapter Eleven)—and here Black gets an extra tempo!

We're back to our traditional Keres game opener again, so here are some Keres statistics: he liked to play everything and keep his opponents guessing, so in 12 games against this line, he played 6...♗g4 three times (2 wins and a draw) 6...f6 three times (2 wins and a draw), and 6...exd4 six times and he *always* played this way against the strongest players, such as Spassky, Mecking and Simagin. And with this critical, and I think objectively best, reply for Black he never had a problem, scoring 3 wins and 3 draws.

Overall against the Delayed Exchange he scored 7 wins and 5 draws; White couldn't win anything and couldn't even draw half the time!

As the following games will show, Black equalizes easily against this system, provided he opens the game quickly for his bishops by capturing when White plays d2-d4.

Game 53
H.Mecking-P.Keres
Petropolis Interzonal 1973

Although Keres leads the way in our journey, some other modern books seem to have forgotten him!

1 e4 e5 2 ♘f3 ♘c6 3 ♗b5 a6 4 ♗a4 d6 5 ♗xc6+

As I mentioned in the notes to Game 7, Andrew Greet recommends this move in his Worrall Attack repertoire book, *Play the Ruy Lopez*, and some of his comments are referenced in this game.

5...bxc6 6 d4

Universally played, as after 6 0-0 ♗g4 Black has easy equality: d2-d4 is then shut down, and Black has the b-file for counterplay.

6...exd4 7 ♕xd4

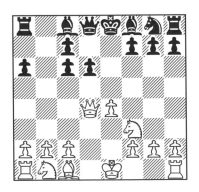

Recommended by Greet and played by Kasparov, as we already saw in

Game 16. I'll cover this move here and in the next game; the slightly more popular 7 ♘xd4 will be seen in Games 55-58.

7...c5

I think this is best, immediately tickling the annoying white queen, though as we saw in Game 16, Short made a reasonably smooth draw against Kasparov with the simple 7...♘f6.

8 ♕d3 ♘e7

8...g6 is quite risky due to the possible pawn sacrifice: 9 0-0 ♗g7 10 e5! (as we saw in the analysis of Game 12).

9 ♘c3

So far 9 e5 has never been played (according to the *Mega*), probably because it gives Black's unopposed light-squared bishop such a beautiful diagonal. I like 9...♗b7 10 0-0 (if 10 exd6 ♕xd6 11 ♕e2 0-0-0 12 0-0 ♕g6 and Black has the typical MS queenside castling and kingside attack set-up) 10...♘g6 11 exd6 ♕xd6 12 ♕e2+ ♗e7 13 ♖d1 ♕c6 14 ♘a3 0-0, when Black does have the doubled isolated pawns that I excoriated in Game 47—but here, he has extremely active pieces and great pressure on the long diagonal, not to mention equals over plus on the *Fritz*ometer—so I'm fine with the weak pawns!

Chess has no rules, only exceptions!

9...♖b8

Greet gives as his main line 9...♘g6 10 0-0 ♗e7 11 ♘d5 ♖b8 12 b3 (after 12 ♗d2 ♗b7 13 ♗c3 0-0 14 ♖fe1 ♗xd5 15 exd5 ♗f6 16 ♕xa6 ♗xc3 17 bxc3 ♖b2 18 ♖ec1 ♕a8 19 ♕xa8 ♖xa8 20 c4 ♖axa2 21 ♖xa2 Black was slightly better but accepted a draw in A.Grosar-D.Sermek, Pula 1991) 12...0-0 13 ♗b2 and calls it "slightly better for White", but Keres reaches the same position by transposition and after 13...♖e8 14 ♖fe1 ♗f8 calls it equal.

I agree with Mr. K—but in a sense this is moot, since Keres plays even more strongly in the main game (though this high-level encounter is not mentioned in Greet's book) and, as we'll see, Black has no difficulties.

10 b3 ♘g6 11 0-0

11 h4!? h5 is called unclear by Keres;

I'll look at a similar line at move 9 in the next game.

11...♗e7 12 ♘d5 ♗f6!

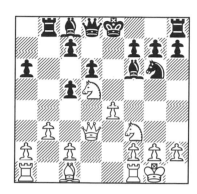

Castle when you should or when you must, but not just because you can! Keres' active move is clearly best. As mentioned above, Greet only gives 12...0-0 13 ♗b2 and stops here with "slightly better", while Keres and I say "equal"—for the record, Greet is quite impressed with the white knight on d5, but as I see it, Black can choose the right time to chase or chop it (...c7-c6 or ...♗b7xd5), so I don't believe he is in any danger.

13 ♘xf6+

If White doesn't take, Black just has a lock on e5.

13...♕xf6 14 ♗g5 ♕e6 15 e5?!

Black might be slightly better after this, but if 15 ♗d2 0-0 16 ♘g5 ♕e7 17 f4 h6 18 ♘f3 ♗b7 gives Black an easy game in any case.

15...d5!

As Keres points out, this is stronger than 15...0-0 16 exd6 cxd6 17 ♖fe1 ♕d7 18 ♖ad1 ♖b6 with equality.

16 ⬛ad1

Keres gives 16 ♕c3 ♕b6 17 ♗c1 d4 as good for Black due to the positional threat of ...♗b7.

16...♗b7 17 ⬛fe1 ½-½

No doubt Mecking offered the draw. Black's light-squared bishop has a great future, with ...d5-d4 always hanging over White's head, and the knight on g6 is ready to join in with a timely ...♘f4/...♘h4. Meanwhile White's e-pawn is static and somewhat weak, and it blocks his only surviving bishop.

The tournament book describes the game as of "little content", but I don't agree: the fact that Black easily shut down White's play is quite important! Remember, Mecking was having the tournament of his life here—he came clear first, in the process mowing down such GMs as Smyslov, Reshevsky, Savon, etc—and yet here he is already slightly worse with White after 17 moves! And as we'll see in the next game, with a similar position against a less redoubtable foe, Keres will not take the draw.

1 e4 ♘c6 2 ♘f3 e5 3 ♗b5 a6 4 ♗a4 d6 5 ♗xc6+ bxc6 6 d4 exd4 7 ♕xd4 c5 8 ♕d3 ♘e7 9 c4

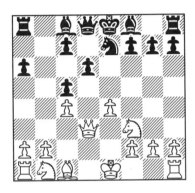

White is trying to set up a Maróczy bind, but it loses its effect due to Black's control of d4. Instead, 9 ♘c3 ⬛b8 gives White nothing, as we saw in the previous game—while if Black plays 9...♘g6 White does have the h2-h4 attack, but this shouldn't be troubling either: 10 h4 h5 11 ♗g5 ♗e7 12 ♗xe7 ♕xe7 13 ♘d5 ♕d8 14 0-0-0 0-0 15 ♘g5 ⬛b8 16 f4 ♗g4 and Black was better and went on to win in J.Kaplan-R.Knaak, Amsterdam 1974; the unclear pawn sacrifice 16 e5 was a more testing continuation, though Black equalizes with 16...dxe5 17 ♘e4 ♗e6.

9...♘c6 10 h3 ♗e7 11 ♘c3 0-0 12 0-0 ⬛e8 13 b3 ♗f6

Keres' simple play is again in evi-dence: the knight and bishop coordinate on the weak d4-square, and Black is slightly better already.

14 ♗b2 ♗b7 15 ♖fe1 ♖e6 16 ♖ad1 ♕d7 17 ♗a1 ♖ae8

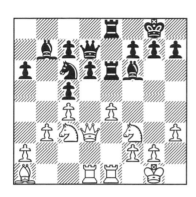

Black has excellent piece play, reminiscent of Lasker's double fianchetto in Game 3, and a target at e4.

18 ♘d5 ♗xa1 19 ♖xa1 ♘b4 20 ♕d2 ♖xe4 21 ♖xe4 ♖xe4 22 ♘xb4 cxb4 23 ♕xb4 c5 24 ♕d2 ♖e6

Black has traded a wing pawn for a centre pawn, and his remaining minor piece is obviously stronger than White's counterpart. And so, about fifty moves later, Black picks up a full point!

25 ♕c3 ♖f6 26 ♘e1 ♕f5 27 ♕e3 ♖e6 28 ♕g3 h5 29 ♔f1 ♕e4 30 ♕d3 ♕e5 31 ♖d1 ♕h2 32 f3 ♕g3 33 ♕d2 ♗c6 34 ♕f2 ♕e5 35 ♘d3 ♕f5 36 ♔g1 a5 37 ♔h1 a4 38 b4 cxb4 39 ♘xb4 ♗b7 40 ♘d5 ♕e5 41 ♕c2 ♗c6 42 ♕d2 a3 43 ♘f4 ♗a4 44 ♖b1 ♖e8 45 ♘d5 ♗c6 46 ♕d3 ♕e2 47 ♕xa3 ♕xc4 48 ♘b4 ♗b7 49 ♕d3 ♕c5 50 a4 ♖e3 51 ♕b5 ♕xb5 52 axb5 ♔f8

It's well known that a rook + bishop is better than rook + knight in this type

of open position—and the author of *Practical Chess Endings* grinds away until he proves this maxim once again!

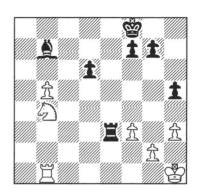

53 ♔g1

If I were trying to draw this as White, I would think as follows: I don't want to have my kingside pawns fixed with a highway through g3 (in other words, don't allow ...h5-h4); and I want to trade knight for bishop. I also know that many rook and pawn endings are drawn, even a pawn down, if one has the active rook. With this in mind, I think White would have good drawing chances after 53 h4! ♖c3 54 ♔h2 ♔e7 55 ♘c6+ ♗xc6 (Black must take, since 55...♔d7 56 ♘a5 gives good counterplay) 56 bxc6 ♖xc6 57 ♖b7+ ♔e6 58 g4, when Black has a very tough rook ending to win, if a win is at all possible—White has kingside counterplay with his mobile pawns and rook on the seventh, while his king can blockade Black's passed pawn.

However, White clings to material... and loses!

53...♔e8 54 ♔f2 ♖c3 55 ♖b2 ♔d7 56

♔e2 h4 57 ♔d2 ♖c5 58 ♘c2 ♔c7 59 ♘d4 ♔b6

Now White's b-pawn is weak, there is a hole at g3, and both minors are still on the board.

60 ♖a2

60 ♘c6 is too late because of 60...♖xb5, since White doesn't want the exchange of rooks.

60...g5 61 ♔d3 f6 62 ♖a1 ♖e5 63 ♖a2 ♗d5 64 ♖c2 f5 65 ♘c6 ♖e1 66 ♔d2 ♖g1 67 ♔e3 f4+ 68 ♔f2 ♖d1 69 ♔e2 ♖g1 70 ♔f2 ♖b1 71 ♘d4 ♖d1 72 ♘f5 ♗b7 0-1

Splendid! 73 ♖b2 ♗c8 74 ♘e7 ♗d7 and the b-pawn goes, while White has (unlike in my recommendation at move 53) absolutely no kingside counterplay.

One sees that the capture on d4 with the queen gives White nothing, so let's look at the more natural 7 ♘xd4.

Game 55
G.Daskalov-P.Keres
Tallinn 1971

1 e4 e5 2 ♘f3 ♘c6 3 ♗b5 a6 4 ♗a4 d6 5

♗xc6+ bxc6 6 d4 exd4 7 ♘xd4

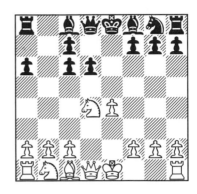

It's slightly more common to take on d4 with the knight, much as in the Sicilian Defence—and in this case White immediately threatens the c6-pawn. However, just as after the queen capture, Black simply advances this pawn and drives the knight out of the centre, after which he should be fine, as this and the next game show.

7...c5

Note that 7...♗d7 is also playable—for which see Games 57 and 58.

8 ♘e2

8 ♘f3 is regarded as best—see the next game.

The invasion 8 ♘c6 gets nowhere: 8...♕d7 9 ♘a5 ♕a4 10 ♕d5 ♖b8 11 ♕c6+ ♕xc6 12 ♘xc6 ♖b6 (White has only opened the game to Black's advantage) 13 ♘a5 f5! (White has been left with a knight on the rim, while Black's bishops scent open diagonals) 14 0-0 fxe4 15 ♘c3 ♘f6 16 ♖e1 d5 17 f3 c4 18 fxe4 ♗c5+ 19 ♔h1 and now, instead of castling as in D.Velimirovic-M.Scekic, Subotica 2002, Black should play more sharply with 19...♖e6!, when he has the edge due to his bishop pair and White's pinned e-pawn.

8...♘f6 9 ♘bc3 ♗b7 10 ♘g3

More aggressive is 10 ♗g5 ♗e7 (but not 10...g6? 11 e5! winning—you can't always fianchetto in the MS!) 11 f3 and since White is setting up for a kingside attack, Black should *not* castle into it. Correct is 11...♗c6!, clearing the b-file and waiting to see where the white king goes. If 12 0-0 then 12...0-0 is fine; but if 12 ♕d2, signalling queenside castling, Black should leave his king in the centre for a bit and play 12...♕b8 with immediate counterplay.

10...g6!

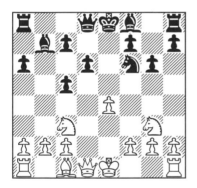

Once again we see Lasker's double fianchetto—in this case Black's last also restricts the g3-knight. With the two bishops and play against the e-pawn, Black is already better.

11 0-0

After 11 h4 ♕d7 12 ♗g5 ♗g7 13 ♕d2 ♘g4 14 ♘f1 f5 15 f3 ♘e5 16 exf5 gxf5 Black had the edge with his two bishops and central control—and as

the second player wrote, he quite regretted taking a draw here: ½-½ D.King-N.Davies, London 1989.

11...♗g7 12 ♖e1 0-0 13 ♗f4 ♖e8 14 ♕d2

If 14 e5 ♘d5 15 ♘xd5 dxe5! is a clever trick that recovers the piece with advantage.

14...♘g4 15 h3 ♘e5 16 b3 ♘c6 17 ♖ad1 ♘d4 18 ♘d5 c6

Black has to take some risks to win after this. As Keres pointed out, 18...a5! is better, keeping the option of ...♗xd5 and stirring up queenside play. If then 19 c3 ♘b5 only weakens White's c-pawn.

19 ♘c3 ♖e6 20 ♘a4 ♕e7 21 c3 ♘b5 22 ♗g5 ♕f8 23 ♗e3 h5 24 f3 ♖ae8 25 ♘e2

25...f5!?

Risky, but Keres is not playing Mecking here so he goes for the win! Of course 25...♕e7 with equality is possible.

26 ♘f4 ♖f6 27 exf5 ♖xf5 28 ♘d3?!

Correct is the bold 28 ♘xg6 ♕f6 29 ♘f4, when Black wins the c-pawn back but his breezy king position causes concern. Now the weaker player is gradually pushed back.

28...♗c8 29 ♘f2 ♖d5 30 ♕c1 ♖de5 31 ♗d2 ♗e6 32 ♖xe5 ♗xe5 33 f4 ♗g7 34 ♖e1 c4! 35 b4 ♗f5

Black has activated both bishops while his kingside remains intact: thus, a clear plus to Black.

36 ♘b6 d5 37 a4 ♘d6 38 ♖xe8 ♕xe8 39 ♗e3 ♘e4!

The c3-pawn is the target, and it's beginning to crack.

40 ♘xe4 ♕xe4 41 ♕d2 0-1

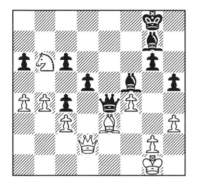

Adjournment analysis convinced Daskalov that his position was hopeless. White resigned in view of 41...♕d3! 42 ♕xd3 ♗xd3, after which 43 b5 is the only try (clearly 43 ♗d2 d4! 44 ♗c1 dxc3 is hopeless, while 44 cxd4 ♗xd4+ 45 ♔h2 ♗xb6 gives Black a clean piece), but it fails to 43...axb5 44 a5 (if 44 axb5 cxb5 45 ♘xd5 ♗e4 46 ♘c7 ♗xc3 and the passed c-pawn + bishops should win) 44...c5! 45 a6 (no better is 45 ♗xc5 d4 46 cxd4 c3 47 ♘d5 c2 48 ♗a3 ♗xd4+ 49 ♔h2 ♗e4 50 ♘b4 ♗c3 51 ♘a2 ♗xa5 and White's last

hope falls) 45...d4 46 a7 ♗e4 (just in time!) 47 cxd4 cxd4 48 ♗c1 d3 49 a8♕+ ♗xa8 50 ♘xa8 b4 and the three pawns beat the piece; e.g. 51 ♘c7 c3 52 ♘b5 b3 etc.

Black's sound structure and especially his bishop pair (in a rather open position) are a heavy counterweight to White's play. Even trivial errors in the opening (8 ♘e2 seen in the main game, or 8 ♘c6 given in the notes) can give Black some advantage. In the next game Spassky plays the correct 8 ♘f3, but still only succeeds in holding the balance.

Game 56
B.Spassky-P.Keres
USSR Championship,
Moscow 1973

---

1 e4 e5 2 ♘f3 ♘c6 3 ♗b5 a6 4 ♗a4 d6 5 ♗xc6+ bxc6 6 d4 exd4 7 ♘xd4 c5 8 ♘f3!

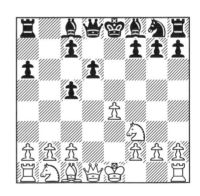

Best: White must at least think of advancing e4-e5 to maintain some play.

8...♘f6

Spassky also got nothing against the alternative knight development, similar to Games 53-54: 8...♘e7 9 0-0 ♘g6 10 ♘c3 ♗e7 11 ♖e1 0-0 12 ♘d5 and now, instead of 12...♗f6 after which Black floundered and lost in B.Spassky-K.Göhring, German League 1981, Black should just kick the knight immediately with equality; e.g. 12...c6 13 ♘xe7+ ♕xe7 14 ♗d2 f6 15 ♗c3 ♗e6, when Black not only has an excellent restraint structure, he can also choose to become active later with ...d6-d5 or ...a6-a5.

Another high-level game went 9 ♘c3 ♘c6 10 h3 ♗e7 11 0-0 0-0 12 ♖e1 ♗e6 13 b3 ♗f6 14 ♗b2 ♘d4 15 ♘a4 ♗d7!? (15...♘xf3+ 16 ♕xf3 ♗xb2 17 ♘xb2 ♕g5 should be equal, but there's something to be said for Black's idea, which is simply that White's extra a-pawn doesn't mean anything!) 16 ♘xd4 cxd4 17 ♗xd4 ♗xa4 18 bxa4 ♖e8 19 ♖b1 ♗e5 20 ♕d3 ♕d7 21 ♕c4 ♗xd4 22 ♕xd4 ♕c6 23 ♖b4 ♕xc2 24 ♖c4 ♕xa2 25 ♖xc7 ♖ab8 26 ♖a7 d5 27 e5 ♕c4 28 ♕xc4 dxc4 29 ♖xa6 ♖ec8 30 ♖c1 c3 31 ♖a5 ♔f8 32 ♖b5 ♖xb5 33 axb5 ♖b8 34 ♖xc3 ♖xb5 35 f4 g5 36 g3 gxf4 37 gxf4 f6 38 ♖c8+ ♔e7 39 exf6+ ♔xf6 40 ♔g2 and for no reason that's apparent to me, this dead-drawn position was continued for more than 30 moves before the inevitable ½-½ A.Stripunsky-R.Hess, New York 2004—note that the young leader of the black pieces is now a GM!

9 0-0

White can carry out his break, but he can't profit from it: after 9 e5 ♕e7 10 ♕e2 dxe5 11 ♕xe5 ♕xe5+ 12 ♘xe5 ♗d6 13 ♘c4 ♗f5 Black's excellent development plus the bishop pair outweigh the damaged pawn structure.

9...♗e7 10 ♘c3 0-0 11 ♖e1

Again, if 11 e5 dxe5 12 ♘xe5 ♕xd1 13 ♖xd1 ♖e8 14 ♗e3 ♗f5 15 ♖d2 ♗f8 with the usual active play. This shows that e4-e5, often breaking Black's pawns, also often activates the black bishop pair to such an extent that the pawn structure doesn't matter.

11...♗b7 12 h3

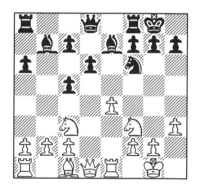

Black has gained the usual marginal plus—I don't see that White has any real compensation for the bishop pair—and I think Black keeps the edge with either 12...♖e8 or 12...♖b8.

12...♘d7

Keres' actual move leads to surrendering the bishop pair, and gives White a slight initiative, though nothing to worry about too much. The strength of Black's position in these lines made me begin to wonder whether the whole line without the tempo gain (that is, 4 ♗xc6 bxc6!) would be sound—and I found out that Larsen, Alekhine and Lasker had wondered the same thing—and better yet, tested this idea out with success!

13 ♘d5 ♗f6 14 ♖b1 ♖b8 15 b3 ♖e8

Not 15...♘b6 16 ♘xb6 cxb6 17 ♗f4 ♗e7 18 ♕d3 which gives White a target at d6.

16 ♗f4 h6 17 ♕d2 ♗e5 18 ♘xe5 ♘xe5 19 ♗g3 ♕d7 20 ♖bd1 ♗xd5 21 ♕xd5 ♕e6 22 ♗xe5 ♕xe5 23 ♕c6

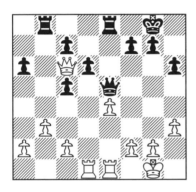

23...♕e7

Black should run for the draw here with 23...♕c3! 24 ♖e2 (or the pawn massacre variation 24 ♕xc7 ♕xc2 25 ♖xd6 ♕xa2 26 ♕xc5 ♖xe4! 27 ♖xe4 ♕b1+ 28 ♔h2 ♕xe4 29 ♖xa6 ♖xb3 resulting in dead equality) 24...♕a5 which is equal and drawish.

24 ♖e3

Boris misses his chance, as 24 e5 finally works! Since 24...dxe5 fails to the rook invasion 25 ♖d7, Black has to defend with 24...♖b6 25 ♕a4 ♕e6 26 f4 ♖e7 27 ♕e4 when White might claim a small pull with his central control—and Black's biggest trump, the bishop

pair, has vanished from the board.

24...♖b6 25 ♕a4 f6

But now White has no good breaks, and so...

½-½

Though Boris did have one middle-game chance for an edge, the opening was, if anything, slightly favourable for Black.

1 e4 e5 2 ♘f3 ♘c6 3 ♗b5 a6 4 ♗a4 d6 5 ♗xc6+ bxc6 6 d4 exd4 7 ♘xd4 ♗d7

This seems perfectly playable, if quieter than 7...c5. Black simply defends and develops, then plans to kick the knight out later (in this game on move 17). The only drawback is that White can try to blockade the queen-side with b2-b4, but that also creates a weakness that allows tactical play (see the following note).

8 0-0 g6

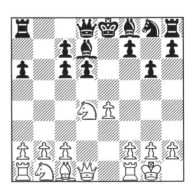

9 ♘c3

Keres also played 7...♗d7 on occasion; here his opponent tries to "punish" him by preventing ...c6-c5—but the punishment falls on White: 9 b4 ♗g7 10 ♗b2 ♘f6 11 ♘b3 0-0 12 ♘1d2 ♖e8 13 f3 ♕b8 (not a bad idea, as Keres creates counterplay on the b-file—but there was also a strong tactic available, based on the undefended bishop at b2: 13...♘xe4!? 14 ♗xg7 ♘xd2 15 ♗b2 ♘xf1 16 ♕d4 ♖e5 17 ♖xf1 f6 18 f4 ♖e8 and White doesn't have enough for the exchange, while 17 f4 ♘e3 18 fxe5 ♘xc2 19 ♕c3 ♘xa1 20 e6 f6 21 exd7 ♘xb3 22 ♕xb3+ ♔g7 23 ♕e6 ♕f8 finally turns in Black's favour, as there is no way to break into his position) 14 a3 a5! 15 bxa5 (Keres' idea is 15 ♘xa5 ♖xa5! 16 ♗xf6 ♕a7+ 17 ♔h1 ♗xf6 18 bxa5 ♗xa1 19 ♕xa1 ♕xa5, when Black has a clear edge in view of White's ragged pawns) 15...c5 16 ♖b1 ♕a7 17 c4 ♗a4 18 ♕c1 ♖ab8 19 ♗c3 ♖b7 20 ♕b2 ♘h5 21 ♗xg7 ♘xg7 22 ♕c3 ♘e6 23 f4 ♘d4 24 ♘xd4 cxd4 25 ♕f3 (if 25 ♖xb7 dxc3+ 26 ♖xa7 cxd2 27 ♖xc7 ♖a8 28 ♔f2 d1♕ 29 ♖xd1 ♗xd1 and I doubt White's three pawns are enough for the piece) 25...♖xb1 26 ♖xb1 ♕xa5 (Black has recovered his pawn with the better game) 27 ♕f2 ♕c3 28 ♖e1 ♗c6 29 f5 gxf5 30 exf5 ♖xe1+ 31 ♕xe1 ♕xa3 32 ♘f1 ♕d3 33 ♕h4 ♕xf5 34 ♕xd4 ♕e4 35 ♕d2 ♕xc4 36 ♕g5+ ♔f8 37 ♘e3 ♕c1+ 38 ♔f2 ♕b2+ 39 ♔g1 ♕c1+ 40 ♔f2 ♕b2+ 41 ♔g1 ♕e5 42 ♕h6+ ♔e8 43 h4 ♕g3 44 ♔f1 ♗e4 (again we see Keres win with the superior minor piece) 45 ♔e2 ♗g6 46 ♔f1 ♗d3+ 47 ♔g1 ♗e4 48 ♔f1 ♔e7 49 ♔e2 c5 50 h5 f6 51 ♘d1 0-1 V.Simagin-P.Keres, Szczawno Zdroj 1950.

9...♗g7 10 ♖e1 ♘e7 11 ♘f3

11 ♗f4 led to one of Alekhine's attacking masterpieces, though Black could have equalized with some sharper play: 11...0-0 12 ♕d2 c5 13 ♘b3 ♘c6 14 ♗h6 (this is Black's chance!—see below)

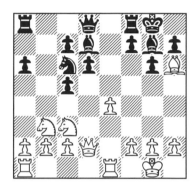

14...♗e6 15 ♗xg7 ♔xg7 16 ♘d5 f6 17 ♖ad1 ♖b8 18 ♕c3 (note the position of the white queen, which both defends his queenside and attacks—Black had to lure the queen out of position, where it only had one function) 18...♕c8 19 a3 ♕b7 20 h3 ♖f7 21 ♖e3 ♕b5 22 ♘xc7!! (Alekhine breaks through, with fireworks) 22...♖xc7 23 ♖xd6 ♗c4 24 a4 ♕xa4 25 ♘xc5 ♕b5 26 ♕xf6+ ♔g8 27 ♘d7 ♖d8 28 ♖f3 ♕b4 29 c3 ♕b5 30 ♘e5! (nothing can be taken!) 30...♖dc8 31 ♘xc6 1-0 A.Alekhine-G.Koltanowski, London 1932.

Going back, 14...♗xh6 15 ♕xh6 a5! is correct: while White's queen is away on the kingside, without back-up, Black attacks on the opposite wing, keeping the defensive resource ...♕f6-g7 in hand; e.g. 16 ♘d5 (if 16 a3 a4 17 ♘d2 ♘d4 and the centralized knight gives Black a plus, or 16 ♖e3 ♖b8 17 f4 c4 18 f5 ♕f6 19 ♘d5 ♕g7 and Black beats off the attack with advantage) 16...♘b4 with equality.

11...f6

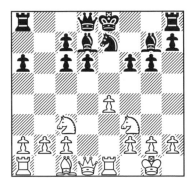

Bronstein prevents e4-e5, but it's possible to ignore White's "threat"; e.g. 11...0-0 12 e5 dxe5 13 ♘xe5 ♗f5 and once again Black's active bishops compensate for the split pawns.

12 ♕d3 0-0 13 ♕c4+ ♔h8 14 ♘d4 ♕e8 15 f4

Of course 15 ♘e6 fails to 15...♕f7.

15...♕f7 16 ♕d3 c5 17 ♘f3

Black has evicted the knight and stands fully equal, but how to win? Given that this was the Lasker Memorial, Bronstein says he decided, Lasker style, to create small difficulties for his opponent—then finally sacrificed a pawn for "purely psychological considerations!"

Actually I think there was a pretty good positional basis for the sac, but in any case he certainly confused his opponent!

17...♗c6 18 ♗e3 ♗b7 19 ♖ad1 c4!?

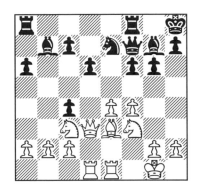

A key move: Black advances and gains space, but at the same time the pawn moves "beyond the reach" of his fellows. However, Bronstein is not concerned with saving the pawn—the very irritation of the pawn on the fifth causes problems: psychological *and* on the board. Even if Black loses the pawn, as happens later, then he just gets some more open lines for attacking purposes!

By the way, Mr. *Fritz* is unimpressed both with Bronstein's psychology and my long note above, and now gives White the dreaded plus equals—but I disagree: I like Black's dynamism which is hard to measure in bytes!

20 ♕d2 ♖fe8 21 ♗f2 h6 22 ♘d5 ♘xd5 23 exd5 ♖xe1+ 24 ♗xe1 ♖e8 25 ♕d4 f5!

Taking over the square e4 is more important than the pawn (says me)—

Fritz is still at plus equals!

26 ♕xc4 c5 27 ♕d3 ♖e4 28 c3 ♕e8 29 ♗f2 ♕b5!

Black confidently exchanges queens a pawn down—his roving rook on the fifth plus the two bishops give him full compensation for the pawn.

30 ♕xb5 axb5 31 ♘d2 ♖a4

Black could trap himself here: 31...♖xf4 32 ♗g3 ♖g4 33 ♗xd6 ♗xd5 34 g3 ♗xa2 looks good until you see 35 ♗f4, which traps Black's rook and so wins the exchange.

32 a3 ♗f8

Now Black threatens to take on f4 with impunity, while d5 is hanging as well. But White does have a way out!

33 b3?!

The Modern Steinitz, unexpected manoeuvres, Bronstein's psychological pawn sac—all this caused so much confusion that White was now in serious time pressure. In such a state, it's not a surprise that he missed the one escape hatch, 33 ♘b3! and then:

a) 33...♖xf4 34 ♘xc5! is the point, sacrificing a knight for a powerful d-

pawn—White could even win after 34...dxc5 35 d6 ♗c6 36 d7 ♗xd7 37 ♖xd7 ♖a4 38 ♔f1 ♔g8 39 ♗e3 h5 40 ♗d2 b4 (40...♖e4 41 ♖b7 wins a pawn) 41 cxb4 cxb4 42 ♗xb4! ♖xb4 43 ♖d4, when he emerges a pawn up with excellent winning chances.

b) 33...♔g8! 34 g3 (the sac fails here because Black's rook can defend: 34 ♘xc5 dxc5 35 d6 ♖a8) 34...♔f7 and Black has full compensation for the pawn, but the game is about even.

33...♖xa3

Now Black recovers his pawn and retains the initiative.

34 c4 ♗a6 35 ♖c1 g5!

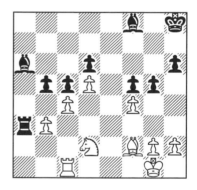

Black attacks on all sides, and the seconds tick away...

36 fxg5 hxg5 37 b4?

Desperation! The passive 37 ♖b1 gives some faint chances to hold.

37...cxb4 38 cxb5 ♗xb5 39 ♗d4+ 0-1

White lost on time, but the position is lost anyway: Black plays 39...♔g8 40 ♗f6 g4 41 ♖b1 ♖a4 and keeps both his bishop pair and his gift passed pawn.

One sees again that Black has no

problems in this Delayed Exchange—the only difficulty Bronstein faced was how to unbalance the position enough to win.

Game 58
N.Short-V.Hort
Dortmund 1983

---

1 e4 e5 2 ♘f3 ♘c6 3 ♗b5 a6 4 ♗a4 d6 5 d4

5 ♗xc6+ bxc6 6 d4 exd4 7 ♘xd4 ♗d7 reaches the game by this chapter's move order.

5...exd4

5...b5! is the simple equalizer—see Games 64-67.

6 ♘xd4 ♗d7 7 ♗xc6

7 ♘c3 is better, with the typical Steinitz Defence (but not Modern Steinitz!) edge.

7...bxc6

We have now transposed back to the previous game.

8 0-0 ♘f6

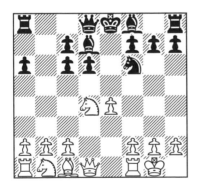

Hort chooses a more restrained de-

velopment than Bronstein's 8...g6—the fact that Black can play in various ways and still count on equality is a sign of the strength of the opening.

9 ♘c3

Another path is 9 ♕f3 c5 10 ♘f5 ♗xf5 11 ♕xf5 ♕d7 12 ♕f3 ♕g4 13 ♕xg4 ♘xg4 14 ♘c3 g6 15 ♘d5 ♔d7 16 ♗d2 ♗g7 17 h3 ♘f6 18 ♗c3 ♘e8 19 ♖ad1 ♗xc3 20 ♘xc3 f6 21 f4 ♖f8 22 e5 fxe5 23 fxe5 ♖xf1+ 24 ♔xf1 ♖b8 25 b3 ♖b4 26 exd6 cxd6 27 ♘d5 ♖e4 28 ♔f2 ♔c6 29 c4 ♘c7 30 ♘xc7 ♔xc7 with dead equality in V.Vasiliev-J.R.Capablanca, Leningrad (simul) 1935.

9...♗e7 10 ♕f3 0-0 11 e5

One always sees White trying to make something with this break, but it rarely accomplishes anything, for whatever damage to Black's structure occurs is offset by the opening of the board for his bishops.

11...♘g4 12 ♘xc6 ♗xc6 13 ♕xg4?!

The brave young Short avoids 13 ♕xc6 ♘xe5 with dead equality, preferring to leave Black with two isolated queenside pawns—but instead of being able to exploit said pawns, he gets a lesson in the power of the two bishops!

13...dxe5 14 ♖e1 ♗d6 15 ♗g5 ♕c8 16 ♕xc8 ♖fxc8

Despite the isolated pawns, the ending actually favours Black with his bishop pair and mobile kingside majority.

17 ♖ad1 f6 18 ♗d2 ♖d8 19 ♘e4 ♗e7 20 f3 ♖d5 21 ♗e3 ♖a5 22 a3 ♖b8 23 ♗c1

♖d5 24 ♖xd5 ♗xd5 25 ♖d1 ♗e6 26 b3 ♖b6 27 ♗b2 ♔f7 28 ♔f1 ♖c6 29 ♖d2 h5 30 ♖e2 ♖b6 31 ♖e3 ♖c6 32 ♖c3 ♖xc3 33 ♘xc3 ♗f5 34 ♘e4 ♔e6 35 ♔e2 g5 36 h3 g4

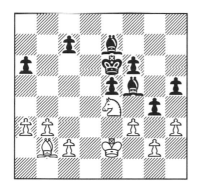

Hort breaks open the kingside—more room for the bishops! Note that Black's isolated queenside pawns have not been any kind of factor: White hasn't been able to effectively attack them at all.

37 hxg4 hxg4 38 a4 ♗g6 39 ♗c1 f5 40 ♘f2 gxf3+ 41 gxf3 ♗h5 42 ♘d3 ♗d6 43 ♔f2 ♗d5 44 ♗e3 f4 45 ♗c1 c5 46 ♗b2 ♗g6 47 c4+ ♔e6 48 ♔e2 e4 49 fxe4 ♗xe4 50 ♗a3

White has finally created a target at c5, but...

50...f3+ 51 ♔e3 ♗xd3! 52 ♔xd3 ♔f5

...it's too late! Black no longer needs both bishops and can win with his passed pawn.

53 ♗c1

White can't keep the black king out: 53 ♔e3 ♔g4 54 ♔f2 ♔f4 55 ♗c1+ ♔e4 56 ♗a3 (or 56 ♔e3 ♔g3+ and the pawn ending is trivial) 56...♗e7 57 ♔g3

(other losers are 57 ♔f1 ♔d3 and 57 ♗b2 ♗h4+ 58 ♔f1 ♗g5 59 a5 ♗e3 60 ♗a3 ♔d3) 57...♔e3 and the pawn goes through.

53...♗e5 54 ♗d2

If 54 ♗a3 ♗d4 55 b4 ♔g4 56 bxc5 ♔h3! 57 c6 f2 and queens with check.

54...♔g4 0-1

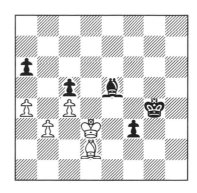

White's only try is 55 b4 (other moves lose simply: 55 ♔e3 ♗f4+ 56 ♔d3 ♗xd2 57 ♔xd2 ♔g3 58 ♔e1 ♔g2 and as always the pawn ending is a breeze, or 55 ♗e1 ♔h3 56 ♔e4 ♗g3 57 ♔xf3 ♗xe1 58 ♔e4 ♔g4 59 ♔d5 ♗b4 60 ♔e4 a5 61 ♔e3 ♔g3 62 ♔e2 ♔g2— even Black's "bad" bishop is good enough to help Black turn the corner— 63 ♔e3 ♔f1 64 ♔d3 ♔e1 65 ♔c2 ♔e2 etc) 55...♔h3! (this well-known Botvinnik manoeuvre has cropped up several times in this ending—White is helpless against the diagonal advance of the king) 56 ♗e1 (or 56 b5 f2 and queens) 56...♗g3 57 ♔e3 ♗xe1 58 ♔xf3 ♗xb4 and Black wins easily.

Hort won in the style of Lasker and Capablanca!

I can't see any serious problems for Black in this variation as long as he plays 6...exd4. After this, there is much scope for individual play: sometimes fianchetto, sometimes ...♘f6/...♗e7, and while ...c6-c5 is my preference right away, these last two games show it can be delayed or, as here, not played at all.

I mentioned in Chapter One that even though such World Champions as Euwe and Capablanca played 6...f6, I did not like Black's cramped game, which I think favours White's knight pair. Let's take a last look at this variation, with White played by a specialist in the Delayed Exchange, Jacob Yukhtman.

Game 59
J.Yukhtman-A.Genin
USSR Team
Championship 1964

When Jacob Yukhtman emigrated to New York around 1970, he was renowned for having defeated Tal with the Göring Gambit (!) and for his bold attacking play. He won tournament after tournament in a brief US career, capped by a stunning double rook sacrifice that took down fellow Soviet émigré Lev Alburt in the New York Open of 1980—and then, so far as I know, he disappeared from the chess world. I had the pleasure of playing him a few times, and the honour of defeating him once—and learned much from my losses, one of which was

with the Modern Steinitz! I had no idea he was a specialist in the white side of the Delayed Exchange in those pre-database days; although I no longer have the game score, I still remember the opening moves (see the note to move 7). But first, take a look at the Tal and Alburt wins:

Tal is brought down by a gambit! 1 e4 e5 2 ♘f3 ♘c6 3 d4 exd4 4 c3! dxc3 5 ♘xc3 ♗b4 6 ♗c4 ♘f6 7 0-0 ♗xc3 8 bxc3 d6 9 e5 dxe5 10 ♘g5 (White sacrifices two pawns in Tal style!)

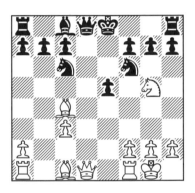

10...0-0 11 ♗a3 ♕xd1 12 ♖axd1 ♗f5 13 ♗xf8 ♖xf8 14 ♖fe1 h6 15 ♘f3 ♗g4 16 ♖b1 e4 17 ♘d4 ♘e5 18 ♗f1 c5 19 ♘b5 c4 20 f3 ♗xf3 21 gxf3 ♘xf3+ 22 ♔f2 ♘g4+ 23 ♔g3 ♘xe1 24 ♖xe1 f5 25 ♗xc4+ ♔h7 26 ♗e2 ♘e5 27 ♔f4 ♘g6+ 28 ♔e3 f4+ 29 ♔d4! (29 ♔xe4 f3! 30 ♗xf3 ♖e8+ would be a typical Tal miracle, but no such luck for Mischa on this day!) ♔h8 30 ♖g1 ♘h4 31 ♔xe4 ♖e8+ 32 ♔d3 f3 33 ♗d1 ♘g2 34 ♔d2 ♘h4 35 ♘d4 ♖d8 36 ♖f1 ♖d5 37 ♔d3 ♖a5 38 ♗b3 g5 39 ♘xf3 1-0 J.Yukhtman-M.Tal, USSR Championship, Tbilisi 1959.

Instead of sac'ing two pawns, here Yukhtman sacs two rooks! 1 d4 ♘f6 2 c4 c5 3 ♘f3 cxd4 4 ♘xd4 e6 5 g3 ♗b4+ 6 ♘c3 0-0 7 ♗g2 d5 8 cxd5 ♘xd5 9 ♗d2 ♗xc3 10 bxc3 e5 11 ♘b3 ♘c6 12 c4 ♘b6 13 ♖c1 ♕e7 14 c5 ♘d7 15 0-0 ♖d8 16 ♘a5 (White plays for positional pressure, but Black regroups creatively) 16...♘db8 17 ♕e1 ♗e6 18 ♘b3 ♗d5 19 ♗e3 ♗xg2 20 ♔xg2 ♘a6 21 ♖c4 ♕e6 22 ♖h4 ♖d7 23 ♕b1 h6 24 f3 ♖ad8 25 ♕b2 ♘ab4 26 ♗f2 g5 27 ♖e4 f5 28 ♖e3 ♘d5 29 ♖d3 e4 30 fxe4 fxe4 31 ♖xd5 (White's exchange sacrifices fall short) 31...♕xd5 32 ♗e3 ♖f7 33 ♖f6 ♘e5 34 ♖xh6 ♕d1 35 ♖h8+ ♔xh8 36 ♕xe5+ ♔g8 37 ♕xg5+ ♖g7 (up two exchanges, Yukhtman feels he has rooks to give...) 38 ♕h5 ♕d5 39 ♕h6 ♕c4 40 ♕h5 ♕f7 41 ♕e5 ♖e8 42 ♕b2 ♖f8 43 ♘d2 ♖g6 44 ♕b4 ♕d5 45 ♕a4 ♖a6 46 ♕b4 ♖xa2 47 c6 ♖xd2! (here's one!) 48 ♗xd2 e3+ 49 ♔g1 ♖f1+! (and here's the other!) 50 ♔xf1 (and resigns in view of mate) 0-1 L.Albert-J.Yukhtman, New York Open 1980.

1 e4 e5 2 ♘f3 ♘c6 3 ♗b5 a6 4 ♗a4 d6 5 ♗xc6+ bxc6 6 d4 f6

I don't recommend this at all, which closes the game for the knight pair—but I was not so sophisticated about the opening in 1972! My game with Yukhtman continued 7 ♘c3 g6 8 ♗e3 ♘h6 9 dxe5 and now I couldn't figure out how to recapture: I didn't like 9...fxe5 10 ♗g5 when I have to play the awkward 10...♕d7, and I didn't like 9...dxe5 10 ♕xd8+ ♔xd8 when I have three isolated pawns in a doubtful ending. But I thought sac'ing a pawn for the two bishops might be promising, so I tried 9...♘g4. My opponent, entirely unfazed, calmly took the pawn with 10 exf6 ♘xe3 11 fxe3 ♕xf6 12 0-0 and as it turned out, White's active knights, plus the central control of his doubled pawns far outweighed my two bishops, and so eventually... 1-0 J.Yukhtman-T.Taylor, New York 1972. That was the very last time I played 6...f6.

Keres himself tried 6...f6 on occasion, against weaker players—here's an example: 7 ♗e3 ♖b8 8 b3 ♘e7 9 ♘c3 ♘g6 10 ♕d3 ♗e7 11 0-0-0 a5 12 h4 (Black has the unpleasantly cramped position typical of this line, but it's complicated, so even though Keres is completely outplayed in the opening and early middlegame, his experience and practical guile give him the win in the end—but such trickery wouldn't have worked against Spassky or Mecking!) 12...♗d7 13 h5 ♘f8 14 ♘h4 a4 15 f4 axb3 16 cxb3 ♘e6 17 d5 cxd5 18 exd5 ♘xf4 19 ♗xf4 exf4 20 h6 g5 21 ♘g6!

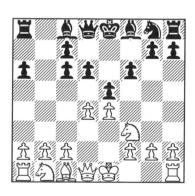

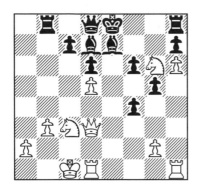

(this surprise blow should win for White; Keres finds the only practical chance: give up an exchange to start activating the bishops, but there's hardly enough compensation) 21...♔f7 22 ♘xh8+ ♕xh8 23 ♕d4 (White should win by manoeuvring his *knight* to this square, not the queen: correct is 23 ♘e2 intending ♘d4, with the knight scenting weak squares at c6 and e6—missing this, White is gradually outplayed, though he is certainly not lost for a long time) 23...f5 24 ♕xh8 ♖xh8 25 ♖d4 ♖c8 26 ♖c4 c5 27 dxc6 ♗e6 28 ♖b4 ♖xc6 29 ♔d2 ♗f6 30 ♘e2 (better is 30 ♖c1 ♔g6 31 a4 and White is still at least equal as his passed a-pawn is a dangerous threat) 30...♗d5 31 ♖g1 ♗e4 32 ♖c4 ♖xc4 33 bxc4 ♗d8 (Black is now better in view of the devalued enemy queenside and the fact that White is using a whole rook to defend a pawn—but if the rook moves, Black takes and wins with his kingside pawn mass) 34 ♘c3 ♗a5 35 ♖c1 ♗xg2 36 ♔d3 ♔e6 37 a4 g4 38 c5 dxc5 39 ♘e2 ♗e4+ 40 ♔c4 f3 41 ♘f4+ ♔f6 0-1 J.Kupper-P.Keres,

Zürich 1961: another great endgame lesson from Mr. K, but please don't follow his opening play!

Keres also occasionally experimented with 6...♗g4 7 dxe5 dxe5 which reaches a structure I warned about in Game 47: Black's excessively split pawns on the queenside are a long-term problem unless he has exceptionally active pieces. That not being the case here, White might try for an endgame grind—but in the following game, another problem arises: White, much lower rated, is happy with a draw and Keres can do nothing, as his position lacks dynamism due to the lamed pawns: 8 ♕xd8+ ♖xd8 9 ♘bd2 (of course not 9 ♘xe5?? ♖d1 mate) 9...♗d6 10 0-0 ♘e7 11 h3 ♗h5 12 ♘c4 f6 13 ♗e3 ♗f7 14 ♘fd2 ♖b8 15 c3 c5 16 f3 (White has parked his knight in front of the doubled pawns, and secured his centre—nothing much happens for the rest of the game, though one can see Keres trying!) 16...♘c6 17 ♖fd1 ♔e7 18 ♔f1 ♖b5 19 ♔e2 ♖hb8 20 a4 ♖5b7 21 ♔d3 ♗e6 22 ♔c2 g6 23 g4 ♖h8 24 ♖g1 h5 25 gxh5 ♖xh5 26 ♖xg6 ♖xh3 27 ♖g7+ ♗f7 28 ♖ag1 ♖b8 29 ♗f2 ♖bh8 30 ♘e3 ♔f8 31 ♖7g3 ♘e7 32 ♖xh3 ♖xh3 33 ♖g3 ♖h8 34 ♖g1 ♗e6 35 ♔d3 ♔f7 36 ♘ec4 ♘g6 37 ♗e3 ♗e7 38 ♖f1 ♖h2 39 b3 ♗f8 40 ♖f2 ♖h3 41 ♘a5 ½-½ H.Hecht-P.Keres, Varna Olympiad 1962.

I wouldn't recommend this against a strong player, who might grind unmercifully against you—and the endgame position is too quiet to beat a weaker player—so I can't recommend 6...♗g4 at all!

7 ♘c3 ♘e7 8 ♗e3

8...♗e6

Another Yukhtman triumph, quite similar to the main game, went as follows: 8...♘g6 9 ♕d2 ♗e7 10 h4 h5 11 0-0-0 ♗e6 12 dxe5 fxe5 13 ♘g5 (we'll see this knight raid again) 13...♗g8 14 g3 ♕c8 15 f4 ♕b7 16 ♘f3 ♗c4 17 b3 ♖b8 18 ♘xe5! (White sacrifices a piece, but will soon get it back with a savage attack) 18...dxe5 19 ♕d7+ ♔f8 20 f5 (the black knight has no squares) 20...♕b4 21 ♔b2 ♘xh4 (after 21...♕a3+ 22 ♔a1 Black can't get through; e.g. 22...♗b4 23 ♘b1 ♕a5 24 fxg6 is too easy, or 23...♗xb3!? with the trick 24 ♘xa3 ♗c3+ 25 ♔b1 ♗e6+, but White doesn't have to fall for it: 24 ♗c5+! ♗xc5 and the black queen is now edible, or 24...♔g8 25 cxb3 and wins) 22 gxh4 ♕a5 23 ♘b1 ♗f7 24 ♕xc6 ♗e8 25 ♕c3 ♗b4 26 ♕c4 ♗f7 27 ♕d3 ♕b5 28 ♘c3 ♕a5 29 ♘d5 ♗d6 30 ♕c3 ♕a3+ 31 ♔a1 ♖b5 32 ♗c1 ♕c5 33 ♕xc5 ♖xc5 34

c4 (White consolidates with his extra pawn—the knight is a powerhouse) 34...♖c6 35 ♗e3 ♔g8 36 ♘b1 ♔h7 37 c5 ♗f8 38 ♘b4 ♖xc5 39 ♗xc5 ♗xc5 40 ♘xa6 ♗d6 41 ♘xc7! (one last beautiful knight blow finishes the game) 41...♖d8 42 ♘e6 ♗xe6 43 fxe6 ♔g6 44 ♖hg1+ ♔f6 45 ♖df1+ 1-0 J.Yukhtman-F.Cheremisin, Moscow 1958.

9 ♕d2 ♕b8 10 b3 ♘g6 11 h4 h5 12 dxe5

Again this capturing dilemma: I think taking with the d-pawn is the lesser evil, as despite the isolated pawns, at least the f8-bishop comes into the game.

12...fxe5?!

Black wants to justify 6...f6 and takes towards the centre—but now White's knights run amok.

13 ♘g5

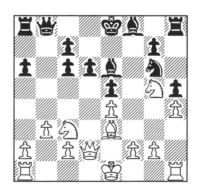

Yukhtman's patented raid!

13...♗g8 14 g3 ♗e7 15 f4 ♗f6 16 f5 ♘e7 17 0-0 a5 18 ♘a4 ♕b4 19 c3 ♕b7 20 ♖ad1 ♕c8 21 c4 c5 22 ♘c3 ♘c6 23 ♘d5

Talk about dominating knights!

23...♘d4 24 ♗xd4

Black is not allowed to enjoy any horsepower.

24...cxd4 25 ♘e6!

Having taken over the fifth rank, the knights now invade the sixth—the knight on e6 is too strong to ignore, but is, as Nimzowitsch would say, "heavily insured against death" by reason of the lines that would be opened in the case of capture.

25...♖a7 26 ♘xf6+ gxf6

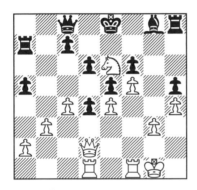

27 ♘xd4!!

The mark of the great master is the willingness to trade one advantage for another: Yukh abruptly gives up both his proud knights—exchanges one and sacrifices the next—but smashes Black's position in the process, while leaving his foe with a helpless and nearly immobile bishop on the back rank.

27...exd4 28 ♕xd4

White gains a tempo on the a7-rook and then lays waste to the black king-side.

28...♖a6 29 ♕xf6 ♖h7 30 e5 dxe5 31

♕g5 ♗f7 32 ♖fe1 ♖d6 33 ♖xe5+ ♔f8 34 ♖xd6 cxd6 35 ♕e7+ ♔g8 36 ♕xd6 ♖g7

If 36...a4 37 ♖b5 ♔g7 38 f6+ with a winning attack.

37 ♖xa5?

After all his great play, Yukhtman is inaccurate at the end. He doesn't need this pawn! Correct is 37 ♖b5! which controls the activity of the black queen and threatens to win same with ♖b8—this move wins easily. Whereas now Black will get one more chance!

37...♕b7 38 f6 ♖g6?

Losing! Here Black had the stunning resource 38...♕e4!! with a perpetual if White takes the rook, and on other moves it's obvious that the active queen puts Black back in the game.

39 ♕d8+ 1-0

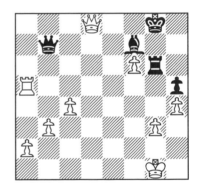

Black resigns as White can force the exchange of queens, when one of the many extra pawns will promote; e.g. 39...♔h7 40 ♖xh5+ (since White got away with taking on a5, that means he's now six pawns up!) 40...♖h6 41 ♕e7 ♕xe7 (41...♕b6+ only keeps the queens on for a moment: 42 c5 ♕e6 43

♖xh6+ ♚xh6 44 ♕xe6 ♗xe6 45 b4
♗xa2 46 g4 ♚g6 47 g5 ♗c4 48 c6 ♗b5
49 c7 ♗d7 50 b5 ♗c8 51 b6 ♗b7 52 h5+
♚f7 53 h6 ♚g6 54 ♚f2 and the white
king marches to e7; another way is
45...♚g6 46 b5 ♗xa2 47 c6 ♗d5 48 h5+
♚xf6 49 ♚f2 ♚g5 50 ♚e3 ♚xh5 51 ♚d4
♗f3 52 ♚c5 ♚g4 53 b6 etc) 42 ♖xh6+
♚xh6 43 fxe7 ♚g7 44 a4 ♚f6 45 a5
♚xe7 46 a6 ♗e8 47 a7 ♗c6 48 h5 ♚f6
49 h6 ♚g6 (49...♗e4 50 h7 ♚g7 51 b4
♚xh7 52 b5 ♚g7 53 c5 ♗a8 54 c6 ♚f7
55 c7 comes to the same thing) 50 b4
♚xh6 51 b5 ♗a8 52 c5 ♚g6 53 c6 ♚f7
54 c7 ♗b7 55 a8♕ ♗xa8 56 c8♕ and
wins.

This and all the subsidiary variations have the same result: a new, winning white queen.

This game was a knightmare!

Conclusion

The Delayed Exchange holds no terrors
for Black, since 6...exd4 is a clean equalizer which holds its own right to the
World Championship match level, and
which can be used to play for the win
against anyone. The bishop pair in the
open position will often give Black a
pull all the way to the endgame, as
Keres and Hort demonstrated.

On the other hand, 6...f6 is not good
at all against someone with an understanding of knight attacks, while
6...♗g4 sacrifices Black's pawn structure for too little.

Chapter Seven
The Duras Variation

The Duras Variation comes about after **1 e4 e5 2 ♘f3 ♘c6 3 ♗b5 a6 4 ♗a4 d6 5 c4!?**, where White (as I mentioned in Game 5) tries to impose a Maróczy Bind on a Ruy Lopez, which is not a good fit! The Duras is virtually never played at a high level today due to the Reshevsky/Yandemirov answer 5...♗g4 that equalizes on the spot, as we will see in Games 60-62. A risky attempt to play in Siesta style with 5...f5!? will be seen in Game 63.

Keres often played this rather off-beat line with White, probably to avoid "playing against himself"—one recalls his draw with Capablanca in the aforementioned Game 5. Capa equalized easily with 5...♗d7 6 ♘c3 g6 7 d4 exd4 8 ♘xd4 ♗g7 9 ♗e3 ♘ge7, but had no winning chances whatsoever. Interestingly enough, on the rare (three) occasions when Keres was faced with the Duras Variation as Black—he was

not entirely successful in avoiding "playing against himself"—he always played quietly, à la Capablanca. Here's an example: 5 c4 ♗d7 6 ♘c3 g6 7 d4 ♗g7 8 dxe5 ♘xe5 9 ♘xe5 ♗xe5 10 0-0 ♘f6 11 ♗g5 h6 12 ♗xd7+ ♕xd7 13 ♗xf6 ♗xf6 14 ♘d5 ♗g7 15 ♖c1 ♖d8 16 ♕f3 0-0 17 ♖fd1 ♔h8 18 ♖c2 c6 19 ♘e3 ♕e7

and one can see that Black's active bishop balances White's Maróczy Bind—the players manoeuvred about for another twenty moves without changing the basic nature of the position, and finally agreed to a draw in N.Karaklajic-P.Keres, USSR-Yugoslavia match, Leningrad 1957.

Now let's take a look at this rather unpromising (for White!) line—with Keres leading the way, on the wrong side!

Game 60
P.Keres-S.Reshevsky
World Championship,
The Hague/Moscow 1948

1 e4 e5 2 ♘f3 ♘c6 3 ♗b5 a6 4 ♗a4 d6 5 c4 ♗g4!

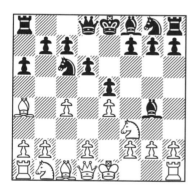

Black continues as in Chapter Five, but the pin is even stronger here as White has not made the useful developing move 5 0-0 and, furthermore, now has a weakness at d4. While we've seen that 5...♗d7 should equalize, it's also evident that Black has no serious winning chances after that—whereas the longer bishop move does give him

chances to win!

6 ♘c3

For 6 d3 and the subvariations 6 h3 and 6 d4, see Game 62.

6...♘e7

Reshevsky is trying to play as in the Knight Defence (Chapter Two), but Yandemirov's 6...♘f6 is stronger, for which see the next game.

7 h3 ♗xf3 8 ♕xf3 ♘g6

Not an ideal square for the knight in this variation, as will be seen.

9 ♘d5 ♖b8 10 ♘b4

Best—if 10 d3 b5 11 cxb5 axb5 12 ♗b3 ♘d4 and Black gets counterplay.

10...♘e7

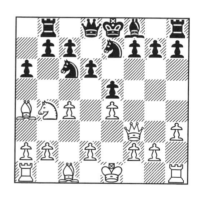

Now Reshevsky has to scurry back with the knight, and White could take over the advantage with the consistent 11 ♕b3 which really puts the pressure on. If Black tries to counter with 11...b5, then 12 ♘xc6 ♘xc6 13 cxb5 axb5 14 ♗xb5 and White is a pawn up. Instead, 11...a5 might be relatively best, but after 12 ♘d5 Black is tied up, unable to shake off the Spanish pin.

11 ♘c2?!

This unmotivated retreat allows Black to disentangle.

11...♕d7 12 d3 ♘c8 13 ♗d2 ♗e7 14 ♕g3 ♗f6 15 ♖c1 ♘b6

Black finally shakes off the pin (after great loss of time).

16 ♗b3

Even now 16 ♗xc6 ♕xc6 17 ♘e3 g6 18 ♘d5 ♗g7 should keep an edge for White with his superior minor pieces. However, Keres, in an unusually defensive mood, retreats again and allows Black to equalize.

16...♕d8 17 0-0 ♘d7 18 a3 ♘c5

Although very delayed, this knight manoeuvre—which we will see Yandemirov do regularly, and efficiently, in the next two games and notes—finally puts Black back on track.

19 ♗a2 0-0 20 b4 ♘e6 21 ♗e3 ♘f4!

Just when one expected a black knight to d4, Reshevsky, with his tactical alertness, finds a clean equalizer with this surprising knight jump.

22 ♕f3

Not 22 ♗xf4 exf4 23 ♕xf4 as 23...♗g5 spears an ox.

22...♘xd3 23 ♖b1 ♘f4 24 b5 ½-½

Black can answer 24...axb5 25 cxb5 ♘e7 26 ♗xf4 exf4 27 ♕xf4 ♖a8 which looks about equal: Black has the half open a-file, but White has a little more influence in the centre.

One sees that Black's king's knight was misplaced in the opening (the poor horse wore himself out, making eleven moves in this short game!

However, the ...♗g4 idea is very strong, when combined with the correct knight placement, as Yandemirov will show us.

Game 61
A.Ayapbergenov-
V.Yandemirov
Volgograd 1994

---

1 e4 e5 2 ♘f3 ♘c6 3 ♗b5 a6 4 ♗a4 d6 5 c4 ♗g4 6 ♘c3 ♘f6

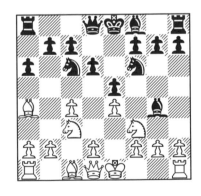

Clearly a more active move than Reshevsky's 6...♘e7, but what's most important is that the knight can be quickly redirected to c5, where it hits

White's Ruy bishop and observes the weak d3-square, and might be further manoeuvred to e6 to take advantage of the weak d4-square!

7 d4

White tries to break immediately. On the slower 7 h3 ♗xf3 8 ♕xf3 ♗e7 9 ♘e2 0-0 10 ♗xc6 bxc6 11 d4 one sees that White has fallen way behind in development in order to cover the d4-weakness—this allows Black to strike back with 11...d5! 12 dxe5 (even worse is 12 exd5 e4 when Black takes over the centre: 13 ♕c3 cxd5 14 c5 ♕d7 15 ♗e3 c6 16 0-0 ♘e8 17 f4 f5 18 b4 ♘c7 19 a4 h6 20 ♕d2 ♔h7 21 ♖ab1 ♖g8 22 ♔h2 g5 and Black won with an attack in S.Tatai-A.Medina Garcia, Wijk aan Zee 1968) 12...♗b4+ 13 ♘c3 ♘xe4 14 0-0 ♗xc3 15 bxc3 ♕e7 16 cxd5 cxd5 17 c4 ♕xe5 18 ♗f4 ♕c3 19 cxd5 ♕xf3 20 gxf3 ♘c3 21 ♗xc7 ♘xd5, and it's worth seeing Smyslov win this seemingly only marginally superior ending: 22 ♗g3 ♖fc8 23 ♖fd1 ♖c5 24 ♖d2 h6 25 ♖e1 ♖ac8 26 ♗d6 ♖c1 27 ♖xc1 ♖xc1+ 28 ♔g2 ♘b6 29 ♗g3 ♖c6 30 ♔f1 f6 31 ♔e2 ♔f7 32 ♔d3 ♖c5 33 ♖b2 ♘d7 34 ♔d4 ♖a5 35 ♖c2 ♔e6 36 ♖c6+ ♔f5 37 ♖c7 ♘e5 38 ♖c5 ♖a3 39 ♗xe5 ♖a4+ 40 ♖c4 fxe5+ 41 ♔d5 ♖xa2 42 ♖g4 g5 0-1 I.Boleslavsky-V.Smyslov, Leningrad 1948—a rare success for Smyslov in the Modern Steinitz!

7...exd4 8 ♗xc6+

Evidently not 8 ♕xd4?? b5! and Black wins a piece. A key motif of the MS is that Black can nearly always break the pin on his queen's knight when he needs to.

8...bxc6 9 ♕xd4 ♘d7

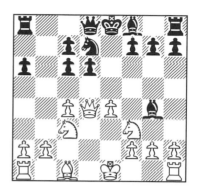

This is the key manoeuvre—the knight goes to c5 and makes room for the king's bishop at f6.

10 ♘d2 ♕h4

Typically aggressive play from Yandemirov!

11 0-0 ♗e7 12 f4

12 ♕xg7?? ♗f6 traps the queen.

12...0-0 13 ♔h1 ♗f6 14 ♕e3 ♖fe8

Now one can see that the white pawns are overextended; furthermore White's position is crippled by his lack of development, all of which means that Black is clearly better already.

15 ♘e2 ♗xe2 16 ♕xe2 ♘c5 17 ♕f3 ♖e6 18 e5

White doesn't want to wait for the second black rook to arrive on e8, and so tries to mix it up... but we all know about seeking complications in a worse position—not advisable!

18...dxe5 19 fxe5 ♖xe5 20 ♕xc6 ♖c8!

A surprisingly effective "discreet use of the energy of the rook" as Nimzowitsch would say. Now the white queen has no targets, and the rest of White's pieces are not in play.

21 ♘f3

Forking queen and rook, but Black's answer is crushing. Two other tries are slightly better, though neither saves White: 21 b3 ♖h5 22 ♘f3 ♕e4 23 ♕xe4 ♘xe4 and White will lose an exchange as both rooks are threatened (...♗xa1 and ...♘g3+), while if 21 ♖b1 ♕e1! with a powerful attack.

21...♕xc4

Threatening ...♕xf1, so now Yandemirov is just up a good pawn and wins quickly and stylishly.

22 ♖d1 ♖e6 23 ♕d5 ♖e1+! 0-1

White has little choice and no good answer (except resigns, which in fact he plays):

a) 24 ♖xe1 ♕xd5 wins the queen.

b) 24 ♘g1 ♘e4 25 h3 ♕xd5 26 ♖xd5 c6 27 ♖d7 (if 27 ♖a5 ♗d4 wins immediately) 27...c5! and there's no real defence to ...♗d4; e.g. 28 ♔h2 ♗e5+ 29 g3 ♗d4 30 ♘f3 ♖e2+ 31 ♔h1 ♘xg3 mate.

c) 24 ♘xe1 ♕f1 mate!

Although White can succeed in pushing through the advance d2-d4, it's far from easy—as in, say, the Accelerated Dragon where the Maróczy Bind is strong. Here White gave up the bishop pair and fell behind in development, so the Bind was weak and soon smashed.

In the next game, White tries a restrained set-up with d2-d3, but gets nothing either.

Game 62
V.Kupreichik-V.Yandemirov
St Petersburg 2001

1 e4 e5 2 ♘f3 ♘c6 3 ♗b5 a6 4 ♗a4 d6 5 c4

Apparently GM Kupreichik really likes the Duras Variation—or else he is very stubborn! He has played it five times vs. Yandemirov, and although always having the white pieces, and with an approximately equal rating to his MS foe, the result was two draws and three wins for Black! Every game

started out as here, 5 c4 ♗g4—but note that against another opponent (and if White wants this), a delayed Duras can be used as a drawing line (groaning sounds in background). I feel I have to put these in, since this "White to play and draw" disease has become epidemic, and as Black you will have to face such variations.

Kupreichik—and Keres himself— have used the following to make short draws: 5 0-0 ♗d7 (of course Yandemirov would play 5...♗g4 here, which is why I said "another opponent" above) 6 c4 ♘f6 7 ♘c3 ♗e7 8 d4 ♘xd4 (the easiest path to equality: Black trades off two pieces, somewhat similar to Game 5, Keres-Capablanca) 9 ♘xd4 exd4 10 ♗xd7+ ♘xd7 11 ♕xd4 ♗f6 12 ♕e3 0-0 13 ♘d5 ♖e8 14 ♘xf6+ ♘xf6 (now a third minor is off the board) 15 f3 c6 16 ♗d2 d5 17 cxd5 cxd5 18 e5 d4 19 ♕f4 ♘d7 20 ♕xd4 ♘xe5 ½-½ V.Kupreichik-Y.Balashov, Minsk 1986.

While Kupreichik was satisfied with a draw here, Keres boldly played on until only one piece on each side re-

mained: 21 ♗c3 ♕xd4+ 22 ♗xd4 ♖ad8 23 ♖fd1 ♖d5 24 ♗c3 ♘d3 25 ♖d2 ♘f4 26 ♖xd5 ♘xd5 27 ♗a5 ♖e2 28 ♖e1 ♖xe1+ 29 ♗xe1 f6 ½-½ P.Keres-S.Gligoric, Los Angeles 1963. Black's centralized knight, which cannot be dislodged by a pawn, is just as strong as White's bishop.

5...♗g4 6 d3

We saw that the natural developing move 6 ♘c3 gave White no advantage in the two previous games, so Kupreichik tries a more restrained set-up, not trying to get in d2-d4 too early. Also possible are:

a) 6 d4 (White gets equality at best from this early thrust) 6...exd4 (simple and good; but 6...b5!? while extravagant, is also playable: 7 cxb5 ♘xd4 8 bxa6+ c6 and it's hard for White to hold the extra pawn, or 8 ♘c3 axb5 9 ♘xb5 ♘xf3+ 10 gxf3 ♗d7 11 ♗b3 ♘f6 12 ♘c3 g6 13 ♗g5 ♗g7 14 ♕d2 0-0 15 h4 ♕b8 with a very double-edged, opposite sides attacking game in J.Florian-J.Banas, Harrachov 1970) 7 ♗xc6+ (of course not 7 ♕xd4?? b5 8 ♕d5 ♘ge7 and Black wins) 7...bxc6 8 ♕xd4 ♗xf3 (also good is 8...♘f6 9 ♘c3 ♘d7, transposing to the previous game) 9 gxf3 ♕f6 with a familiar Yandemirov type position, where the doubled pawns on both sides balance each other.

b) 6 h3 (another Kupreichik try which induces an exchange on f3, but in fact Black does not mind removing a defender of d4) 6...♗xf3 7 ♕xf3 ♘f6 8 d3 ♘d7 9 ♗e3 ♗e7 occurred in two

Kupreichik-Yandemirov games: Black has equalized as the knight pair are well suited to the closed position, and if White captures on c6, Black gets the b-file for counterplay. Here's a quick look at the games in question:

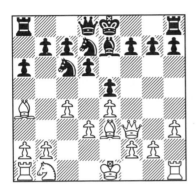

b1) 10 ♘c3 0-0 11 ♘e2 ♗g5 12 0-0 ♖b8 13 ♖ad1 ♗xe3 14 ♕xe3 ♘c5 15 ♗xc6 bxc6 16 ♖d2 ♘e6 (Black has solid equality, or perhaps one should say that White has finally covered his weakness at d4; Kupreichik now heads for an even ending) 17 f4 exf4 18 ♘xf4 ♕g5 19 ♖f3 ♘xf4 20 ♖xf4 ♕a5 21 b3 ♕c3 22 ♖f3 a5 23 d4 ♕xe3+ 24 ♖xe3 a4 25 bxa4 ♖b4 26 ♖a3 ♖a8 27 a5 ♖a6 28 ♖c2 ♔f8 29 ♔f2 ♖b7 30 ♔e3 ♖ba7 31 ♖cc3 ♖xa5 32 ♖xa5 ♖xa5 33 a3 (some might agree to a draw here, but Yandemirov makes an heroic effort to win) 33...♔e7 34 ♔d2 c5 35 dxc5 ♖xc5 36 a4 ♖a5 37 ♖a3 ♔e6 38 ♔c3 c5 39 ♖a1 ♔e5 40 ♔d3 ♔f4 41 ♖f1+ ♔e5 42 ♖xf7 ♖xa4 43 ♖xg7 ♖a3+ 44 ♔e2 ♔xe4 45 ♖xh7 ♖a2+ 46 ♔f1 d5 47 ♖e7+ ♔d4 48 cxd5 ♔xd5 49 h4 c4 50 ♖c7 ♔d4 51 h5 c3 52 h6 ♖a1+ 53 ♔f2 ♖h1 54 h7 ♔d3 55 ♔f3

c2 56 g4 ♖h3+ 57 ♔f4 ½-½ V.Kupreichik-V.Yandemirov, Miedzy-brodzie 1991—drawn as White's pawn holds off Black's rook after 57...♖xh7 58 ♖xc2 ♔xc2 59 g5 ♔d3 60 g6 ♖a7 61 ♔f5 ♔d4 62 ♔f6.

b2) 10 ♕g3 0-0 11 ♘d2 ♗f6 12 ♗xc6 bxc6 13 c5 ♕b8 (simpler is 13...♘xc5 14 ♗xc5 dxc5 15 ♘c4 ♖b8 16 0-0 ♕d4 with some advantage for Black, who has an extra, if tripled pawn; and those triplets control a lot of squares, while White retains a weakness at d3—note that Black has no opening difficulties in any of these games) 14 cxd6 ♕xb2 15 ♖b1 ♕c3 16 dxc7 ♖fc8 (this chaotic position might be objectively worse than the previous bracket, but it suits Yandemirov's style) 17 ♖b7 (17 0-0 is better) 17...♕xd3 18 ♕g4 c5 19 ♕e2 ♕d6 20 ♘c4 ♕c6 21 ♘a5 ♕a4 22 ♕d2 ♘f8 23 0-0 ♘e6 24 ♖c1 ♖xc7 25 ♖c4?! (allowing a game-changing tactic; correct is the simple 25 ♖xc7 ♘xc7 26 ♖xc5 ♖d8 27 ♕c2 when White might have a marginal superiority due to his better bishop) 25...♕xc4! 26 ♘xc4 ♖xb7 27 ♕d5 ♖b1+ 28 ♔h2 ♖d8 29 ♕c6 h5 30 ♕xa6 ♖dd1, when Black's active rooks are better than the queen and he won the ending in V.Kupreichik-V.Yandemirov, Minsk 1994.

6...♗e7

We already saw in Game 60 that ...♘ge7 is a less active move. Nonetheless, in Keres-Sokolsky, Black fully equalized by move 16 as follows: 6...♘e7 7 h3 ♗xf3 8 ♕xf3 ♘g6 9 ♘c3

♗e7 10 ♗e3 ♗g5 11 0-0 0-0 12 ♕g4 h6 13 ♘e2 ♗xe3 14 fxe3 ♕g5 15 ♕g3 ♕xg3 16 ♘xg3 ♘ge7 with complete equality, even double zero on the *Fritz*! So far so good, yes? But in P.Keres-A.Sokolsky, Moscow 1947, Keres kept at it... and at it... and finally turned a drawn rook ending into a win and collected the full point on move 89!

As I often say, success in the opening is not the whole story! You must also play well in the middlegame and especially the ending!

7 ♗e3

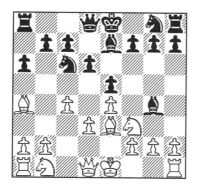

7...♗xf3?!

Essentially losing a tempo (Black should wait for White's h2-h3), and Black is not developed enough for the plan he has in mind.

7...♘f6 is correct as we have seen previously, when Black has no difficulties; e.g. 8 ♘c3 0-0 9 ♗xc6 bxc6 10 h3 ♗xf3 11 ♕xf3 ♖b8 12 ♖b1 ♘d7 13 0-0 ♗g5 14 b4 c5 15 b5 axb5 16 ♖xb5 ♖xb5 17 ♘xb5 ♗xe3 18 fxe3 ♘b6 19 ♖b1 ♕d7 20 ♕f5 ♕e7 21 ♘c3 ♖a8 (note that Black has now obtained a slightly superior

pawn structure—White has three islands to one for Black—which is similar to the rook ending Yand tried forever to win in note 'b1' to move 6 above) 22 ♖b3 ♕d8 23 ♕f2 h6 24 ♕b2 ♕g5 25 ♕f2 ♕d8 ½-½ P.Clarke-I.Szabo, Hastings 1956. In the final position Black has an .03 plus from the *Fritz*ter—I'm sure Yandemirov would play on!

8 ♕xf3 ♗g5?

This game could have been an object lesson in overreaching. Black had a perfectly good opening, and if he played like Szabo above, he would have had an equal game that most likely would have been a draw. However, by trying for more (moving both bishops twice while his king's knight is undeveloped—of course 8...♘f6 was again preferable), he allows White finally to rid himself of the weakness at d4 and get the better game.

9 d4! ♗xe3

White exploits the fact that 9...exd4 10 ♗xd4 b5? fails to 11 ♗xg7, highlighting Black's undeveloped kingside.

10 fxe3!

White finally covers the weakness at d4, threatens d4-d5, and opens the f-file. Yand is in trouble! He tries confusion...

10...♕h4+!? 11 ♔d1?!

...and gets away with it! After the natural 11 g3 Black is in big trouble; e.g. 11...♕f6 12 ♕xf6 ♘xf6 13 d5 b5 14 cxb5 ♘b4 15 bxa6+ ♔e7 16 a3 ♘d3+ (no better is 16...♘xa6 17 ♘c3 ♘c5 18 ♗c2 ♖hb8 19 ♖b1 ♘b3 20 ♔e2 ♘d7 21 ♘a2 ♘dc5 22 ♘b4 and Black has no real compensation for the pawn) 17 ♔e2 ♘c5 (not 17...♘xb2? 18 ♗b5 ♖hb8 19 a4 ♘xe4 20 ♖a2 winning the trapped knight) 18 ♗c2 ♘cxe4 19 ♖c1 ♘c5 20 b4 ♘xa6 21 ♘c3 and White has a clear advantage in view of Black's backward c-pawn.

11...exd4 12 exd4

White should bail out here with the move 12 ♗xc6+!? and approximate equality.

12...b5!

Because 11 ♔d1 did not win a tempo (like the correct 11 g3), Black has time for this typical MS counterblow—and so takes over the initiative.

13 cxb5 ♘xd4 14 b6+ ♔f8 15 ♕e3 ♕h5+ 16 g4!?

White tries some confusion of his own, since if 16 ♔d2 ♕a5+ 17 ♘c3 ♕xb6 or 16 ♔c1 ♕c5+ and in both cases Black emerges a pawn up for not much.

16...♕xg4+ 17 ♔c1 c5! 18 ♘c3 ♘f6 19 e5 ♘d5! 20 ♘xd5 ♕g2

A clever fork!

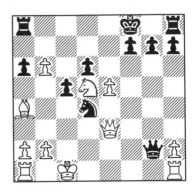

21 ♖e1 ♕xd5 22 exd6

22 b3 keeps White in the game, but Kupreichik probably never dreamed his bishop could be taken, given his two passed pawns on the sixth.

22...♕c4+!

Fearless!

23 ♔b1 ♕xa4 24 ♕e7+ ♔g8 25 b3 ♕b5 26 ♔b2 h5

26...h6!? might be safer (not Yandemirov's forte).

27 d7

27 b7! is a better try.

27...♕xb6 28 ♖e5 ♕f6! 29 ♕e8+ ♔h7 30 ♖xh5+ ♔g6 31 ♖xh8 ♕f2+

This queen and knight attack justifies Black's wild play.

32 ♔a3 ♘c2+ 33 ♔b2 ♘b4+ 34 ♔a3 ♘c2+ 35 ♔b2 ♘d4+

No draw!

36 ♔a3 ♘b5+ 37 ♔a4 ♕d4+ 38 ♔a5 ♕b4+ 39 ♔b6 ♘d6+ 40 ♔c6?!

40 ♔c7 is slightly better in view of the ensuing skewer, though Black now has a material advantage and should win in any event.

40...♘xe8 41 ♖g1+ ♔f6 42 ♖f1+ ♔g6 43

♖g1+ ♔f6 44 ♖f1+ ♔g5 45 ♖g1+ ♔f5 46 ♖f1+ ♔g4 0-1

White is out of good checks and must lose shortly; e.g. 47 ♖g1+ ♔f3 48 ♖g3+ ♔f2 49 dxe8♕ (49 ♖xe8 ♖xe8 50 dxe8♕ ♕b5+ is the same) 49...♖xe8 50 ♖xe8 ♕b5+ and the skewer strikes!

Clearly Szabo and Yandemirov have shown that 5...♗g4 equalizes with ease. The plan is to take the f3-knight if hit by h2-h3, and meanwhile develop with ...♘f6—this is an extremely sound set-up.

Here Yandemirov tries to escape his own box—and I think this wild game is both entertaining and instructive. Black goes beyond the safety limits, and "should" be punished—but his enterprising and risky play is rewarded with the full point, whereas Szabo's solidity only gave him a draw.

You must decide how much risk *you* are willing to take.

The following game was thought to knock out the Duras/Siesta combination, but as is often the case with "re-ceived wisdom", it's not quite true. In the main line (not the game, where Black goes under quickly), which has never been played according to my database, White gets an attack for a pawn—but nothing is decisive and bold players might want to try this out—if the calm equalizer we saw in the notes to the last game is too boring!

Game 63
E.Böök-Er.Andersen
Warsaw Olympiad 1935

1 e4 e5 2 ♘f3 ♘c6 3 ♗b5 a6 4 ♗a4 d6 5 c4

Can Black play the Siesta here? After all, White has moved his c-pawn and weakened the key d3-square, so important in that gambit.

5...f5!?

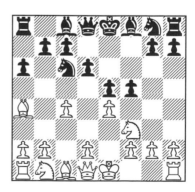

Black tries it! But now consider a true Siesta, and keep the 11th move position in your mind as a mental exercise: 5 c3 f5 6 d4 fxe4 7 ♘xe5 dxe5 8

♕h5+ ♔e7 9 ♗xc6 bxc6 10 ♗g5+ ♘f6
11 dxe5 ♕d5!, when my note from
Game 42 reads as follows: "Capablanca's great defensive move, planning
to pin along the rank, makes White
struggle to draw."

6 d4!

This doesn't do anything against
the Siesta, as we have seen, and almost
everything is the same here—but note
that the white c-pawn is one square
forward—what difference could that
single square make?

For the record, 6 exf5 ♗xf5 7 d4
might also be a real try for advantage,
since Black, in the main line Siesta,
must soon play ...d6-d5 here, which is
now discouraged by White's c-pawn.
Furthermore there are lines where
White plays c2-c3 and then c3-c4 (for
example, the note to move 9 in Game
41) and here White might save a
tempo.

But let's continue with our "refutation".

6...fxe4 7 ♘xe5! dxe5 8 ♕h5+ ♔e7

Black continues as in the Siesta—
others are worse; e.g. 8...g6 9 ♕xe5+ ♔f7
10 ♕xh8 ♗g7 (or 10...♘f6 11 ♘c3 ♘xd4
12 ♗g5 and Black has nothing real for
the exchange) 11 ♕xh7 ♘xd4 12 ♘c3
♘f6 13 ♕h4 ♘f5 14 ♕f4 ♕e7 and now,
instead of the retrograde 15 ♕d2 of
Michal-B.Petkevic, Prague 1935, White
should win with 15 h3, when again
Black doesn't have real compensation
for the sacrificed material.

9 ♗xc6

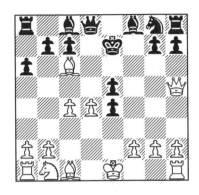

9...♕xd4?

Black panics! No doubt he was
counting on "Capa's great defensive
move" as noted above: 9...bxc6 10
♗g5+ ♘f6 11 dxe5 ♕d5, but then had a
terrible shock when he realized that the
"harmless" little white c-pawn, up one
square, actually prevents this key
move! Seeing that, Black collapsed and
lost quickly.

But there was no necessity for this!
Instead, he should just go ahead and
give back the piece: 11...♕d4! (the
queen also moves up one square) 12
exf6+ gxf6 13 ♗c1 (stronger than 13
♗d2 ♕xb2 14 0-0 ♕e5, when 15 ♕h4
♖g8 16 ♗c3 ♕f5 17 ♘d2 ♖g4 looks
good for Black, so White should probably take the draw: 15 ♗b4+ ♔e6 16
♕e8+ ♔f5 17 ♕h5+ etc) 13...♕xc4 14
♘c3 ♗g7 15 ♗d2 ♖b8 16 0-0-0 and
White has a good attack for the pawn,
but I certainly wouldn't consider
Black's play "refuted".

10 ♕e8+

Decisive! White finishes in problem
style.

10...♚d6 11 ♗e3 ♛xc4 12 ♘c3 ♗g4

This looks like a chaotic 19th century chess problem, and amazingly enough—despite being an actual game—it is in fact "White to play and mate in two!"

13 ♖d1+! 1-0

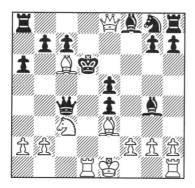

It's incredible that every reply allows mate in one: 13...♛d3 14 ♘xe4 mate, or 13...♗xd1 14 ♛d7 mate are the main variations.

Yes, Capa's defensive line in the Si-esta is prevented, but 11...♛d4 is possible, if not quite as strong—and even if Black's king is floating a bit, one could experiment with this line. On the other hand, is it worth it? White might also try to prove the worth of 5 c4 in the 6 exf5/7 d4 line as noted—and meanwhile, one can equalize easily against the Duras with 5...♗g4 and ...♘f6.

Conclusion

Given the rarity of the Duras now, I don't think it's worth studying the ramifications of the Duras/Siesta when you might never get it in your lifetime! I have played the MS off and on for 40 years, and intensively over the last few months—and I have never once faced the Duras. My recommendation is to play for a win with the positional 5...♗g4—when White has absolutely nothing, but Black can complicate as necessary à la Yandemirov!

Chapter Eight
White Plays an Early d2-d4

This chapter is devoted to lines where White plays an early and unsupported d2-d4, either on the fifth or sixth move, similar to the way he plays in the original Steinitz Defence. In general, Black can either easily equalize against this, or force White (if he wants to play for advantage) to transpose to previously covered main lines.

The move order 1 e4 e5 2 ♘f3 ♘c6 3 ♗b5 a6 4 ♗a4 d6 5 d4 will be covered in Games 64-67. Then, for purposes of comparison, I have put in one example (Game 68) of the original Steinitz Defence (3...d6 4 d4 ♗d7 5 0-0 ♘f6 6 ♘c3) where White obtains a strong position. Finally, the last four games of the chapter (Games 69-72) cover the line 4 ♗a4 d6 5 0-0 ♗d7 6 d4 which usually transposes into Chapter Three (e.g. after 6...♘f6 7 c3), though there are some independent lines—and traps!—worth knowing.

1 e4 e5 2 ♘f3 ♘c6 3 ♗b5 a6

If Black plays 3...d6 (the original Steinitz) then 4 d4 is strong.

4 ♗a4 d6 5 d4

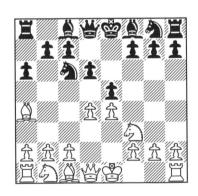

And now, with the interpolation of 3...a6 and 4 ♗a4, the same advance is

206

weak! We saw this move in Game 2, where Steinitz replied with the okay but hardly scintillating 5...♗d7, which is similar to his original Steinitz Defence. As I pointed out then, the advantage of the MS is that Black can break out with 5...b5—played by Capablanca, Alekhine, Spassky, and of course our hero Keres—and so cleanly equalize. The proof of that will be seen in this and the following three games.

5...b5! 6 ♗b3

White has nothing else. 6 d5 bxa4 7 dxc6 ♘e7 8 c3 ♘xc6 9 ♕xa4 ♗d7 was already good for Black in T.Diamant-A.Papista, Hungarian Team Championship 2001, as he has a central pawn majority and the two bishops.

6...♘xd4 7 ♘xd4 exd4 8 ♗d5

8 ♕xd4? is a blunder that allows the Noah's Ark trap—see Capablanca give an instructive lesson in the next game. 8 c3 can be a doubtful gambit (Game 13 in the "World Champions" chapter, or Game 67 here) or a drawing line (see Game 66).

Keres gives a trenchant comment on Hort's actual move, 8 ♗d5: "It is interesting to note that this tame continuation is played time and time again, despite the fact that with it White can only hope for equality."

Keres continues that if White wants a draw, he would do better to try to force it with 8 c3, which I agree is relatively best—but if White is already reduced to such desperation, then 5 d4 has no theoretical value whatsoever.

8...♖b8 9 ♗c6+

Alekhine, who also had the pleasure of winning on the black side of this variation, remarked that if White thought he could obtain a draw just by simplifying the position, he was certainly ill advised.

9...♗d7 10 ♗xd7+ ♕xd7 11 ♕xd4 ♘f6 12 0-0 ♗e7 13 ♘c3

It amazes me that, despite all the heavy hitters weighing in against this line (and the fact that from this position White scores an appallingly low 29% out of 90 games in the *Mega*), the line is still played today by strong players! For example, as we'll see in the note to move 14, the Croatian IM Mrkonjic goes down in flames with this line as recently as 2004, to an opponent about 200 Elo points below him!

Basically, White's centre is slightly weak and he can't stop Black's queen-side expansion, so White is slightly worse already—but I think the real reason the score is so lopsided is that Black's game (as we'll see through many examples) is very easy to play, whereas White has a difficult and un-pleasant defensive job.

13...0-0 14 a4

Here's Alekhine's smooth win: 14 ♗d2 ♖fe8 15 ♕d3 b4 16 ♘e2 ♕c6 17 f3 d5 18 exd5 ♘xd5 (Alekhine notes that he already has a clear advantage in view of White's weakness at e3) 19 ♖ae1 ♗f6 20 c4 ♕c5+ 21 ♖f2 ♘e3 22 b3 ♖bd8 23 ♗xe3 ♖xe3 24 ♕c2 ♗h4 25 g3 ♖xf3 26 ♖ef1 ♗g5 27 ♔g2 ♖xf2+ 28 ♖xf2 ♕c6+ 29 ♔h3 ♗e3 30 ♖f1 ♖d5! (launching the attack) 31 ♘f4 ♕d7+ 32 g4 ♖d4 33 ♕g2 c6 34 ♘h5 ♗g5 35 ♕e2 g6 36 ♘g3 h5 37 ♘e4 ♕xg4+ 38 ♕xg4 hxg4+ 39 ♔xg4 ♖xe4+ 40 ♔xg5 ♔g7 (the piquant final point: since 41 h4 f6+ winning a rook would be even more embarrassing, White is forced to enter a lost king and pawn ending with 41 ♖f4, and so he resigns) 0-1 G.Stoltz-A.Alekhine, Bled 1931.

Like every other MS player, it seems, I also have had the pleasure of defeating this variation, though I can't say I worked too hard. While I no longer have the scoresheet from this early 70's tour-nament game, I remember the trap very well—and also the fact that my oppo-nent played on for a very long time with a missing piece! NN-T.Taylor, Washing-ton DC, ca. 1973, continued 14 ♗g5 b4 15 ♘d5? (the craven 15 ♘d1 is neces-sary) 15...♘xd5 16 ♕xd5 ♖b5 and with this unusual skewer on the rank, Black won a piece and eventually the game.

Finally, we should note that, despite the crushing position Keres obtained

against Hort, another Czech, FM Frantisek Blatny, tried his luck against Keres eight years later—with the same result: 14 a3 a5 15 ♖e1 ♖fe8 16 ♕d3 ♗f8 17 ♗d2 c6 18 f3 ♕b7 19 a4 b4 20 ♘e2 d5 21 exd5 ♘xd5—as usual, Black gains space on the queenside and then attacks in the centre.

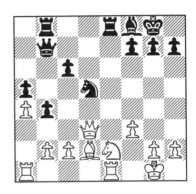

We also see, just as in Stoltz-Alekhine above (about 40 years earlier!) the white weakness at e3. Keres won as follows: 22 c4 bxc3 23 bxc3 ♖ed8 24 ♘d4 c5 25 ♖ab1 ♘b6 26 ♗g5 ♖d7 27 ♕f5 cxd4 28 ♖xb6 ♕xb6 29 ♕xd7 dxc3+ (White avoids the loss of a piece, but the monster passed pawn is just as good) 30 ♗e3 ♕b7 31 ♕d3 ♕c6 32 ♖e2 ♖c8 33 ♖c2 ♕xa4 34 ♗d4 ♖d8 (now the piece goes anyway and Black still has a passed pawn to queen) 0-1 F.Blatny-P.Keres, Luhacovice 1969.

14...♖fe8

Flash forward about another forty years, and nothing much has changed: in this modern game that I referenced above, Black immediately advances on the queenside and then the centre, and easily defeats his higher-rated opponent: 14...b4 15 ♘e2 d5 16 exd5 ♕xd5 17 ♗f4 ♖bd8 18 ♕xd5 ♖xd5 19 ♖fd1 ♖fd8 20 ♖xd5 ♖xd5 21 ♖c1 (if 21 ♗xc7 ♖d2 recovers the pawn with a typical seventh rank advantage) 21...c5 22 ♔f1 g5 23 ♗g3 ♘e4 24 ♔e1 ♗f6 25 ♖b1 c4 26 f3 ♘c5 27 b3 cxb3 28 cxb3 ♖d3 29 ♖c1 ♘xb3 30 ♖c6 ♗g7 31 ♖xa6 ♘c5 32 ♖b6 b3 33 ♘c1 ♗c3+ 34 ♔e2 ♖d2+ 35 ♔e3 b2 36 ♗e5+ ♗xe5! 37 ♔xd2 ♗f4+ (this pretty finish forces promotion) 0-1 N.Mrkonjic-A.Vajda, Zalakaros 2004.

15 ♕d3 b4 16 ♘d5 a5 17 b3 ♘xd5 18 exd5

18 ♕xd5 ♗f6 19 ♖b1 ♖e5 also puts the pressure on White.

18...♗f6 19 ♖b1 c5!

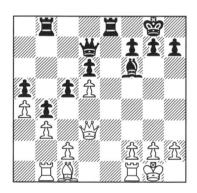

20 ♗f4

Keres comments that if 20 dxc6 ♕xc6, White's weakness at c2 is more significant than Black's at d6, and I agree. Black has easy defences of d6 such as ...♖e6 or ...♗e5/...♗e7, whereas White will have a very hard time defending c2 as he can't use his bishop, while Black can easily double or per-

haps triple on the target. However, by not taking, White allows Keres a large advantage in space and play against White's artificially isolated d-pawn.

20...♗e5 21 ♗e3?!

Exchanging bishops would give White more drawing chances.

21...♖bc8 22 ♕c4 ♕f5 23 ♕b5

A desperate attempt—but if White tries to sit tight with 23 ♖bd1, then Black makes progress by 23...♗d4; e.g. 24 ♗xd4 cxd4 25 ♕xd4 ♕xc2 with a continuing advantage.

23...♕xc2 24 ♕xa5 f5

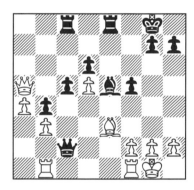

"The game is already decided from the strategic point of view," writes Keres, and Mr. *Fritz* agrees, giving Black a decisive advantage. White has no reasonable defence to ...f5-f4 and in some cases onwards to f3.

25 f3

There is nothing better:

a) 25 f4 ♕d3 26 fxe5 (26 ♗xc5 ♖xc5 wins a piece) 26...♕xe3+ 27 ♔h1 ♕xe5 and Black enjoys a solid extra pawn.

b) 25 h3 f4 26 ♖bc1 ♕xb3 and again a pawn goes.

c) 25 g3 f4 26 gxf4 ♕g6+ 27 ♔h1 ♕e4+ 28 ♔g1 ♗xf4 and Black has a winning attack.

25...♗b2

Black starts down the road to madness...

This would never have become a famous game had Keres (as he himself points out) played the simple 25...♕d3 26 ♗f2 ♕xd5 which wins easily—for as Keres writes, "Black pockets a pawn" without giving White the slightest counter-chance.

26 ♕a6 ♕xb3 27 ♗f2 c4 28 ♕b7!

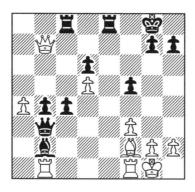

The first hint that White is getting some counterplay: Hort actually threatens to win (if Black carelessly plays 28...c3?) with 29 ♗d4!. With each curious turn from move 25 on the game gets stranger and stranger (which is why I picked it for this book!) and culminates with Keres making a *positional* sacrifice of a whole queen!

Of course Black could also win without complications on the next move—but chess is still played by humans, and the mutual mistakes and

Keres colossal imagination make this game a treasure—as opposed to, for example, Alekhine's technical win against Stoltz that we saw above.

28...♖b8

28...♕a3 (Keres) wins easily—but who wants simple chess?

29 ♕a7 ♖a8

Even here 29...♕c2 30 ♖xb2 ♕xb2 31 ♗d4 ♖b7! wins without complications—but then we would be deprived of the brilliant insanity that follows!

30 ♕b7 ♖eb8 31 ♕d7 ♕c2 32 ♕xd6 b3 33 ♕e6+ ♔h8 34 d6

Now White has real counterplay!

34...♗f6 35 ♖fc1

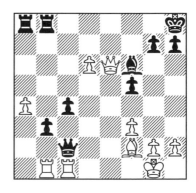

35...♕xc1+!!

A shock! And an unapproved one, according to *Fritz*—but I like it! Keres has just casually traded a queen for a rook, and he's not done sacrificing!

36 ♖xc1 b2 37 ♖b1 c3 38 ♕e2

White can get some drawing chances by taking pawns and reducing material; e.g. 38 ♕xf5 ♖xa4 39 ♗e1 ♖a1 40 ♗xc3 ♗xc3 41 ♔f2 ♖d8 42 f4 ♖xb1 43 ♕xb1 ♖xd6 44 ♔f3 g6 45 ♕c2

♖c6 46 ♕b3 h5, when Mr. *Fritz* says Black is slightly better but clearly White is still playing.

38...♖xa4 39 d7 h6

Black needs to make a square for his king—he could even lose in a variation like 39...♖g8 40 ♕d3 ♖a1 41 ♗e1 g6? 42 ♗xc3 ♖xb1+ 43 ♔f2.

40 ♕e8+ ♔h7

After sterling defence a queen up (how's that for an oxymoronic sentence!) Hort must seal his move. He makes the obvious promotion, winning a rook—but it turns out that he loses while up a full queen!

41 d8♕

Correct is to give back material as quickly as possible with 41 ♕xb8 c2 42 ♕xb2! ♗xb2 43 ♖f1 ♖a8 44 ♗b6 ♖a1 45 d8♕ ♖xf1+ 46 ♔xf1 c1♕+ 47 ♔f2 ♗c3 which "would probably gain him a pawn and good practical winning chances" (Keres); e.g. 48 g3 ♗f6 49 ♕d6 ♕h1 50 h3 ♕xh3 51 ♔g1, when despite Keres' optimism, I think White could legitimately hope for a draw.

41...♖xd8 42 ♕xa4 ♖d2

Black is unbelievably down a full queen, without a single piece for her majesty—"the most curious position that I have ever had in my whole long chess praxis" (Keres). And yet it seems, even more incredibly, that Black wins no matter what White does!

43 ♖xb2

I checked Keres' analysis with *Fritz*, and it does seem that Black wins in all variations, despite the "trifle" of White's extra queen. Evidently the two passed pawns on the seventh are not just the equivalent of the queen, they are actually worth more: 43 ♕c4 (43 ♕b5 c2 44 ♕f1 transposes) 43...c2 44 ♕f1 ♖d5! 45 h3 ♖a5 and wins shows the main idea—Black's rook travels to the a-file and plans to invade on a1.

43...cxb2 44 ♕b3 ♖d8 45 ♕c2 ♖b8 46 ♕b1

If 46 ♕xf5+ g6 47 ♕d7+ (or 47 ♕b1 ♖a8! again) 47...♗g7 and the pawn goes through.

46...g6 47 g4 ♖a8 48 ♔g2 ♖a1 49 ♕c2 b1♕ 50 ♕c7+ ♗g7 51 ♗d4 ♕f1+ 52 ♔g3 f4+!

Finally! The win is now clear after this last tactical blow.

53 ♔xf4

This loses at once, as does 53 ♔h4 g5+ 54 ♔h5 ♛h3 mate. Therefore the only try is 53 ♛xf4, but this still fails after 53...♖a2 54 ♛c7 (if 54 ♗xg7 ♛g2+ 55 ♔h4 g5+ and mate next move, or 54 ♛f7 ♛g2+ 55 ♔f4 ♛d2+ 56 ♗e3 ♛d6+ 57 ♔e4 ♖a4+ and mates) 54...♛g2+ 55 ♔f4 (or the familiar 55 ♔h4 g5+ 56 ♔h5 ♛h3 mate) 55...♛xh2+, winning the queen.

53...♛c1+ 0-1

The queens come off and Black wins.

An incredibly brilliant game from the great Keres—not flawless of course, but stunningly imaginative. From the opening point of view, the whole 5 d4 and ♗b3-d5-c6+ variation can be considered refuted. Black gets an easy game with excellent winning chances.

Game 65
E.Steiner-J.R.Capablanca
Budapest 1929

1 e4 e5 2 ♘f3 ♘c6 3 ♗b5 a6 4 ♗a4 d6 5 d4 b5! 6 ♗b3 ♘xd4 7 ♘xd4 exd4 8 ♛xd4?

As White players still venture the poor 8 ♗d5, so this even worse blunder is still played today (see the note to move 16). Black now wins a piece for two pawns, as should be easy to see.

White could save the bishop with 8 a4, but he will have a hard time both regaining the pawn and avoiding bishop shut-in—here Spielmann manages to inflict both of these on White and wins with a nice (what he would call "sham") sacrifice of a rook: 8...♗b7 9 0-0 (or 9 ♛xd4 c5 10 ♛e3 c4 11 ♗a2 ♘f6 and White's development left something to be desired in Pardeep007-Taylor, playchess.com blitz 2010) 9...♘f6 10 ♖e1 ♗e7 11 ♛xd4 c5 12 ♛e3 c4 (White's bishop is shut in) 13 ♗a2 ♘xe4 (Black snatches a button) 14 ♘c3 ♘xc3 15 bxc3 ♛d7 16 ♗a3 f6 17 ♖ad1 ♔f7 18 ♛f4 ♖he8 19 h4 ♗f8 20 ♖xe8 ♖xe8 21 ♖d4 ♖e5 22 axb5 axb5 23 ♛d2 ♛e6 24 ♗xd6 ♗xd6 25 ♖xd6 ♖e1+ 26 ♔h2 ♛g4! (go ahead, take my rook!) 0-1 G.Stoltz-R.Spielmann, Stockholm (2nd matchgame) 1932. One notices that Stoltz, quite a strong player, was hammered both by Alekhine (in the notes to the previous game) and Spielmann here when he essayed the dubious 5 d4.

8...c5 9 ♛d5 ♗e6 10 ♛c6+ ♗d7 11 ♛d5 c4

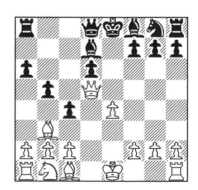

Noah's Ark! It's instructive to see how Capablanca wins—he recognizes that the piece will not win "by itself" and so constantly seeks the initiative and is alert to small combinations.

12 ♗xc4 bxc4 13 ♕xc4 ♘f6 14 ♘c3 ♗e7 15 0-0 0-0 16 a4

Now here's a modern example: 16 ♗g5 h6 17 ♗h4 ♗e6 18 ♕d3 ♕c7 19 ♖fd1 ♖fd8 20 ♗g3 ♘h5 21 ♘d5 ♗xd5 22 exd5 ♘xg3 23 hxg3 ♗f6 (the exchange of minor pieces has left White without recourse) 24 c3 ♕b6 25 ♖ab1 ♖e8 26 c4 a5 27 b3 ♕b4 28 ♔f1 ♖e7 29 ♖e1 ♖ae8 30 ♖xe7 ♖xe7 31 ♕c2 ♕c3 32 ♕d1 ♗g5 33 ♕f3 ♕c2 34 ♕d1 ♕xa2 (with this key pawn gone, it's really time for White to resign, but nowadays so many people play out routine losses to the bitter end) 35 ♖a1 ♕d2 36 ♕xd2 ♗xd2 37 ♖d1 ♗b4 38 ♖a1 ♔f8 39 ♖b1 ♔e8 40 f3 ♔d7 41 ♔f2 ♔c7 42 f4 ♔b6 43 ♔f3 ♔c5 44 ♖d1 ♗c3 45 ♖d3 ♔b4 46 c5 dxc5 47 d6 ♖d7 48 ♔e4 c4 0-1 D.Lutz-A.Heinz, Postbauer 2000; White decides not to test Black's patience further, for if 49 bxc4 ♔xc4 50 g4 ♗b4 51 ♖d4+ ♔b5 52 ♖d5+ ♗c5 53 ♔e5 ♖xd6 54 ♖xd6 ♗xd6+ 55 ♔xd6 a4 and White will soon be looking at a new black queen.

And note that the White player was rated over 2100! Evidently many people do not study the Modern Steinitz at all.

16...♗e6 17 ♕d3 ♕a5!

Capablanca transfers the queen to the kingside, which creates fresh tactical opportunities.

18 ♗d2 ♕h5 19 h3 ♖fc8 20 b3 d5 21 exd5 ♖d8

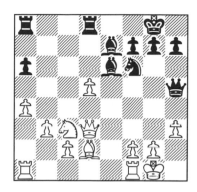

The open position favours the extra piece, while the "extra pawns" at c2 and b3 have nothing to say.

22 ♕g3 ♘xd5 23 ♘e4 ♗h4 24 ♕h2 ♘f6 25 ♘d6 ♕g6 26 ♗a5 ♖d7 27 c4 ♘e4 28 ♕f4 ♗xf2+!

Capa finishes with his usual elegance.

29 ♖xf2 ♘xf2 30 ♔xf2 ♖xd6 31 ♕xd6 ♕f6+ 32 ♔g3 ♕xa1 0-1

The extra rook should be enough!

There's nothing to say about this opening, other than: hone your technique, just in case your opponent blunders!

Game 66
P.Schlosser-M.Stangl
Lippstadt 1995

1 e4 e5 2 ♘f3 ♘c6 3 ♗b5 a6 4 ♗a4 d6 5 d4 b5 6 ♗b3 ♘xd4 7 ♘xd4 exd4 8 c3

This is what we like to see! A GM vs. GM encounter, where they come at each other with guns blazing! Here White offers a pawn sacrifice!

8...dxc3 9 ♕d5

Oh.

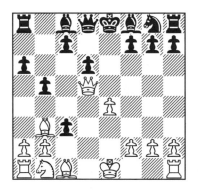

There are 35 draws in the *Mega* with this move. We'll look at ways in which both sides can avoid the draw in the next game.

9...♗e6 10 ♕c6+ ♗d7

Supposedly Steinitz analysed 10...♔e7? to avoid the draw at this point (though I have not found a source), but concluded that after 11 ♘xc3 White's attack is too powerful to justify the king move; I quite agree.

11 ♕d5 ♗e6 12 ♕c6+ ½-½

No blazing guns—just a rest day.

If your opening so terrifies White that he tries to force the draw on move 9, I say take it—and enjoy your rest.

Game 67
N.De Firmian-R.Hübner
San Francisco 1995

1 e4 e5 2 ♘f3 ♘c6 3 ♗b5 a6 4 ♗a4 d6 5

d4 b5 6 ♗b3 ♘xd4 7 ♘xd4 exd4 8 c3 dxc3

Black can avoid the draw with 8...♗b7, but I don't recommend it: 9 cxd4 ♘f6 (not 9...♗xe4?! 10 0-0 with a typical Open Game e-file attack) 10 f3 ♗e7 11 0-0 0-0 12 ♘c3 c5 13 ♗e3 (I prefer White's strong centre to Black's queenside majority—in this game Black barely manages to draw, and in fact is still worse in the final position) 13...c4 14 ♗c2 d5 15 e5 ♘e8 16 f4 f5 17 g4 g6 18 gxf5 gxf5 19 ♔h1 ♘g7 20 ♖g1 ♕e8 21 ♕f3 ♔h8 22 ♖g3 ♕f7 23 ♖ag1 ♖g8 24 ♘e2 ♖af8 25 ♖h3 ♘e8 26 ♘g3 ♗c8 27 ♖h5 ♘g7 28 ♖h6 ♘e8 29 ♖c6 ♘g7 30 ♖h6 ♘e8 31 ♗d1 ♖g6 32 ♕h5 ♖xh6 33 ♕xh6 ♕e6 34 ♕h3 ♘g7 ½-½ A.Bisguier-V.Ciocaltea, Tel Aviv Olympiad 1964, though I would play on with 35 ♗f3, when Black will have a hard time covering his weaknesses.

9 ♕h5

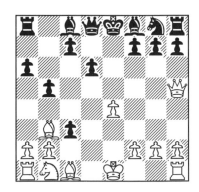

9 ♘xc3 ♘f6 10 0-0 (in Game 13 we saw how Spassky brushed off the 10 e5 "attack" by simply taking the pawn) 10...♗e7 11 ♕f3 0-0 12 e5 ♗g4 13 exf6

♗xf3 14 fxe7 ♕xe7 15 gxf3 c6 16 ♗e3 d5 and Black was much better in K.Richter-G.Machate, Swinemünde 1933, as his extra pawns shut out White's pieces.

9...♕d7!

The more complicated 9...g6 is also possible; e.g. 10 ♕d5 ♗e6 11 ♕c6+ ♗d7 12 ♕xc3 which turns in Black's favour after 12...♕f6! as one sees that the c7-pawn is taboo—but I think Hübner's simple move is the best: Black refuses to weaken his structure and already I can see no compensation for the sacrificed pawn.

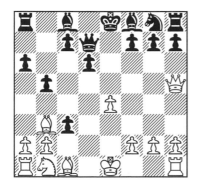

10 ♘xc3 ♘f6 11 ♕e2 ♗e7

Black develops his kingside rapidly; there is no attack; and the American Grandmaster must now face a world-class player a pawn to the bad!

12 0-0

Or 12 a4 b4 13 ♘d5 ♘xd5 14 exd5 0-0 15 a5 ♗f6 16 0-0 ♕g4 17 ♖e1 ♕xe2 18 ♖xe2 ♗g4 and White was just a pawn down in A.Kosten-M.Yeo, British Championship, Brighton 1984.

12...0-0 13 h3 ♗b7 14 ♖d1 ♖ae8 15 ♗f4

If 15 e5 ♗d8 16 f4 ♕c6 is much better for Black.

15...♘xe4!

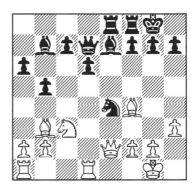

A nice tactic, forcing exchanges.

16 ♘xe4 ♕f5 17 ♗xd6 ♗xd6 18 ♘xd6 cxd6 19 ♕g4 ♕f6 20 ♕d7?

20 ♖d2 is relatively best, though I'm sure Dr. Hübner would have converted the extra pawn in the end.

20...♖e7! 21 ♕g4

Not 21 ♕xd6 ♖e1+ 22 ♔h2 ♕xd6+ 23 ♖xd6 ♖xa1, picking off a rook.

21...♕xb2 22 ♖ac1 ♕f6 23 ♗d5 ♗xd5 24 ♖xd5 ♕b2 25 ♖cd1 ♕xa2 26 ♖xd6 g6 27 ♖1d2 ♕a1+ 28 ♔h2 ♖fe8

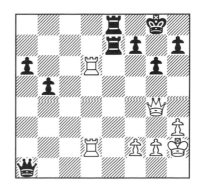

Black has two extra pawns and will

win after any queen exchange—but avoiding said exchange allows Hübner to attack.

29 ♕f4 ♖e6 30 ♖6d4 ♕c3 31 ♖2d3 ♕c5 32 ♖d5 ♕e7 33 ♖d7 ♕f6 34 ♕g3 ♕e5 35 f4 ♕f6 36 f5 ♖6e7 37 ♖7d5 ♖e5 38 ♖d6 ♕xf5 39 ♖xa6 ♖e1 40 ♖f3 ♕b1

White's persistent avoiding of exchanges has led to this—but who would not prefer a quick death?

41 ♕f2 ♖h1+ 42 ♔g3 ♕c1 43 ♕a7 ♕g5+ 44 ♔f2 ♖f1+! 0-1

White resigns, as 45 ♔xf1 ♕c1+ 46 ♔f2 ♕e1 is mate.

As I noted in Game 13, Alekhine pronounced 8 c3 "a gambit of doubtful value" almost a hundred years ago, and nothing has changed that assessment. Indeed, it's *only* value is that White can pretty much force the draw we saw in Game 66.

Unfortunately (as I often face such lines) I might run into this from a lower-rated player who wishes to draw with someone higher rated—but this is not, I think, the way to play chess. In any case, from an objective point of view, 5 d4 can be considered refuted as a winning attempt for White.

Does the d2-d4 break have a point if delayed one move? I will consider that question over the final four games of this chapter—but before we get there, let's take a look at the original Steinitz Defence, which will prove useful for understanding these more modern positions.

1 e4 e5 2 ♘f3 ♘c6 3 ♗b5 ♘f6

3...d6 4 d4 ♗d7 5 0-0 ♘f6 is the more typical original Steinitz order, which reaches the same position as the game.

4 0-0 d6 5 d4 ♗d7 6 ♘c3 ♗e7

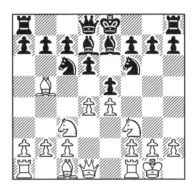

7 ♗xc6

Trap alert—please pay attention! If 7 ♖e1 Black should play 7...exd4, with a normal Steinitz Defence where White is a little better. But what if he plays the natural 7...0-0? - ? Let's take a look: 8 ♗xc6! ♗xc6 9 dxe5 dxe5 10 ♕xd8 ♖axd8 11 ♘xe5 ♗xe4 12 ♘xe4 ♘xe4 13 ♘d3 f5 14 f3 ♗c5+ 15 ♘xc5 ♘xc5 16 ♗g5 ♖d5 17 ♗e7 ♖e8 18 c4 (and Black resigns, as he loses the exchange and has a bad position as well) 1-0 S.Tarrasch-G.Marco, Dresden 1892.

This is the original "Tarrasch Trap" into which many people have fallen (I will show a modern example in Game

70). Of course Black doesn't have to lose the exchange, and can just drop a pawn if he bails out early, but this is certainly not what you want!

7...♗xc6 8 ♖e1 exd4

Correct and necessary, as 8...0-0? 9 dxe5 transposes back into the trap.

9 ♘xd4 ♗d7 10 h3 0-0 11 ♕f3

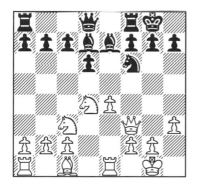

Take a good look at this very typical Steinitz position; something very similar, yet crucially different, will appear in Game 71. Note that White is playing on five ranks, while Black only has three. Also one of Black's "bishop pair" has no legal moves! But perhaps the most serious problem is this: White's queen is active and well developed, while Black's plays no role in the game.

11...♖e8

Although Black can play different moves, his strategical difficulties remain—here are two examples from practice:

a) 11...g6 (this kingside weakening does not help Black) 12 ♗h6 ♖e8 13 ♖ad1 ♕c8 14 e5 dxe5 15 ♖xe5 ♗d6 16 ♖ee1 ♖xe1+ 17 ♖xe1 (White's advantage is already decisive; note the awkward black queen and the non-playing black rook, not to mention the dark square holes on the kingside!) 17...♘h5 18 g4 ♘g7 19 ♘d5 ♕d8 20 ♕f6! ♗f8 21 ♘e7+ (now it's too late to just lose a piece, Black must give up the queen!) 1-0 Jos.Sanchez-C.Marzano, Genoa 2004.

b) 11...c6 12 ♗f4 ♕b6 (the black queen wanders out, but can't find anything to do) 13 ♖ad1 ♖ad8 (if 13...♕xb2? 14 ♖b1 ♕a3 15 ♘d5 snags a piece) 14 b3 ♖fe8 15 ♖e3 ♗c8 16 ♖ed3 h6 17 ♘de2 ♕c7 18 ♘g3 ♘d7 19 ♕e3 ♘f8 and now, instead of 20 ♘h5 when White won messily in Z.Lanka-R.Callergard, Jyvaskyla 1991, either 20 ♕d2 or 20 ♕xa7 (even simpler) wins a pawn for basically nothing.

12 ♗f4 c6 13 ♖ad1 ♕b6 14 ♘b3

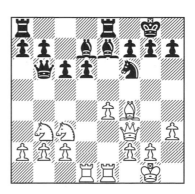

The simple 14 b3, as in the Lanka game above, is also good for White. Black's dual problems are that his queen is ineffective and his d-pawn weak.

14...a5

The lesser evil was 14...c5, which weakens the d5-square but at least temporarily holds the vital d6-pawn.

15 ♗xd6 ♗xd6 16 ♖xd6 a4 17 ♘d2 ♛xb2

17...♗e6 is necessary, but then Black is just a pawn down.

18 e5

Unfortunately for Black, he now loses a piece!

18...♛xc2 19 ♖e2 ♗f5 20 exf6 ♖xe2 21 ♘xe2 ♗g6 22 a3 ♖e8 23 ♛e3! 1-0

That's all folks! It's clear that Black has no compensation for the piece.

Now I'm sure this looked like a very easy win for Anand—and it was!—but the similar position from the Modern Steinitz gives Black new resources. Before we get there (Game 71) let's look at some inaccurate, but instructive opening play in the next two games.

Game 69
W.Kim-T.Taylor
Los Angeles (rapid) 2010

---

1 e4 e5 2 ♘f3 ♘c6 3 ♗b5 a6 4 ♗a4 d6 5 0-0 ♗d7 6 d4

6...b5

As we will see, 6...♘f6! with an improved Steinitz Defence is correct.

7 ♗b3 ♘xd4 8 ♗xf7+?

My opponent panicked, as he noticed the Noah's Ark Trap which would occur after 8 ♘xd4 exd4 9 ♛xd4? c5 when Black wins, and so sacrificed unsoundly. However, unlike in Game 67, White can offer a strong pawn (not piece!) sacrifice. The reason it works here and not there is the inclusion of 0-0 for White and ...♗d7 for Black. White's move is good for the attack, putting the king out of danger and preparing the king's rook for action; meanwhile Black's ...♗d7 prepares a solid defence in a closed position, but is useless in an open attack.

Therefore White should play 8 ♘xd4 exd4 9 c3! dxc3 10 ♛h5! and *now* Black is struggling, as the defensive move that killed the white attack in De Firmian-Hübner, ...♛d7, is no longer on, Black must try more awkward defences—here are two examples:

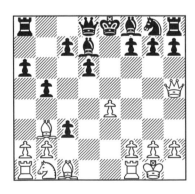

a) 10...g6 11 ♛d5 ♗e6 (note the loss

of tempo) 12 ♕c6+ ♗d7 13 ♕xc3 f6 (if 13...♘f6 14 ♗g5 ♗g7 15 f4 with a strong attack; and furthermore, 13...♕f6 fails to 14 ♕xc7—this worked for Black in the note to move 9 in Game 67, but here White has the extra move 0-0, and so the c1-bishop is protected) 14 f4 c6 15 e5! (White has a strong attack against Black's undeveloped position) 15...b4 (if 15...d5 16 e6! wins) 16 ♕xb4 d5 17 ♕c3 ♔f7 18 ♘d2 ♕b6+ 19 ♔h1 ♗b4 20 ♕d3 ♘e7 21 exf6! ♔xf6 22 ♘e4+ ♔g7 23 ♗e3 dxe4 24 ♗d4+! (winning the queen) 1-0 R.Sanguinetti-C.Guimard, Argentina 1968.

b) 10...♕f6 11 ♘xc3 (Everyman editor John Emms wins with a nice 19th century-looking attack) 11...♘e7 12 ♖e1 ♕g6 13 ♕f3 c6 14 ♗f4 ♗g4 15 ♕e3 ♘c8 16 e5 dxe5 (Black can't keep lines closed, for if 16...d5 17 ♘xd5! gives White a decisive attack for a mere knight) 17 ♕xe5+ ♗e7 18 ♕c7 0-0 19 ♖xe7 ♘xe7 20 ♕xe7 ♖fe8 21 ♕c5 a5 22 ♕g5 a4 23 ♕xg6 hxg6 24 ♗c2 (White cruises to the win with two pieces for a rook) 24...a3 25 b4 ♖ad8 26 ♗e3 ♗f5 27 ♗xf5 gxf5 28 g3 f6 29 h4 ♔f7 30 ♖c1 ♖e6 31 ♔g2 ♖d3 32 h5 ♖d8 33 ♘e2 ♖e4 34 ♖xc6 ♖xb4 35 ♖c7+ ♔g8 36 ♘f4 ♖e8 37 h6 gxh6 38 ♘d5 ♖xe3 39 ♘xb4 ♖e4 40 ♘c2 b4 41 ♔f3 h5 1-0 J.Emms-R.Granat, British League 2009.

8...♔xf7

Happy that White played the wrong sacrifice, I simply take material, consolidate, and win.

9 ♘g5+ ♔e8 10 ♘c3 ♘f6 11 ♗e3 h6 12 ♗xd4

Desperation.

12...exd4 13 ♕xd4 hxg5 14 e5 dxe5 15 ♕xe5+ ♔f7 16 ♕xg5 ♗d6

Black has a winning attack, which is pretty easy with two extra bishops!

17 h3 ♖h5 18 ♕d2 ♗xh3! 19 ♖ad1 ♗g4 20 f3 ♗c5+ 21 ♖f2 ♕xd2 22 ♖dxd2 ♗xf2+ 23 ♔xf2 ♗e6 0-1

Despite Black's easy success, my answer to 6 d4 cannot be recommended because of White's gambit continuation: 6...b5 7 ♗b3 ♘xd4 8 ♘xd4 exd4 9 c3!.

Therefore Black should play a more circumspect developing move, as Keres did—namely 6...♘f6, which is the subject of the final three games of this chapter.

Game 70
M.Tal-B.Ivkov
Belgrade-Moscow match 1974

1 e4 e5 2 ♘f3 ♘c6 3 ♗b5 a6 4 ♗a4 d6 5 0-0 ♗d7 6 d4 ♘f6!

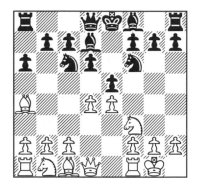

I like this move, not only because Keres always played it (well, 8 times out of 9—once he played 6...b5 as I did in Game 69, but he never repeated it and I doubt I will either), but mainly because I feel it's objectively best. When Black plays 5...♗d7 (instead of going for the Yandemirov Gambit with 5...♗g4), he is planning to enter one of the solid lines seen in Chapters Two or Three. He is not looking for an open fight, as the tactics after 6 d4 this time favour White (unlike when he breaks prematurely with 5 d4). Therefore, Black should keep the position as closed as possible, develop rapidly, and prepare to castle. 6...♘f6 does all these things—not to mention that none of Keres' high-class foes could make a dent in it over his long career!

That being said, Black still has to watch out for a 19th century trick!

7 ♗xc6 ♗xc6 8 ♖e1 ♗e7

Captures don't work: 8...♘xe4? 9 d5 wins a piece, or 8...♗xe4 9 ♘c3 and White recovers his pawn with attack.

9 ♘c3 0-0?

9...exd4 is correct, for which see the next game—but the well-known GM Ivkov was evidently not conversant with opening theory circa 1892!

10 dxe5 dxe5 11 ♕xd8 ♖axd8 12 ♘xe5

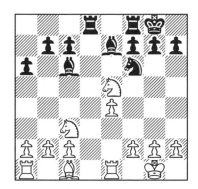

Now he sees it! The fact is, this position is exactly the same as Tarrasch-Marco (as played in 1892 and seen in the notes to Game 68), except for the fact that Black has the extra tempo ...a7-a6, which here means *nothing*—though in the next game it will mean *something*.

12...♗d7

If Black tries to get his pawn back, then the Tarrasch trap slams shut again like the casket of an undead ghoul: 12...♗xe4 13 ♘xe4 ♘xe4 14 ♘d3 f5 15 f3 ♗c5+ 16 ♘xc5 ♘xc5 17 ♗g5 ♖d5 18 ♗e7 ♖e8 19 c4 and wins—note that Black can resign on move 19 here, instead of on move 18 in the original, due the inclusion of ...a7-a6 and ♗a4.

13 ♘xd7 ♖xd7

Tal is a clear pawn up and converts by methodically exchanging down to a winning king and pawn endgame.

14 ♗g5 ♖fd8 15 ♖ad1 h6 16 ♗xf6 ♗xf6
17 ♖xd7 ♖xd7 18 e5 ♗e7 19 ♖d1 ♖xd1+
20 ♘xd1 ♗c5 21 ♔f1 g5 22 ♘e3! ♗xe3

Not exchanging will also lose in the end, though I think that's the better practical chance.

23 fxe3

White wins the pawn ending despite the doubletons, since Black's kingside pawns are so weak.

23...♔g7 24 g4 h5

No better is 24...♔g6 25 ♔e2 h5 26 gxh5+ ♔xh5 27 ♔f3 ♔g6 28 ♔e4 and Black will soon be in zugzwang, or 24...♔f8 25 ♔e2 ♔e7 26 ♔d3 ♔e6 27 ♔e4 a5 28 a4 c6 29 c4 b6 30 b3 c5 31 h3 and again Black is out of tempi.

**25 gxh5 ♔h6 26 ♔g2 ♔xh5 27 ♔g3 g4
28 ♔f4 ♔h4 29 b4 b6 30 a4 c6 31 c4 b5
32 axb5 axb5 33 c5 ♔h3 34 ♔g5 ♔xh2
35 ♔xg4 ♔g2 36 ♔f5 ♔f3 37 e6! 1-0**

Tal finds a way to queen far ahead of Black; e.g. 37...fxe6+ 38 ♔xe6 ♔xe3 39 ♔d6 ♔d4 40 ♔xc6 ♔c4 41 ♔d6 ♔xb4 42 c6 and White is too fast.

The moral is: 19th century traps are still alive!

Game 71
D.Stellwagen-E.Tomashevsky
World Junior Ch'ships,
Heraklio 2004

**1 e4 e5 2 ♘f3 ♘c6 3 ♗b5 a6 4 ♗a4 d6 5
0-0 ♗d7 6 d4 ♘f6 7 ♗xc6**

Just as in the previous game. I'll go through all reasonable alternatives for White in the next and final game of this chapter—but first, let's see how Black should answer Tal's line, when White tries to force Black into an original Steinitz.

7...♗xc6 8 ♖e1 ♗e7 9 ♘c3 exd4!

Please don't fall into an ancient trap like Ivkov did! *Not* 9...0-0? 10 dxe5 winning at least a pawn.

10 ♘xd4 ♗d7 11 ♕f3 0-0 12 h3

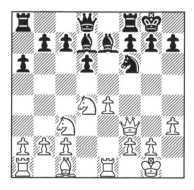

Do you remember this position? This is *almost* Anand-Milos (Game 68) after White's 11th move. Note that the similar position here has one higher move number: White made a useless extra move (♗b5-a4-c6) instead of Anand's ♗b5-c6. Meanwhile Tomashevsky (whose play impressed me in this game when he was a mere 2500—now I see the young Russian GM is over 2700!) has the gift tempo ...a7-a6, which Anand's opponent did not have. How can one use this seemingly very modest extra move?

I noted before that one big problem Black has is the development of the queen: in the regular Steinitz it's hard to find a good place for Her Majesty, and she often must either shuttle behind the lines or, as Milos tried, go out among the enemy where she faces grave dangers. But Tomashevsky finds both a safe and active square for his strongest piece...

12...♖e8 13 ♗f4 ♕c8 14 ♖ad1 b5!

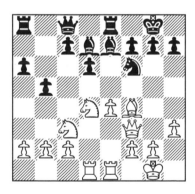

Black uses the extra tempo to gain space and open an active square for his queen on b7.

15 a3

Ivkov had bad luck with this variation. After the Tal debacle, he found the correct line as here, and equalized cleanly, but then: 15 ♖e3 b4 16 ♘ce2 a5 17 ♘g3 ♗f8 18 ♘df5 ♗xf5 19 exf5

(if 19 ♘xf5, not 19...♘xe4 20 ♘xg7 ♗xg7 21 ♖xe4 ♖xe4 22 ♕xe4 ♗xb2 23 ♖d3 and White's attacking chances against the weakened king position outweigh Black's extra pawn, but instead 19...♕b7 20 ♘g3 ♖e6 21 ♖de1 ♖ae8 and Black has a good Steinitz/Nimzowitsch restraint position, or if 20 ♕g3 Black shakes off the pressure with 20...g6 and the white e-pawn is weak) 19...h6 20 ♖de1 ♕d7 21 ♘h5 ♘xh5 22 ♕xh5 ♕b5 23 ♕g4 ♖xe3 24 ♖xe3 ♕c4 25 b3 ♕d4 (Black could take some risks and go for the win with 25...♕xc2 26 ♗xh6 ♕xa2, when it's not clear if White has compensation for the pawn) 26 ♔h2 a4 27 ♕f3 axb3! (a cool sacrifice) 28 axb3 (Black's point is 28 ♕xa8? ♕xf4+ 29 ♔g1 ♕xe3! 30 fxe3 b2 and queens!) 28...♖a5 29 ♗g3 ♕d5 30 ♕g4 ♕xf5 31 ♕xb4 ♕b5 32 ♕c3 (Ivkov has played well and has reached a completely equal, double zero kind of position—only to leave a pawn en prise and so lose the game!) 32...♖a8?? (of course 32...♖a7 is dead equal) 33 ♕xc7 and White chopped it off and took the full point 40 moves later in G.Sigurjonsson-B.Ivkov, Amsterdam 1976.

15...♕b7

Now we see two critical differences between this game and Anand-Milos: one, the black queen is well activated, attacking not the inconsequential b-pawn but rather White's crucial centre pawn; and two, Black achieved this without playing ...c7-c6 (as Milos did), which just weakens the d-pawn. So that one small extra tempo, ...a7-a6, means a lot!

16 ♗g5 ♖ad8 17 ♘f5 ♗xf5 18 ♕xf5 h6 19 ♗h4 ♘d7 20 ♗xe7 ♖xe7 21 ♘d5 ♖e5 22 ♕g4 c6

Now that Black has so much activity, he can afford this move which drives back the formerly active white knight.

23 ♘c3 ½-½

After 23...♖e6 Black is at least equal: he can double on the e-file, and both f6 and e5 are good squares for his knight; meanwhile he can continue to expand on the queenside with moves like ...a6-a5 and ...b5-b4, which also threaten to remove a defender of e4. I'd play on with Black, but in fact a draw was agreed here.

If you know both your Tarrasch *and* your Tomashevsky, this variation should hold no terrors, as the Modern Steinitz is dramatically stronger than the older version—thanks to that little a-pawn!

Game 72
A.Hermlin-P.Keres
USSR Team
Championship 1968

1 e4 ♘c6 2 ♘f3 e5 3 ♗b5 a6 4 ♗a4 d6 5 0-0 ♗d7 6 d4 ♘f6

Clearly White is not forced to give up bishop for knight as in the previous two games, so as promised, here is a round-up of the other possibilities, usually with Keres' responses.

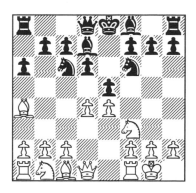

7 dxe5

As we'll see in the main game, Keres has zero problems with this. Other tries in order of their popularity in the *Mega* follow:

a) 7 c3 g6 returns to the Bishop Defence of Chapter Three, for example Parma-Keres (Game 25).

b) 7 ♖e1 b5 (now this is good, as Black is one development tempo—6...♘f6—closer to castling; so Keres accepts White's gambit, then returns the pawn at the right moment to go all medieval on his foe!) 8 ♗b3 ♘xd4 9 ♘xd4 exd4 10 c3 dxc3 11 ♘xc3 ♗e7 12 f4 0-0 13 ♕f3 b4 14 ♘e2 d5! (this counterblow gives Black the advantage already) 15 ♗xd5 ♗c5+ 16 ♔h1 c6 17 ♗c4 ♗g4 18 ♕d3 ♕xd3 19 ♗xd3 ♖fd8 20 ♗c2 ♗f2 (Black exploits the weak back rank to win material and...) 21 ♖f1 ♗xe2 22 ♖xf2 ♗d3 23 ♗xd3 ♖xd3 24 g3 ♘xe4 25 ♖c2 c5 26 b3 ♖d1+ 27 ♔g2 ♖ad8 28 a3 ♘d2 29 ♖aa2 ♘xb3 30 ♗e3 ♖1d3 31 ♔f2 h5 32 axb4 cxb4 33 ♖xa6

♘d2 34 ♖b6 ♘e4+ 35 ♔f3 ♘c3 (...finishes with this crushing blow!—there is no good defence to the threat of ...♖xe3+ and ...♘d5+) 0-1 R.Bogdanovic-P.Keres, Sarajevo 1972.

c) 7 ♗xc6 ♗xc6 was seen in the previous two games—please follow the second one!

d) 7 ♘c3 (Lasker and Spassky take the sting out of this—note especially Lasker's cool defensive play after White sacs a piece) 7...exd4 8 ♘xd4 and then:

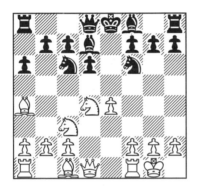

d1) 8...♘xd4 9 ♗xd7+ ♕xd7 10 ♕xd4 ♗e7 11 ♗f4 0-0 12 ♖ad1 ♖ad8 13 h3 ♖fe8 14 ♖fe1 h6 15 ♕d3 ♕e6 16 ♕f3 c6 ½-½ J.Nunn-B.Spassky, London 1986. Black has neutralized any space problems he had by the double exchange of minor pieces, and now takes a somewhat premature draw—Spassky, like Tomashevsky, could certainly play on and try to prove that White's e-pawn is more a weakness than a strength.

d2) 8...♗e7 (this simple move is also acceptable) 9 ♗xc6 bxc6 10 f4 (White tries to overrun Black's solid position,

but doesn't succeed) 10...0-0 11 b3 c5 12 ♘de2 ♗c6 13 ♘g3 ♖e8 14 ♗b2 ♗f8 15 ♕d3 a5 16 ♖ae1 a4 17 ♘d1 ♖b8 18 c4 ♗b7 19 ♖f3 axb3 20 axb3 ♗c8 21 ♘e3 ♗b7 22 ♘ef5 g6 23 ♕c3 ♖e6 24 ♘h5 gxh5 (just take it!) 25 ♖g3+ ♔h8 26 ♕f3 h4 27 ♘xh4 h6 28 ♕h5 ♕e8 29 ♘f5 ♔h7 30 ♗xf6 ♖xf6 31 ♘h4 ♖xf4 32 ♘f3 f6 (White's attack is broken) 33 ♕xe8 ♖xe8 0-1 J.Showalter-Em.Lasker, New York 1893.

e) 7 c4 ♗e7 8 d5 (closing the position, but then Black gets typical King's Indian style play; otherwise 8 ♘c3 ♘xd4 9 ♘xd4 exd4 10 ♗xd7+ ♘xd7 11 ♕xd4 ♗f6 with equality is a line from the Duras Variation—see the note to move 5 in Game 62) 8...♘b8 9 ♗c2 0-0 10 ♘c3 a5 11 h3 ♘a6 12 ♗e3 ♘e8 13 a3 g6 14 ♗h6 ♘g7 15 ♖b1 and now—instead of 15...c5 as in A.Bisguier-A.Medina Garcia, Palma de Mallorca 1971, when I think White could have obtained a positional advantage with 16 ♗a4—Black might get a good game by 15...f5 16 exf5 gxf5 17 ♕e2 ♖f6 (17...♕e8 intending ...♕h5 and ...f5-f4 is also good) 18 ♗g5 ♖g6 with active kingside play.

f) 7 ♗g5 ♗e7 (it's already clear that the white bishop is misplaced, as Black threatens ...♘xe4, while an exchange on f6 favours Black) 8 ♖e1 b5 9 ♗b3 ♘xd4 10 ♘xd4 exd4 11 e5 dxe5 12 ♖xe5 0-0 13 ♕f3 (not 13 ♕xd4? c5 with a certain ark) 13...♗d6 14 ♗xf6 ♕xf6 and Black was a sound pawn up in S.Dabus-J.Godois, Vacaria 1978.

I would say that 7 c3, transposing to main lines, is relatively speaking White's best move, as the others can be handled with little difficulty.

7...♘xe5

Better than 7...dxe5 8 ♕e2 ♗d6 9 ♖d1, when Black had been forced into a defensive position in W.Hoover-M.Shulman, Canadian Championship 1963.

8 ♗xd7+ ♘fxd7 9 ♘c3 ♗e7 10 ♘d4 0-0 11 ♘f5 ♖e8

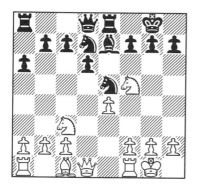

12 b3

12 ♘xe7+ ♕xe7 13 ♘d5 ♕d8 14 ♖e1 h6 15 ♗f4 ♘f6 is quiet equality, while 12 f4 ♘c6 13 ♖f3 ♗f8 14 ♗e3 g6 is sharper and more complicated, but in either case I don't think Black has much to worry about—his kingside is solid and he always gets counterplay against the white e-pawn.

12...♗f6 13 ♗b2 g6 14 ♘h6+ ♔g7 15 f4!

Since "normal" play gets nowhere— e.g. 15 ♘g4 ♘xg4 16 ♕xg4 ♘c5 17 f3 c6 18 ♘d1 d5 19 exd5 cxd5 20 ♕f4 ♘d7 21 ♗xf6+ ♕xf6 22 ♕xf6+ ♘xf6 23 ♘b2

and the ending is slightly better for Black because of his more active rooks and the somewhat weak c2-pawn— White decides to mix it up with this bold pawn sacrifice that Keres should probably not accept.

15...♔xh6!?

Keres often took such risks against weaker players, but I think 15...♘c6 is objectively correct, which seems to favour Black without complications; e.g. 16 ♘g4 ♗d4+ 17 ♔h1 ♘c5 and White still has problems with his e-pawn and the pressure on the long diagonal, especially as his bishop is undefended.

16 fxe5 ♖xe5

16...♘xe5 17 ♘d5 ♗g5 18 ♗xe5 dxe5 19 ♖xf7 c6 20 ♕f3 cxd5 21 ♕h3+ ♗h4 22 g3 dxe4 reaches a double-edged position where White has compensation for the material, while if 16...dxe5 17 ♕g4 ♖e6 18 ♖ad1 and again there's annoying pressure. No recapture exempts Black from difficulties.

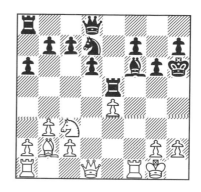

17 ♕d3?

But this just loses a tempo, and the

compensation vanishes like a handful of pixie dust. Correct is the forceful 17 ♕d2+! with good play in all variations:

a) 17...♔g7? 18 ♘d5 ♖e6 19 ♘xf6 ♘xf6 20 ♖xf6 ♖xf6 21 ♖f1 and White wins by pin.

b) 17...g5 18 h4! and Black's kingside will be broken up.

c) 17...♗g5 18 ♕e1 f5 19 ♕g3 and White's attack is worth the pawn.

17...♖e6!

Keres' risk pays off—again! As 17 ♕d3 didn't threaten anything, Black uses his free move to consolidate; Keres never gives his opponent another chance.

18 ♖xf6 ♖xf6 19 ♘d5 ♘e5! 20 ♕h3+ ♔g7 21 ♘xf6 ♕xf6 22 ♖f1 ♕e7 23 ♗c1 ♖e8 24 ♕h6+ ♔g8 25 ♗g5 ♕f8

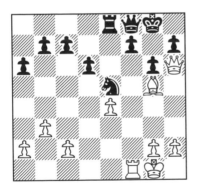

Keres calmly shakes off the attack, and retains his extra pawn.

26 ♕h3 ♖e6 27 ♗f6 ♘d7 28 ♗b2 ♕e7 29 ♖f3 ♖xe4

Make that two.

30 ♕h6

Note that the old trick 30 ♕xh7+ ♔xh7 31 ♖h3+ fails to 31...♔h4.

30...♘e5 31 ♖f1 ♖e2 32 ♕c1 ♘g4 33 ♗d4 ♕e4 0-1

The counter-attack triumphs.

It's clear that White can't get anything more than equality with this central exchange (7 dxe5).

Conclusion

We see now that 5 d4 leads to a draw at best for White. On the other hand, 5 0-0 ♗d7 6 d4 is quite playable, and contains traps, some very old! However, Black can follow Keres and obtain a safe game with 6...♘f6 when, as far as I can see, White has nothing better than 7 c3 with a return to the main lines of the Bishop Defence in Chapter Three. Note that this move order does eliminate the Knight Defence (with ...♘ge7) of Chapter Two, as Black is basically compelled to put the knight on f6.

Chapter Nine
Four Fishes

So far in this book, I have covered the critical and important lines that occur after 1 e4 e5 2 ♘f3 ♘c6 3 ♗b5 a6 4 ♗a4 d6, namely 5 c3, 5 0-0, 5 ♗xc6, 5 c4 and 5 d4. But there are also other lines that are often played, which have no theoretical importance, but are of great practical value. These are 5 ♘c3, 5 d3, 5 ♕e2 and 5 h3. As can easily be seen, all are defensive moves—when White is not even attacked! I am not an advocate of such passive play with White, but you *will* face such moves as Black, as I have, and the following five games are a guide on how to deal with them.

Game 73
G.A.Thomas-P.Keres
Margate 1937

---

1 e4 e5 2 ♘f3 ♘c6 3 ♗b5

3 ♗c4 ♘f6 4 ♘g5 d5 5 exd5 ♘d4 6

c3 b5 7 ♗f1 is the Fritz Variation (that's Alexander Fritz the 19th century German master, not Mr. *Fritz*, my computing alter ego!) of the Two Knights Defence where Black gets good counterplay—but he will get an improved version of this in the main game.

3...a6 4 ♗a4 ♘f6 5 ♘c3 b5 6 ♗b3 d6

Transposing to our opening—the MS order would be 4...d6 5 ♘c3 b5 6 ♗b3 ♘f6, reaching this position.

7 ♘g5

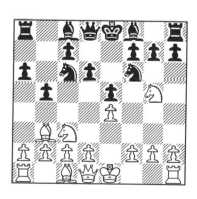

White doesn't seem to have anything better than this Two Knights style attack, but the results in practice have been abysmal. My database gives 14 games with this move and the Yates/Keres counter 7...d5, of which White won two (one of these being a 1600 rated blunderfest), drew three, and lost nine! Keres' analysis, plus my own supported by *Fritz*, shows this to be a dangerous venture for White.

The quiet 7 d3 ♘a5 reaches the next game by transposition, where Black gets the advantage right in the opening—and a flank attack gets nowhere: 7 a4 b4 8 ♘d5 ♘xe4 and White is struggling to equalize after the loss of his centre pawn.

7...d5!

Black is prepared to go into a Fritz Variation with a number of improved factors. First, let's note that even though the d-pawn moved twice, Black did not lose a tempo: the white king's bishop moved three times to get to the Italian diagonal (♗b5-a4-b3), while Black also used three moves (...a6/...d6/...d5) to arrive at the "Fritz similar position"—Black's ...b7-b5 is played in both lines—which makes the tempo count even.

However, the current position contains advantages to Black: the white bishop can no longer retreat to f1, which is normal in the Fritz Variation as given above—and therefore g2 is unprotected, and indeed the decisive blow is struck there in the game. On

the other side, the b5-pawn is protected, usually a weak point for Black in the Fritz Variation proper.

To quote Keres: "White must play most carefully in the ensuing phase of the game so as not to fall victim to a withering attack on the part of his better developed opponent."

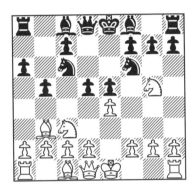

8 ♘xd5

When this gambit line was introduced by the great British player F.D.Yates, White answered with the pawn capture 8 exd5, much as in the Two Knights Defence—but after 8...♘d4 9 d6 ♘xb3 10 dxc7 ♕xc7 11 axb3 ♗b7 "Black obtains a fine position with excellent attacking prospects," says Keres, and I couldn't agree more. Yates won as follows: 12 0-0 h6 13 ♘f3 ♗d6 (the "Two Knights style" 13...e4 also looks good for Black) 14 d3 0-0 15 ♖e1 ♖ad8 16 ♕e2 ♖de8 17 ♘e4 ♘xe4 18 dxe4 f5! (Black opens lines, attacks...) 19 ♖d1 fxe4 20 ♘e1 ♖e6 21 ♗e3 ♖ef6 22 ♖d2 ♗c5 23 ♖ad1 ♖xf2! (...and crashes through in style!) 24 ♗xf2 ♖xf2 25 ♕xf2 ♗xf2+ 26 ♔xf2

♕f7+ 27 ♔g1 ♕h5 28 ♖d8+ ♔h7 29 ♖a1 ♕f5 30 ♖dd1 e3 31 ♘d3 ♕g4 32 ♘e1 ♕e2 33 ♘f3 ♕f2+ 34 ♔h1 e2 35 ♖g1 e4 36 ♘e1 h5 37 ♖b1 h4 38 ♖a1 (there is no defence: 38 h3 ♕g3 39 c4 e3 40 ♘f3 ♗xf3 41 gxf3 ♕xh3 mate) 38...h3 39 ♖b1 e3 40 ♖a1 ♕f1 0-1 J.Lewis-F.Yates, British Championship, Oxford 1910.

8...♘d4

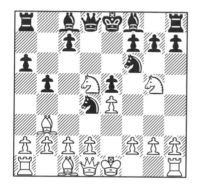

Now it's surprisingly hard to find a good move for White.

9 ♘e3

Keres gets a strong attack after this, so let's look at some alternatives.

a) 9 ♘xf6+ ♕xf6 10 ♗xf7+ (if 10 ♘xf7 ♘xb3 11 ♘xh8 ♘xa1 12 ♕h5+ g6 13 ♕xh7 ♘xc2+ 14 ♔d1 ♘d4 15 ♕xg6+ ♕xg6 16 ♘xg6 ♗g7 and Black's piece should beat the three pawns, or 10 d3 h6 11 ♘h3 ♕g6! and the weakness at g2 is fatal) 10...♔e7 11 d3 h6 12 h4 (12 ♗d5 c6 13 ♘f7 ♖h7 also favours Black—one recalls I used this knight-trapping idea in Game 44) 12...hxg5 13 ♗xg5 ♕xg5! is a pretty win pointed out by Keres.

b) 9 d3 ♘xb3 10 axb3 (not 10

♘xf6+? gxf6! winning a piece) 10...♘xd5 11 exd5 ♕xd5 and Black has two good bishops and material equality.

c) 9 ♘c3 ♘xb3 10 axb3 ♗g4 11 f3 (if 11 ♘f3 b4 12 ♘a4 ♘xe4 13 d3 ♘f6 14 ♕e2 ♗e7 15 ♕xe5 0-0 and Black has good play for the pawn) 11...♗h5 12 0-0 ♗c5+ 13 ♔h1 h6 14 ♘h3 0-0 and again Black has good compensation with his two bishops and attacking chances.

d) 9 c3 ♘xb3 10 ♕xb3 ♘xd5 11 ♕xd5 ♕xd5 12 exd5 ♗b7 13 0-0 ♗xd5 14 ♖e1 f6 15 ♘e4 0-0-0!, when Black has recovered his pawn with the better game, which so disheartened White that he made a losing blunder. 16 b4 was necessary with slight drawing chances, but instead White played 16 d4? exd4 17 cxd4 ♖e8! 0-1 D.Janosevic-G.Tringov, Sarajevo 1967—White will lose a piece.

9...♘xb3 10 axb3 h6 11 ♘f3 ♘xe4

12 ♘xe5

In the highest level recent game with this variation, the strong French GM Fontaine tried 12 d3 here, perhaps unaware that this had already been analysed by Keres with an unfavourable verdict for White! His lower-rated FM opponent followed Keres and scored after 12...♗b4+!

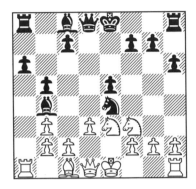

13 c3 ♘xc3 14 bxc3 ♗xc3+ 15 ♗d2 ♗xa1 16 ♕xa1 f6 (Keres gives 16...♕xd3 with advantage here, but Somborski's move is not bad: he secures his centre and maintains a rook + two pawns vs. two knights balance, which will favour Black in the long run) 17 ♕c3 0-0 18 0-0 ♖f7 19 ♘h4 ♗e6 20 ♕c6 ♕e8 21 ♕e4 ♖d8 22 ♘ef5 ♗xf5 23 ♘xf5 ♕d7 24 ♕g4 ♔h7 25 ♕h5 ♕e8 26 ♕f3 ♖fd7 (now the weak d-pawn goes and the position clarifies to Black's advantage) 27 d4 exd4 28 ♖e1 ♕f7 29 ♖e4 d3 30 h3 ♕xb3 31 ♗xh6 d2! (a beautiful illustration of the "passed pawn's lust to expand"! Black leaves both his opponent's bishop and his own queen en prise—and so forces the win!) 32 ♕xb3 d1♕+ 33 ♕xd1 ♖xd1+ 34 ♔h2 gxh6 35 ♖e7+ ♔h8 36 ♖xc7 ♖b8 37 ♘e7 b4 38 ♘g6+ ♔g8 39 ♘e7+ ♔f8 40 ♘c6 ♖c1 41 ♖h7 ♖b6 42 ♘d4 b3

43 ♖h8+ ♔g7 0-1 R.Fontaine-N.Somborski, Serbian Team Championship 2005.

12...♕f6 13 ♘f3

13 ♘5g4 is a better try, though Black has good compensation after 13...♕e6.

13...♗b7 14 ♕e2 0-0-0

Yet another MS long castle!

15 0-0 ♗d6

We now see a perfect version of a development/attack/two bishops pawn sacrifice. I think White's chances of holding this position in a practical game are virtually nil.

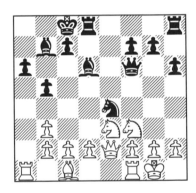

16 ♘g4 ♕f5

Keres gives 16...♕g6 as more accurate, so he can meet 17 d3 ♘g5 18 ♘h4 with 18...♕h5.

17 d3 ♘g5 18 ♘h4 ♕d5 19 c4?

19 f3 is necessary, when Black has a strong attack with 19...♘e6 followed by a kingside pawn storm, but White is at least still playing. Now instead, Black immediately forces a winning position.

19...♘h3+! 20 ♔h1 ♕h5

It's all over.

21 c5 ♖he8 22 ♕c2

22 ♗e3 ♕xh4 23 cxd6 ♗xg2+ 24 ♔xg2 ♘f4+ winning the queen is another way—note again the weakness of g2.

22...♕xh4 23 cxd6

Making it short, but there are no saves in any case: 23 c6 ♗xc6 24 ♕xc6 ♘xf2+ 25 ♔g1 ♘xg4 is another pretty win given by Keres; and even after the relatively best 23 f3 (White must block the long diagonal if he wants to continue playing) 23...♘f2+ 24 ♕xf2 (forced) 24...♕xf2 25 ♘xf2 ♗xc5 26 ♘e4 ♗b6 27 ♗d2 f5 28 ♘g3 ♖xd3 29 ♗c3 g6 Black emerges with all he needs to win: an extra pawn and the two bishops.

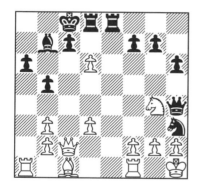

23...♗xg2+!

The weak square tells again, as Black forces mate.

24 ♔xg2 ♕xg4+ 25 ♔h1 ♕f3 mate

The Four Knights Game (1 e4 e5 2 ♘f3 ♘c6 3 ♘c3 ♘f6 4 ♗b5) is a quite reasonable opening, which forestalls the counter 4...a6 due to 5 ♗xc6 dxc6 6 ♘xe5, when Black will have a terrible

time getting his pawn back—if he can do so at all—since the white e-pawn is already protected. However, to enter a Four Knights "type" of position by playing an early ♘c3 when Black has ...a7-a6 in *already* is asking for trouble. White was struggling in the opening here, as his sharp play rebounded against him—and the quiet play he tries in the next game doesn't promise any more.

Game 74
R.Hermansen-J.A.Peters
Irvine, California 1998

1 e4 e5 2 ♘f3 ♘c6 3 ♗b5 a6 4 ♗a4 ♘f6 5 d3 d6 6 ♘c3

This position could have been reached via a strict MS order by 4...d6 5 d3 ♘f6 6 ♘c3.

In any move order, the knight on c3 is misplaced in the Ruy, and Black promptly takes advantage by gaining space and seizing the two bishops.

6...b5 7 ♗b3 ♘a5

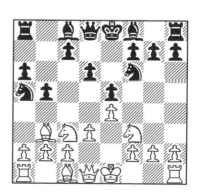

White only scores 45% from this position; it's evident that Black already has the more comfortable game with the bishop pair (he's going to take the b3-bishop soon!) and a solid centre.

8 h3

A good example of dominating black bishops can be found in the following game—of course Anderssen was a great, indeed "Immortal", player, but he could do nothing with this opening, and 130 years have not improved the line: **8 0-0 ♗e7**

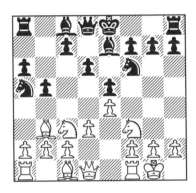

9 h3 0-0 10 ♘e2 ♘xb3 11 axb3 c5 12 ♘g3 ♘e8 13 ♗d2 g6 14 ♗a5 ♕d7 15 b4 f6 16 c3 ♘g7 17 bxc5 dxc5 18 d4 cxd4 19 cxd4 exd4 20 ♗b6 ♘e6 21 ♗xd4 ♘xd4 22 ♘xd4 ♔h8 23 ♖c1 ♗b7 24 ♖c3 ♗d6 (Black's bishops are already overwhelming) 25 ♘de2 ♖ad8 26 ♖d3 ♕e7 27 ♘c3 ♗xg3 28 fxg3 b4 29 ♘d5 ♕xe4 (White is losing a pawn—when he tries to get it back, he loses a piece!) 30 ♖f4 ♕e5 31 ♖xb4 ♗xd5 32 ♖bd4 ♗b3 33 ♖xd8 ♗xd1 34 ♖xf8+ ♔g7 35 ♖fd8 ♗a4 36 ♖3d4 ♗c6 37 ♔h2 g5 38 ♖d2 h5 39 ♖8d3 h4 40 ♖c3 f5 41 ♖f2 hxg3+ 42 ♖xg3 f4 43 ♖c3 f3+ 44 g3 ♕e1 45 ♖cc2 ♗e4 46 ♖cd2 ♗d3! 0-1 A.Anderssen-L.Paulsen, Krefeld 1871. Perhaps not "Immortal" or "Evergreen", but this was a fine positional win by Paulsen.

8...♗b7 9 ♘e2

White follows Anderssen but meets a similar fate: the knight will find no green pastures on g3. Our friend Mr. *Fritz* claims that White holds the balance with the simple 9 0-0, but I like the long-term prospects of Black's bishop pair after the simple 9...♘xb3 10 axb3 ♗e7.

9...g6 10 ♘g3 ♗g7 11 ♗g5 h6 12 ♗d2 c5 13 ♕e2 0-0 14 ♘h2 d5!

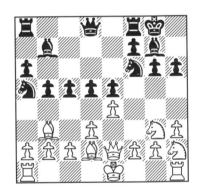

Black breaks in the centre and stands obviously better.

15 c3 c4 16 dxc4

16 ♗c2 cxd3 17 ♗xd3 dxe4 18 ♘xe4 ♘xe4 19 ♗xe4 ♗xe4 20 ♕xe4 f5 21 ♕e2 ♘c4 is also much better for Black.

16...♘xb3 17 axb3 ♘xe4

White's centre is destroyed, and Black has the two bishops.

18 ♘xe4 dxe4 19 ♖d1 ♕b6 20 ♗e3 ♕e6 21 g4

This desperate attempt at kingside counterplay just hastens the end. After the stronger 21 cxb5 axb5 22 ♕xb5 ♖fb8 23 ♕c4 ♕xc4 24 bxc4 ♗a6 25 b4 ♗xc4 White's endgame prospects are poor, but at least he can still attempt to resist.

21...♖fc8 22 ♘f1 bxc4 23 bxc4 ♕xc4

Black has an extra pawn supported by the bishop pair—the rest is technique.

24 ♕xc4 ♖xc4 25 ♖d7 ♗c6 26 ♖c7 ♗b5 27 ♖xc4 ♗xc4 28 ♘g3 ♖b8 29 ♗c1 ♗d3 30 ♔d1 ♖f8 31 ♗e3 f5 32 gxf5 gxf5 33 ♘h5 ♗h8 34 ♗xh6 ♖b8 35 ♔c1 f4 36 ♗g5 ♔f7 37 ♘xf4 exf4 38 ♗xf4 ♖b5 39 ♗d2 ♖a5 40 ♗e1 ♗e5 41 c4 0-1

An appealing conclusion. Black mates in two: 41...♗f4+ 42 ♔d1 ♖a1 mate.

Once again it's easy to see that ♘c3 is the cuckoo in the Lopez nest: this move just doesn't fit in with White's system after Black has played the freeing ...a7-a6—which simply means White is struggling and Black has good play.

Game 75
Al.David-S.Mamedyarov
Mainz (rapid) 2006

1 e4 e5 2 ♘f3 ♘c6 3 ♗b5 a6 4 ♗a4 ♘f6 5 d3

We know that Lasker defeated this passive move in the nineteenth century, and more than a hundred years of chess technique have not improved it!
5...d6

Of course 4...d6 5 d3 ♘f6 reaches the game position by the MS order.
6 c3

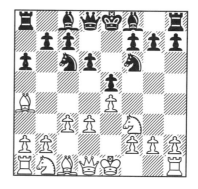

We've seen this innocuous for White position before in the World Champions chapter—four times in fact, with White getting nothing out of the opening in all four cases. Lee-Lasker went 6...b5, Smyslov-Botvinnik saw 6...♗e7, and Karpov-Ravinsky and Topalov-Anand continued 6...♗d7. Mamedyarov, who often plays the MS, goes for yet another move—which shows, as I pointed out before, that the complete lack of pressure on Black's position allows him to choose any reasonable set-up and count on equality.

6...g6 7 0-0

Another quick Mamedyarov win went as follows: 7 ♘bd2 ♗g7 8 0-0 0-0 9 ♖e1 ♘d7 10 ♘f1 ♘c5 11 ♗c2 ♘e6 12 h3 h6 13 a4 ♕f6 14 ♘e3 ♘f4 15 ♘d5 ♘xd5 16 exd5 ♘e7 17 c4 ♘f5 18 a5 ♘h4 19 ♘xh4 ♕xh4 20 b4 f5 (once you see this move it's obvious that Black has outplayed his opponent, as only Black's kingside attack is real, whereas White has nothing on the opposite wing—still, one doesn't expect the game to last just two more moves!) 21 ♖b1 f4 22 f3 ♖f5 0-1 M.Zulfugarli-S.Mamedyarov, Dubai 2003. White resigned in the face of the attack. A possible finish is 23 ♖e2 (or 23 ♕e2 ♖g5 24 ♕f2 ♕xh3 with an extra pawn and a still powerful attack) 23...♖g5 24 ♔h2 (or 24 ♔f1 ♗xh3 with a winning attack) 24...♗xh3 25 gxh3 ♕g3+ 26 ♔h1 ♕xf3+ 27 ♔h2 ♖g3 28 ♗a4 ♖xh3+ 29 ♔g1 ♖h1 mate.

7...♗g7 8 ♖e1 0-0 9 h3 ♗d7 10 d4 h6 11 d5 ♘e7 12 ♗xd7 ♘xd7

White reaches a typical Chapter Three pawn chain position, but here Black is a tempo up in view of White's stutter-step: 5 d3, 10 d4.

13 c4 f5

White has the theoretically better bishop, but the white king position is very weak, as the kingside is Black's strong side according to the pawn chain, and one already sees several black pieces in the vicinity!

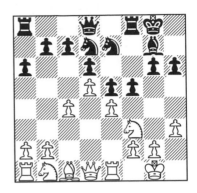

14 ♘c3 ♘f6 15 b4 ♕e8 16 ♖b1 g5 17 exf5 ♘xf5 18 ♕d3 ♕g6 19 ♘e4 g4 20 ♘xf6+ ♖xf6 21 hxg4 ♕xg4 22 ♖e4 ♕h5 23 g4?

An unexpected error from the Luxembourg GM—White can hardly create such a weakness on Black's strong side. However, even after 23 ♗d2 ♖g6 24 ♖b3 ♖f8 Black has a strong attack.

23...♕g6 24 ♖b3 ♖af8

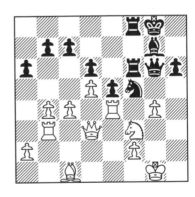

Every black piece is attacking, and the f- and g-files are full of weak points. I don't see any way White can hold this position, though his actual move is a quick death.

25 ♗d2

White can also lose swiftly with 25 ♕c2 ♘d4 26 ♘xd4 ♖xf2 27 ♕xf2 ♖xf2 28 ♔xf2 ♕xe4, and even the relatively best 25 g5 (trying to keep lines closed) can't save him: 25...hxg5 26 ♖g4 (26 ♗xg5 ♘d4 also wins) 26...♕h5 27 ♖xg5 ♖g6 28 ♕b1 (28 ♖xg6 ♕xg6+ 29 ♔f1 e4 30 ♕xe4 ♘g3+ picks up the queen) 28...♗f6 29 ♖xg6+ ♕xg6+ 30 ♔f1 e4 31 ♘e1 ♗d4 with a decisive attack, as Black's bishop finally comes into the game with deadly threats.

25...♘g3!

Black's attack breaks through. White has only two tries (retreat his rook or take the knight) and both lose:

a) 26 ♖e3 e4 27 ♕b1 ♘e2+ 28 ♔h2 ♘d4! 29 ♘xd4 ♖xf2+ 30 ♔h3 h5! with a winning attack.

b) 26 fxg3 ♖xf3 27 ♖e3 ♕xd3! 28 ♖bxd3 ♖f1+ 29 ♔g2 ♖8f2+ 30 ♔h3 ♖h1 mate! How about that for a drastic exploitation of doubled pawns: the hapless creatures do nothing but take away their own king's flight squares.

Seeing all this, White chose variation 'c'—and resigned!

0-1

It's more than evident that Black should have no problems against a move like 5 d3.

Game 76
E.Paljusaj-I.Nei
Pula 1997

1 e4 e5 2 ♘f3 ♘c6 3 ♗b5 a6 4 ♗a4 d6

Let's let Fischer give us a lesson: 4...b5 5 ♗b3 ♘a5 6 0-0 ♘xb3 7 axb3 d6 8 d4 (here is the reason this Norwegian Defence has never caught on—Black is behind in development and can barely hold his centre) 8...f6 9 ♘h4 ♘e7 10 ♘c3 ♗e6 11 ♗e3 g5 12 ♕f3! ♗g7 13 dxe5! dxe5 14 ♘f5 ♗xf5 15 exf5 0-0 16 ♖ad1 ♕c8 17 ♗c5 ♘xf5 18 ♗xf8 ♗xf8 19 ♘d5 ♔g7 20 g4 1-0 R.J.Fischer-R.Walker, US Junior Championship 1957. That was a nice crush! But the difference between a crush for White and a good position for Black can be a single tempo—keep the position after Fischer's 8th move above in mind as we go through the main game.

5 h3

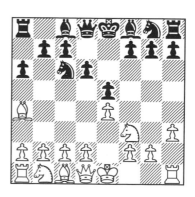

White defends against... nothing! Any reasonable move is possible for Black: one can't go wrong developing a piece with attack.

5...♘f6 6 0-0 b5 7 ♗b3 ♘a5

Iivo Nei, perhaps best known for co-authoring *Both Sides of the Chessboard* with Robert Byrne, on the Fischer-Spassky match, shows he really does know his Fischer from both sides! He seizes the bishop pair (Fischer's favourite), but at the same time avoids Fischer's attack above, since White has lost a tempo with 5 h3.

8 c3

If 8 d4 ♘xb3 9 axb3 and one sees Black is a full tempo up on the Fischer-Walker game (h2-h3 is meaningless, but the black knight on f6 is not!) and so should at least equalize with his two bishops; e.g. 9...♗b7 10 dxe5 dxe5 11 ♕xd8+ ♖xd8 12 ♘xe5 ♘xe4 and the bishop pair gave Black the edge in C.Bognarne-S.Vajda, Budapest 1994.

8...♘xb3 9 axb3 ♗b7 10 ♖e1 g6 11 d4 ♕e7 12 ♗e3 ♗g7 13 b4

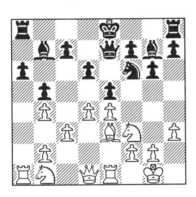

13...♘d7

Nei is content with his bishops, but it seems to me that Black, having consolidated his position, could just go ahead and snatch the pawn on e4: 13...♘xe4 14 ♘bd2 ♘xd2 15 ♕xd2 f6, when White's compensation is doubtful.

14 ♕b3 0-0 15 ♘bd2 h6 16 g4

This "attack"—which, strangely enough, we have seen in this as well as the previous two games—is bad once again: White only weakens his kingside. The logical 16 c4 is correct, creating some play for White, with approximate equality.

16...♔h7 17 g5 f6 18 gxh6 ♗xh6 19 ♗xh6 ♔xh6 20 c4

Too late, since Black's next prepares ...♖h8 with good play against White's weakened kingside.

20...♔g7 21 ♔h2?

A tactical error in a difficult position.

21...exd4!

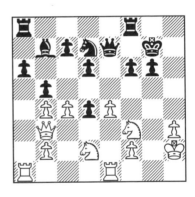

Black has won a pawn—so, rather than lose technically, White pitches a piece for a desperate counter-attack!

22 ♘xd4 ♕e5+ 23 ♕g3 ♕xd4 24 ♘f3 ♕b6 25 ♖g1

Paljusaj enjoys, for a moment, his threat of mate in two.

25...♔f7 26 ♕xg6+ ♔e7 27 ♕f5 ♖f7 28 ♘h4 ♘e5 29 f4 ♕f2+ 0-1

But now the moment's gone.

White resigns in view of 30 ♖g2 (or 30 ♘g2 ♘f3+ 31 ♔h1 ♕g3 and mates)

30...♛xh4 31 fxe5 fxe5, when Black has an extra piece *and* the attack.

All 5 h3 does is present Black with a useful development tempo.

Game 77
C.H.Alexander-M.Cuellar Gacharna
Munich Olympiad 1958

1 e4 e5 2 ♘f3 ♘c6 3 ♗b5 a6 4 ♗a4 d6

4...♘f6 5 0-0 (or 5 ♕e2) 5...♗e7 6 ♕e2 is the Worrall Attack, but in the main game Black has more options.

5 ♕e2

Defending a pawn that isn't attacked—but that's typical of the sidelines in this chapter. Also the white queen is slightly exposed, so it's clear that Black should have no problems.

5...♗e7

There's nothing wrong with this (any good developing move is fine against White's non-threatening opening), but it does lead to positions more reminiscent of the Worrall (see the

note to move 8, where a transposition was possible).

I would probably stay in Steinitz territory with 5...♗d7 6 0-0 (of course 6 c3 ♘f6 7 d4 ♗e7 transposes back to Game 30) 6...♘ge7 7 c3 ♘g6 and the Knight Defence (Chapter Two) looks very promising, as the white queen is in range of both black knights; e.g. 8 d3 ♗e7 9 ♗e3 0-0 10 ♘bd2 ♘d4 (one knight hits the white queen!) 11 cxd4 ♗xa4 12 ♘c4 ♗f6 13 b3 ♗d7 14 h3 exd4 15 ♗xd4 ♖e8 16 ♘e3 ♘f4 (the second knight strikes—clearly the white queen position aids Black) 17 ♕d1 ♗xd4 18 ♘xd4 and now, instead of 18...♕f6 which eventually led to a draw in L.Hilburt-I.Loktiev, Arvier 2004, I think 18...♕g5! 19 ♔h1 d5 would lead to a different result: Black is hitting hard in the centre and kingside, and both his minor pieces are more active than White's—and having the only bishop is a long-term asset.

6 c3 b5 7 ♗c2 ♘f6 8 d4 ♗g4

In a recent high-level game (which reached this position via the Worrall move order 4...♘f6 5 ♕e2 ♗e7 6 c3 b5 7 ♗c2 d6 8 d4) Black played 8...exd4, with the idea of direct counterplay after 9 cxd4 ♗g4—but White actually took with the knight, and it's worth seeing Black's crushing counter-attack when White attempts to mate Black without further ado: 9 ♘xd4 ♗b7 10 ♘f5 0-0 11 ♗g5 ♘d7 12 h4 (of course 12 ♘xe7+ ♘xe7 is correct, when Black, as Marin has pointed out, will find counterplay with ...f7-f5, although at this moment White still has a slight edge) 12...♗f6 13 ♘d2 b4 14 ♖h3 (White wants to attack immediately...) 14...♔h8 15 f4 bxc3 16 bxc3 ♘e7 17 ♖b1 ♗c6 18 ♗xf6 ♘xf6 19 ♘d4 ♗d7 20 e5 ♘fd5 21 ♖h1 (...but this move probably wasn't part of the plan!) 21...♘xf4 22 ♕e4 ♘eg6 23 h5 dxe5 24 hxg6 fxg6 (now only Black is attacking: for the slight cost of a piece, he brings up all the big guns to bear on White's "centralized" king) 25 ♘c6 ♗xc6 26 ♕xc6 ♕g5 27 ♗e4 ♖ad8 28 ♖b2 ♖d6 29 ♕xc7 ♖fd8 30 ♘f1 ♘e6! (White is unable to defend his loose queen, rook and bishop) 31 ♕b8 ♖d1+ 32 ♔f2 ♕f4+ 33 ♗f3 ♖xb8 34 ♖xb8+ ♖d8 35 ♖xd8+ ♘xd8 36 ♘g3 h6 and Black won easily in I.Nepomniachtchi-I.Khairullin, Russian Championship, Moscow 2006.

9 d5 ♘a5 10 a4 ♗d7 11 b4 ♘c4 12 ♗d3 c6!

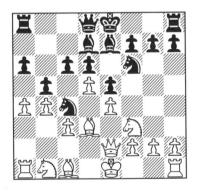

White's overly cautious play has allowed this strong pawn sacrifice: Black gets the two bishops, and open queenside lines for pressure against White's undeveloped position—more than enough for the pawn.

13 ♗xc4 bxc4 14 ♕xc4 cxd5 15 exd5 0-0 16 0-0 ♕b6 17 ♕b3 ♖fc8 18 ♘a3 ♖ab8 19 ♗d2 ♘e4 20 ♗e3 ♕b7 21 ♖ac1 ♘c5 22 ♗xc5

White must give up his last bishop, as otherwise Black just recovers his pawn with advantage.

22...♖xc5 23 ♖fd1 ♖a5?

Overall this is an excellent game from the Colombian IM, probably best known for participating in the famous Leningrad Interzonal to find a successor to Fischer—but this is a bobble, seen immediately by *Fritz*, though not, fortunately, by Cueller's human opponent! Correct is 23...♗g4!, when Black pressures both kingside and queenside, and retains more than enough compensation for the pawn.

24 b5?

White misses his chance! 24 ♘b5! suddenly unpins and wins the trapped rook! After 24...♖xb5 25 axb5 axb5 26 ♖a1 Black hardly has enough for the exchange.

24...axb5 25 ♘xb5 ♗xb5 26 axb5 ♖xb5

But now Black has recovered his pawn with the better game, and from here onward Cueller controls the game until White resigns.

27 ♕c4 ♖c5 28 ♕e4 ♕c8 29 c4 f5!

Black's advantage goes across the whole board.

30 ♕e2 ♗f6 31 g3 ♖b4 32 ♘d2 e4 33 ♕e3 h6 34 ♕a3 ♕b7 35 ♖b1 ♗b2 36 ♕e3 ♗e5

The difference between the white and black minor pieces is drastic.

37 ♔g2 ♖c8 38 ♖xb4 ♕xb4 39 ♖b1 ♕c3 40 ♖b6 ♕c2 41 ♖c6 ♖f8 42 ♘f1 f4

The kingside majority asserts itself: Black has a winning attack.

43 gxf4 ♗xf4 44 ♕a7 ♕e2 45 ♖c7 ♕f3+ 46 ♔g1 ♕g4+ 47 ♔h1

If 47 ♘g3 e3 wins at once.

47...♖f5 48 ♕d4 e3!

49 ♘xe3

Not 49 fxe3 ♕f3+ 50 ♔g1 ♖g5+ 51 ♘g3 ♗xg3 and Black forces mate.

49...♕f3+ 50 ♔g1

Or 50 ♘g2 ♖g5 with an easy win.

50...♖g5+

Black covers White's mate threat with tempo, and wins cleanly—though the computer informs us that 50...♗xh2+! is quicker, forcing mate with all checks.

51 ♔f1 ♗xe3 52 ♖c8+

If 52 ♕xe3 ♕h1+ 53 ♔e2 ♖e5 pins the queen.

52...♔h7 53 ♕d3+ ♖f5 0-1

Again Black's rook both defends and attacks—while White is left a piece down, facing a mating attack.

Although Cueller won stylishly, I think I would avoid the Worrall type positions of the main game in favour of the more Steinitzian 5...♗d7, when Black should equalize with ease, given the rather misplaced white queen, which has no function on e2 in the MS.

Conclusion

None of the Four Fishes are any threat to Black's health and welfare: in general Black equalizes with ease against any of these needlessly defensive moves, and can then play for the win.

This chapter concludes my coverage of the Modern Steinitz proper—but as I pointed out early on, White does have one (and only one!) way of staying in Ruy territory while avoiding the MS—and that is the Exchange Variation with 4 ♗xc6, the subject of the last two chapters of this book.

Chapter Ten
Ruy Exchange: Main Line with 4...dxc6

By capturing the queen's knight on the fourth move, White avoids just about everything: the Modern Steinitz, the Marshall Gambit, the Open Ruy, the Archangel, the Zaitsev, etc, etc. In short, White avoids all the most interesting variations and settles for (or perhaps hopes for) a very drawish position with slight winning chances.

In this chapter we'll see Keres' main line defence with 4...dxc6.

Game 78
A.Adorjan-P.Keres
Budapest 1970

1 e4 e5 2 ♘f3 ♘c6 3 ♗b5 a6 4 ♗xc6

White avoids the Modern Steinitz, which otherwise will terrify him on the next move!

4...dxc6

The most popular move, always played by Keres, but is it the best? After the inevitable d2-(d3)-d4, Black will have to count on his bishop pair to hold the game, as otherwise White will have a good kingside pawn majority (4 vs. 3), while Black has a lamed "majority" on the queenside, where he *cannot* force a passed pawn. The final position of this game is a case in point.

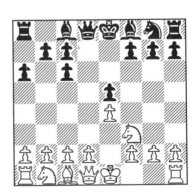

After my experiences with this main line, I lean towards the other recapture: take towards the centre à la Larsen with 4...bxc6, which will be covered in Chapter Eleven.

5 0-0

The Barendregt Variation, popularized by Fischer, is considered best—though White has two major alternatives here: 5 ♘c3 and 5 d4, for which see Games 80 and 81.

5...♗g4

I chose this as a main line repertoire variation to dovetail with Chapter Five, as Black gets a more favourable Yandemirov Gambit here, though he has a hard time generating any fireworks.

A year after playing Adorjan, Keres claimed that 5...♕d6 was "less boring" than either 5...♗g4 (as here) or 5...f6—and then produced the following 16 move draw. Tell me if this is less boring than the 19 move draw of the main game: 5...♕d6 6 d3 (for 6 d4 see the first note to Game 82) 6...♘e7 7 ♗e3 ♘g6 8 ♘bd2 ♗e6 9 ♕e2 ♗e7 10 d4 0-0 11 c3 ♖ad8 12 ♘c4 ♗xc4 13 ♕xc4 ♖fe8 14 ♕b3 exd4 15 ♘xd4 c5 16 ♘f5 ♕c6 ½-½ V.Savon-P.Keres, Petropolis Interzonal 1973.

The most popular defence of e5 is the simple 5...f6, but while it's very solid, it also has an excruciatingly high drawing percentage (43% according to the *Mega*). A typical draw at the World Championship level is: 6 d4 ♗g4 7 dxe5 ♕xd1 8 ♖xd1 fxe5 9 ♖d3 ♗d6 10 ♘bd2 ♘f6 11 ♘c4 ♘xe4 12 ♘cxe5 ♗xf3 13 ♘xf3 0-0 14 ♗e3 b5 15 c4 ♖ab8 16 ♖c1 bxc4 17 ♖d4 ♖fe8 18 ♘d2 ♘xd2 19 ♖xd2 ♖e4 20 g3 ♗e5

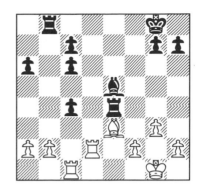

(the mighty Spassky has obtained the advantage with Black against the formidable Fischer, but the drawing nature of the position is so great that Fischer draws without even breaking a sweat, though Boris plays on with an extra pawn for another forty moves) 21 ♖cc2 ♔f7 22 ♔g2 ♖xb2 23 ♔f3 c3 24 ♔xe4 cxd2 25 ♖xd2 ♖b5 26 ♖c2 ♗d6 27 ♖xc6 ♖a5 28 ♗f4 ♖a4+ 29 ♔f3 ♖a3+ 30 ♔e4 ♖xa2 31 ♗xd6 cxd6 32 ♖xd6 ♖xf2 33 ♖xa6 ♖xh2 34 ♔f3 ♖d2 35 ♖a7+ ♔f6 36 ♖a6+ ♔e7 37 ♖a7+ ♖d7 38 ♖a2 ♔e6 39 ♔g2 ♖e7 40 ♔h3 ♔f6 41 ♖a6+ ♖e6 42 ♖a5 h6 43 ♖a2 ♔f5 44 ♖f2+ ♔g5 45 ♖f7 g6 46 ♖f4 h5 47 ♖f3 ♖f6 48 ♖a3 ♖e6 49 ♖f3 ♖e4 50 ♖a3 ♔h6 51 ♖a6 ♖e5 52 ♔h4 ♖e4+ 53 ♔h3 ♖e7 54 ♔h4 ♖e5 55 ♖b6 ♔g7 56 ♖b4 ♔h6 57 ♖b6 ♖e1 58 ♔h3 ♖h1+ 59 ♔g2 ♖a1 60 ♔h3 ♖a4 ½-½ R.J.Fischer-B.Spassky, Reykjavik (16th matchgame) 1972.

6 h3 h5

As in the Yandemirov Gambit, this is the whole point of the bishop pin—but the lines in this chapter are far less risky for Black; just as in Chapter Five the lines with an early ♗xc6 were much easier to meet than the 7 d4 line, where Black had to work to eliminate the white king's bishop.

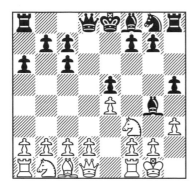

GM Wedberg comments on the game position: "This is probably one of Black's safest ways to play against the Exchange Variation. The downside is that if White knows the main line Black has absolutely no winning chances."

I checked this out in the *Mega* and found Wedberg to be absolutely correct—at the highest level the draws run about 70%!

And what of our hero Keres? As mentioned above, he always recaptured with 4...dxc6—though he played various lines afterwards, always seeking something "less boring". How did this search work out for Mr. K? According to my database, he faced the Exchange Variation nine times in his career, with the result of one win, *eight draws* and no losses. A good percentage score with Black, but booooooring!

Let's look at a great player of our time: Mr. Number One rated in the

world, Raw model Magnus Carlsen, has faced the Ruy Exchange as Black seven times according to my database—and his score is virtually identical to Keres: one win, *six draws* and no losses. Booooooring!

7 d3

On the other hand, if someone is greedy, then Black can have some fun! I will cover every chance to take the intrepid bishop on g4 in the course of this game, but as one will see, mostly such captures are just good for Black: 7 hxg4? hxg4 8 d4 (if 8 ♘e1 ♕h4 9 f4 g3 and mates) 8...gxf3 9 ♕xf3 ♕h4 10 g3? (White can hold on to a lost position with 10 ♕h3 ♕xh3 11 gxh3 exd4) 10...♕h2 mate, A.Gusev-L.Murzin, Tula 2000.

Also possible is the drawing line 7 c3—see the first note in Game 80.

7...♕f6

Black continues with the usual Yandemirov ideas: here he wants to double the white f-pawns, which, as we already saw in Game 18, generally leads to complete (and drawish) equality.

8 ♘bd2

Again dubious is 8 hxg4 hxg4 9 ♘g5 (or 9 ♗g5 ♕g6 10 ♘h4 ♕xg5 and Black recovers the piece with advantage) 9...♕h6 10 ♘h3 (not 10 f4? ♗c5+! 0-1 M.Maslik-K.Pagac, Hlohovec 1996) 10...♕h4 11 ♗g5 ♕h5 and again Black gets his piece back with the better game and went on to win in N.Moe Nilssen-K.Mork, Norwegian Team Championship 1990.

A sound alternative is 8 ♗e3, as White now threatens to defend f3 with no inconveniences (8 ♘bd2, as played by Adorjan, blocks the queen's bishop) with 9 ♘bd2, so Black must take the knight—and all this means is that the world champion—or practically anyone else—can make an easy draw with White: 8...♗xf3 9 ♕xf3 ♕xf3 10 gxf3 ♗d6 11 ♘d2 ♘e7 and the doubled pawns on both sides balanced each other out, with a draw coming soon in V.Anand-R.Kasimdzhanov, World Blitz Championship, Moscow 2007.

8...♗d6

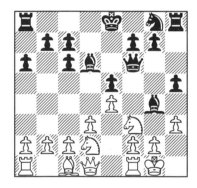

In the next game, Topalov tries the newer but no less boring 8...♘e7.

9 ♖e1

Bad as usual is 9 hxg4 hxg4 10 ♘h2? ♕h4 and wins.

9...♘e7 10 d4

Still questionable is 10 hxg4 hxg4 11 ♘h2 ♖xh2! 12 ♔xh2 ♕h4+ 13 ♔g1 ♗c5 and now:

a) 14 ♕e2 g3 wins for Black.

b) 14 ♖e3 ♗xe3 15 fxe3 0-0-0 "with a violent attack for Black" is given by

Panczyk and Ilczuk in their book *Ruy Lopez Exchange*.

c) 14 ♖e2 g3 15 ♘f3 (or 15 ♖e3 ♗xe3 with a winning attack) 15...♗xf2+ 16 ♖xf2 gxf2+ 17 ♔f1 ♕h1+ wins the queen.

d) 14 g3 ♕xg3+ 0-1 M.Ben Kassem-K.Willenberg, African Junior Championship 2004.

Better not take it yet!

10...♘g6

The idea of White's last move is 10...exd4? 11 e5 ♗xe5 12 hxg4 hxg4 13 ♘e4 ♕f5 14 ♘xe5 ♕xe5 15 ♘g3 and for the first time White can take the piece and win!

11 hxg4

Finally! White takes—but not to win a piece, rather to force a very drawish ending that he can't lose: in a word, boring!

11...hxg4 12 ♘h2 ♖xh2!

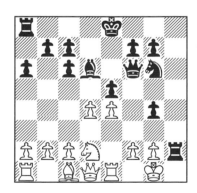

Black has no choice, for as we now know, 12...exd4? 13 e5 ♘xe5 14 ♘e4! ♕h4 15 ♘xd6+ cxd6 16 ♗f4 wins for White.

13 ♕xg4

And White has no choice either, though the players who go in for this as White are not looking for excitement in any case—for the record, White shouldn't try to keep the material: 13 ♔xh2? ♕xf2 14 ♖e2 exd4+ 15 e5 (not 15 ♔h1? ♕h4+ 16 ♔g1 ♕h2+ 17 ♔f1 ♕h1+ 18 ♔f2 g3+ 19 ♔f3 ♕h5 mate) 15...♗xe5+ 16 ♔h1 (Black wins the queen after 16 ♖xe5+? ♘xe5 17 ♘e4 ♘f3+ 18 ♕xf3 ♕h4+ 19 ♔g1 gxf3) 16...♕h4+ 17 ♔g1 0-0-0 18 ♖xe5 ♖h8 19 ♕e2 (both 19 ♖e4 ♕h1+ and 19 ♖e1 ♘f4 lose for White) 19...♕h2+ 20 ♔f2 ♘xe5 and Black has four pawns for the piece and a strong attack.

13...♕h4

A clean equalizer. In *My 60 Memorable Games* Fischer only considers 13...♖h4 14 ♕f5, when he claims a slight advantage for White—and *Fritz* agrees—though in the following game the young lady playing Black stubbornly resists Ruy Exchange specialist GM Khachiyan, and makes her draw: 14...♘e7 15 ♕xf6 gxf6 16 ♘f3 ♖h7 17 ♗e3 0-0-0 18 g3 ♖g8 19 ♔g2 ♖g4 20 ♘d2 exd4 21 ♗xd4 f5 22 ♗f6 fxe4 23 ♗xe7 ♗xe7 24 ♖xe4 ♖xe4 25 ♘xe4 f5 26 ♘d2 ♗f6 27 c3 ♖d7 28 ♘f1 ♖d5 29 ♖c1 b5 30 ♘e3 ♖d2 31 ♖c2 ♖xc2 32 ♘xc2 ♔d7 33 ♔f3 c5 34 ♔f4 ♔e6 35 ♘e3 ♗e5+ 36 ♔g5 ♗f6+ 37 ♔g6 b4 38 ♘xf5 bxc3 39 bxc3 ♗xc3 40 f4 ♗d4 41 g4 ♗f2 42 ♘g7+ ♔d5 43 ♘e8 ♔e4 44 ♘xc7 ♔xf4 45 ♘xa6 ½-½ M.Khachiyan-B.Tuvshintugs, Philadelphia 2007.

14 ♕xh4 ♖xh4 15 ♘f3 ♖h5 16 dxe5

♘xe5 17 ♘xe5 ♗xe5 18 c3

Premature is 18 f4 ♗d4+ 19 ♔f1 ♖h2 and Black's active pieces compensate for his inferior pawn structure.

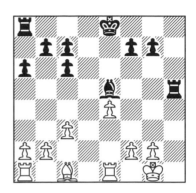

18...0-0-0?!

18...g5! is recommended by Panczyk and Ilczuk, and I emphatically agree: White's kingside pawn majority must be restrained. Practical results for this move have been very good (that means Black can draw!) as can be seen:

a) 19 g3 0-0-0 20 ♗e3 g4 21 ♔g2 ♖dh8 22 ♖h1 ♖xh1 23 ♖xh1 ♖xh1 24 ♔xh1 ♔d7 25 ♔g2 ♔e6 26 ♗f4 ♗d6 27 ♔f1 f5 28 exf5+ ♔xf5 29 ♗e3 ♔e4 with a dead draw in I.Nataf-D.Anic, Enghien les Bains 1997.

b) 19 f3 ♗g3 20 ♖d1 ♔e7 21 ♗e3 ♖ah8 22 ♔f1 ♖h1+ 23 ♔e2 ♖xd1 24 ♖xd1 ♖h2 25 ♖g1 f6 26 ♗f2 ♗d6 27 ♗d4 c5 28 ♗e3 ½-½ J.Nunn-M.Corden, Birmingham 1974.

c) 19 ♗e3 ♔d7 20 f3 ♔e6 21 ♔f2 f6 22 ♖h1 ♖ah8 23 ♖xh5 ♖xh5 24 ♖d1 ♗d6 25 c4 ♖h8 26 c5 ♗e5 and now—instead of 27 ♖d3 when Black got play with 27...♖h1 and amazingly managed to win in T.Bjornsson-R.Hardarson, Sel-foss 2003—White should prefer 27 b3 with an absolutely dead draw.

19 ♗e3? ½-½

Evidently with a draw offer, which was accepted.

Instead, 19 f4! takes advantage of Black's mistake to activate the kingside pawn majority. Since Black does not have either the two bishops or the rook penetration after ...♗d4+ we saw earlier, he is just worse and will suffer either a long painful defeat, or luckily, after hours of suffering, a long painful draw. Here's a typical example—note the helplessness of Black's lamed queenside majority in the pawn endgame: 19...♗f6 20 ♗e3 ♖dh8 21 ♔f1 ♗h4 22 ♗f2 ♗xf2 23 ♔xf2 ♖d8 24 ♖ad1 ♖b5 25 ♖xd8+ ♔xd8 26 ♖d1+ ♔e7 27 ♖d2 c5 28 ♔e3 ♖b6 29 a3 ♖d6 30 e5 ♖xd2 31 ♔xd2 f6 32 exf6+ gxf6 33 ♔e3 ♔e6 34 ♔e4 f5+ 35 ♔f3 b5 36 g4 fxg4+ 37 ♔xg4 ♔f6 38 f5 a5 39 ♔f4 b4 40 ♔e4 c6 41 ♔f4 b3 42 ♔e4 a4 43 ♔f4 c4 44 ♔e4 1-0 Z.Fic-P.Bartas, Moravian Championship 2003.

Black resigned here, but I think the winning method is instructive—Black should know how bad this ending is! White can handle any resistance as follows: 44...♔f7 45 ♔e5 ♔e7 46 f6+ ♔f7 47 ♔f5 c5 (or 47...♔f8 48 ♔e6 ♔e8 49 f7+ ♔f8 50 ♔f6 c5 51 ♔e6 and queens) 48 ♔e5 ♔f8 49 ♔d6 ♔f7 50 ♔xc5 ♔xf6 51 ♔xc4 ♔e5 52 ♔b4 ♔e4 53 ♔xa4 ♔d3 54 ♔xb3 and White lays waste to the queenside.

Keres was fortunate that his bobble on move 18 didn't cost. Against a determined opponent he would have had a tough time drawing after 19 f4!—if a draw was at all possible. On the other hand, had he played the correct 18...g5, he would have held the draw comfortably, though there would be no winning chances against a good opponent.

Note that, overall, Keres (or Carlsen, for that matter) was unable to inject any life or winning prospects into the black side of the Exchange Variation. His 5...♕d6 was just as boring as the main game, and his one win came against the much lower ranked Kagan, from a dead equal position, when the Israeli IM lost his head in time pressure.

In the next game we'll see Topalov grapple only semi-successfully with the same problems in the modern day. If Keres and Topalov could not solve these problems—that is, reaching a position where three results are possible, besides the two usually seen in this variation: win for White and draw—then what can an IM, or a club player do?

Game 79
A.Shirov-V.Topalov
Madrid (rapid) 1997

1 e4 e5 2 ♘f3 ♘c6 3 ♗b5 a6 4 ♗xc6 dxc6 5 0-0 ♗g4 6 h3 h5 7 d3 ♕f6 8 ♘bd2 ♘e7

This is fashionable move now; you can put it to the music of "Another Way to Die", or in this case, another way to draw!

9 ♖e1

Just as in Keres' 8...♗d6 line, White can (but probably won't) take the g4-bishop, as this almost always leads to a good game for Black: 9 hxg4 hxg4 and White must immediately return the piece; while 9 ♘c4 ♗xf3 10 ♕xf3 ♕xf3 11 gxf3 is an even endgame, which the World Champion drew easily—with Black this time—as we saw in Game 18.

9...♘g6 10 d4

If 10 hxg4 hxg4 and again the piece must come back right away, since 11 ♘h2? ♗c5 12 ♕e2 g3 wins for Black.

10...♘f4 11 dxe5

Still bad is 11 hxg4 hxg4 12 ♘h2 ♘xg2! 13 ♘df1 (or 13 ♔xg2 ♖xh2+ 14 ♔xh2 ♕xf2+ 15 ♔h1 g3 and mates) 13...♘xe1 14 ♕xe1 0-0-0 15 ♗d2 ♗d6 16 d5 cxd5 17 exd5 e4 18 ♕xe4 ♗xh2+ 19 ♘xh2 ♖xh2 0-1 E.Brondum-G.Iskov, Esbjerg 1972.

11...♕g6 12 ♘h4

Still can't take it: 12 hxg4 hxg4 13 ♘h2? ♖xh2! 14 ♔xh2 g3+ 15 ♔g1 (or 15 fxg3 ♕h6+ 16 ♔g1 ♗c5+ 17 ♔f1

♕h1 mate) 15...gxf2+ 16 ♔xf2 ♕xg2+ 17 ♔e3 ♕g3+ 0-1 Walther-Hornig, correspondence 1985.

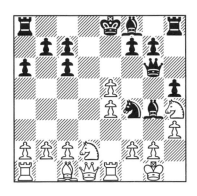

12...♗xd1

It's the end of the line (where White might misplay in taking the bishop), so Black must now enter another dreary, very drawish, very slightly better for White ending.

Impossible is 12...♕h7? 13 hxg4 hxg4 14 ♕xg4 ♕xh4 15 ♕xh4 ♖xh4 16 ♘f3 and White is up a good pawn.

13 ♘xg6 ♘xg6 14 ♖xd1 0-0-0 15 ♖e1 ♘xe5 16 ♘f3 ♘xf3+ 17 gxf3 ♗b4 18 c3 ♗c5 19 ♔f1 ♖d3 20 ♔e2 ♖hd8 21 ♖g1 g6 22 ♗f4

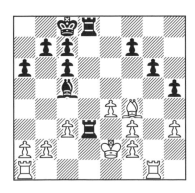

Boring? – check.

Marginally better for White? – check.

Black struggles but makes the draw? – check.

Great!

22...b5 23 ♖ac1 ♔b7 24 ♖c2 a5 25 ♖f1?!

25 c4! is better, which takes advantage of the doubled c-pawns and makes it hard for Black to completely equalize—as far as I can see best play is 25...b4 26 ♖g5! ♔b6! (not 26...♗b6 27 c5, shutting out the bishop) 27 ♗xc7+ ♔xc7 28 ♖xc5 ♔b6 29 ♖e5 a4, when it's quite conceivable that Black makes a draw a pawn down thanks to his d-file play, but no doubt there would be a lot of suffering before that blessed result.

25...a4 26 ♖d2 ♖xd2+ 27 ♗xd2 ♗e7 28 ♗e3 ♗f6 29 ♗c5 ♗g5 30 ♖d1 ♖xd1 31 ♔xd1 ♔c8 32 b3 axb3 33 axb3 ♔d7 34 ♔e2 ♔e6 35 ♗e3 ♗e7 36 c4 ♗d6

37 ♔d3 ½-½

Instead of this move and a draw offer, White could try 37 f4 ♗a3 38 ♔d4 ♗d6 39 ♔e3 c5 40 ♗c3 b4 41 ♗b2 ♗e7 and now *Fritz* claims equality—but my point of view (I'm not sure what Euro-

pean players would think) is that in American sudden death with five second delay, this is still hard to hold. Black's queenside is fixed and he can undertake absolutely nothing active (...f7-f5 or ...g6-g5 just open lines for White and could lead to undoubling his pawns). All Black can do is wait, while White tries to set up the f4-f5 break—and White can manoeuvre until Black's time runs out without risking anything whatsoever.

Against Topalov with a 30 second increment it is, of course, a dead draw.

These games are not just boring—they're painful! Black is barely hanging on to the draw at the GM level—so how does that work for an IM?

GM Melikset Khachiyan and I are friendly rivals in Los Angeles. Since we are two of the few titled players in the area, we play fairly often, usually about twice a year. In 2004 and 2005 I beat him twice in succession with the white pieces (a Bird and a Grünfeld), and published the games in my books *Bird's Opening* and *Beating the King's Indian and Grünfeld*.

The chess gods, offended by my hubris, rewarded me with *ten* Blacks in a row against the GM—a streak that shows no signs of stopping! And the result was I made a few draws—and more losses—with no wins.

I tried practically every opening, trying in vain to win. Finally, I studied the Keres and Topalov games above, with the aim of simply making a draw, and I was convinced I could do just that against Melik's favourite Ruy Exchange—so let's see how that turned out...

Game 80
M.Khachiyan-T.Taylor
Los Angeles 2010

1 e4 e5 2 ♘f3 ♘c6 3 ♗b5 a6 4 ♗xc6 dxc6 5 ♘c3

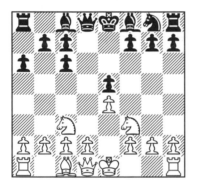

Since my friend Melik is a GM, and I a mere IM, I did not expect the following continuation which he had played before—but against a GM: 5 0-0 ♗g4 6 h3 h5 7 c3 ♕d3 8 hxg4 hxg4 9 ♘xe5 ♗d6 (looking this up now, I notice that this position has been reached 197 times in the *MegaBase*—all draws of course!—it is a "rest day" favourite of such GMs as Guseinov, Smirnov, Gavrikov, Sorokin, Kholmov, and many more) 10 ♘xd3 ♗h2+ 11 ♔h1 ♗d6+ ½-½ M.Khachiyan-G.Serper, Los Angeles 2001.

5...f6

While I was armed to the teeth with Keres' drawing line vs. Adorjan and had the improvement on his game of 18...g5 ready, I was not so prepared for my opponent's actual move, which was more popular in Lasker's day—and although Keres did face it, as one will soon see, I fail to follow my mentor on move 9.

6 d4

Necessary: if 6 0-0 ♗g4 and White can't get d2-d4 in without concessions—White only scores 43% with this line.

6...exd4 7 ♘xd4

The phenomenal endgame expert Lasker was willing to play both sides of the ending after 7 ♕xd4, and his near superhuman patience and subtlety allowed him to win with both colours! Here are two epic World Champion vs. World Champion battles.

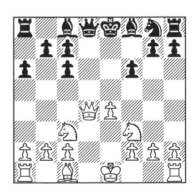

a) Lasker as White: 7...♗d6 8 ♗e3 ♘e7 9 ♘d2 c5 10 ♕d3 b5 11 ♕e2 c4 12 ♕h5+ g6 13 ♕h6 ♔f7 14 f4 ♕f8 15 ♕h4 ♘c6 16 ♘d5 f5 17 ♕f6+ ♔g8 18 ♕xf8+

♗xf8 19 ♘xc7 (Lasker picks off a dou-bled pawn and...) 19...♖b8 20 0-0-0 ♔f7 21 ♘f3 h6 22 e5 ♗e7 23 ♘d5 ♗d8 24 h4 ♖g8 25 ♖he1 ♗e6 26 ♗c5 b4 27 ♘e3 ♖b5 28 ♗d6 c3 29 b3 a5 30 ♖d3 a4 31 ♘d4 ♘xd4 32 ♖xd4 ♗xh4 33 ♖e2 axb3 34 cxb3 ♗e7 35 ♘c2 g5 36 ♗xe7 ♔xe7 37 ♘xb4 gxf4 38 ♘c6+ ♔f7 39 ♖xf4 ♖g4 40 ♖d4 h5 41 ♘d8+ ♔e7 42 ♘xe6 ♔xe6 43 ♖d6+ ♔e7 44 ♖h6 ♖e4 45 ♖f2 ♖bxe5 46 ♖xh5 ♔e6 47 ♖h6+ ♔d5 48 ♖f6 ♔d4 49 ♖d6+ ♔c5 50 ♖d8 ♖e2 51 ♖f3 ♖xa2 52 ♖xc3+ ♔b4 53 ♖c2 ♖xc2+ 54 ♔xc2 (...now, 35 moves later, has finally reached a single rook ending with two pawns to one, which...) 54...♖e2+ 55 ♖d2 ♖e4 56 ♖f2 ♖g4 57 ♔b2 ♖e4 58 g3 ♖e5 59 ♖f4+ ♔b5 60 ♔a3 ♖d5 61 ♖f3 ♔a5 62 b4+ ♔b5 63 ♔b3 ♔b6 64 ♔c4 ♔c6 65 ♖b3 ♖e5 66 b5+ ♔b6 67 ♔d4 ♖e4+ 68 ♔d5 ♖e8 69 ♔d6 ♖e1 70 ♖f3 ♔xb5 71 ♖xf5+ (...he finally converts to a rook and one pawn vs. rook ending which is clearly won—no need to consult the *Tablebase*!) 71...♔c4 72 g4 ♔d4 73 g5 ♖g1 74 ♔e6 ♔e4 75 ♔f6 ♖a1 76 g6 ♖a7 77 ♖e5+ ♔f4 78 ♖e7 1-0 Em.Lasker-W.Steinitz, Moscow (14th matchgame) 1896.

b) Lasker as Black: 7...♕xd4 8 ♘xd4 ♗d6 9 ♗e3 ♘e7 10 0-0-0 0-0 11 ♘b3 ♘g6 12 ♗c5 ♗f4+ 13 ♔b1 ♖e8 14 ♖he1 b6 15 ♗e3 ♗e5 16 ♗d4 ♘h4 17 ♖g1 ♗e6 18 f4 ♗d6 19 ♗f2 ♘g6 20 f5 ♗xb3 21 axb3 ♘f8 22 ♗xb6 ♗xh2 23 ♖h1 cxb6 24 ♖xh2 b5 25 ♖e1 ♘d7 26 ♘d1 a5 27 ♖h3 b4 28 ♘f2 ♘c5 29 ♖he3 a4 30 bxa4 ♘xa4 31 e5 fxe5 32 ♖xe5 ♖eb8

33 ♘e4 b3 34 ♖e2 ♘b6 35 cxb3 ♘d5 36 g4 h6 37 g5 hxg5 38 ♘xg5 ♔f6 39 ♖e7 ♖xb3 40 ♖g2 ♘d5—Lasker's superla-tive defensive play has eliminated all dangers to his position, and the evalua-tion would seem to be dead drawn.

White should accept equality and play 41 ♖e1 when, with two pawns on each side, none passed, it's impossible to see how either side could win. In-stead, Alekhine makes a catastrophic blunder, losing the exchange and even-tually, the game: 41 ♖d7?? ♖d3! 42 ♖xd5 (astonishingly enough, despite the simplified position, White must give up the exchange as 42 ♔c2 ♘b4+ wins a rook; 42 ♖b7 ♖d1+ 43 ♔c2 ♘e3+ wins a different rook; and 42 ♔c1 ♖a1+ 43 ♔c2 ♘b4 is mate!) 42...♖xd5 43 ♘e6 ♔f7 44 ♖xg7+ ♔f6 45 ♖c7 ♖d6 46 ♘c5 ♔xf5 (Lasker now manoeuvres pa-tiently for 30 moves in order to induce White to play b2-b3, where it is slightly weaker than b2!—now that shows 1. Patience; and 2. He is playing a slow time limit without sudden death!) 47 ♖f7+ ♔e5 48 ♔c2 ♖h6 49 ♘d3+ ♔d6 50

♖f5 ♖b8 51 ♔c3 ♔c7 52 ♖f7+ ♔b6 53 ♖d7 ♖h3 54 ♖d4 ♖bh8 55 ♖b4+ ♔c7 56 ♔c2 ♖8h4 57 ♖b3 ♖h2+ 58 ♔c3 ♖4h3 59 ♖b4 ♖h5 60 ♖g4 ♖2h3 61 ♔c2 ♖d5 62 ♘f4 ♖c5+ 63 ♔b1 ♖h1+ 64 ♔a2 ♖a5+ 65 ♔b3 ♖b5+ 66 ♔c3 ♔b6 67 ♘d3 ♖h3 68 ♔c2 ♖d5 69 ♖b4+ ♔c7 70 ♖b3 ♖h2+ 71 ♔c3 ♔d6 72 ♖a3 ♖g2 73 ♖a1 ♖g3 74 ♖d1 ♔c7 75 ♖d2 ♔b6 76 ♖d1 ♔b5 77 ♔c2 ♔c4 78 b3+ (phase one completed!) 78...♔b5 79 ♖d2 ♖h3 80 ♖d1 ♖h2+ 81 ♔c3 ♖d8 82 ♖g1 ♖h3 83 ♖d1 ♖dh8 84 ♖g1 ♖8h5 85 ♔c2 ♖d5 86 ♖d1 ♖g5 87 ♖d2 ♖hg3 88 ♘c1 ♖g2 89 ♘e2 ♔b6 0-1 A.Alekhine-Em.Lasker, St Petersburg 1914—the exchange of rooks is now forced.

To prove to myself this is a win (I wouldn't say Black's win is obvious) I analysed further, and came up with the following main line: 90 ♔d1 ♖d5 91 ♖xd5 (giving Black a passed pawn, but if the rook exchange occurs on d2, the knight remains fatally pinned) 91...cxd5 (the rest of the winning procedure involves shepherding the pawn down the board, using any and all tactical tricks to justify the strategical imperative) 92 ♔d2 ♔c5 93 ♔d3 ♖g4 94 ♔e3 d4+ 95 ♔f3 d3 96 ♘c3 ♖d4 97 ♔e3 d2 98 ♔e2 ♔b4 99 ♘d1 ♔xb3 100 ♘e3 ♔c3 101 ♔d1 (if 101 ♘d1+ ♔c2 102 ♘e3+ ♔c1 is an easier win for Black) 101...♖d3 102 ♘f1 ♖h3 103 ♔e2 (if 103 ♘xd2 ♖d3 wins the knight) 103...♖h2+! (one still has to be awake, alert, and have time on your clock to find this nice tactic on *move 103* if your oppo-

nent plays on, as he would, nowadays!) 104 ♘xh2 (if 104 ♔d1 ♖h1 105 ♔e2 ♖xf1 wins) 104...♔c2 and the pawn finally promotes!

7...c5 8 ♘de2 ♕xd1+ 9 ♘xd1

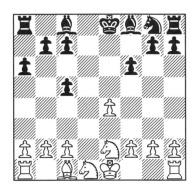

9...♗d7?

If I had known at this time every Keres/Black/MS/Exchange game (I do now!) I would have gone for the more active 9...♗e6! as played by Keres. Of course I should also have found this at the board. In a few moves we will see the crucial difference between the two bishop developments.

But first, let's see a nice technical draw by Keres: 9...♗e6! 10 ♗f4 0-0-0 11 ♘e3 ♘e7 12 ♖d1 (White has to lose time to exchange rooks, since long castling is illegal) 12...♖xd1+ 13 ♔xd1 g6 14 ♔c1 ♗g7 15 ♖d1 ♖d8 16 ♖xd8+ ♔xd8 ½-½ A.Lutikov-P.Keres, USSR Team Championship 1969. Black's bishops are active enough to hold the draw if White plays on; e.g. 17 ♗g3 f5 18 ♘f4 ♗d7 19 exf5 ♘xf5 20 ♘xf5 ♗xf5 21 ♘d5 ♗h6+ 22 ♗f4 (or 22 ♔b1 c6 23 ♘f6 g5 and the bishop pair holds)

22...♗e4! 23 ♗xh6 ♗xd5 and despite the inferior pawn structure, the opposite bishops should secure the draw—but even so, this is marginally, marginally better for White (+.03 on *Fritz*, which is about right). Why does this matter? Because in sudden death White will play this on, and you will suffer for another two hours to make your draw!

10 ♗f4 0-0-0 11 ♘e3 ♘e7

About a month later, in another Los Angeles open tournament, Khachiyan tried this line again. His young opponent, Michael Brown, *also* did not know his Keres, and instead followed me on the 9th move—not a good choice! At this point Brown deviated from my play, though without scoring a better result: 11...♖e8 12 ♘c3 ♗c6 13 f3 ♘e7 14 0-0-0 (notice White's effective long castle here, as in the main game, which Keres prevented by having his bishop on e6 while the d-file was open) 14...♘g6 15 ♗g3 ♘e5 16 ♖he1 g6 17 ♘ed5 ♗h6+ 18 ♔b1 ♗g7 19 f4 ♘d7 20 f5 ♘e5 21 ♘f4 ♗d7 22 ♘cd5 ♖hf8 (after 22...b6 White is only marginally better) 23 ♘d3 ♘xd3 24 cxd3 (Black is in trouble because White has cleared the diagonal for his bishop) 24...gxf5 25 ♘xc7 ♖d8 26 ♘d5 ♖de8 27 ♗d6 ♖f7 28 exf5 ♖xe1 29 ♖xe1 ♗f8 30 ♗xf8 ♖xf8 31 ♘b6+ ♔d8 32 ♘xd7 ♔xd7 33 ♖e6 (White has secured a pawn plus in a rook endgame, and GM technique takes over) 33...♖f7 34 ♔c2 ♔c7 35 ♔d2 ♔d7 36 ♔e3 ♔c7 37 ♔e4 b6 38 g4 a5

39 h4 h6 40 b3 ♖g7 41 ♔f4 ♖f7 42 g5 hxg5+ 43 hxg5 fxg5+ 44 ♔xg5 ♖g7+ 45 ♔g6 ♖d7 46 f6 ♔d6 47 ♖g7 ♖d8 48 ♔g6 ♖e8 49 f7 ♖f8 50 ♔f6 1-0 M.Khachiyan-M.Brown, Los Angeles 2010.

12 0-0-0

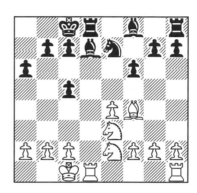

Again, the clear difference between Keres and Taylor is revealed: White castles smoothly without loss of time, and so stands slightly better with his superior pawn structure. The two bishops don't mean much, since the white knights are coming to d5 (0-0-0 is useful for this plan as well) and Black will have to take one off with a bishop soon.

Bottom line: White is better, Black is struggling for a draw. For a time I play well, but never *completely* equalize, and a mistake on move 23 sends me further downhill.

12...g5 13 ♗g3 ♗g7 14 h4 h5!

I have to fight for every inch of space. This advance gives me counter-chances that approach very near to a draw—but as we'll see later, the draw is never forced. The even sadder thing is that Black can hope for *nothing more than a draw*, and even Keres never even tried to win such positions, as was clear from the Lutikov game above.

15 ♘c3 ♗e6 16 ♖xd8+ ♔xd8 17 ♖d1+ ♔c8 18 ♘cd5 ♘xd5 19 ♘xd5 gxh4 20 ♗xh4 ♗h6+ 21 ♔b1 ♗g5 22 g3 ♗xd5 23 ♖xd5

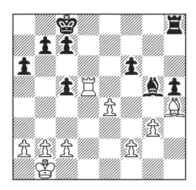

23...♗xh4?!

When I looked at the game immediately afterwards, I thought this was a classic example of playing moves in the wrong order. As one sees in the game, taking the white bishop loses control of c1, so White solves his back rank problem and enters a superior rook ending where I have both doubled pawns and split kingside pawns. However, by playing 23...♖g8! first, don't I draw? I threaten to take on h4 winning a piece, and White can't (very unusual for a Ruy Exchange) exchange off all pieces, as here the king and pawn ending wins for Black! So it seems that Black draws, as White will be forced back onto defence. When I got home I checked it on *Fritz*: Yes, said the iron man, 23...♖g8!— equal! In fact my computer still says

this now, as I write. For a while I thought it was nice that I just missed a draw against a GM by one careless move; I had not been outplayed, a mere blunder had cost me the game.

But then my "good angel"—that is, my "truth in chess" angel—kept bothering me. If Black has lost his bishop pair, and still has the same defects in his pawn structure that he started with (the doubled c-pawns, no pawn majority—and here Black has additional isolated pawns on the kingside) then why should Black be drawing here? I kept looking at the ending off and on as I worked on the book, and after many hours defying my "genius computer" I found... it's not a draw after all. *Fritz* failed to display the "sorry" function when I proved White was better, but the monster did change its evaluation. While it's not nice to prove that one's position is bad, I did learn a lot about difficult rook endings!

Here is my analysis: 23...♖g8! 24 ♗xg5 (24 b3 ♗xh4 25 gxh4 ♖g4 26 ♖xc5 ♖xh4 27 ♔c1 ♖xe4 28 ♖xh5 ♖f4 really is a draw) 24...♖xg5 25 ♖d1! (yes, White has to defend for a while, but the key feature of the better pawn structure is, in the long run—and of course, given exact play by White—more important than Black's temporary initiative; but note that Black wins after 25 ♖xg5?? fxg5 26 ♔c1 h4 and gets good counterplay after 25 ♖d3 h4—both of these lines show the importance of my strong 14...h5! earlier)

25...♖e5 26 f3 ♖g5 27 ♖g1 f5 (no better is 27...h4 28 g4 ♖g8 29 ♖h1 ♖h8 30 ♔c1 ♔d7 31 ♔d2 ♔e6 32 ♔e3 ♔e5 33 f4+ ♔e6 34 ♔f3 c4 35 ♖h2 ♖h7 36 g5 fxg5 37 fxg5 ♔e5 38 ♔g4 ♔xe4 39 g6 ♖g7 40 ♔g5 and White wins, or 27...♔d7 28 ♔c1 ♔e6 29 ♔d2 f5 30 ♔e3 fxe4 31 ♔xe4 h4 32 g4 ♖e5+ 33 ♔d3 ♔f6 34 f4 c4+ 35 ♔d2 ♖e8 36 ♖h1 ♖h8 37 ♖h3 b5 38 ♔e2, when White retains a plus in view of his connected passed pawns) 28 exf5 ♖xf5 29 f4 h4 (if 29...♖f8 30 ♔c1 ♖g8 31 ♔d2 ♔d7 32 ♔e3 ♔e6 33 ♔e4 b5 34 ♖h1 ♖xg3 35 ♖xh5 and White still has a pull: he has a passer, and Black doesn't, though this worse ending might be Black's best hope to draw) 30 gxh4 ♖xf4 31 ♖h1 ♖f6 32 h5 ♖h6 33 ♔c1 ♔d7 34 ♔d2 ♔e6 35 ♔d3 ♔f5 36 ♔c4 b6 37 a4 and White has a permanent advantage with the rook behind the passed pawn, as Black can't go into the king and pawn ending; e.g. 37...♔g5 38 a5 ♖xh5 39 ♖xh5+ ♔xh5 40 axb6 cxb6 41 ♔d5 ♔g4 42 ♔c6 wins. Therefore Black must answer 37 a4 with 37...♔e5, and stay in the somewhat worse rook ending. This might draw—and it might not—what is beyond dispute is that White can legitimately play this ending to win, and Black will have to defend precisely for hours in the hope of a draw.

It is true that 23...♖g8 is much stronger than the move I played, and as White can try to win, Black also has legitimate drawing hopes, especially if I had Lasker on the lifeline!

24 gxh4 ♖g8 25 ♔c1

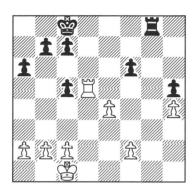

Now White has solved his back rank problems and, with targets on the fifth rank, has a clear advantage in the rook ending.

25...♖g4 26 ♖xh5 ♖xe4 27 ♔d2 ♔d7 28 f3 ♖b4 29 b3 c4!?

This leads to the loss of a pawn, but I succeed in activating my king. All in all, it seems no worse than the following alternatives, as nothing seems to really save the game: 29...♔d6 (or 29...♖d4+ 30 ♔e3 b6 31 ♖h7+ and White is in effect a pawn up, with good winning chances) 30 c3 ♖b5 31 c4 ♖a5 32 a4 c6 33 ♖h8 b5 34 h5 ♔e7 (not 34...bxa4? 35 h6 and wins) 35 ♖c8 35...♔f7 36 axb5 cxb5 37 ♖xc5 ♖a2+ 38 ♔d3 bxc4+ 39 bxc4 ♖h2 when Black has the active rook, but White probably wins anyway due to his two passed pawns.

30 ♔c3 ♖b6

Black fails to queen after 30...cxb3? 31 ♔xb4 b2 32 ♖d5+ ♔e6 33 ♖d1.

31 ♔xc4 ♖e6 32 ♖h7+ ♔d6 33 ♖f7 b5+ 34 ♔d3 ♔e5 35 h5 ♔f4

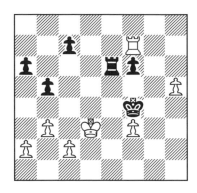

Black has a great king, but meanwhile the white h-pawn has made a lot of progress. The alternative 35...♖d6+ also fails: 36 ♔e3 ♖c6 37 h6 ♖xc2 38 h7 ♖h2 39 ♖xc7 etc.

36 h6 f5

There are no saves: 36...♔xf3 37 h7 ♖e3+ (or 37...♖e8 38 ♖xf6+ ♔g3 39 ♖g6+ ♔f3 40 ♖g8 and wins) 38 ♔d4 ♖e4+ 39 ♔d5 ♖h4 40 ♖xf6+ ♔e3 41 ♖f7 and White will win the game on the queenside.

37 h7 ♖h6 38 ♖xc7 ♔xf3 39 c4 bxc4+ 40 bxc4 f4

Black's counterplay comes too late.

41 c5 ♔f2 42 ♖f7 f3 43 c6 ♔e1 44 c7 f2 45 c8♕ 1-0

This game shows how the Ruy Exchange can be used as a weapon by a strong player: White aims for a marginally better position and then grinds away—yes, Black might draw, like Keres, but remember, even at the end of that game White was very slightly better. If White also has a rating advantage, you can be sure you will be tormented for hours!

Is it possible for *Black* to win in this main line Exchange? Yes, but it's quite difficult—see the next game.

Game 81
A.Hughes-T.Taylor
US Open, Irvine 2010

1 e4 e5 2 ♘f3 ♘c6 3 ♗b5 a6 4 ♗xc6 dxc6 5 d4 exd4 6 ♕xd4 ♕xd4 7 ♘xd4 ♗d7 8 ♘c3

Let's look at two instructive World Champion games: in the first, Smyslov tries to defeat Keres—but can only draw; and in the second, Miles (with White) tries to draw with Karpov, and succeeds. Both games continued 8 ♗e3 0-0-0 and then:

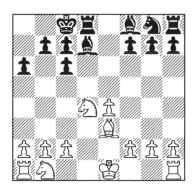

a) 9 ♘c3 ♖e8 10 0-0-0 ♗b4 (Keres and I are on the same page this time—this game was played a month or so after the previous one—Black doesn't mind giving up the bishop pair if he can shatter White's queenside; this threat causes White to retreat, which in turn allows the following break, opening up the game for the bishops) 11 ♘de2 f5 12 exf5 ♗xf5 (clearly Black's active bishops fully compensate for the worse pawns; Smyslov tries for a long time—but can't get anywhere against Keres' precise and active defence) 13 a3 ♗d6 14 ♗f4 ♗c5 15 ♘g3 ♗g6 16 f3 ♘f6 17 ♖he1 ♗f2 18 ♖f1 ♗c5 19 ♖fe1 ♖xe1 20 ♖xe1 ♖f8 21 ♗e5 ♖e8 22 ♖e2 ♗g1 23 ♘f1 ♗c5 24 ♗g3 ♖xe2 25 ♘xe2 ♗d6 26 ♔d2 ♔d7 27 ♘f4 ♗e8 28 ♘d3 c5 29 c4 b6 30 b3 ♘h5 31 ♗e5 ♔e6 32 ♗c3 ♘f4 33 ♘xf4+ ♗xf4+ 34 ♔d1 g5 35 g3 ♗d6 36 ♘d2 ♗e5 37 ♘e4 ♗xc3 38 ♘xc3 ♔e5 39 ♔d2 ♗h5 40 ♔e3 ½-½ V.Smyslov-P.Keres, USSR Championship, Moscow 1940. After 40...♗g6 41 ♘e4 h6 Black's strong bishop just holds the draw despite White's still superior pawns.

b) 9 ♘d2 (Miles avoids the pin, and if you really want a draw—even against Karpov!—this move can't be beat... so to speak; which illustrates another problem with the 4...dxc6 line for Black: a lower-rated White player can very successfully play for a draw) 9...♘e7 10 0-0-0 f6 11 f3 ♘g6 12 h4 (White needs some kingside play—this is the move my opponent didn't make in the main game) 12...h5 13 ♘c4 c5 14 ♘f5 ♗e6 15 ♖xd8+ ♔xd8 16 ♘d2 b6 17 b3 ♔c8 (17...♗xf5 18 exf5 ♘e7 19 g4 is also equal) 18 ♗f2 ♘f4 19 g3 g6! 20 ♘e7+ ♗xe7 21 gxf4 f5 22 ♖g1 ♖g8 23 ♘c4 ♗f6 24 a4 ♔b7 25 ♖g2 ♗xc4 26 bxc4 ♖g7 27 ♔b1 ♗c3 28 ♔a2 ♖e7! 29 ♔b3 ♗h8 30 e5! (Black's idea was 30

♖xg6 fxe4 31 fxe4 ♖xe4 32 f5 ♖f4 with a fork, but Miles dodges this) 30...♖e6 31 ♖g1 ♗g7 32 ♖d1 ♔c8 33 a5 ♗h6 34 ♗e3 ♗f8 35 ♖a1 ♔b7 36 ♖d1 ♗e7 37 ♗f2 ♔c8 38 ♖a1 ♔b7 39 ♖d1 ♔c8 40 ♖a1 ♔b7 41 ♖d1 (it's been even for a long time, despite the over 100 point rating disparity—Karpov finally accepts the inevitable) ½-½ A.Miles-A.Karpov, Biel 1992.

8...♗b4

À la Keres!

9 ♗d2 0-0-0

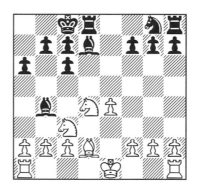

10 f3

10 0-0-0 is more accurate; e.g. 10...♘e7 11 ♘ce2 ♗d6 12 ♗f4 with equality. The tactical 10...♗g4 is worse: 11 ♘de2 ♗xc3 (or 11...♗xe2 12 ♘xe2 ♗xd2+ 13 ♖xd2 ♘f6 14 ♖xd8+ ♖xd8 15 f3 ♘d7 16 ♖d1 with the usual White pull) 12 ♗xc3 ♖xd1+ 13 ♖xd1 ♗xe2 14 ♗xg7 and White emerges with the better minor piece in the end. Note that both these variations lead to the kind of exchanges Black does not want—remember the king and pawn ending is hopeless for Black if the pawn structure

hasn't changed, and Black must get some compensation if he gives up the bishop pair.

10...♘e7 11 0-0-0 ♘g6

12 ♘ce2

12 h4 is necessary, as in Miles-Karpov. White needs some space on his strong side and, despite my best efforts, after this I, like Karpov, would probably have to give up the draw to a lower-rated player.

12...♗d6 13 ♘f5?

13 h4 is still necessary. White needs both to gain space on his strong side, and also to remove this pawn from the d6-bishop's diagonal.

13...♗xf5

I'm willing to give up the bishop pair, since I double White's pawns in return and seize the e-file.

14 exf5 ♘h4 15 ♗g5 ♖de8 16 ♗xh4 ♖xe2 17 g3 ♖he8 18 ♖d2 ♖2e5!

Keeping the pressure on. Instead, Black can win a pawn here, but I'm not sure the resulting bishop ending can be won: 18...♖e1+ 19 ♖d1 ♖xh1 20 ♖xh1 ♖e5 21 g4 ♖e3 22 ♖e1 ♖xe1+ (but not

22...♖xf3?? 23 ♖e8+ ♔d7 24 ♖d8 mate!) 23 ♗xe1 ♗xh2 and even though Black is a pawn up, it's very hard to see how he makes progress, as there is no evident way to make a passed pawn (because of the doubletons).

19 g4 ♖a5 20 ♔b1 ♖e3

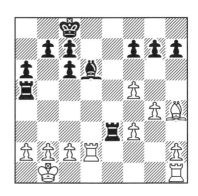

It's clear that every black piece is more active than its white counterpart, and h2 is still weak. I think Black should win this position, though it's not easy, and as one will see, I bobble the ball a bit before I score the point.

21 ♖e1 ♖ae5 22 ♖f1 ♖e2 23 ♔c1 ♖xd2 24 ♔xd2 ♖d5+ 25 ♔e3 ♖a5 26 a3 ♖b5

26...♗xh2 is premature, as 27 f4 shuts the door.

27 b4 c5!

Exchanging the doubled pawn is a big step forward for Black.

28 c4

If 28 c3 cxb4 29 axb4 c5 30 bxc5 ♗xc5+ 31 ♔d3 ♖b2 and Black has both a passed pawn and the superior pawn structure—two rarities in this line!

28...♖b6 29 ♖c1 f6?

Black's bishop has been observing

the h-pawn for so long, I failed to real-ize that now was the time to take it! Black should win after 29...♗xh2! and then:

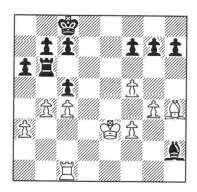

a) 30 f4 (this fails to catch the bishop this time) 30...cxb4 31 ♖h1 (or 31 axb4 ♖xb4 32 ♖h1 ♖b2 and the bishop is defended) 31...bxa3! 32 ♖xh2 ♖h6 and the pin is too strong; e.g. 33 g5 a2 34 ♖xa2 (after 34 gxh6 a1♕ the new queen holds g7) 34...♖xh4 and Black wins with two extra pawns.

b) 30 bxc5 ♖b3+ 31 ♔e4 ♖xa3 and Black is up a good passed pawn.

c) 30 ♔e4 cxb4 31 ♗f2 ♖d6 32 axb4 ♖d2 and the extra pawn should even-tually be decisive.

Note that, besides the inaccurate move that I played, 29...cxb4 also gives White counterplay after 30 c5 ♖c6 31 axb4.

30 g5!

Suddenly White activates his pawn majority and gets counterplay: Black played quite well through the ending until the previous move—then one in-accuracy and... nothing.

30...♗e5

The moment has gone: 30...fxg5 31 ♗xg5 cxb4 32 c5 ♖c6 33 axb4 ♗xh2 34 f4 is dangerous for Black.

31 bxc5 ♖c6 32 ♔e4 ♖xc5 33 f4 ♗b2 34 ♖c2 ♗xa3 35 g6?

White blunders in turn. 35 gxf6 gxf6 36 ♗xf6 is correct, when White, with dangerously passed f-pawns, stands at least equal.

35...hxg6 36 fxg6 f5+

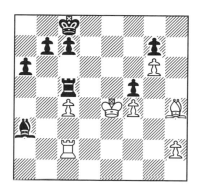

Black meets the threat of ♗xf6 and once again stands better, as all the white pawns are weak, and none are passed—whereas Black has one extra passed pawn.

37 ♔d4 ♖c6 38 ♔e5

If 38 ♖g2 ♖e6 and White can't hold all the weak pawns.

38...♖xg6

The win should now be a matter of technique, and I handle that pretty well—but that doesn't mean there isn't a bizarre occurrence still to come!

39 ♔xf5 ♖c6 40 ♗f2 ♖f6+ 41 ♔e4 g6 42 c5 ♔d7 43 ♗d4 ♖e6+ 44 ♔d5 c6+ 45 ♔c4 ♖e4 46 ♖a2 ♗c1 47 ♔d3 ♖xf4 48

♖c2 ♖f1 49 ♔g2 g5 50 h4 gxh4

So far so good: Black is significant material up, and even though White can regain a pawn or two, Black is clearly winning. Obviously White has no legal way of resisting—so here my opponent tried something I have never seen in 40 years of tournament chess. He had been away from the board when I captured on h4. When he came back, he didn't like the black h-pawn there—so he picked it up, put it aside, and put a white pawn in its place! I could not believe my eyes! I finally managed a kind of strangled, "You can't do that!" and picked up his white pawn, moved it off the board, and put my black pawn back on h4!

Then my opponent made a face very similar to that of my one year old son when you take his bottle away—and quickly played out the rest of the moves.

51 ♖g7+ ♔e6 52 ♖xb7 ♖f7 53 ♖b6 ♔d5 54 ♖xa6 h3 55 ♖a8

If 55 ♖a2 ♖f3+ 56 ♔e2 h2 wins.

55...♖f3+ 56 ♔e2 h2!

The winning combination begins:

the black rook is always immune with the pawn (the *black* pawn!) one square from queening. Meanwhile the white king has been diverted from its protection of the bishop.

57 ♖h8 ♖f8!

Still immune!

58 ♖xh2

58 ♖h4 would drag the game out one more move, but after 58...♗g5 something's gotta give!

58...♔xd4 0-1

Black is a clear piece up and still has the c-pawn for queening purposes— my opponent chose not to replace it with a white pawn (now that would be a theoretical draw) and resigned.

So I finally won with 4...dxc6— though of course the verdict on the opening position must still be "extremely drawish".

Conclusion

"Everybody knows" that you have to take back with the d-pawn when White plays 4 ♗xc6. And then it is certainly possible to study every variation of this main line Exchange—5 ♘c3 and 5 d4 as well as the theory-heavy 5 0-0—and practice your endgame defence until you can draw these positions. That's exactly how Keres handled it, and it's how Carlsen deals with the variation now. You might win a game here and there against a lower-rated player, but most of the time you will draw.

Despite my mentor's endorsement, I find this a dreary prospect! My per-

personal experience in the last two games above prompted me to question what "everybody knows"—and I discovered that I was not the only one. The great Bent Larsen passed away as I was working on this book (I will always remember how he taught me to play queen endings by winning one a pawn down against me!) and I wondered, did that independent thinker ever face the Exchange Variation? Yes! And against his highest rated foe, he did *not* do what everyone else did. In Bent's honour, I am going to call the line I will examine in the next and final chapter of this book, Larsen's Variation.

I pointed out in my book on Bird's Opening how Larsen loved to take towards the centre (and that is the rule anyway)—so *why not 4...bxc6! - ?*

As to my conclusion about the "regular" 4...dxc6 seen in this chapter—all I can say is, life is too short to play such a boring variation!

Chapter Eleven
Ruy Exchange: Larsen's Variation, 4...bxc6

In Chapter Six we saw that Black equalized with unparalleled ease in the tempo-loss line 1 e4 e5 2 ♘f3 ♘c6 3 ♗b5 a6 4 ♗a4 d6 5 ♗xc6+ bxc6 6 d4, so long as he opened the game for his bishops with 6...exd4!. Frequently Black was better right out of the opening, and in no case could White prove any kind of advantage.

So if Black has such an easy game, might not the variation also be good with one less tempo? I say, Yes!

Since Keres wouldn't do something so unorthodox as capture towards the centre—though, interestingly enough, in principle he had no problem with it; see his note about 4...bxc6 in Game 84—I will lead with and dedicate this chapter to the late, great Bent Larsen.

Finally—even if you didn't see the player's name, you would suspect this was a Larsen game because both rook pawns advance to the fifth rank!

Game 82
U.Andersson-B.Larsen
Las Palmas 1972

1 e4 e5 2 ♘f3 ♘c6 3 ♗b5 a6 4 ♗xc6 bxc6!

One can see the position is identical to Chapter Six—*except* that Black does not have the extra move ...d7-d6 on the board. The question Larsen asks is: does that extra tempo matter?

I think Black has sufficient resources despite the tempo, and here are some onboard advantages: the bishop pair of course; a more flexible pawn structure than in the main line Exchange, which means pawn endings are by no means lost, and even though one would like to keep the pair of bishops, exchanging one is hardly fatal here; and the b-file for counterplay.

There are also some psychological advantages: one good point is that White can't (as in Game 79, for example) simply roll out a long series of book moves and end up with a small plus—there really isn't much book on this line at all! So your opponent must already think with his own head.

An even bigger advantage is that Black can go into this line with the thought, I can really try to win here! This is huge, in my opinion—White has zero chance of setting up a "classic Ruy Exchange grind", as Larsen, on the other side, shows us yet again: 4...dxc6 5 0-0 ♕d6 6 d4 exd4 (for the rest of the game Black will have to contend with White's superior pawn majority) 7 ♘xd4 ♗d7 8 ♗e3 0-0-0 9 ♘d2 ♘h6 10 h3 ♕g6 11 ♕f3 f5 12 ♖ad1 fxe4 13 ♕xe4 ♕xe4 14 ♘xe4 (White gets the queens off and stands marginally better) 14...♘f7 15 ♖fe1 ♖e8 16 ♗d2 c5 17 ♘f3 ♗e7 18 ♘fg5 ♘xg5 19 ♘xg5 ♗xg5 20 ♗xg5 (even in this extremely simplified and drawish position with opposite bishops, White's superior pawn majority gives him the usual tiny pull,

while Black can't even dream of winning) 20...♖xe1+ 21 ♖xe1 ♖e8 (one imagines that Portisch offered a draw here—but Bent said, play on!) 22 ♗e3 ♗f5 23 c4 b5 (23...b6 is correct when Black is effectively a pawn down, but the opposite bishops and exact defence should give a draw—I, for one, am thrilled!) 24 ♖c1!

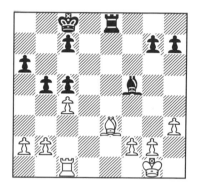

(Bent now has plus equals and commences to grind) 24...bxc4 25 ♖xc4 ♖e5 26 ♗xc5 ♗e6 27 ♖c1 ♗xa2 28 ♗d6 ♖e6 29 ♖xc7+ ♔d8 30 ♗g3 (White is a pawn up and, with rooks on, has real winning chances... after many moves of course!) 30...♖e7 31 ♖c6 ♖e6 32 ♖c1 ♔e8 33 f3 ♗d5 34 ♖c5 ♗c6 35 ♗e5 g6 36 ♔f2 h5 37 g4 hxg4 38 hxg4 ♗b7 39 ♗c3 ♖c6 40 ♖a5 ♖d6 41 ♔e3 ♖d7 42 ♗b4 ♔f7 43 ♖c5 ♔f6 44 ♗c3+ ♔f7 45 ♖c1 ♗d5 46 ♖a4 ♗b7 47 ♖b4 ♗d5 48 ♔f2 ♖e7 49 ♖d4 ♔e6 50 ♖a4 ♖a7 51 ♔g3 ♗c6 52 ♖a1 ♖f7 53 f4 ♗b5 54 ♖e1+ ♔d6 55 ♔h4 ♔c5 56 ♔g5 ♗d3 57 ♖e5+ ♔c4 58 ♖e3 ♖b7 59 ♖xd3! (after 30 moves of grinding, the immortal Bent finds a winning combination!)

59...♔xd3 60 ♔xg6 ♖b6+ (White also wins after 60...♔e4 61 f5 ♔f4 62 f6 ♔xg4 63 f7 ♖b6+ 64 ♗f6 ♖b8 65 ♗e7 etc) 61 ♔f5 ♖h6 62 g5 ♖h5 63 ♔g6 ♖h2 64 f5 1-0 B.Larsen-L.Portisch, Rotterdam (7th matchgame) 1977.

As I plan to play 4...bxc6 at the next opportunity, the realization that I will not have to face such a grind cheers me immensely! I will certainly try to win, and as we see, Larsen had good chances to win this one...

5 d4

White has a few alternatives:

a) 5 0-0—see Game 85.

b) 5 c3 is virtually untried but looks too slow to be effective: Black can hit back in the centre with either 5...♘f6 or even 5...d5!?, which certainly gets the tempo back by advancing to d5 in one go!

c) 5 ♘xe5

5...♕e7! (this looks stronger than 5...♕g5, when Black trades his centre pawn for White's g-pawn; e.g. 6 ♘f3 ♕xg2 7 ♖g1 ♕h3 8 ♘c3 d6 9 ♖g3 ♕d7 10 ♕e2 and White was better and even-tually won in V.Gusev-K.Klaman, Sevastopol 1973) 6 d4 (if 6 ♘d3 ♕xe4+ 7 ♕e2 ♕xe2+ 8 ♔xe2 ♗b7 9 ♖e1 0-0-0 10 ♔f1 ♘h6 11 ♘c3 f6 12 ♘e4 ♘f5 13 c3 d6 14 b4 a5! and Black's two bishops gave him the better ending and eventually the full point in K.K.Olsen-J.R.Pedersen, Esbjerg 2006) 6...d6 7 ♘xc6 ♕xe4+ 8 ♕e2 ♕xe2+ 9 ♔xe2 ♗b7 and now we have:

c1) 10 d5 (almost always played) 10...♔d7 (simplest: White can't keep the extra pawn) 11 c4 (or 11 ♘b4 a5) 11...♗xc6 12 dxc6+ ♔xc6 with an equal game that was soon drawn in A.Arakeljan-S.Sviridonov, Volodarskij 2007. But note that Black has no worries about White's permanent pawn majority here, and the position is slightly unbalanced. A player who wanted to win could take this position and try to gradually outplay his opponent, something that's rarely possible in the main line.

c2) 10 ♘a5 appears only three times in the *Mega*, and Black won them all. Basically in this line Black keeps the two bishops, gets a more open game, and is freed of his doubled pawns—not what White wants. Here's a typical example: 10...♗xg2 11 ♖e1 ♔d7 12 ♘c3 ♖e8+ 13 ♗e3 ♘f6 14 f3 g6 15 ♔f2 ♗h3 16 ♖e2 ♗g7 17 ♖ae1 ♖b8 18 ♘c4 ♗e6 19 b3 ♖he8 20 ♘d2 ♗f5 21 ♘c4 ♗e6 22 ♘d2 ♗f5 23 ♘c4 ♖e7 24 d5 ♘h5 25 ♘d1 ♗f6 26 ♔g1 ♖be8 27 ♘a5 ♗h4 (Black trades off his bishops—but soon wins two pawns!) 28 ♘c6 ♗xe1 29 ♘xe7 ♖xe7 30 ♖xe1 ♗xc2 31 ♔f2 ♗xd1 32 ♖xd1 ♖e5 33 f4 ♖f5 34 ♔f3 ♘f6 35 ♖d4 ♘xd5 36 ♖a4 ♘xe3 37 ♔xe3 a5 38 b4 axb4 39 ♖xb4 ♖a5 40 a4 ♖a7 41 ♔e4 c5 42 ♖c4 ♔c6 0-1 A.Breuer-S.Baier, Görlitz 1999.

d) 5 d3 is worse than pointless—Black, having a nice central pawn mass and the two bishops, easily takes over the advantage:

5...d6 6 ♘c3 ♘f6 7 h3 g6 8 ♗g5 ♗g7 9 ♕d2 ♗e6 10 ♘h2 ♕b8 and given his solid centre, two bishops and the b-file, one can see that Black (in this case, me!) is already better, and I went on to win in Blauelagune2-Taylor, play-

chess.com (blitz) 2010.

e) 5 ♘c3 shouldn't give Black any trouble—as long as he keeps his move order straight and is aware of the missing tempo (compared to Chapter Six). For example, after 5...d6 6 d4 exd4 7 ♘xd4,

the immediate 7...c5 8 ♘c6 ♕d7 9 ♘a5 gives Black a cramped game, for unlike in Velimirovic-Scekic (in the notes to Game 55), Black does not have 9...♕a4 to chase the white knight—keep an eye out for that extra tempo, here 5 ♘c3.

Instead, 7...♘e7! is my rather obvious novelty, when White has no good way to stop the coming ...c6-c5. Finding no games in the database, I took on the intrepid *Fritz 11*—and confounded the machine as follows: 8 0-0 c5 9 ♘f3 ♘g6 10 ♗g5 f6 11 ♗e3 ♗e7 12 ♕d5 ♖b8 13 ♖ab1 ♕d7 14 ♖fd1 ♕e6 15 a3 0-0 16 h4 f5! and Black had good counterplay in Comp Fritz 11-T.Taylor, Los Angeles 2010.

5...exd4 6 ♘xd4

This and the next game see White

recapturing on d4 with the knight, while the remaining two will feature the queen recapture (the final one being on move seven due to the order 5 0-0 d6 6 d4 exd4 7 ♕xd4).

6...g6!?

I like the ambition of this move, and Bent may have been counting on psychological factors: his opponent, Andersson, is noted for quiet positional play—but such quietness here would just allow Black an excellent game, so he forces Ulf into unfamiliar territory. But despite all that, from a sound opening point of view, we notice that there is a point of attack at f5, and White has a lead in development. Therefore I recommend 6...c5 as in Chapter Six, which will be seen in the next game.

7 ♘c3 ♗g7 8 0-0

After the sharp 8 h4 h5 9 ♗g5 ♘e7 10 ♕d2 f6 11 ♗e3 d6 12 0-0-0 ♗d7 13 f3 ♕c8 14 ♖dg1 a5 15 ♘de2 ♖b8 16 ♘f4 ♕b7 17 b3 ♕b4 18 ♘d3 ♕a3+ Black got good counterplay in J.Magem Badals-B.Sahl, Ubeda 1996—note how

Black has been careful not to commit his king.

8...♘e7

Larsen is trying a typically creative set-up. As we saw in Chapter One (in the note to move 9 in Game 12), if Black plays an early ...d7-d6 and ...g7-g6, White often has a strong break with e4-e5. But here, Larsen uses the missing tempo to deprive (for now) the e4-e5 thrust of a point of contact.

9 f4 c5 10 ♘b3 d6

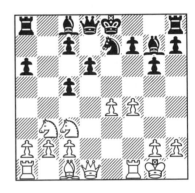

11 f5!

Larsen has delayed ...d7-d6 until he is ready to castle, so now 11 e5 0-0 12 ♕e2 ♖e8 is somewhat better for Black, as White's pawn advances get nowhere. The problem is that White has a stronger lever, and Ulf goes for it: an uncharacteristically blunt attack and pawn sacrifice, no doubt thinking that if he didn't mix it up quickly, Black's bishops would eventually prevail. While the move is correct, Larsen was right to think that Andersson would be a fish out of water in such a wild position and would not continue correctly.

Really White has no choice: on the quiet 11 ♗e3 0-0 12 ♕d2 ♖e8 13 ♖ae1 ♖b8 Black has good counterplay with the open b-file and the long dark diagonal.

11...gxf5 12 ♕h5!

Andersson makes another sound and correct attacking move! How long can this go on?

12...0-0 13 ♗h6?!

Three is not the charm, and Bent's psychological play works.

Correct is 13 exf5! which casts grave doubt on Black's set-up. Since 13...♘xf5 14 ♖xf5 ♗xf5 15 ♕xf5 gives White an easy advantage with two knights for the rook, 13...f6 is necessary, but then Black is in trouble with a buried king's bishop; e.g. 14 ♗d2 ♕d7 15 ♖ae1 ♘xf5 16 ♘d5 ♔h8 17 c4 ♘d4 18 ♗c3 with a very strong attack.

13...♗xh6 14 ♕xh6 f6

After the bishop exchange, this pawn move is fine, as it doesn't shut in a missing piece!

15 ♖ae1 ♖f7 16 ♘d5 ♘xd5 17 exd5 ♕f8 18 ♕xf8+ ♔xf8 19 ♘d2 ♗d7

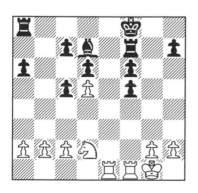

Andersson has floundered trying to reach his comfort zone, the quiet ending—now Black is a pawn up (even if doubled) and has the superior minor piece. Note one very important fact: unlike in the main line Exchange Variation, *White has no pawn majority*.

20 ♖f3 ♖b8 21 b3 ♖g7 22 ♖e2 ♖g5 23 ♖f4 ♖g4 24 g3 ♔f7 25 ♔f2 ♖b4 26 c4 ♖b8?!

Bent misses his chance! 26...♖xf4+ 27 gxf4 c6 pries open lines for bishop and rook, and leaves White desperately struggling to draw. After missing this, we see the game shift as Andersson's famed ability in quiet positions gradually gives him the better game.

27 h3 ♖g7 28 ♖e3 ♖bg8 29 ♘f1 h5 30 ♖ef3 ♖h8 31 ♘e3

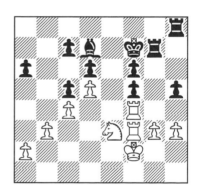

A fine regrouping by Andersson, who now recovers his pawn.

31...h4!

And Bent responds with his patented rook pawn confusion!

32 ♖xh4 ♖xh4 33 gxh4 ♖h7 34 ♔g3 ♔g6 35 ♘g2 ♖h6 36 ♘f4 ♖e7 37 ♖f1 ♖e3+ 38 ♔f2 ♖e4 39 ♔f3 ♗e8 40 ♖g1

♗f7 41 ♖g2 a5 42 ♖e2 ♖e5 43 ♖e3 ♗h5+ 44 ♔f2 ♗e8 45 ♘e6 c6 46 dxc6 ♗xc6 47 ♘d8 ♗e8 48 ♖d3 ♗h5 49 ♖xd6 ♖e2+ 50 ♔f1 ♖xa2 51 ♖xf6+ ♔h7 52 ♘e6 a4 53 bxa4 ♗e2+ 54 ♔e1 ♗xc4

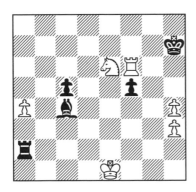

55 ♘g5+

Now *White* misses his chance! After 55 ♘xc5 Andersson retains rook pawns on both sides of the board. Although many such positions are theoretically drawn, it's clear that Larsen would still have a long uphill fight to make the half point—whereas now the game ends quickly.

55...♔g7 56 ♖xf5 ♖a1+ 57 ♔d2 ♖xa4 58 h5 ♔h6 ½-½

White's extra h-pawn doesn't mean anything, so a draw was agreed here.

But just take a moment and think how lively this game was! Attack! Counter-attack! Sacrifices on both sides—11 f5!, 31...h4!. Best of all, either player could have won. Now you can follow Keres or Carlsen, and give six or eight draws to win one, but that has never been my style, and was never Larsen's either.

Let's look at some more enterprising play.

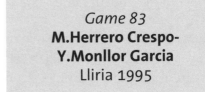

Game 83
M.Herrero Crespo-
Y.Monllor Garcia
Lliria 1995

1 e4 e5 2 ♘f3 ♘c6 3 ♗b5 a6 4 ♗xc6 bxc6 5 d4 exd4 6 ♘xd4 c5

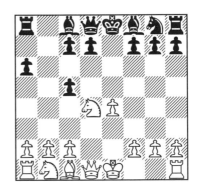

Just as in Chapter Six (and with apologies to Bent, but I think his "over-optimistic"—as Kasparov would say—6...g6 is too risky), Black drives the white knight out of the centre and declares the missing tempo to be meaningless.

7 ♘f3

7 ♘e2 ♗b7 8 ♘bc3 ♘f6 9 f3 d6 (better than 9...c6?! 10 e5 ♘d5 11 ♘e4, when Karpov took the d6-square and squeezed out a win in his inimitable style on move 60 in A.Karpov-V.Kalashnikov, Zlatoust 1961—this Karpovian grind terrifies chess masters the world over, but evidently didn't

faze Kirsan!) 10 0-0 ♗e7 and Black has a typically equal Chapter Six position where, indeed, one can't find anything important to do with White's extra move.

7...♗b7 8 ♘c3 ♘e7 9 0-0 h6 10 ♖e1 ♘g6

Black sets up in Knight Defence style.

11 ♗e3 ♗e7 12 ♘d5 0-0!

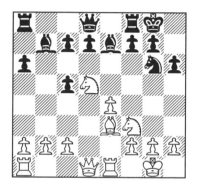

What a relief not to have to worry about exchanging off the bishop pair! With no "endgame panic" in mind, Black settles down to enjoy a nice equal position. Note again that White has no pawn majority.

13 ♘xe7+ ♕xe7 14 ♘d2 d6 15 f3 ♖ab8 16 ♘c4 ♕e6 17 b3 ♖fe8 18 ♕d2 f5 19 e5 d5

This is rather over-aggressive (perhaps Larsen inspired!) and while it works in the game, I think the simpler continuation 19...♘xe5 20 ♘xe5 dxe5 21 ♗xc5 ♕g6 is a little better for Black—note that here it is actually *Black* who has an effective kingside pawn majority!

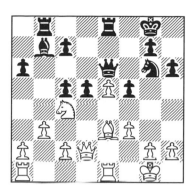

20 ♘a5 d4 21 ♗f2 ♗a8 22 ♖ad1?

White can get a small advantage with 22 c3!, breaking up Black's pawns—the actual text just loses a pawn.

22...♘xe5 23 ♗g3

Not 23 f4 ♕g6 with a withering attack.

23...♕f6 24 f4?!

This opens the long diagonal for Black. 24 ♗xe5 is the best try.

24...♘g4 25 ♘c4 ♕c6 26 h3 ♘e3! 27 ♘xe3 dxe3

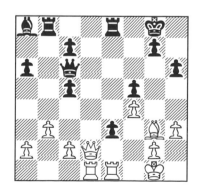

Obviously the e-pawn is immune—so now the powerful queen/bishop battery, plus the extra passed pawn, gives Black a decisive advantage.

28 ♕e2 ♔h7 29 c4 ♖e6 30 ♕c2 ♖e4 31 ♖e2 ♕g6 32 ♔h2 ♖be8 33 ♖de1 ♕e6 34 ♖g1 ♖d8 35 ♕c1 ♖d3 36 ♕c2 ♖ed4 37 ♕c1 ♖d2

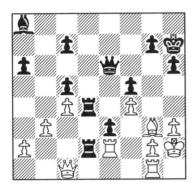

Both sides have played reasonably well so far, especially Black, who now has manoeuvred to a clearly winning position. However, the final few moves of the game are either time pressure madness or someone put the moves in wrong! Objectively White has no defence and **38 ♕f1 ♖xe2 39 ♕xe2 ♖d2 40 ♕f1 ♕e4** with a decisive advantage for Black would be a reasonable continuation. Instead, a bunch of silly moves were "played" or "inputted" which I will not comment on—although, if you like, you can watch rooks being tossed back and forth like hot potatoes!

38 ♖xe3? ♖xg2+? 39 ♔h1? ♕g6? 40 ♗f2? ♖xf2+

Finally!

0-1

Disregarding the last few doubtful moves, we saw an excellent way for

Black to handle the opening. White gained nothing from her extra tempo, while Black (having no fear of a pawn majority win) was able to give up the bishop pair to buy time to castle with complete equality—and was able to outplay her opponent in the subsequent double-edged position.

1 e4 e5 2 ♘f3 ♘c6 3 ♗b5 a6 4 ♗xc6 bxc6

"Though unusual, this variation appears to me eminently practicable. In any case it has the advantage of not allowing White the majority of pawns on the kingside as happens after 4...dxc6 5 d4 exd4 6 ♕xd4 ♕xd4 7 ♘xd4 etc," writes Alekhine.

I couldn't agree more!

5 d4 exd4 6 ♕xd4

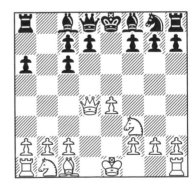

6...♕f6

"Black concludes that his somewhat

cramped position will be more easily defendable after the exchange of queens, and the sequel confirms the correctness of his judgment," continues Alekhine and gives his move an exclam—but it's not the only good choice:

a) 6...c5 is one move I *don't* recommend: although good in Chapter Six, here the missing tempo counts, as White has a nasty check: 7 ♕e5+ (obviously not possible when the black d-pawn is already on d6!) 7...♕e7 (the only move that doesn't lose a pawn: if 7...♗e7 8 ♕xg7 or 7...♘e7 8 ♕xc5) 8 ♕xc7 ♕xe4+ 9 ♗e3 (weaker is 9 ♔d1 ♕d5+ 10 ♗d2 ♗d6 with counterplay in Y.Gusev-V.Shcherbakov, Moscow 1955) 9...♕xc2 10 ♘c3 ♕xb2 11 ♕e5+ ♘e7 12 ♖b1 ♕c2 13 ♗xc5 and White has more than enough for the pawn.

b) 6...♘e7 7 ♘c3 ♘g6 (as in the previous game, the solid Knight Defence development works well here) 8 h4 h5 9 ♗g5 f6 10 ♗d2 ♕e7 11 0-0-0 ♕c5 12 ♕d3 ♕d6 13 ♕e3 ♕c5 14 ♕e2 ♘e5 (it's true that Black gained ground by threatening to draw with queen repetitions, but now has obtained an ideal position) 15 ♗f4 d6 16 ♗e3 (or 16 ♘xe5 fxe5 17 ♗e3 ♕a5 18 ♕c4 ♗d7 19 ♕b3 ♗e7 20 ♔b1 ♗f6 21 a3 ♔e7 22 ♔a1 ♖hb8 23 ♕c4 ♖b7 with good play for Black) 16...♕c4 17 ♘xc5 ♕xe2 18 ♘xe2 fxe5 19 ♗g5 ♗e7 20 ♗xe7 ♔xe7 21 ♖d3 ♖f8 22 f3 ♗e6 23 b3 a5 24 a4 and Black is evidently slightly better in the ending with the superior minor piece,

solid centre and initiative on the queenside. Gritty defence finally saved the draw for White after about 40 more moves in K.Beckmann-B.Vonach, Bad Wörishofen 2003—but note that here *Black* got to grind in the endgame!

c) 6...♗b7—there are no master games with this rather natural developing move: how's that for a plus? Unexplored on move six of a Ruy Lopez?? This looks quite playable: Black prepares ...d7-d6 and ...c6-c5, or even ...d7-d5 in one go, and queenside castling might be possible.

d) 6...d6 returns us directly to Chapter Six, but with an extra tempo for White. The question is, can he do anything with it? The great Lasker asked this question back in 1904 and the answer he got was: Not much!

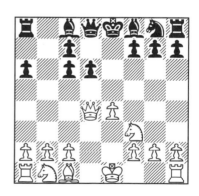

7 0-0 ♘e7 8 ♘c3 (8 ♗g5 is seen in the next game) 8...♘g6 9 ♖e1 f6 (9...c5 10 ♕d3 ♗e7 is easier equality) 10 ♘e2 (10 ♕c4 is best, with real chances of advantage since Black can't castle and his queenside is also under fire—though this wouldn't have happened had Lasker

been more accurate on the previous move) 10...♗e6 (you only get one chance, my friend!) 11 ♘g3 c5 12 ♕c3 ♗e7 13 ♘f5 0-0 (once again, Black has no worries about the two bishops, and stands fully equal) 14 ♘g5 ♗xf5 15 exf5 fxg5 16 fxg6 hxg6 (Lasker is quick to see the virtues of his tripled pawns—open f-file, bases for his pieces at f5 and f6—and begins to outplay his opponent) 17 ♕d3 ♖f5 18 g4 ♖f7 19 ♕xg6 ♗f6 20 c3 ♖b8 21 ♖e3 ♕d7 22 ♕h5 ♖e7 23 ♖xe7 (if 23 ♖h3 ♖e1+ 24 ♔g2 ♕c6+ 25 f3 ♕b5! and Black's attack is more deadly) 23...♕xe7 (Black is clearly better, as White has no good way to develop his queenside) 24 ♗d2 ♖xb2 25 ♖e1 ♗e5 26 ♗xg5 ♕f8 27 ♗h4 ♕f7 28 ♕xf7+ ♔xf7 29 ♖e3 ♖c2 30 ♗d8 ♗xc3 31 ♖e7+ ♔f8 32 ♖xc7 ♗e5 (material is still even, but Lasker has connected passed pawns on the queenside—not very likely after 4...dxc6—and thus a clear advantage) 33 g5 ♔e8 34 ♗e7 d5 35 ♖xc5 ♖d2! 36 ♖a5 ♔xe7 37 ♔g2 ♔e6 38 ♖xa6+ ♔f5 39 h4 ♗d4 40 ♖a8 ♔g4 41 ♖f8 ♖xa2 42 ♖f7 ♖xf2+! (Emanuel is too cool for school) 43 ♖xf2 ♗xf2 44 ♔xf2 ♔xh4 45 ♔e3 ♔xg5 0-1 A.W.Fox-Em.Lasker, Cambridge Springs 1904.

7 0-0

Alekhine recommended 7 e5 here, with a pawn sacrifice on the next move, which is probably best—White needs to keep the queens on if he is to have any hope of advantage (completely contrary to the main line Exchange, where White *wants* to exchange queens—you can see how this line will disconcert your opponent). After 7...♕g6 8 0-0 ♕xc2 (I don't think Black should take this, though he wins the following game) 9 ♘c3 ♘e7 10 ♖e1 (White has good development and central compensation for the pawn) 10...♕g6 11 ♗g5 ♕e6 12 ♘e4 ♘f5 13 ♕c3 ♗e7 14 ♘f6+!? (14 ♗xe7! is even stronger) 14...♔f8 15 g4 h6 16 gxf5 ♕xf5 and now, instead of 17 ♗h4 when White went slowly downhill and eventually lost in H.Daurelle-A.Sermier, French Team Championship 2003, he can get a winning position with 17 ♘xd7+! ♗xd7 (or 17...♕xd7 18 e6 fxe6 19 ♘e5) 18 ♗xe7+ ♔xe7 19 ♘d4 ♕g4+ 20 ♔h1, since Black's king is too exposed.

Instead of this risky pawn capture, Black should play 8...♗b7, when White has various tries but nothing particularly convincing:

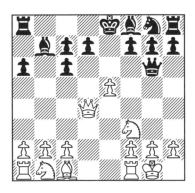

a) 9 c4 0-0-0 10 ♗f4 c5 11 ♕e3 ♘e7 12 ♗g3 ♘f5 13 ♕f4 h5 14 h4 ♗e7 and Black had good play in M.Muhutdinov-A.Lutikov, Sverdlovsk 1957.

b) 9 e6 looks strong but has a brilliant refutation: 9...fxe6 10 ♘e5 ♕xg2+! 11 ♔xg2 c5+ and wins.

c) 9 ♘bd2 0-0-0 10 ♘b3 c5 11 ♕c3 f6 with approximate equality according to Keres, citing the game N.Krogius-A.Lutikov, Leningrad 1955. I found this note in Keres' book *Spanisch bis Französisch*, where he says of 4...bxc6 that there is no convincing way for White to obtain advantage against it!

d) 9 ♗f4 ♘e7 10 ♖d1 0-0-0 11 ♘bd2 ♘d5 12 ♗g3 c5 13 ♕c4 h5 14 h4 ♗e7 15 ♖e1 f5 16 exf6 gxf6 17 ♕b3 ♖h7 18 ♖ad1 ♘b4 19 c3 ♘c6, and in this violently double-edged position a draw was agreed: ½-½ R.Vera Gonzalez-F.Perez Perez, Havana 1978.

As far as I can see, Black holds his own, even with the queens on.

7...♕xd4 8 ♘xd4 ♖b8

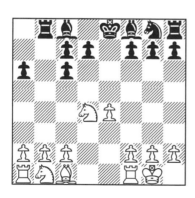

One can already say that Black has equality, with the two bishops (while the white cleric is at least temporarily prevented from moving) and pressure down the b-file.

9 ♘b3 ♘e7 10 ♗d2 ♘g6 11 ♗c3 ♘f4 12

♖e1 ♗e7! 13 ♘1d2

Not 13 ♗xg7? ♖g8 14 ♗c3 ♘xg2 and Black has a strong attack even without queens.

13...0-0 14 ♘c4 ♖e8

Alekhine writes that he didn't play the natural 14...d6 due to the following draw: 15 ♘ca5 ♗d7 16 ♘d4 ♖b6 17 ♘c4 ♖bb8 18 ♘a5 etc.

Nonetheless, this is a theoretical success for Black, and the draw is not at all obvious and even perhaps dodgeable, if Black is willing to give up his bishop pair. In any case, I'll take this—where White must push accurately to maybe draw—to almost any main line Exchange, where Black must suffer for hours to reach the same result.

15 ♘ca5 ♗f8 16 ♖ad1 c5 17 e5 ♘e6

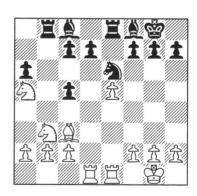

Black has a very cramped game (yes, plus equals according to Mr. *Fritz*!), but it's also hard to find anything to attack. Amazingly enough, Alekhine finds a way to attack out of this position with *Black*, though White could have avoided the combination to come with a timely a2-a3.

18 ♘c4 h6 19 h4 ♗e7 20 g3 g5 21 hxg5 hxg5 22 ♘ba5 ♔h7 23 ♔g2 ♔g6 24 ♖h1

Here 24 a3! is best, when 24...♖h8 maintains the status quo of a very slight edge to White—though I don't see how Duras could really improve his position. White's actual move looks logical but allows a hidden and spectacular blow, based on the heretofore unseen power of Black's unopposed light-squared bishop.

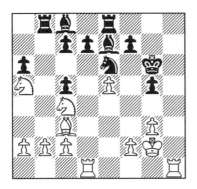

24...♘d4!! 25 ♗xd4 cxd4 26 ♖xd4 ♗b4!

The hidden point, which White could have prevented with 24 a3—now Black threatens to take a knight on a5, after which he will be able to capture either White's e- or b-pawn.

27 ♘b3 d5!

The second point: if the pawn is taken either way, Black's light-squared bishop becomes amazingly powerful, as the next note demonstrates.

28 ♘e3

Obviously if 28 ♖xd5 ♗b7 wins the exchange; but harder to see is 28 exd6 ♗b7+! 29 f3 ♖e2+ 30 ♔g1 ♖be8 31 ♖h2 ♖e1+ 32 ♔g2 f5 33 d7 ♖8e2+ 34 ♔h3

♗xf3! and now it's clear that 35 d8♕ loses straight away to 35...♖xh2+ 36 ♔xh2 ♖h1 mate! So White must try 35 g4 ♗xg4+ 36 ♖xg4 fxg4+ 37 ♔xg4 ♗e7 when Black stops the passed pawn with advantage.

28...c5!

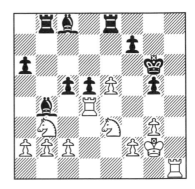

The third point, winning material—for if 29 ♖dd1 d4, levering open the long diagonal, is too strong.

29 ♖xd5 ♗b7 30 c4 ♖xe5 31 a3 ♗xa3 32 ♘a5 ♗xd5+ 33 cxd5 ♖xe3

In view of numerous threatened knight forks, Alekhine gives back the exchange at once to reach a pawn up ending with the superior minor piece.

34 fxe3 ♖xb2+ 35 ♔f3 f5! 36 g4

Black wins after both 36 d6 g4+ 37 ♔f4 c4 and 36 ♘c4 g4+ 37 ♔f4 ♖b4—the key tactical motif is the pin on the fourth rank.

36...fxg4+ 37 ♔e4 ♖b4+ 38 ♔d3 ♗b2 39 d6 ♗f6 40 ♖f1 g3 41 d7 ♖b8 42 ♖d1

42 ♘c6 g2 43 ♖xf6+ ♔xf6 44 ♘xb8 ♔e7 45 ♘c6+ ♔xd7 46 ♘e5+ ♔e6 47 ♘f3 g4 48 ♘g1 ♔e5 is a beautiful win given by Alekhine.

42...g2

Now Black wins technically, much as I did in Game 81—with the black g-pawn on the seventh rank, the rook can easily "sacrifice" itself.

43 ♔e2 ♖b2+ 44 ♔f3 ♖d2! 45 ♖g1 ♖xd7 46 ♖xg2 ♖d3 47 ♖c2 ♖c3 48 ♖xc3 ♗xc3 49 ♘c4 a5 50 ♘b6 ♗b4 0-1

As Alekhine remarks, the black king simply marches to the queenside.

White failed to achieve any opening advantage, and even when Alekhine riskily played for a win, the slight plus White had was never enough to give real winning chances—whereas the resources in Black's position (the two bishops especially) allowed his later combination after an infinitesimal White slip.

Game 85
F.Künzner-B.Sahl
Isle of Man 1993

1 e4 e5 2 ♘f3 ♘c6 3 ♗b5 a6 4 ♗xc6 bxc6

If World Champions like Lasker and Alekhine could play this move, why are present day GMs (with the notable exception of the late Bent Larsen) so afraid?

Meanwhile some IMs do have the courage! Norwegian IM Sahl specializes in this move—see also the note to White's 8th move in Game 82, where Sahl drew with a much higher-rated GM! What does his fellow Norwegian, Mr. Magnus, think of all this I wonder?

As we know, Magnus Carlsen has a very Keres-like score when facing the Exchange Variation. Here's a typical example of the fun Magnus has had with the approved fourth move recapture: 4...dxc6 5 0-0 ♗e6 6 ♘xe5 ♕d4 7 ♘f3 ♕xe4 8 ♘g5 ♕g6 9 ♘xe6 fxe6 10 d3 0-0-0 11 ♕e2 ♗d6 12 ♘d2 ♘f6 13 ♘e4 ♘xe4 14 ♕xe4 ♕xe4 15 dxe4 ♗c5 16 ♗g5 ♖d7 17 ♖ad1 ♖xd1 18 ♖xd1 ♖f8 19 ♘h4 b5 20 ♗g3 h5 21 h4 ♖d8 22 ♖xd8+ ♔xd8 23 ♗e5 g6 24 b3 ♗e7 25 g3 c5 26 c4 c6 27 ♔g2 ♔e8 28 ♔f3 ♗f8 29 a4 ♔e7 30 ♗b8 ♔f6 31 ♗c7 e5 32 ♗d8+ ♔e6 33 ♗g5 ♗d6 34 ♔e3—despite the fact that Magnus tried to play actively in the opening, look what he ended up with!

Here's the same old dreary ending of the type I lost to Khachiyan, the kind of ending a great player might draw, but even a Carlsen or an Anand could never win. Let's run it down again: Black's queenside majority is lamed by the doubled c-pawns, so the three white pawns there hold four.

On the kingside, White has a good pawn majority, and is able to make a passed pawn. All Black can hope to do is grimly hold, without the slightest hope of a win—and although Carlsen succeeds here, I wouldn't like to play this position. Meanwhile his countryman in the main game gets a full-blooded, interesting position that I, for one, find much more enjoyable than holding to the draw like grim death!

Carlsen held on as follows: 34...♗f8 35 ♔d3 ♗d6 36 ♗h6 ♗e7 37 ♔e2 ♗d6 38 ♔e3 ♗e7 39 ♗g5 ♗d6 (39...♗xg5+ 40 hxg5 ♔d6 41 f4 is lost for Black, which shows just how limited his options are) 40 f4 ♗c7 41 ♔f3 ♗d6 42 ♗h6 ♗e7 43 ♗g7 exf4 44 ♔xf4 ♔f7 45 ♗e5 ♔e6 46 ♗c7 ♔d7 47 ♗b8 ♗e6 48 e5 ♗d8 49 ♗d6 ♗a5 50 ♔g5 ♔f7 51 ♔h6 ♗d2+ 52 ♔h7 g5 53 ♗xc5 gxh4 54 gxh4 ♗e1 55 ♔h6 ♗xh4 56 ♔xh5 ♗g3 57 ♔g4 ♗xe5 58 ♔f5 ½-½ A.Naiditsch-M.Carlsen, Sarajevo 2006.

5 0-0 d6 6 d4 exd4 7 ♕xd4

Of course this is Mecking-Keres (Game 53), except that in that game

(due to the extra tempo used on ♗b5-a4xc6) White had not yet castled. There Keres immediately attacked the white queen with ...c6-c5, but Sahl omits this in favour of a quick ...♘e7-g6 development (as Lasker played in the notes to the previous game).

On 7 ♘xd4,

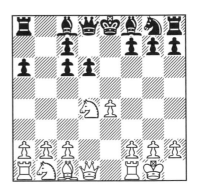

I recommend 7...♗b7 (now we know where the white king lives, it's a good idea to aim our unopposed bishop at it!—besides that, Black takes the c6-square under control before playing ...c6-c5) 8 ♘c3 ♘f6 9 ♗g5 h6 10 ♗h4 ♗e7 (I also like 10...c5 11 ♘f5 g5 12 ♗g3 ♕d7 13 f3 0-0-0 14 ♕d2 ♖g8 with good counterplay, as Black's rook on g8 may well be able to join forces with the bishop on b7) 11 ♖e1 ♕d7 12 e5 dxe5 13 ♖xe5 0-0-0 with a typical MS long castle and a wild struggle in prospect, which was won by Black in L.Stirling-I.McNab, Scottish Championship, Ayr 1974.

The alternate way of covering c6 is much weaker: 7...♘e7 8 ♖e1 c5 9 ♘f5 ♗xf5 (this can't be good, but it's a simul!) 10 exf5 ♕d7 11 ♕f3 ♖c8 12 ♘c3 ♔d8 13 f6 and the World Champion crushed his luckless foe in G.Kasparov-H.Xanthoudakis, Corfu (simul) 1996.

7...♘e7

The above-mentioned 7...c5 is also good and playable. After 8 ♕d3 (8 ♕d5 only helps the opponent develop: 8...♗e6 9 ♕c6+ ♗d7 10 ♕d5 ♘f6 11 ♕d1 ♗e7 and Black was already slightly better in Premtimi-Taylor, playchess.com blitz 2010) 8...♘e7 Aronian and Rozentalis couldn't even make a half point between them from this position—with White!

a) 9 b3 ♘g6 10 ♗b2 ♗e7! 11 ♖e1 (if White takes the bait with 11 ♗xg7, then 11...♖g8 12 ♗h6 ♗h3! gives Black a strong attack) 0-0 12 ♘bd2 ♗e6 13 ♕c3 ♘e5 14 ♘xe5 dxe5 15 ♖ad1 f6 16 ♘f1 ♕e8 17 ♘e3 ♕b5 18 ♘d5 ♗d6 19 a4 ♕c6 20 ♕c4 ♔h8 21 ♗a3 f5 22 exf5 ♖xf5 23 f3 ♖af8 24 ♖c4 ♖h5 25 ♖e2 (White should play 25 h3 with an even game—the text allows a devastating combination) 25...e4! 26 fxe4 ♗xh2+ 27 ♔h1 ♗g3+ 28 ♔g1 ♗xd5 29 ♕xc5

♖h1+! 0-1 L.Aronian-A.Vajda, Bucharest 1995.

b) 9 ♗f4 (Rozentalis tries a different bishop development, with no better result) 9...♘g6 10 ♗g3 ♗e7 11 ♘c3 0-0 12 ♖ad1 ♖b8 13 b3 f5 14 exf5 ♗xf5 15 ♕c4+ ♔h8 16 ♘d5 ♕d7 17 ♖fe1 ♗d8 18 ♘d2 a5 19 ♘e4 ♕f7 20 a4 h6 21 ♕e2 ♗h4 22 ♕d2 (White is trying to prove an advantage, but his slow manoeuvres allow Black finally to activate his bishops) 22...♖be8 23 ♘ec3 ♗g5 24 f4 ♗d8 25 ♘e3 ♗d7 26 ♘c4 ♖xe1+ 27 ♖xe1 ♘xf4 28 ♘xa5 ♗g5 (White fails to sense the danger) 29 ♕f2?! ♗f6! 30 ♖e3 ♗d4 31 ♘c4 ♗xe3 32 ♘xe3 ♗c6 33 a5 ♘e6 34 ♕xf7 ♖xf7 35 ♘cd5 ♘d4 36 h3 ♘xc2! (White's whole position collapses) 0-1 E.Rozentalis-L.Shevelev, Lithuanian Championship, Kaunas 1980.

8 ♗g5

As we have already seen, 8 ♘c3 ♘g6 9 ♖e1 gives White nothing after 9...c5 10 ♕d3 ♗e7.

8...f6 9 ♗e3

9...♘g6?!

9...♗e6 is mandatory, when Black can complete his development normally; e.g. 10 ♘c3 c5 11 ♕d3 ♘g6 12 ♖ad1 ♗e7 with equality.

10 ♘bd2

10 ♕c4, the same move Fox missed vs. Lasker (see 6...d6 in the previous game), again gives White a clear plus.

10...♗d7 11 b4 ♗e7 12 c4

The queen should have gone here: now Black castles with a good game.

12...0-0 13 c5 f5 14 cxd6 cxd6 15 ♕c4+

Too late!

15...♔h8 16 exf5 ♖xf5

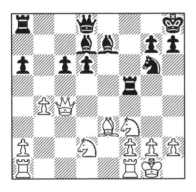

With a little help from his opponent, Black has gotten rid of his doubled pawns, activated his two bishops, and opened the f-file! Black is already somewhat better.

17 ♖fe1 d5 18 ♕c3 ♗d6?!

The a8-rook is not in the game, whereas the white rooks are connected and can play on any file. Therefore Black should exchange one rook and focus play on the f-file. Correct is 18...a5! 19 a3 axb4 20 axb4 ♖xa1 21 ♖xa1 ♘f4 and Black keeps the edge.

19 ♗c5 ♕c7 20 ♗d4 ♖g8 21 ♘f1 h6 22 ♘g3 ♖f7 23 ♕c2 ♘f4 24 ♘e5 ♗xe5 25 ♗xe5 ♕d8 26 ♘e2 ♘xe2+ 27 ♖xe2 ♕g5 28 ♖ae1

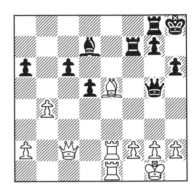

White's doubled rooks are now obviously better than Black's defensive castles (especially the one on g8!) and the white bishop is better as well. At this point it looks like Black can only hope for a drawn opposite-coloured bishop ending.

28...♕f5 29 ♕d2 ♔h7 30 ♗d4 ♕g6 31 ♖e3 ♖f4 32 ♗e5 ♖g4 33 ♖g3

33 f4 is best, when Black has no attack and a deplorable game.

33...♖e8 34 a3 ♗f5 35 ♗c3 d4!

After a few second-rate moves by White, Black jumps right back in the game and actually stands better again!

36 ♗b2

Not 36 ♖xe8 ♕xe8 37 ♗xd4? ♖xd4!.

36...♕g5 37 ♕d1 ♖xe1+ 38 ♕xe1 d3 39 ♗c1 ♖e4 40 ♕d1 ♕e7 1-0

Evidently Black lost on time in this slightly favourable position: after 41 ♖e3 ♖xe3 42 ♗xe3 ♕e5 one could say that Black could not lose—but oh that clock!

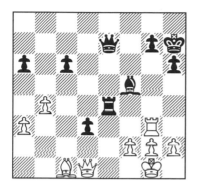

The main game was messy but interesting, and it was fun to see future big guns Aronian and Rozentalis (they were both juniors during the games given in the notes) crash and burn in this strategically complicated variation.

Conclusion

Summing up Larsen's Variation, I find it, as Alekhine said, eminently practicable. The extra tempo for White requires caution, but I think Black has sufficient resources. And if Black wants to win, he has much better chances here than in the booked-up drawing lines of Chapter Ten—just cast your mind back to Adorjan-Keres and Shirov-Topalov, not to mention (please don't) Khachiyan-Taylor!

Then blot that bad memory out with a picture of Alekhine's bishops coming to life after the spectacular 24...♘d4!. I am certainly looking forward to my first Ruy Lopez Exchange, Larsen's Variation!

Afterword

This book has been an enormous undertaking for me, and I am a little sad to see it finish—but we are now at the end of our journey, and I trust you are well armed to Slay the Spanish! As you now see, the Modern Steinitz is an amazingly rich opening. There is a sound gambit, the Siesta, and an extremely risky one, the Yandemirov. There are solid lines that are solid, and "solid" lines with opposite side castling and fierce attacks! Indeed, I have never seen so many long castles for Black in any other Open Game—so always be alert for this possibility.

As I mentioned in the Introduction, one of the great and unexpected discoveries I made while writing this book was that Black does not need to suffer in the Exchange Variation with 4...dxc6 but can fight back with 4...bxc6!.

Also, in my seven recent games over the board, I found out that very few people study this opening for White, so you may get quick advantages—or even quick wins—against opponents who *only* know what to do against 4...♘f6, and are already clueless when facing 4...d6.

Finally, if there is one chapter in this book you should study most diligently, that is Chapter Three, the Bishop Defence. This is the closest thing to a universal system in the whole Modern Steinitz, and it can come about through all kinds of confusing move orders—but if you can master this line, you will have the foundation you need to start playing this opening in practice.

Many thanks to my faithful readers, and I wish you, as always, good luck!

Index of Variations

Chapter Two: The Knight Defence
5 0-0 ♗d7 6 c3 ♘ge7 7 d4 ♘g6

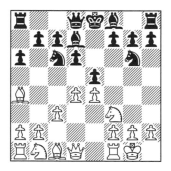

8 ♖e1

 Alternative move order:
5 c3 ♗d7 6 d4 ♘ge7 7 ♗b3

Chapter Three: The Bishop Defence
5 0-0 ♗d7 6 c3 ♘f6 7 d4 g6 (or 5 c3 ♗d7 6 d4 ♘f6 7 0-0 g6)

8 ℤe1

    8 ♘bd2 – *83*; 8 d5 – *93*; 8 ♕e2 – *96*; 8 ♗xc6 – *98*

8...b5 9 ♗b3

    9 ♗c2 – *74*

9...♗g7

    10 ♘bd2 – *80*; 10 dxe5 – *82*

    Alternative move orders:

a) **5 c3 ♗d7 6 0-0**

    6 d4:   6...g6 7 ♗g5 – *87*

            6...♘f6 7 0-0 ♗g7 – main line; 7 ♕e2 ♗e7 – *89*

6...g6 7 d4

    7...♘f6 – main line; 7...♗g7:

        8 ℤe1 b5 9 ♗b3 ♘f6 – main line; 8 dxe5 – *35*; 8 ♗g5 – *22*

b) **5 0-0**

    5...♗d7 – main line; 5...♘f6 6 c3 ♗d7 – main line; 5...g6 – *22*

Chapter Four: The Siesta
5 c3 f5

6 exf5

> 6 d3 – *137*
>
> 6 d4 fxe4
>
>> 7 ♘xe5 – *133*; 7 ♘g5 exd4 8 ♘xe4 – *18, 136*

6...♗xf5 7 d4

> 7 0-0 ♗d3 8 ♖e1 ♗e7
>
>> 9 ♕b3 – *130*
>>
>> 9 ♖e3 e4 10 ♘e1 ♗g5 – *124, 128*
>>
>> 9 ♗c2 ♗xc2 10 ♕xc2 ♘f6 11 d4 e4 – *117, 121*

7...e4 8 ♘g5 d5 9 f3

> 9...h6 – *112*

9...e3 10 f4

> 10...♗d6 – *103*; 10...♘f6 – *109*

Chapter Five: The Yandemirov Gambit
5 0-0 ♗g4

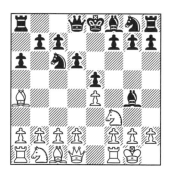

6 h3

> 6 c3 – *144*

6...h5 7 d4

> 7 ♗xc6+ bxc6
>
>> 8 d3 ♕f6 9 ♘bd2 ♘e7 10 ♖e1 ♗d7 – *31, 150*
>>
>> 8 d4 ♗xf3 9 ♕xf3 exd4 – *154, 158*

7...b5 8 ♗b3 ♘xd4 9 hxg4 ♘xb3

> 9...hxg4 – *162*

10 axb3 hxg4 11 ♘g5 ♕d7 12 c4 ♖b8

> 13 cxb5 – *164*; 13 ♕d5 – *168*; 13 ♖xa6 – *169*

Chapter Six: Delayed Exchange Variation
5 ♗xc6+ bxc6 6 d4

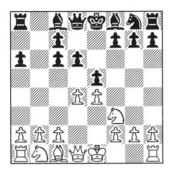

6...exd4

    6...f6 7 c4 – *25*; 7 ♘c3 – *188*

7 ♘xd4

    7 ♕xd4 c5

        7...♘f6 – *46*

    8 ♕d3

        8...g6 – *38*; 8...♘e7 – *174, 176*

7...c5

    7...♗d7 8 0-0

        8...g6 – *182*; 8...♘f6 – *186*

8 ♘f3 – *180*

    8 ♘e2 – *178*

Chapter Seven: The Duras Variation
5 c4

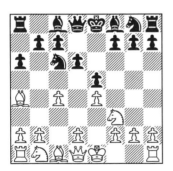

Chapter Eight: White Plays an Early d2–d4
5 d4 or 5 0-0 ♗d7 6 d4

a) **5 d4 b5 6 ♗b3 ♘xd4 7 ♘xd4 exd4**

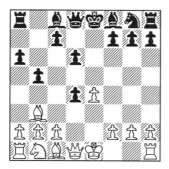

b) **5 0-0 ♗d7 6 d4**

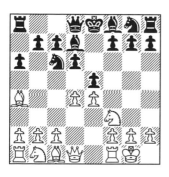

6...♘f6

6...b5 – *218*

6...♞ge7

7 c3 ♞g6 – Chapter Two; 7 ♝g5 – *15*

7 ♝xc6

7 c3 g6 – Chapter Three; 7 dxe5 – *223*

7...♝xc6 8 ♖e1 ♝e7 9 ♞c3

9...0-0 – *219*; 9...exd4 – *221* (and cf *216*)

Chapter Nine: Four Fishes

5 d3

5 h3 – *235*

5 ♛e2

5...♞f6 – *96*; 5...♝e7 – *237*

5 ♞c3 b5 6 ♝b3 ♞f6

7 d3 – 5 d3; 7 ♞g5 – *227*

5...♞f6

6 ♞c3 b5 7 ♝b3 – *231*

6 c3

6...b5 – *17*; 6...♝e7 – *28*; 6...g6 – *233*

6...♝d7 7 0-0 g6 – *44, 47*

Chapter Ten: Exchange Variation, Main Line
4...dxc6

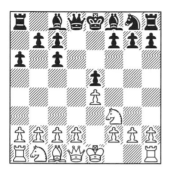

5 0-0

5...♗g4 6 h3 h5 7 d3 ♕f6 8 ♘bd2

Chapter Eleven: Exchange Variation, Larsen's Variation
4...bxc6

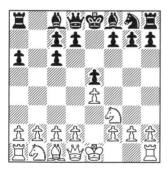

5 d4

5...exd4

6 ♘xd4

Index of Complete Games